LORDSHIP AND P
IN THE NORTH OF S(

LORDSHIP AND POWER
IN THE NORTH OF SCOTLAND

The Noble House of Huntly, 1603–1690

Barry Robertson

First published in Great Britain in 2011 by
John Donald, an imprint of Birlinn Ltd

West Newington House
10 Newington Road
Edinburgh
EH9 1QS

www.birlinn.co.uk

ISBN 978 1 906566 34 0

The publishers gratefully acknowledge the support
of the Scouloudi Foundation in association
with the Institute of Historical Research,
and the Centre of Irish-Scottish and Comparative Studies
at Trinity College Dublin towards the publication of this book

British Library Cataloguing-in-Publication Data
A catalogue record for this book is available on request
from the British Library

Typeset in Minion by
Koinonia, Manchester
Printed and bound in Britain by
Bell and Bain Ltd, Glasgow

To Edda

Contents

Acknowledgements		ix
Note on Dates and Currency		x
Abbreviations		xi
Maps		xii
Gordon Family Tree		xviii

Introduction   1

1 The House of Huntly and the North of Scotland   9

2 Power-broking and Popery: the House of Huntly, 1603–1625   36

3 Religion, Fire and Sword: the House of Huntly, 1625–1637   62

4 The Bishops' Wars, 1638–1641   87

5 The Wars of the Stuart Kingdoms, 1642–1660   121

6 Restoration and Revolution, 1660–1690   155

Conclusion   183

Bibliography   188
Index   209

Acknowledgements

I would like to begin by expressing my gratitude for the funding I received from the University of Aberdeen in order to conduct my research for the PhD thesis upon which this book is based. The Research Institute of Irish and Scottish Studies provided me with a three-year scholarship, which covered my university fees during that time, and I also received a number of travel grants from the School of Divinity, History and Philosophy.

I would also like to acknowledge the help I received from staff at the following repositories: Aberdeen City Council Archives; Aberdeen University Special Collections; Angus Archives, Forfar; British Library, London; Drum Castle Archives; Dundee City Archives; Edinburgh University Special Collections; Lambeth Palace Library, London; National Archives of Scotland, Edinburgh; National Library of Scotland, Edinburgh; The National Archives, London; and West Sussex Record Office, Chichester.

I would especially like to thank my PhD supervisor, Professor Allan Macinnes, for all the help, advice and guidance he has given me over the years, as well as my former supervisor, Professor Jane Ohlmeyer, for encouraging me to begin my research in the first place. Thanks also to the examiners of my PhD thesis, Dr John Young and Professor Thomas Bartlett, for their insightful and helpful comments. I would also like to thank a number of other individuals who provided help, friendship and encouragement along the way. They are in no particular order: Dr Steve Murdoch, Dr David Worthington, Dr Aonghas MacCoinnich, Dr Scott Spurlock, Dr Iain Macinnes, Dr Alan Fimister, Professor David Dickson, Dr David Ditchburn, Dr Andrew Mackillop, Dr Micheál Ó Siochrú, Dr Robert Armstrong, Dr Cathy Hayes, Professor David Stevenson, Russell Simpson, Tadhg O' Bric and Thomas Brochard. I also have a great debt of gratitude to my family and in particular to my mother, Anne Robertson.

I am also very grateful for the generous subvention grants that were provided by the Scouloudi Foundation in association with the Institute of Historical Research, and by the Centre of Irish-Scottish and Comparative Studies at Trinity College Dublin. The publication of this book would not otherwise have been possible. Many thanks also to the Duke of Richmond and Gordon, and James Peill for the free use of images of portraits in the Goodwood collection.

Finally I would like to thank my wife Edda Frankot for all her love and support.

Note on Dates and Currency

DATES

Dates throughout are given according to the Old Style (Julian) Calendar, which was used in contemporary Britain. The New Year is taken to begin on 1 January according to Scottish usage, not 25 March as was the case in England. It has been assumed that British persons writing from Catholic Europe dated their correspondence according to the New Style (Gregorian) Calendar, which was ten days ahead of the Julian Calendar.

CURRENCY

The merk was valued at two-thirds of the pound Scots, twelve of which were equivalent to a pound sterling.

Abbreviations

APS   Acts of the Parliaments of Scotland
BL   British Library
CSPD   *Calendar of State Papers, Domestic Series*
CSPI   *Calendar of State Papers, relating to Ireland*
CSPV   *Calendar of State Papers and Manuscripts, relating to English Affairs, existing in the Archives and Collections of Venice and in other Libraries of Northern Italy*
HMC   Historical Manuscripts Commission
NAS   National Archives of Scotland
NLS   National Library of Scotland
ODNB   *Oxford Dictionary of National Biography*
RGSS   *Registers of the Great Seal of Scotland*
RPCS   *Registers of the Privy Council of Scotland*
WSRO   West Sussex Record Office

Scotland

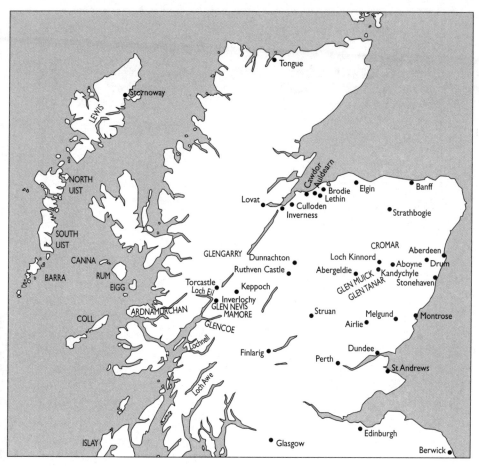

Central and North Scotland

East Aberdeenshire

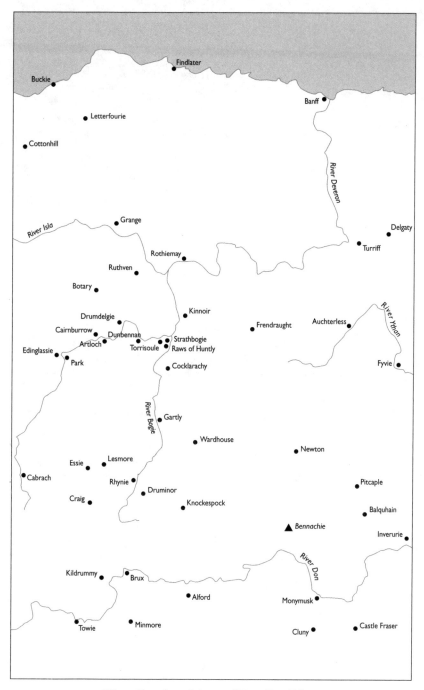

West Aberdeenshire and East Banffshire

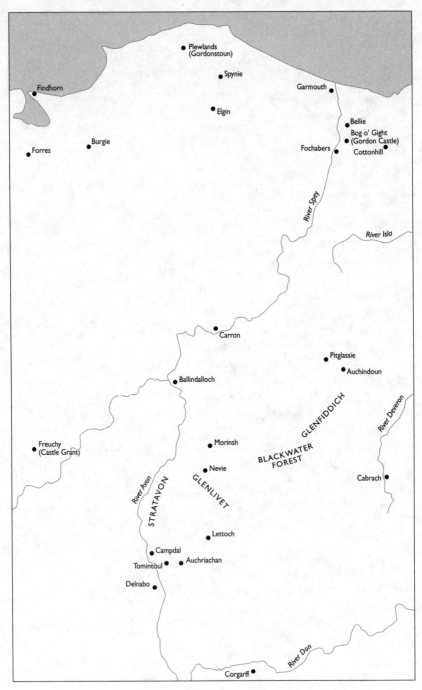

Moray and West Banffshire

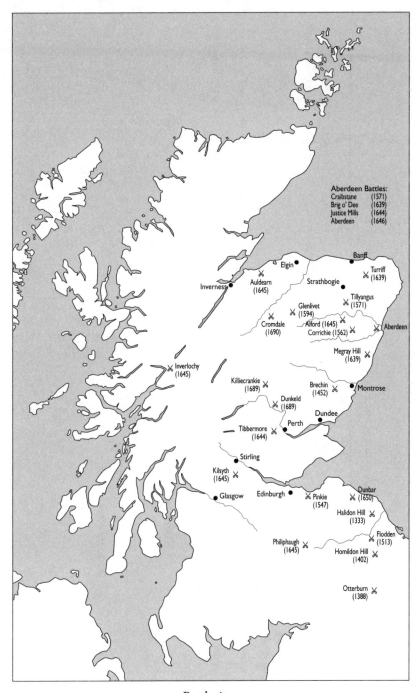

Aberdeen Battles:
Craibstane (1571)
Brig o' Dee (1639)
Justice Mills (1644)
Aberdeen (1646)

Banff

Elgin

Turriff (1639)

Inverness

Auldearn (1645)

Strathbogie

Tillyangus (1571)

Glenlivet (1594)

Cromdale (1690)

Alford (1645)

Corrichie (1562)

Aberdeen

Megray Hill (1639)

Inverlochy (1645)

Killiecrankie (1689)

Brechin (1452)

Montrose

Dunkeld (1689)

Dundee

Tibbermore (1644)

Perth

Stirling

Kilsyth (1645)

Glasgow

Edinburgh

Pinkie (1547)

Dunbar (1650)

Halidon Hill (1333)

Flodden (1513)

Philiphaugh (1645)

Homildon Hill (1402)

Otterburn (1388)

Battlesites

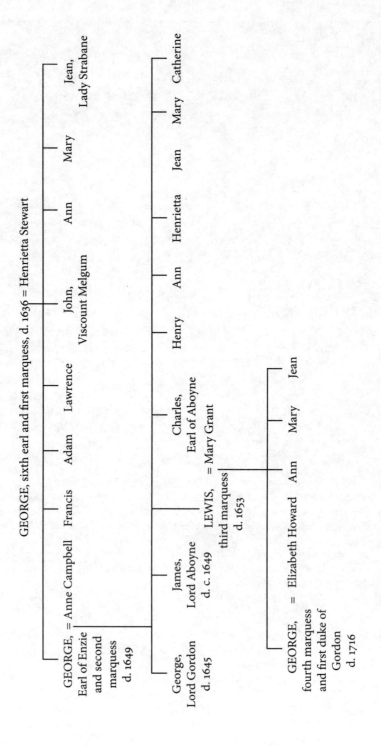

Gordon Family Tree

GEORGE, sixth earl and first marquess, d. 1636 = Henrietta Stewart

GEORGE, = Anne Campbell   Francis   Adam   Lawrence   John,   Ann   Mary   Jean,
Earl of Enzie   Viscount Melgum   Lady Strabane
and second
marquess
d. 1649

James,   George,   Charles,   Henry   Ann   Henrietta   Jean   Mary   Catherine
Lord Aboyne   Lord Gordon   Earl of Aboyne
d. c. 1649   d. 1645   = Mary Grant

LEWIS,
third marquess
d. 1653

GEORGE, = Elizabeth Howard   Ann   Mary   Jean
fourth marquess
and first duke of
Gordon
d. 1716

Introduction

Introduction

In many respects the nobility of early modern Scotland has been well studied in recent years. A number of monographs and articles have been published concentrating on aspects as diverse as aristocratic finances, indebtedness, anglicisation, the drawing up of bonds of association, feuding, and Crown-noble relations.[1] A range of more general studies have also been made which either seek to look at Scottish noble society as a whole or at the aristocracy and gentry of a particular region of the country.[2] Many of these are seminal works that go a long way to placing the Scottish nobility firmly within the historiography of the period. However, there remains a significant gap in all of this. Whereas a wealth of material has been produced that considers the aristocracy as a whole, relatively little modern research has been published which concentrates on individual households and nobles.[3] This is all the more surprising given how powerful

1 See, for example, K.M. Brown, 'Noble Indebtedness in Scotland between the Reformation and the Revolution', *Historical Research*, 62, no. 149 (Oct. 1989), 260–275; D.J. Menarry, 'Debt and the Scottish Landed Elite in the 1650s', in R.J. Morris and L. Kennedy (eds.), *Ireland and Scotland: Order and Disorder, 1600-2000* (Edinburgh, 2005), 23–33; K.M. Brown, 'The Scottish Aristocracy, Anglicization and the Court, 1603-38', *Historical Journal*, 36, no. 3 (1993), 543–576; J. Wormald, *Lords and Men in Scotland: Bonds of Manrent, 1442–1603* (Edinburgh, 1985); J. Wormald, 'Bloodfeud, Kindred and Government in Early Modern Scotland', *Past and Present*, no. 87 (1980), 54–97; K.M. Brown, *Bloodfeud in Scotland, 1573-1625. Violence, Justice and Politics in an Early Modern Society* (Edinburgh, 1986); M. Lee, 'James VI and the Aristocracy', *Scotia*, 1, no. 1 (1977), 18–23; J. Goodare, 'The Nobility and the Absolutist State in Scotland, 1584–1638', *History*, 78, no. 253 (June 1993), 161–182.

2 K.M. Brown, *Noble Society in Scotland. Wealth, Family and Culture, from Reformation to Revolution* (Edinburgh, 2000); M.M. Meikle, 'The Invisible Divide: the Greater Lairds and the Nobility of Jacobean Scotland', *Scottish Historical Review*, 71, nos. 191/2 (Apr., Oct. 1992), 70–87; S. Nenadic, *Lairds and Luxury: Highland Gentry in Eighteenth Century Scotland* (Edinburgh, 2007); M.M. Meikle, *A British Frontier? Landed Society in the Eastern Anglo-Scottish Borders, 1540–1603* (East Linton, 2004).

3 The list of works on individual families or nobles is slowly growing, but much remains to be done. For some of the material already available, see H.L. Rubinstein, *Captain Luckless: James, First Duke of Hamilton, 1606–1649* (Edinburgh, 1975); P.D. Anderson, *Robert Stewart, Earl of*

many of the families were and given their important role in early modern Scottish history. There was something of a boom in family histories during the nineteenth and early twentieth centuries but these provided little more than basic chronological narratives appended with transcriptions of letters, charters and other documents. Little was provided in the way of analysis.[4] All-in-all it would seem opportune to offer a study of one of the most prominent Scottish noble families: the Gordons of Huntly.

For much of the late medieval and early modern period the noble House of Huntly was a key player in Scottish political and social life, both at a regional and national level. The family owned extensive tracts of land stretching across the north of Scotland, commanded the allegiance of a powerful network of cadet families, and controlled the reins of local justice through a myriad of franchise courts and hereditary offices. It is all the more surprising, therefore, that so little has been published on them over the years. A couple of family histories emerged in the eighteenth century[5] and some narrative accounts in the early twentieth century, but not much else.[6] As such, while addressing the general imbalance already mentioned, this book also has the key aim of providing the first modern account of the House of Huntly.

The focus throughout is on the seventeenth century. There is a key reason for this. During the sixteenth century successive earls of Huntly gained the nickname 'Cock of the North' – a direct reference to the level of power they wielded in that part of the world as well as to their strutting, confident

---

Orkney, Lord of Shetland, 1533–1593 (Edinburgh, 1983); P.D. Anderson, *Black Patie. The Life and Times of Patrick Stewart, Earl of Orkney, Lord of Shetland* (Edinburgh, 1992); J.E.A. Dawson, *The Politics of Religion in the Age of Mary Queen of Scots. The Earl of Argyll and the Struggle for Britain and Ireland* (Cambridge, 2002). A number of biographies have also emerged devoted to James Graham, 1st marquis of Montrose. See, for example, J. Buchan, *Montrose* (London, 1928); R. Williams, *Montrose. Cavalier in Mourning* (London, 1975); M. Hastings, *Montrose. The King's Champion* (London, 1977); E.J. Cowan, *Montrose: For Covenant and King* (Paperback edn, Edinburgh, 1995).

4　See in particular the output of Sir William Fraser. Examples of his work include: W. Fraser, *The Book of Carlaverock*, 2 vols (Edinburgh, 1873); W. Fraser, *The Chiefs of Grant*, 3 vols (Edinburgh, 1883); W. Fraser, *The Sutherland Book*, 3 vols (Edinburgh, 1892).

5　W. Gordon, *A Concise History of the Ancient and Illustrious Family Of Gordon*, 2 vols (Edinburgh, 1726–7); C.A. Gordon, *A Concise History of the Ancient and Illustrious House of Gordon* (Aberdeen, 1890). The latter was originally published in 1754.

6　C. [Gordon], eleventh Marquis of Huntly, *The Records of Aboyne, 1230-1681* (Aberdeen, 1894), 353-553; J.M. Bulloch, *The First Duke of Gordon* (Huntly, 1908); J.M. Bulloch, *The Polish "Marquises of Huntly"* (Peterhead, 1932); C. [Gordon], eleventh Marquis of Huntly, *The Cock o' the North* (London, 1935). Bulloch also produced an edited volume that concentrated in the main on some of the cadet branches of the family. See J.M. Bulloch (ed.), *The House of Gordon*, 3 vols (Aberdeen, 1903–12). He also wrote a short book which focused on the House of Aboyne. See J.M. Bulloch, *The Earls of Aboyne* (Huntly, 1908).

demeanour. In 1547 George, fourth earl of Huntly, reportedly raised 8000 men of the North to fight at the Battle of Pinkie, and in 1594 George, sixth earl of Huntly, defeated a royal army that had been sent against him under the command of Archibald Campbell, seventh earl of Argyll.[7] However, fast-forward some 95 years to 1689 and it can be seen that George, first duke of Gordon, demonstrated little of the confident, fighting spirit of his forefathers. This was the year that the so-called 'Glorious Revolution' came to Scotland and for his part Gordon did little else other than surrender Edinburgh Castle to the forces of William of Orange after a somewhat inglorious siege. On top of this there seemed to be not much in the way of committed support for this nominally Jacobite duke amongst cadet families in the North-East, and certainly nothing like that afforded to previous generations of Gordon lords.[8] To compare the generations in this way raises the question of what might have changed in the meantime. Was the family less powerful than it had been in the previous century? Had it undergone a process of decline?

This becomes all the more intriguing in light of recent research on the early modern nobility, both at a Scottish and European-wide level. In the past a traditional view among historians held that the seventeenth century witnessed a period of marked decline of the European nobility, both politically (due to the centralising processes of state-building) and economically (due to the rise of a middle class). This has since been challenged and the consensus now rests with the idea that the nobility as a group showed remarkable resilience during the crises of the time, as well as through the state-building process, to emerge just as powerful as it had always been.[9] Indeed, to take England as an example, the years 1688 to 1788 can be seen as nothing less than the 'golden days' of its aristocracy.[10]

The same pattern has also been traced in Scotland. Although the fortunes of many individual families may have 'waxed and waned' during the seventeenth century, it is asserted that as a group the nobility was as strong as ever at the time of the union with England in 1707.[11] And although there were partic-

7 H. Potter, *Bloodfeud. The Stewarts and Gordons at War in the Age of Mary Queen of Scots* (Stroud, 2002), 40, 213–221.

8 P. Hopkins, *Glencoe and the End of the Highland War* (revised reprint, Edinburgh, 1998), 138, 146–147.

9 H.M. Scott and C. Storrs, 'Introduction: the Consolidation of Noble Power in Europe, c.1600–1800', in H.M. Scott (ed.), *The European Nobilities in the Seventeenth and Eighteenth Centuries*, 2 vols (Harlow, 1995), I, 8–9; H.M. Scott, 'Conclusion: the Continuity of Aristocratic Power', in *ibid.*, II, 274; S. Clark, *State and Status. The Rise of the State and Aristocratic Power in Western Europe* (Cardiff, 1995), 373; R.G. Asch, *Nobilities in Transition, 1550–1700. Courtiers and Rebels in Britain and Europe* (London, 2003), 4.

10 J. Cannon, 'The British Nobility, 1660–1800', in Scott (ed.), *European Nobilities*, I, 62.

11 K.M. Brown, *Kingdom or Province? Scotland and the Regal Union, 1603–1715* (Basingstoke and London, 1992), 33–34.

ular periods in the seventeenth century when the lesser landed proprietors, the lairds, extended their political power at the expense of the higher nobility (relatively speaking), the fact remains that they can be regarded as a lower tier of the nobility anyway.[12] More specifically, though lairds and administrators rose to positions of power during the reign of James VI and there was a corresponding increase in new peers, such 'new men' merely adopted the attitudes and lifestyles of the existing magnates. In short, the nobility as a unit retained its power and dominance.[13] Indeed, it has been asserted that at a European level it was this constant replenishment through the rise of new families that helped keep the nobility strong.[14]

As such, with the example of the House of Huntly in mind, this all poses a double question. Did that family indeed experience a relative decline in power, and if so, to what extent does this present an exceptional case? As has been seen, recent historians have asserted that while individual families may have gone into decline, as a group the nobility prospered. How, then, would findings pointing towards the relative decline of the Gordons affect such a thesis? Would the Gordons just have to be regarded as one of the unlucky households who had seen better days? Such questions form the heart of much of what follows and highlight the key overall theme that runs through all of the chapters.

A study based on the Gordons during the seventeenth century also provides the opportunity to gain a fresh perspective on a number of key events and historical themes. Many of these themes run throughout the book and most of them feed into and inform the overall topic of the House of Huntly and noble decline. The relationship between the monarch and the state on one hand, and

---

12 John Young has argued that with the increasing political power of the lairds and burgh commissioners a 'Scottish Commons' emerged in the Scottish Parliament during the 1640s. This was a direct consequence of the doubling of the vote of the Commissioners of the Shires (the parliamentary estate composed of the lairds) in 1640. See J.R. Young, 'The Scottish Parliament and the Covenanting Movement: the Emergence of a Scottish Commons', in J.R. Young (ed.), *Celtic Dimensions of the British Civil Wars* (Edinburgh, 1997), 164–184. For a case study showing how the vote doubled in Aberdeenshire in 1640, see J.R. Young, 'The Scottish Parliament in the Seventeenth Century: European Perspectives', in A.I. Macinnes, T. Riis and F.G. Pedersen (eds), *Ships, Guns and Bibles in the North Sea and the Baltic States, c.1350–c.1700* (East Linton, 2000), 161. While accepting this was the case, Keith Brown maintains that the lairds should be regarded, along with the parliamentary peers, as part of the nobility anyway; indeed, in his view, the lairds can be termed the 'lesser nobility'. As such, for Brown, the Scottish Parliament remained a body dominated by the nobles, particularly following the restoration of the Stuart monarchy in 1660. See K.M. Brown and A.J. Mann, 'Introduction. Parliament and Politics in Scotland, 1567–1707', in K.M. Brown and A.J. Mann (eds), *Parliament and Politics in Scotland, 1567–1707* (Edinburgh, 2005), 22, 40.

13 Meikle, 'Invisible Divide', 86–7; K.M. Brown, 'Nobility of Jacobean Scotland, 1567–1625', in J. Wormald (ed.), *Scotland Revisited* (London, 1991), 61–72, at 72.

14 Scott and Storrs, 'Consolidation of Noble Power', 15–16.

successive heads of the House of Huntly on the other, proves a common thread. Connected to this is the question of the autonomy of the Gordon lords as regional magistrates and the extent to which the Crown looked to impinge on this over the course of the century. The role of the Gordon lords as Highland landowners also comes under scrutiny, particularly in relation to their activities as agents of the Crown and as power-brokers in that part of the country. Religion forms an important thread, a number of the Gordon lords having been Catholic: how did this impact on their relationship with the Crown and with the Kirk? How was the overall standing of the household affected? And looming large at the centre of the story are the civil wars of the mid-seventeenth century. As a key royalist family, the Gordons of Huntly played a major role in these conflicts and so warrant more extensive treatment than has hitherto been afforded them. The historiography of Scottish Royalism is still dominated by the numerous studies devoted to James Graham, first marquess of Montrose, thus making it impera- tive that another side to the story be presented.[15] More generally, given that the Scottish historiography of the civil war period is generally lacking in modern regional studies and in biographies of key nobles, this book will help in filling an important gap.[16]

The Civil Wars have also been at the centre of a lengthy debate among historians over the so-called 'New British and Irish History'.[17] Early formulations

15 See footnote 3 for the key biographies of Montrose. The Montrose narrative also lies at the heart of the following: S. Reid, *The Campaigns of Montrose* (Edinburgh, 1990); R. Williams, *The Heather and the Gale: Clan Donald and Clan Campbell during the Wars of Montrose* (Colonsay, 1997). David Stevenson provided an extremely important new perspective on the wars in D. Stevenson, *Highland Warrior: Alasdair MacColla and the Civil Wars* (Edinburgh, 1994). This was originally published in 1980 under the title *Alasdair MacColla and the Highland Problem in the Seventeenth Century*. Also of note is Jane Ohlmeyer's biography of the Gaelic lord, Randal MacDonnell, marquess of Antrim. See J.H. Ohlmeyer, *Civil War and Restoration in the Three Stuart Kingdoms: the Career of Randal MacDonnell, Marquis of Antrim* (2nd edn, Dublin, 2001).

16 Important modern works in this vein include: A.I. Macinnes, 'Scottish Gaeldom, 1638–1651: the Vernacular Response to the Covenanting Dynamic', in J. Dwyer, R.A. Mason and A. Murdoch (eds), *New Perspectives on the Politics and Culture of Early Modern Scotland* (Edinburgh, 1982), 59–94; A.I. Macinnes, *Clanship, Commerce and the House of Stuart, 1603–1788* (East Linton, 1996), 88–121; S. Adams, 'The Making of the Radical South-West: Charles I and his Scottish Kingdom, 1625–1649', in Young (ed.), *Celtic Dimensions*, 53–74; S. Adams, 'A Regional Road to Revolution: Religion, Politics and Society in South-West Scotland, 1600–1650' (unpublished PhD thesis, University of Edinburgh, 2002); L.A.M. Stewart, *Urban Politics and the British Civil Wars: Edinburgh, 1617–1653* (Leiden, 2006); J. Scally, 'The Political Career of James, Third Marquis and First Duke of Hamilton (1606–1649) to 1643' (unpublished PhD thesis, Selwyn College, University of Cambridge, 1992).

17 For the origins of this, see J.G.A. Pocock, 'British History: a Plea for a New Subject', *Journal of Modern History*, vol. 47, no. 4 (1975), 601–628. A range of works have since contributed to the debate. See, for example, D. Stevenson, 'The Century of the Three Kingdoms', *History Today*, vol. 35, no. 3 (March 1985), 28–33; C. Russell, 'The British Problem and the English Civil War',

of this approach looked to adopt a wider contextual framework within which to explain the origins of the English Civil Wars. It was deemed necessary that consideration be given to how the political situations in Scotland and Ireland impacted on England and helped spark the revolutionary process there. However, it has remained open to the criticism that this simply involves the writing of an enriched English history that remains Anglocentric in its overall scope.[18] In response a number of scholars have advocated a more holistic approach that stresses the need for a balanced treatment of all the separate nations that formed part of the multiple-monarchy of the seventeenth-century Stuart kings, and the need that the key interactions between them be fully understood.[19] From this comes the formulation of a two-level approach in which British and Irish history consists of individual histories of England, Ireland, Scotland and Wales running alongside a 'macro-narrative' that examines the interactions and the overall process of state-building.[20]

Others remain cautious about 'New British History' and point out that concentrating as it does on high-level politics it runs the danger of underestimating social and economic considerations.[21] And some scholars are convinced that 'New British History' is now a redundant concept that remains Anglocentric in its approach and which underplays transoceanic aspects as well as Scottish and Irish links to the continent.[22] From this it would seem that a much more complex history needs to emerge, one that does not remain dogmatic about

---

History, vol. 72, no. 236 (1987), 395–415; H. Kearney, *The British Isles. A History of Four Nations* (Cambridge, 1989); J.S. Morrill (ed.), *The Scottish National Covenant in its British Context, 1638–51* (Edinburgh, 1990); C. Russell, *The Fall of the British Monarchies, 1637–1642* (Oxford, 1991); R.G. Asch (ed.), *Three Nations – a Common History? England, Scotland, Ireland and British History, c.1600–1920* (Bochum, 1993); J. Morrill, *The Nature of the English Revolution* (Harlow, 1993), 252–272; Ohlmeyer, *Civil War and Restoration*; S.G. Ellis and S. Barber (eds), *Conquest and Union: Fashioning a British State, 1485–1725* (Harlow, 1995); B. Bradshaw and J. Morrill (eds), *The British Problem, c.1534–1707: State Formation in the Atlantic Archipelago* (Basingstoke and London, 1996); Young (ed.), *Celtic Dimensions*; J. Ohlmeyer, 'The Wars of the Three Kingdoms', *History Today*, vol. 48, no. 11 (Nov. 1998), 16–22; G. Burgess (ed.), *The New British History. Founding a Modern State, 1603–1715* (London, 1999); N. Canny, *Making Ireland British* (Oxford, 2001); A.I. Macinnes and J. Ohlmeyer (eds), *The Stuart Kingdoms in the Seventeenth Century: Awkward Neighbours?* (Dublin, 2001); A.I. Macinnes, *The British Revolution, 1629–1660* (Basingstoke and New York, 2005), 1–7.

18 This criticism has been directed by John Morrill and others at the work of Conrad Russell. See G. Burgess, 'Introduction: The New British History', in Burgess (ed.), *New British History*, 4.

19 This has been the approach most strongly advocated by Morrill. See, *ibid.*, 3.

20 S.G. Ellis, 'Introduction. The Concept of British History', in Ellis and Barber (eds), *Conquest and Union*, 1–7.

21 N. Canny, 'The Attempted Anglicization of Ireland in the Seventeenth Century: an Exemplar of "British History"', in Asch (ed.), *Three Nations*, 50.

22 Macinnes, *British Revolution*, 2–3.

having to fit into any one formulation of what some scholars think British and Irish history should be. As wide a contextual framework should be adopted as possible and naturally should be adapted to the needs of whatever question a given historian is seeking to answer. This seems only common sense. From all this should come not only a multi-level history that encompasses regional, national, pan-national and international perspectives but also one that encompasses political, religious, social and economic aspects as well as the history of ideas and so forth.

This book certainly seeks to hold with this view. In some sections the Britannic dimension becomes apparent, and is duly referred to when this is the case. Other aspects of the history of the family solely require Scottish contextualisation, while other sections need to reflect an awareness of what was going on in the wider world. When studying nobles such as the Gordon lords it soon becomes apparent that they themselves operated across what historians might want to designate to be 'boundaries'. Politically, socially and culturally there was a great mix there. While on the one hand they could be found acting as royal agents and power-brokers in the Highlands, they could also be found operating as Lowland landowners and sometime members of the Privy Council of Scotland. At other times they were at the British courts of the Stuart kings as well as on the continent as soldiers and travellers. In many ways the family was by no means just a 'Scottish' or a 'British' household. This book aims to reflect that. It also looks to adopt the aforementioned multi-disciplinary approach; that is to say it is not just a political, family, cultural, religious or military history, but is a mix of all these elements.

To turn briefly to a discussion of sources: although what remains in the way of personal correspondence is patchy, on the whole the family is well served in terms of primary printed material. Indeed, when looking at the period from 1603 to around 1635 the family has been so well served that very little Gordon-related primary material remains unpublished.[23] Added to this is a canon of excellent published chronicles that remain especially useful when looking at the North of Scotland during the early to mid-seventeenth century.[24] For the

---

23 Of particular note in this regard are the following collections of royal and state correspondence: *State Papers and Miscellaneous Correspondence of Thomas, Earl of Melros*, ed. J. Maidment, 2 vols (Edinburgh, 1837); *Letters and State Papers during the Reign of King James the Sixth*, ed. J. Maidment (Edinburgh, 1838); *Original Letters relating to the Ecclesiastical Affairs of Scotland, chiefly written or addressed to his Majesty King James the Sixth after his Accession to the English Throne*, ed. B. Botfield, 2 vols (Edinburgh, 1851); *The Earl of Stirling's Register of Royal Letters relative to the Affairs of Scotland and Nova Scotia from 1615 to 1635*, ed. C. Rogers, 2 vols (Edinburgh, 1885).

24 R. Gordon, of Gordonstoun and G. Gordon, of Sallach, *A Genealogical History of the Earldom of Sutherland from its Origin to the Year 1630 ... with a Continuation to the Year 1651* (Edinburgh,

late 1630s onwards considerably more is available in the form of unpublished manuscript material. In the National Archives of Scotland the Hamilton papers contain a wealth of material for the years 1638 and 1639, while in the Gordon papers there are a number of letters and other documents covering the period from the 1640s onwards.[25] There is another repository containing important family letters and documents at the West Sussex Record Office in Chichester, England.[26] Inveraray Castle Archives houses essential material relating to the dealings between the families of Argyll and Huntly, while the British Library has the extensive correspondence that was conducted between the Gordons and John Maitland, second earl of Lauderdale during the 1660s and 1670s.[27]

A chronological approach is adopted throughout the book. Chapter 1 follows the history of the family from its origins through to 1603 thus providing a necessary base of background material. The years 1603 to 1636 are examined in chapters 2 and 3, while chapters 4 and 5 consider the involvements of the House of Huntly in the Civil Wars. Chapter 6 concentrates on the Restoration years and culminates with the Williamite Revolution of 1688–9. Interpolated throughout are the stories of the patriarchs of the family during this period: the first four marquesses of Huntly, the last of whom became the first duke of Gordon. Overall, this is a story of their aspirations, trials and tribulations, set against a backdrop of a century of turbulent national history.

1813); J. Gordon, Parson of Rothiemay, *History of Scots Affairs from 1637 to 1641*, eds J. Robertson and G. Grub, 3 vols (Aberdeen, 1841); P. Gordon, of Ruthven, *A Short Abridgement of Britane's Distemper from 1639 to 1649*, ed. J. Dunn (Aberdeen, 1844); J. Spalding, *Memorialls of the Trubles in Scotland and in England, A.D. 1624-A.D. 1645*, ed. J. Stuart, 2 vols (Aberdeen, 1841–2).

25 NAS, GD 406, Hamilton MSS; NAS, GD 44, Gordon MSS. The holdings in the latter are extensive but in the main they consist of the minutiae of countless land transactions across the centuries.

26 WSRO, Goodwood MSS.

27 Inveraray Castle Archives, Miscellaneous bundles; BL, Additional MSS – The Lauderdale Papers.

ONE

The House of Huntly
and the North of Scotland

INTRODUCTION

By the time of the accession of King James VI to the throne of England in 1603 the Gordons of Huntly had risen to become one of the foremost dynasties in what was now the northernmost state in James's new multiple-kingdom. Indeed, as recently as April 1599 George Gordon, sixth earl of Huntly, had been elevated by royal decree to the title of marquess of Huntly, earl of Enzie, Lord Gordon and Badenoch.[1] On top of this he already held title to extensive tracts of territory stretching from rural Aberdeenshire, through Banffshire and the Cairngorms to the Highland vastnesses of Badenoch and Lochaber, and in addition could potentially command the allegiance of a large number of associated followers. Cadet branches bearing the Gordon surname remained plentiful across the North-East of Scotland and the household retained influence in the localities and associated burghs through sheriffships and through franchise courts. On paper, at least, the power and status of the House of Huntly certainly remained apparent.

How, then, was all this achieved and in reality just how stable was the position of the household immediately prior to the dawn of the new age of Jacobean Britain? This chapter provides an overview of their rise as a family of national standing and examines the extent of their hold over the North of Scotland. It outlines the landholdings and strongholds gained by the family, examines the cadet-based kin network, details the relationship between the Gordons and other key north-east families, touches on the position the household held in the main burghs of the area, and lastly shows how the Huntly earls operated in their Highland lordships. It also looks in some detail at the complex political situation that developed during the years 1589 to 1599 – a period that witnessed foreign intrigue, Catholic rebellions, political manoeuvring at the royal court, a couple of notable murders, a pitched battle and a level of violence across the North-East of Scotland that seemed at times to verge on civil war. The Catholic

1 NAS, GD44/13/2/4.

sixth earl of Huntly was deeply implicated in all of this and so some under-standing of what resulted is important in order to assess the overall state of the House of Huntly around the turn of the century. Were there any signs of decline? What was the standing of the family both in the North-East and in the Highlands and how had the troubles of the 1590s affected the situation?

THE RISE OF THE GORDONS

As is the case for most Scottish noble households, the true origins of the Gordons of Huntly remain elusive. From the Middle Ages onwards a number of Gordon histories and genealogies did attempt to shine a light into the dark recesses of the family's early years, but the veracity of what was presented in such accounts is open to serious question.[2] It was claimed, for example, that the Gordons originated in France and came across to England with William the Conqueror.[3] This seems largely fanciful. Given the available evidence, it is probably safer to postulate that their origins lay in the North of England and that they eventually occupied the lands of Gordon in Berwickshire sometime between the years 1058 and 1153.[4]

The first member of the family to make a marked impact in national polit-ical affairs was Sir Adam Gordon in the early fourteenth century. He initially backed the English Crown during the Wars of Independence, but latterly, and in timely fashion, saw fit to lend his support to Robert the Bruce. Later, as a Scottish ambassador to Pope John XXII, he became one of those responsible for the delivery of the letter that was later to gain the title of the Declaration of Arbroath. On account of such service, belated though it was, Sir Adam was rewarded with new lands in the form of the recently forfeited north-east barony of Strathbogie.[5] His descendents looked to demonstrate similar levels of loyal service to the Scottish Crown, most notably in a military capacity at the battles of Halidon Hill (1333), Otterburn (1388) and Homildon Hill (1402).[6] The steady rise of the household continued unabated and seems to have been little compromised by the fact that the line of male heirs actually died out in 1408. At this point the estates fell to a female, Elizabeth Gordon, and to her husband,

2 G. Ross, 'The Royal Lieutenancy: Case Studies of the Houses of Argyll and Huntly, 1475–1567' (unpublished MPhil thesis, University of Aberdeen, 2002). For a chronological list of the various histories, see Bulloch (ed.), *House of Gordon*, I, xxxi–xxxix.

3 Gordon, *Family of Gordon*, I, 4; Gordon, *House of Gordon*, 2; [Gordon], *Records of Aboyne*, 353.

4 Most sources venture the arrival of the Gordons in Scotland as having taken place during the reign of Malcolm III. See Gordon, *Family of Gordon*, I, 2–5; Gordon, *House of Gordon*, 4; [Gordon], *Records of Aboyne*, 353. Graeme Ross has suggested that the family first moved from England during the reign of David I. See Ross, *Royal Lieutenancy*, 13–14.

5 GD44/2/1/1–2.

6 [Gordon], *Records of Aboyne*, 363–371.

Alexander Seton of that Ilk. Seton was happy to adopt the title, lord Gordon, and the eldest son of this marriage, another Alexander, eventually forsook his given surname in favour of that of Gordon.[7]

It was this particular Alexander who found himself elevated by James II to the title of earl of Huntly.[8] Essentially he had succeeded in making a series of shrewd political moves during the 1440s and 1450s, backing the correct factions at the correct times, and in particular had strongly supported the king in his bitter struggle with the Douglas family. Indeed, Huntly had done much to ensure royal victory over the latter, not least of all with his success in battle against the Douglas-aligned earl of Crawford at Brechin in 1452.[9] Clearly, the Gordons had by this time arrived as a major force in Scottish politics, a situation that they looked to build on and exploit.

The Gordon earls were certainly never to be found too far away from the political spotlight in the decades that followed. They were, for example, present at the battles of Flodden (1513) and Pinkie (1547).[10] They also occupied some of the highest offices in the land. In 1497 George, second earl of Huntly obtained the chancellorship of Scotland, as did his great grandson, George, fourth earl of Huntly, for periods during the 1540s and 1550s.[11] Following the demise of James IV in 1513, Alexander, third earl of Huntly became one of those appointed as a councillor to the queen mother, Margaret Tudor, a position similar to that held by the fourth earl upon the death of James V in 1542.[12] This last earl had also been one of the regents of Scotland for a period of months from 1536 to 1537 when James V was in France in search of a bride.[13]

At the same time successive members of the household remained adept at managing to weather the storm during periods of political uncertainty or when they themselves stood in temporary disgrace. In the 1490s, for example, Alexander, master of Huntly (the future third earl) was received back into political favour by James IV in spite of formerly backing the party of the deposed James III. This had probably been facilitated by the fact that the second earl

---

7 *Ibid.*, 372–380.

8 N. Macdougall, *James III. A Political Study* (Edinburgh, 1982), 13.

9 *Ibid.*, 12–13, 23–28.

10 N. Macdougall, *James IV* (East Linton, 1997), 275; M. Merriman, *The Rough Wooings. Mary Queen of Scots, 1542–1551* (East Linton, 2000), 262.

11 Macdougall, *James IV*, 152; Merriman, *Rough Wooings*, 202; Potter, *Bloodfeud*, 39, 45; P.E. Ritchie, *Mary of Guise in Scotland, 1548–1560* (East Linton, 2002), 125.

12 R.D. Oram, 'Gordon, Alexander, Third Earl of Huntly (*d.* 1524)', *Oxford Dictionary of National Biography* [henceforth *ODNB*], Oxford University Press, 2004, http://www.oxforddnb.com, accessed 27 August 2009; D. Franklin, *The Scottish Regency of the Earl of Arran. A Study in the Failure of Anglo-Scottish Relations* (Lampeter, 1995), 9–10.

13 J. Cameron, *James V. The Personal Rule, 1528–1542* (East Linton, 1998), 133.

had remained neutral during the struggle between the royal father and son in 1488 and had subsequently given his backing to James IV's new regime from its inception.[14] In 1554, George, fourth earl of Huntly likewise recovered from a period spent temporarily out of favour with the Crown for having failed to satisfy the queen mother, Mary of Guise, that he had taken sufficient action to subdue a Highland rising involving Clan Cameron and John Moidart, chief of Clanranald.[15]

The family even survived a period spent in rebellion against the regime of Mary, Queen of Scots. During the Reformation crisis of 1559–60, the fourth earl followed a political path which he felt would guarantee the future wellbeing of his household. Initially he vacillated but by April 1560 he had abandoned the cause of Mary of Guise and had backed the reforming Lords of the Congregation. In essence he traded religious reformation in return for the assurance that political revolution would not occur and that he would retain his lands, local offices and privileges.[16] However, the following year he changed tack, offering to raise a Catholic army for Mary Queen of Scots and to enforce counter-reformation at the point of a sword. Unfortunately for Huntly, the young queen had her eye firmly on the prize of the throne of Protestant England and so with the advice of her half-brother, Lord James Stewart (soon-to-be confirmed as earl of Moray), she spurned these advances. Relations quickly deteriorated between the Crown and Huntly and culminated in the rebellion of the latter in 1562 and his defeat by Moray at the Battle of Corrichie in October of that year. Huntly died of a seizure while being led prisoner from the field and his third son, John, was subsequently executed in Aberdeen.[17] The Gordons, however, soon benefited from the fluid political situation that developed as the 1560s wore on, and in 1565, George, fifth earl of Huntly, found himself restored to his titles and to the queen's favour.[18] The following decade, in spite of his support for Mary Queen of Scots (deposed in 1567), he again managed to secure the future of his household by making peace with the regime headed by James Douglas, fourth earl of Morton, then regent to the young James VI.[19]

---

14 Macdougall, *James IV*, 29–42, 61–76, 121. The crisis of 1488 had ended with the victory of the rebel forces of James IV at the Battle of Sauchieburn and the death of James III.

15 Potter, *Bloodfeud*, 49–50; Ritchie, *Mary of Guise*, 164–165; A. Cathcart, *Kinship and Clientage: Highland Clanship, 1451–1609* (Leiden, 2006), 187–189; [Gordon], *Records of Aboyne*, 454–455.

16 A. White, 'Gordon, George, Fourth Earl of Huntly (1513–1562)', *ODNB*, http://www.oxforddnb.com, accessed 27 August 2009.

17 Potter, *Bloodfeud*, 57–76; J. Wormald, *Mary Queen of Scots. A Study in Failure* (London, 1988), 123–124.

18 G. Donaldson, *All the Queen's Men. Power and Politics in Mary Stewart's Scotland* (London, 1983), 74–92.

19 This peace was secured in February 1573. See G.R. Hewitt, *Scotland under Morton, 1572–80*

By the late 1580s it seemed as though the House of Huntly was once again in the ascendant. This largely stemmed from the deep personal regard that had developed between James VI and George, sixth earl of Huntly during the decade. On one level, Huntly had provided vital political support at a time when James had been seeking to extricate himself from the control of the zealously Protestant Gowrie faction. Indeed, the Gordon earl had been among those responsible for co-ordinating the king's flight from their hands in June 1583.[20] On another level, Huntly may have functioned as a replacement for the king's great (now deceased) favourite, Esmé Stewart, duke of Lennox. Like Stewart, Huntly was reportedly handsome and had spent a number of years in France. Prior to his return to Scotland in 1581 it seems that he had been enrolled in the University of Paris and had attended the court of Henry III. He may thus have exuded the same refined air that James had found so attractive in Lennox.[21] The king certainly took a keen interest in the internal affairs of the Gordon household. From 1586, for example, he was instrumental in helping arrange the marriage of Huntly to Henrietta Stewart, Lennox's daughter. He even began to write a masque especially for the occasion, and the wedding itself – which took place in July 1588 – reportedly used up a full 5 per cent of the royal household's expenditure for that year.[22] The Gordon earl also benefited from the king's favouritism in terms of grants and titles. In 1584 he was appointed one of the Lords of the Articles, while in November 1588 he was made Captain of the Guard.[23]

(Edinburgh, 1982), 25–26. The fifth earl later died a somewhat inglorious death. On 20 October 1576 he was taken ill while playing football and expired around three hours later, probably of an internal haemorrhage. See [Gordon], *Records of Aboyne*, 497–498.

20 Potter, *Bloodfeud*, 127; A. Stewart, *The Cradle King. A Life of James VI and I* (London, 2003), 72. The Gowrie faction had been in possession of the king's person for a matter of ten months. Headed by the earls of Gowrie and Mar, the members of this group had been concerned that James had been too much under the influence of his cousin, the Catholic sympathiser, Esmé Stewart, duke of Lennox. In August 1582 they had thus engineered a *coup d'état*, luring James to Huntingtower Castle (near Perth) and refusing to let him leave. They then proceeded to become the *de facto* power in the land for the period James remained under their influence. Lennox subsequently died in France in May 1583.

21 P. Croft, *King James* (Basingstoke, 2003), 33; Potter, *Bloodfeud*, 124, 128. David Mathew put it well when he stated that 'James VI was always taken by a man of rank who combined martial vigour with an experience of the manners of the court of France.' See D. Mathew, *Scotland under Charles I*, (London, 1955), 138.

22 Potter, *Bloodfeud*, 138–139; R.J. Lyall, 'James VI and the Sixteenth-Century Cultural Crisis', in J. Goodare and M. Lynch (eds), *The Reign of James VI* (East Linton, 2000), 66–67; J. Wormald, '"Tis True I am a Cradle King": the View from the Throne', in Goodare and Lynch (eds), *The Reign*, 252–253; Croft, *King James*, 33.

23 J.R.M. Sizer, 'Gordon, George, First Marquess of Huntly (1561/2–1636)', *ODNB*, http://www.oxforddnb.com, accessed 27 August 2009.

LANDHOLDING AND POWER IN THE NORTH

By this time the Huntly earls had managed to acquire large quantities of territory stretching across the North of Scotland. These included the lands of Strathbogie, Aboyne, Glen Tanar, Glen Muick, the Enzie, Auchindoun, as well as the Highland lordships of Badenoch and Lochaber.[24] For the most part these had accumulated piecemeal, usually in the form of gifts from successive monarchs. The household also maintained a number of castles and strongholds, chief amongst them being Bog of Gight (now Gordon Castle) in the Enzie, Ruthven Castle (subsequently Ruthven Barracks) in Badenoch, and their main seat, Strathbogie Castle (now Huntly Castle), at the heart of the lordship.[25] On top of this the earls had also secured positions as the hereditary sheriffs of the shires of Inverness and Aberdeen.[26] These remained important as it was through them and the associated courts that the Gordon earls established and maintained themselves as legitimate power-brokers and law-givers in the North of Scotland. Sheriffs performed a number of different functions but most commonly they would be involved in judging criminal cases and administering land titles.[27] Meanwhile as major landholders the earls also retained the right to hold barony and regality courts. The remit of baron courts mainly stretched to trying lesser criminal cases such as assault and to regulating local land laws. The regalities were far more powerful, and possessed a right to try serious cases of crime, including what were known as the four pleas of the Crown: murder, robbery, rape and arson.[28]

Also important was the Gordon hold over successive lieutenancies of the North. These originally appear to have been granted mainly with the Highland dimension in mind, particularly in connection with the need to uphold law and order and the royal will in that part of the world following the forfeiture of the Lordship of the Isles in 1493. They also seem to have appertained to Lowland areas of the North, the third earl of Huntly's commission of 1501 designating him lieutenant-general north of 'the Mounth'. The powers invested remained very wide-ranging, encompassing the right to grant tacks of land, hunt down

---

24 [Gordon], *Records of Aboyne*, 391, 417–418; Potter, *Bloodfeud*, 61.

25 Bog of Gight was founded by George, second earl of Huntly. See L. Shaw and J.F.S. Gordon, *The History of the Province of Moray*, 3 vols (Glasgow and London, 1882), I, 50–51. Alexander, first earl of Huntly received Ruthven Castle along with the lordship of Badenoch as a gift from James II in 1451. See [Gordon], *Records of Aboyne*, 387; Cathcart, *Kinship and Clientage*, 40–41.

26 James IV granted the former position in 1509. See Macdougall, *James IV*, 190. The fourth earl of Huntly was granted the hereditary position of sheriff of Aberdeen in the early 1540s. See *Records of the Sheriff Court of Aberdeenshire*, ed. D. Littlejohn, 3 vols (Aberdeen, 1904–7), I, 425.

27 For the role of the sheriffs in Scottish local government, see J. Goodare, *The Government of Scotland, 1560–1625* (Oxford, 2004), 176.

28 *Ibid.*, 183–185.

and prosecute 'broken men' (ostracised and outlawed servitors or clansmen), execute the law of the land, make law in the king's name, and grant pardons for all crimes against the king (excepting treason). Alongside this came the right to reap financial benefits, mainly through appropriation of forfeited land and gifts of escheat (goods belonging to denounced rebels).[29]

The power of regional families such as the Gordons of Huntly was also made evident by the manner in which local feuds and disputes were regulated and resolved. Essentially by the 1570s a system had developed whereby, in the event of a dispute of some kind, the aggrieved party would normally approach an authoritative figure such as Huntly in order that reparations could be pursued. The next step would then involve arbitration with a view to resolution based upon the aggrieved party receiving compensation of some kind. Crucially, in most cases the key factor remained that both sides should emerge from the affair believing that justice had been fairly served. In early modern Scotland animosities could easily develop into protracted feuds and so peaceful resolutions, as brokered by nobles such as Huntly, proved vital if extensive bloodshed was to be avoided. At any rate, in a world where local power was all, individuals had scarcely anywhere else to turn other than to the justice of the local power-broker. In the case of the earls of Huntly, this proved another aspect of their hold over the North.[30]

Not only that, but the household could also look to the support of an extended kin network. It has been postulated that by around the middle decades of the sixteenth century the number of families sporting the Gordon surname exceeded 150. Not all could claim a direct bloodline relationship to the Huntly household and indeed some had no doubt merely looked to affiliate themselves to the strongest power in the area, for protection if for no other reason. Successive Huntly earls, with an eye to their own expanding power and influence, had naturally been only too keen to welcome them.[31] For the most part, though, it seems that the majority of the Gordon cadet families – particularly the more

---

29 See Ross, 'Royal Lieutenancy', 33–40. Essentially, 'the Mounth' was a term used in reference to the natural upland barrier of the Grampian Mountains. The jurisdiction of the lieutenancy of the North encompassed the territory stretching from Caithness in the Far North to the eastern edge of the Grampian Mountains at Cairn o' Mount just south-west of Aberdeen. In practice this included everything north of the River North Esk on the east coast, as well as the Highland lordships of Badenoch and Lochaber and the Western Isles north of Coll. For more detail on the rise of the Gordons as a power in the Highlands, see Cathcart, *Kinship and Clientage*, 159–166.

30 For full discussion of bloodfeud in Scotland, see Wormald, 'Bloodfeud'; Brown, *Bloodfeud in Scotland*.

31 Potter, *Bloodfeud*, 28. Jenny Wormald, in her seminal work on lordship in early modern Scotland, has noted that loyalty associated with kinship was a very strong force throughout the period. See Wormald, *Lords and Men*, 80.

important ones – looked to claim some form of link by blood. There were two main strands to this. Some families were of Seton-Gordon stock in that they claimed descent from the earls of Huntly themselves. These included such notable branches as the Gordons of Abergeldie, Gight, Letterfourie and Cluny.[32] Also influential amongst this grouping were the Gordons of Sutherland – a branch that stemmed from the marriage of Adam Gordon, a son of George, second earl of Huntly, to Elizabeth, heiress to the earldom of Sutherland, sometime prior to 1514. A grandson of theirs, John, had gone on to become the first earl of Sutherland to bear the Gordon surname.[33] Other cadet families looked to claim kinship stretching back somewhat further to the pre-Seton-Gordon lords. Notable branches in this instance included the Gordons of Haddo, Cairnborrow, Lesmore, Craig and Buckie.[34]

What all this amounted to was a situation where, for the most part, such families remained willing and able to take the part of the House of Huntly should this be required. Such support was, for example, to be seen in abundance at the battles of Flodden and Pinkie.[35] It was likewise highly evident during a period of confrontation between the House of Huntly and another notable regional family, the House of Forbes, in the early 1570s.[36] The support of some of the cadet lines even seems to have remained fairly firm during the Corrichie campaign of 1562, a remarkable occurrence given that George, fourth earl of Huntly was in rebellion against the Crown. Indeed, although two or three Gordon lairds, including Haddo, did eventually take the field against Huntly it is noteworthy that more did not follow the same path. Admittedly, many lairds must have retained a neutral stance on this occasion but the case remains that most of Huntly's support, such as it was, was garnered from his Gordon kindred.[37]

32 See 'The Balbithan MS', ed. J.M. Bulloch, in Bulloch (ed.), *House of Gordon*, I, 9, 15, 18–19.

33 *Ibid.*, 14; 'Tables compiled and collected together by the great paines and industrie of Sir Robert Gordon, Knight Baronett of Gordonstoun sone to Alexander, Earl of Southerland, copied out of his papers and continued be Maister Robert Gordon, his son', 1659, ed. J.M. Joass, in Bulloch (ed.), *House of Gordon*, II, 130–131.

34 'Balbithan MS', 26–68.

35 Examples of Gordon notables killed at Flodden included Gight, Tillyminnat and Craig. Those killed at Pinkie included Pittlurg, Cairnborrow, Craig, Proney, Knowen, Ardbroglach and Abergeldie. See *ibid.*, 15, 31, 33, 42, 50, 59–61; J.M. Bulloch, 'Abergeldie', in Bulloch (ed.), *House of Gordon*, I, 78.

36 'Balbithan MS', 22, 46, 57; J.M. Bulloch, 'Gight', in Bulloch (ed.), *House of Gordon*, I, 192.

37 At least 28 Gordon lairds appear to have been with Huntly at Corrichie. See Donaldson, *All the Queen's Men*, 53. Named Gordons present included Blelack, Terpersie, Coclarachie, Easter-migvie, Auchiniff and Abergeldie. See 'Balbithan MS', 42, 46, 52, 59, 62; Bulloch, 'Abergeldie', 79; S. Lee, 'Coclarachie', in Bulloch (ed.), *House of Gordon*, I, 123. Sons of certain lairds may also have been present in their fathers' stead, an example seemingly being Patrick Gordon of Oxhill, fifth son of the Laird of Lesmore. See D. Wimberley, 'Lesmoir', in Bulloch (ed.), *House of Gordon*, II, 171–172.

Having said that, the defection of a key laird such as Gordon of Haddo must have had a detrimental effect and overall the Corrichie campaign can in no way be portrayed as the finest moment of the family. It remained, however, an aberration, not to be repeated amongst the Gordons of the North-East during the sixteenth century. The point is that with the full and undivided support of the cadet lines the Gordon earls could put on a considerable show of strength, particularly so in comparison with neighbouring households.

The Sutherland earldom certainly remained a jewel in the Gordon crown. The earls of Sutherland were of noble status in their own right, a fact of which the Huntly earls were keenly aware. It is noticeable that of all the cadet lines the Sutherland family was the only one with which the House of Huntly was prepared to engage in intermarriage. Two marriages form the root of this assertion, one in 1573 between Alexander, eleventh earl of Sutherland, and Jane Gordon, daughter of the fourth earl of Huntly; and the other between Jean, second daughter of John, tenth earl of Sutherland, and Thomas, ninth son of the said Huntly earl.[38] Politically, both the tenth and eleventh earls of Sutherland remained close to their Huntly counterparts, and were allies throughout the Corrichie affair and during the Forbes feud of the early 1570s.[39] Clearly, by the 1580s, the Gordons had created a commanding kin-based power-bloc in the North of Scotland. Indeed, it can be asserted that by that time there existed a 'Gordon conglomerate, controlled by the earls of Huntly and Sutherland'.[40]

Outside of kinship, the Huntly earls would often look to use bonds of manrent as a means by which to build political alliances with other families in the North. These bonds consisted of a written agreement whereby the subject promised to serve a particular lord in any way that might be required, perhaps providing him with counsel on occasion, or defending his person should the need arise. In return that particular lord would look to protect and maintain the subject in question.[41] In other words it was an attempt to extend the natural obligations

---

38 Fraser, *Sutherland Book*, I, 137; J.B. Paul, *The Scots Peerage*, 9 vols (Edinburgh, 1904– 14), VIII, 343–344.

39 Fraser, *Sutherland Book*, I, 120, 134–135.

40 A. MacCoinnich, '"His Spirit was given only to Warre": Conflict and Identity in the Scottish Gàidhealtachd, c.1580–c.1630', in S. Murdoch and A. Mackillop (eds), *Fighting for Identity. Scottish Military Experience, c.1550–1900* (Leiden, 2002), 152. It should be remembered that familial expansionism was by no means solely a Gordon phenomenon. Other notable Lowland families also developed kin networks and cadet branches. Allan Macinnes has noted that by the early seventeenth century the earls of Hamilton had created a family household consisting of estate managers, dependents and feuars. See A.I. Macinnes, *Charles I and the Making of the Covenanting Movement, 1625–1641* (Edinburgh, 1991), 5.

41 Wormald, *Lords and Men*, 2, 73. The complementary document outlining the obligations of the lord was known as a 'bond of maintenance'.

of kinship to those outside the circle of the extended family.[42] The Gordons extracted bonds from a number of families across the North-East of Scotland and in many cases much farther afield.[43] The earls were making their presence felt in the Highlands, successive bonds being struck with the Mackintosh chiefs of Clan Chattan, the chiefs of Clan Cameron, the Frasers of Lovat and the Grants of Freuchy.[44] The earls also sought to ally themselves by similar means with the Farquharsons of Invercauld.[45] In addition, during the 1580s bonds were drawn up with the Mackenzies of Kintail (1585 and 1586), Torquil Macleod of Lewis (1585), Donald Gorm of Sleat (1586), and perhaps most surprisingly, with Archibald Campbell of Lochnell (1587) and Duncan Campbell of Glenorchy (1588).[46] During the period the Gordons even looked to stretch their influence southwards into the Perthshire Highlands, with a couple of bonds being made with the Robertsons of Struan.[47]

Similar to bonds of manrent were what were known as 'bonds of friendship'. In essence these operated in the same way as the former, but with the subtle difference that they were entered into by men of equal status.[48] A number of these were drawn up by the earls of Huntly from the mid-fifteenth century, perhaps the most important of these being with the Hays of Erroll, another key north-east family.[49] With their main seat at Slains on the Buchan coast the Hays held an earldom in their own right, their elevation to the peerage dating to around the same time as that of the House of Huntly. They were also designated hereditary High Constables of Scotland and remained notable landowners in that part of the world.[50] This alliance between the Gordons and the Hays was

42 *Ibid.*, 78.

43 At least three bonds, for instance, were received from the Hume family in the Borders of Scotland, one in 1490, one in 1538, and the third in 1549. No doubt on these occasions the House of Huntly was looking to retain influence close to the original Gordon heartlands. See *ibid.*, 88, 280, 284, 300. However, there appears to be no evidence of an attempt to keep this up beyond 1549. For a comprehensive calendar of the Huntly bonds, see *ibid*, 278–303. In addition a large percentage of the Gordon bonds (of all varieties) were transcribed in the nineteenth century by John Stuart for the Spalding Club. See *The Miscellany of the Spalding Club*, ed. J. Stuart, 5 vols (Aberdeen, 1841–52), IV, 179–260.

44 The Mackintosh bonds date from 1475, 1497, 1532, 1543 and 1568. See Wormald, *Lords and Men*, 281, 283–285, 288, 298–299, 300. The Cameron bonds date from 1543 and 1547. See *ibid.*, 285–287. The Lovat bonds date from 1543 and 1570. See *ibid.*, 285, 289. The Grant bonds date from 1483, 1546, 1569 and 1586. See *ibid.*, 286, 289, 292, 299.

45 *Ibid.*, 3.

46 *Ibid.*, 290–293. It should be noted that Campbell of Lochnell did retain his allegiance to Argyll in the wording of his particular bond.

47 These bonds date from 1509 and 1586. See *ibid.*, 282, 291.

48 *Ibid.*, 3.

49 These were from 1466 and 1546. See *ibid.*, 375, 386.

50 See K.M. Hay, *The Story of the Hays* (Edinburgh, 1977), 5–6.

of great importance for the simple reason that between them they could look to dominate the political scene in the North of Scotland, albeit with the Hays remaining the junior partner.[51] The two dynasties could even look to intermarry in order further to cement their ties, two notable examples of this occurring in 1467 and around the year 1476.[52] Indeed, part of the 1546 bond of friendship between the families concentrated on a proposed union between John, third son of the fourth earl of Huntly, and Margaret, second daughter of George, seventh earl of Errol, 'for manteining of amite and kindness betwyx the houssis of Huntlie and Errol in tyme cummyng' – an ideal example of how local politics could interact with the aristocratic marriage market.[53]

Relations between the House of Huntly and another key north-east family, the Forbeses, were considerably more fraught. Like the Gordons, the House of Forbes had been actively involved in north-east life for centuries and branches of the family occupied lands stretching from Strathdon, through Alford and Monymusk and the lower slopes of the mountain of Bennachie to as far afield as the Lowlands of Buchan. Bonding and intermarriage had occurred between the two families, most notably during the 1460s, but this seems to have done little to alleviate what has been described as something akin to a 'state of cold war'. Essentially the problem boiled down to the fact that these two powerful and acquisitive households were situated in very close proximity to each other geographically. So much so, that it can even be claimed that the chief Forbes seat of Druminor was practically 'hemmed in by Gordon strongholds'.[54]

The earliest roots of animosity between the two families can be traced back to the 1430s when Alexander Forbes of that ilk lent support to one time player in north-east politics, Sir Robert Erskine, in the latter's attempt to build a dynastic opposition to Alexander Seton (later first earl of Huntly).[55] Trouble later erupted in earnest between George, fourth earl of Huntly, and John, sixth Lord Forbes,

51 Wormald, *Lords and Men*, 88, 100.
52 These were between Elizabeth, second daughter of the first earl of Huntly and Nicolas, second earl of Errol and between George, second earl of Huntly and Elizabeth, sister of the aforesaid Nicholas (the second earl's third marriage). See [Gordon], *Records of Aboyne*, 395, 413.
53 *Miscellany of the Spalding Club*, IV, 217. Marriage was the third main method, after kinship and bonding, by which to build up connections and influence within the localities. See Wormald, *Lords and Men*, 90. In this particular case the marriage does not seem to have come off, the said John opting to marry Elizabeth Gordon, widow of Alexander Ogilvy of Findlater. See [Gordon], *Records of Aboyne*, 468. The relationship between the House of Huntly and the House of Errol itself, however, does not seem to have been too adversely affected by the breakdown of these marriage plans.
54 Wormald, *Lords and Men*, 278–279, 283; [Gordon], *Records of Aboyne*, 391, 395, 469; J. Wormald, *Court, Kirk, and Community. Scotland, 1470–1625* (London, 1981), 34.
55 S. Boardman, 'The Burgh and the Realm: Medieval Politics, c.1100–1500', in E.P. Dennison, D. Ditchburn and M. Lynch (eds), *Aberdeen before 1800. A New History* (East Linton, 2002), 214–215.

over profits on some lands held of Huntly in the barony of Strathbogie. Legal proceedings were instigated with the result that in 1536, at the end of a three-year case, Forbes found himself ordered to hand over all profits gained from the said lands during the years 1528–31. Huntly also pursued Lord Forbes for damage done to land in the forest of Corennie in the intervening period, and in 1537 went so far as to accuse the latter and his son of having plotted to kill King James V. Lord Forbes was eventually acquitted but his son was convicted and subsequently executed.[56]

The relationship reached its nadir in the early 1570s when, during the Marian civil war, William, seventh Lord Forbes supported the king's party, thus setting himself up in opposition to the Gordons. Renewed animosities during this period may well also have been fuelled by the fact that the marriage between John, master of Forbes, and Margaret, eldest daughter of the fourth earl of Huntly, had broken down. What resulted in the North-East of Scotland was essentially a destructive and extremely bitter local feud which grafted itself onto the wider national conflict. In this the Gordons, led by the fifth earl's brother, Adam of Auchindoun, soon gained the upper hand, particularly following the battles of Tillyangus and Craibstane (both 1571), each of which ended in defeat for the Forbes faction. In fact, Gordon raiding of Forbes land and property remained extensive throughout the second half of this particular year, the strongholds of Druminor and Corgarff coming in for some particularly harsh treatment.[57] Active feuding continued in bursts until the early 1580s, notable incidents including an attempt by one Arthur Forbes to assassinate Adam of Auchindoun on the streets of Paris, and a skirmish in 1579 between members of the two households at Dundee. Needless to say, the peace that had established itself by 1583 remained a precarious one.[58]

Nevertheless, the Forbes feud had allowed the House of Huntly to reassert its superiority in the North following the disastrous Corrichie affair of 1562. In itself it also provided the opportunity to neutralise (in the short term at least) what had seemed to be a powerful and dangerous rival family. The secret of the Gordon success appears to have been the ability of the family (including the extended kin network) to unite in the face of local opposition. The House of Forbes was apparently unable to do this to the same degree and defeat had been the inevitable result.[59] The fact that the House of Huntly had managed to obtain

---

56 Potter, *Bloodfeud*, 29.
57 Brown, *Bloodfeud in Scotland*, 110; P. Marren, *Grampian Battlefields. The Historic Battles of North-East Scotland from A.D. 84 to 1745* (Aberdeen, 1990), 118–127. The Gordons sacked the castles of Druminor and Corgarff sometime during the period between the two battles.
58 Marren, *Grampian Battlefields*, 123; Brown, *Bloodfeud in Scotland*, 110–112.
59 Wormald, *Lords and Men*, 77.

bonds of manrent from a number of Forbes cadets over the years may well have contributed towards this. These were with the families of Corsindawe (1544), Brux, Towie (both 1549), Balfour (1552) and Monymusk (1554).[60] Granted, in most of these cases it was stipulated that the grantee would not be required to take any action against the head of the Forbes household; nevertheless it remained a process that must have drawn the families in question somewhat closer to the Gordon earls.[61]

By comparison, more peaceful relations were enjoyed with some of the other households in the North-East. For example, the House of Huntly does seem to have been on reasonably amicable terms with that other great local aristocratic family, the Keiths, hereditary earls marischal of Scotland. Again, intermarriage may have helped in fostering this, most notably the union between George, fourth earl of Huntly and Elizabeth Keith, daughter of William, fourth earl Marischal.[62] Having said this, the relationship never seems to have reached the same level of closeness as that enjoyed with the House of Errol. Meanwhile, for the most part, relations appear to have been good with a number of other north-east households including most branches of the Aberdeenshire Leslies, the Cheynes, the Barclays and the Bairds of Auchmedden.[63]

Such amicability remained much less in evidence with regards to relations between the Gordon earls and the Stewart earls of Moray. This latter earldom with its rich fishings had long been coveted by the Gordons and between 1549 and 1562 had been in the *de facto* possession of George, fourth earl of Huntly. But the victory of Lord James Stewart at Corrichie had brought all this to an end, and he went on to consolidate his position as first earl of Moray in Huntly's stead. Upon Moray's assassination in 1570, title to the earldom passed to his eldest daughter, Elizabeth, and in 1581 through her to a newly acquired husband, James Stewart, eldest son of James, first lord Doune. This in itself had provided

---

60 *Ibid.*, 286–288.
61 See the wording of the Towie, Brux and Balfour bonds in *Miscellany of the Spalding Club*, IV, 219–222.
62 [Gordon], *Records of Aboyne*, 369, 402, 432.
63 The adherence given by such families to the House of Huntly during the Marian civil war would seem to confirm this. Unlike most of the other Leslies, however, the family of Balquhain actually supported the king's party during this conflict. See Donaldson, *All the Queen's Men*, 109–110. This was in spite of previous close ties with the fourth earl of Huntly. See C. Leslie, *Historical Records of the Family of Leslie from 1067 to 1868–9*, 3 vols (Edinburgh, 1869), III, 27. By the 1580s they seem have been back on close terms with the Gordons. See K.M. Brown, 'Burghs, Lords and Feuds in Jacobean Scotland', in M. Lynch (ed.), *The Early Modern Town in Scotland* (London, 1987), 108. The support of the Bairds of Auchmedden appears to have remained consistent throughout the second half of the sixteenth century. They did, for example, take the field against Moray at the Battle of Corrichie. See W. Baird, *Genealogical Collections concerning the Sir-Name of Baird and the Families of Auchmedden, New Byth, and Sauchton Hall* (London, 1870), 18.

the Gordons with additional cause for resentment, the hand of the said Elizabeth having reportedly been promised to the future sixth earl of Huntly while
the two were still in infancy.[64] From the outset tensions were only too apparent
between the latter and the newly installed second earl of Moray. Indeed, the two
were soon at loggerheads over prized fishing rights on the River Spey. Legally
these did appertain to Moray, but Huntly had taken up possession some years
previously. By the late 1580s the stage seemed set for a bitter confrontation.[65]

Over much of the period the Huntly earls also looked to build ties in some
of the key burghs of the North. This was particularly the case with regards
to Aberdeen. To some extent it is a truism to suggest that links between this
particular burgh and the House of Huntly were close. As early as 1463 a bond
of manrent had been drawn up between the two and from the early years of
the sixteenth century the Gordon earls had held the associated sheriffship.
In addition, the Huntly earls were in alliance with the key burgess family, the
Menzies of Pitfoddels for much of the period.[66] The Menzies family were the
major power within the burgh during this time, a fact attested to by their near-
monopoly on the post of provost from at least 1501.[67] On two occasions the
Gordons also succeeded in installing their nominees as bishops of Aberdeen.
Indeed, the second of these was none other than William Gordon, uncle of the
fourth earl of Huntly.[68] Having said this, the relationship between the House of
Huntly and the burgh, while often close, rarely involved total subservience on
the part of the latter. For example, in the early 1540s Aberdeen associated itself
with James Hamilton, third earl of Arran, the then rival of the fourth earl of
Huntly.[69] In addition, during the Corrichie affair of 1562 it seems that a similarly
independent line was also adopted, the burgh on this occasion opting to distance

---

64 Potter, *Bloodfeud*, 19, 45, 59–76, 107, 117, 122, 125.

65 *Ibid.*, 131. The fishings, along with lands appertaining to Spynie Palace, had been granted to the
first earl of Moray by George Douglas, bishop of Moray, and had subsequently come down to
the second earl. Huntly had proceeded with litigation to have the titles withdrawn and in the
meantime had taken possession of the fishings along with Spynie Palace.

66 Wormald, *Lords and Men*, 279; Boardman, 'Burgh and the Realm', 222. Referring to the situation as it stood by the early 1500s Boardman uses the term 'political overlordship' with regard
to the relationship of the Huntly earls vis-à-vis Aberdeen.

67 See A. White, 'The Menzies Era: Sixteenth-Century Politics', in Dennison, Ditchburn and
Lynch (eds), *Aberdeen before 1800*, 224. For a list of the sixteenth-century provosts of Aberdeen,
see W. Kennedy, *Annals of Aberdeen, from the Reign of King William the Lion, to the End of the
Year 1818*, 2 vols (London, 1818), II, 232.

68 B. McLennan, 'The Reformation in the Burgh of Aberdeen', *Northern Scotland*, vol. 2, no. 1
(1974–75), 129

69 A. White, 'The Impact of the Reformation on a Burgh Community: the Case of Aberdeen', in
M. Lynch (ed.), *The Early Modern Town in Scotland* (London, 1987), 84.

itself from the same earl.[70] Finally, in 1568, during the Marian civil war, George, fifth earl of Huntly, had to use the threat of force to get the town to yield to him.[71]

In essence, during periods when the House of Huntly appeared strong and was prepared to be proactive, Aberdeen seems to have been more willing to toe the Gordon line. In 1545, for instance, following a relative decline in Arran's fortunes, the fourth earl managed to regain influence in the town, and even managed to install himself as provost for a period of two years.[72] Some two decades later George, sixth earl of Huntly, was especially energetic in his attempts to build closer relations with the burgh, first of all ensuring the election of himself, his uncle, Adam of Auchindoun, and a number of other Gordons as honorary burgesses.[73] He also ensured that Gilbert Menzies of Pitfoddels was re-elected provost in 1587 and then obtained a bond of manrent from him the following year. In 1588 the town was dependent on Huntly's ability to mediate in a potentially explosive dispute between it and John Leslie, Laird of Balquhain.[74] By the end of this particular year it must have seemed to contemporaries that the House of Huntly had regained its position of pre-eminence in the town.

Although overall evidence is sketchy, the Gordon earls may have exercised a more assured hold over two other key northern burghs, Elgin and Inverness. It can, for example, be argued that as the former was considerably smaller than Aberdeen, the earls would have found it that much easier to gain a more consistent level of control.[75] Indeed, their influence was of such a level that Elgin Cathedral even became the burial place of a number of the earls.[76] It is also recorded that from at least 1540 (and probably long before that) they retained a house in the burgh.[77] In Inverness, meanwhile, the earls retained a powerful presence as hereditary sheriffs and as holders of the castle.[78]

By the 1580s the Gordons of Huntly had also managed to extend their influence into the Highlands of Scotland. In this they shared a common position

70 *Ibid.*, 94; M. Lynch, 'The Crown and the Burghs, 1500–1625', in *ibid.*, 62.

71 Potter, *Bloodfeud*, 93.

72 White, 'Impact of the Reformation', 86; Kennedy, *Annals of Aberdeen*, II, 232.

73 McLennan, 'Reformation in the Burgh of Aberdeen', 129–130.

74 Brown, 'Burghs, Lords and Feuds', 106–108. Brown goes on to posit that Huntly may even have unleashed Balquhain on Aberdeen, thus ensuring that his protection would be required.

75 *Ibid.*, 105.

76 This was in what was known as St Mary's Aisle and it appears that the first, fourth and fifth earls were interred there. See [Gordon], *Records of Aboyne*, 394, 468; Paul, *Scots Peerage*, IV, 19; Shaw and Gordon, *Province of Moray*, I, 59–60. In 1636 it would also become the resting place of the first marquess of Huntly.

77 Shaw and Gordon, *Province of Moray*, I, 378.

78 M. Mackintosh, *A History of Inverness* (Inverness, 1939), 72–73. Upon instructions from James IV, Alexander, third earl of Huntly, even carried out extensive rebuilding of the castle, reportedly at his own expense.

with the Campbells of Argyll, the latter family for the South-West and the Gordons for the North. Put simply, they were the two main Scottish families who were able to straddle both the Lowland and the Highland worlds.[79] The first real commissions of lieutenancy had been instituted as early as the 1470s, but it was not until the period following the forfeiture of the Lordship of the Isles that they really began to come into their own.[80] For the Gordons of Huntly, in particular, the period 1501–1509 saw a vast increase in their power, with grants of land and offices being made as reward for their part in successful expeditions against Highland rebels such as Torquil MacLeod and Donald Dubh (grandson of John MacDonald, the recently forfeited Lord of the Isles). The grant of the heritable sheriffship of Inverness was one of the key gains. Inverness Castle also passed into the custodianship of the Gordon earls at this time.[81] Occasionally, the incumbent monarch would mount full-blown royal expeditions to the Highlands with a view to perpetuating the illusion of some kind of direct central rule, but it was through the lieutenants that any form of real control was maintained.[82] Respective monarchs seemed well aware of this reality. In April 1587 James VI could be found writing a letter to his great favourite, George, sixth earl of Huntly, willing him as royal lieutenant to take action against the Clanranald and the Macleods of Lewis and Harris, 'commanding thame to contene themselffis in quietnes and that they forbeare to mak any maner of conventioun or gadderingis, to the hinder and disturbance of our good deliberatioun.'[83] Clearly by this time the Gordons were still perceived as being a key force in that part of the world.[84]

Naturally, through their hold on the lordships of Badenoch and Lochaber alone, the Gordon earls came into close contact with a number of Highland clans. Undoubtedly of most import was the somewhat stormy relationship fostered

---

79 Gordon Donaldson observed that: 'No Highland chief was of much importance in comparison with these two semi-Lowland families.' See G. Donaldson, *Scotland. James V–James VII* (paperback edn, Edinburgh, 1978), 14.

80 Ross, 'Royal Lieutenancy', 23, 33.

81 Macdougall, *James IV*, 178–191; Cathcart, *Kinship and Clientage*, 43–44, 165.

82 Ross, 'Royal Lieutenancy', 3. A good example of a royal expedition mounted with a view to 'daunting the Isles' was that of James V during the summer of 1540. Even then, nobles such as Argyll and Huntly remained very much to the fore in terms of providing men and material. For more detail on this expedition, see Cameron, *James V*, 245–248.

83 *Miscellany of the Spalding Club*, III, 214–215 (James VI to Huntly, 20 April 1587).

84 Graeme Ross portrays the Campbells as being the pre-eminent force in the Scottish Highlands from 1567 and asserts that from the Corrichie debacle of 1562, the Gordons became less and less influential. See Ross, 'Royal Lieutenancy', 115–117. Although there is a degree of truth to this statement, such a view probably underestimates the extent to which the sixth earl of Huntly was re-establishing Gordon dominance in the North during the 1580s. His energetic appropriation of bonds of manrent made this evident; two of them, after all, were drawn up with Campbell chieftains (Lochnell and Glenorchy).

with the Clan Chattan. Essentially Clan Chattan was a conglomeration of clans as opposed to being a single clan in its own right. The chief of the Mackintoshes traditionally held nominal leadership and matters were conducted under what was in effect a band of friendship. Associated clans included, amongst others, the Macphersons, Davidsons, Macbeans, Macphails, Macgillvrays and MacQueens, all as a unit occupying lands stretching from Moray and Speyside to Badenoch and the Grampian and Cairngorm Mountains.[85] Clan Chattan remained important to the earls of Huntly on at least two levels. Firstly, some of its members were key tenants within the lordship of Badenoch. Secondly, it appears that whenever the earls looked to conduct any kind of expedition into the Highlands, they would invariably look to Clan Chattan to provide much of the manpower. This was evident, for example, with regard to an expedition of 1544 and an abortive one of 1554.[86] However, the relationship between the Gordon earls and the Mackintosh chiefs could often be a problematic one.

In the first instance an ongoing dispute existed regarding the right to hold courts in the lordship of Lochaber. Prior to 1493 the chiefs of Mackintosh had two main feudal superiors, the Gordons of Huntly for their eastern holdings, and the Lords of the Isles for lands in the West. It was from the latter that they received the hereditary stewardship of Lochaber, an office which in effect provided them with a jurisdiction and the right to hold courts throughout the territory. With the later grant of the lordship of Lochaber to Alexander, third earl of Huntly, this began to become a problem. From this point on the Mackintosh chiefs held Crown jurisdiction within a hereditary lordship pertaining to the Gordon earls, from whom they themselves held lands, and to whom they owed allegiance. It was hardly a situation conducive to the fostering of ideal relations between the two. Having said this, things were allowed to stand, and with the passage of time and the occasional confirmation by the central authorities, the Mackintosh stewardship became a mainstay.[87] Naturally the Gordon earls remained uncomfortable with the situation. For example, it is recorded that in 1587, Lachlan, chief of Mackintosh, continued to hold a number of courts throughout Lochaber, despite the evident displeasure of George, sixth earl of Huntly.[88]

Such enmity certainly seemed to colour the dealings between the Mackintosh chiefs and the Gordon earls over much of the sixteenth century. The earls would generally seek to bring the Mackintoshes closer to them through occasional

85 Macinnes, *Clanship, Commerce and the House of Stuart*, 10; Cathcart, *Kinship and Clientage*, 20–22.
86 A.M. Mackintosh, *The Mackintoshes and Clan Chattan* (Edinburgh, 1903), 125–126, 137.
87 Cathcart, *Kinship and Clientage*, 147, 184. In 1545, William Mackintosh of Dunnachton was confirmed in the office by Mary of Guise.
88 W. Macfarlane, *Genealogical Collections concerning Families in Scotland*, ed. J.T. Clark, 2 vols (Edinburgh, 1900), I, 243.

shows of favouritism and through bonding; failing that, however, other means would be sought with a view to curbing any potential growth in their power. In 1549, for instance, the fourth earl of Huntly looked to assert his superiority by depriving William Mackintosh of Dunnachton of the office of deputy-lieutenant of Inverness. The following year, he instigated the trial of Dunnachton on a trumped-up charge of treason, and the latter was executed at Bog of Gight.[89] It is perhaps not surprising that during the Corrichie affair of 1562 the Mackintoshes took the side of the Crown. Later, following the death of Regent Moray in 1570, the clan declared themselves of the king's party, thus setting themselves up against the Gordons once again. This was in spite of previous adherence to the queen's party and the exchange of bonds of manrent and maintenance with the fifth earl of Huntly in 1568. Such moments of formal reconciliation were rare and by the end of the 1580s the situation remained tense.[90]

There is less need to mention the dealings between the House of Huntly and other clans in the area in any great detail other than to indicate that the potential for long term animosity was never as great as with Clan Chattan. Admittedly, over the course of the sixteenth century, expeditions occasionally had to be made into the western Highlands with a view to restoring order should the occasion demand, a situation that in effect could result in the Huntly earls acting against Lochaber clans such as the Camerons and the MacDonalds of Keppoch. In 1544, for example, the fourth earl of Huntly campaigned against these clans and against John Moidart of Clanranald following the disruption that resulted from rivalries over the chieftainship of the last clan.[91] Having said this, there seems to be little evidence of any major resentments being built up as a result. Further to the North-East, meanwhile, relations with the Clan Grant seem to have been largely amicable – a situation that was reinforced by the drawing up of a bond of manrent between the sixth earl of Huntly and John Grant of Freuchy (the clan chief) in 1586.[92]

Taking all of this into account, what can be seen is that a number of different factors had contributed towards a situation where the Gordons wielded great power in the North. On one level the earls themselves held vital regional posts such as the sheriffships and the royal lieutenancy of the North. On another level they could also exert a great deal of influence via the likes of kin networks and the widespread practice of bonding. All in all, Scotland remained a highly decentralised state. The monarch certainly acted as its head and was accepted as such, but in effect much power was regionally based and was in the hands

89 Cathcart, *Kinship and Clientage*, 185–187.
90 *Ibid.*, 190–192.
91 Mackintosh, *Mackintoshes*, 125–127.
92 Fraser, *Chiefs of Grant*, I, 159–160.

of nobles such as the Gordon earls. It was as agents of the Crown within this 'crucial layer in Scottish society' that the Gordons excelled.[93] Along with the Campbells of Argyll they had become regional lords of national significance.

REBELLION AND RESURRECTION

However, from the late 1580s and into the decade that followed, any feelings of quiet contentment that George, sixth earl of Huntly, may have had with his situation would soon prove seriously misplaced. Indeed, 1589 saw the first of a series of scandals that would threaten his position as a key figure in Scottish political life. In February of that year it was revealed that Huntly, along with his Catholic co-religionists, the earls of Errol and Crawford, had been in correspondence with the Spanish noble, the Duke of Parma. In these letters they commiserated with Parma over the recent failure of the Spanish Armada, and expressed a hope that another attack could be mounted, this time with a view to landing in Scotland. The reaction to this amongst the Protestant establishment in both Scotland and England was one of outrage and it is from this point that Huntly began to be associated with the cause of counter-reformation. Nevertheless, James VI's initial reaction was mild to say the least. In fact it was only after much persuasion that he was moved to confine Huntly to Edinburgh Castle, and then only for a little over a week. But by April tensions had seemingly increased with the result that the Catholic earls, supported by the erratic Protestant noble, Francis Stewart, fifth earl of Bothwell, saw fit to mount a rebellion. In response to this, James marched an army northwards and forced a confrontation at the Bridge of Dee just outside Aberdeen with the result that the earls backed down and surrendered. Once again Huntly received lenient treatment. After initially being tried for treason, he was confined for a matter of four months before being set at liberty and restored to favour.[94]

Renewed squabbling between Huntly and the earl of Moray ensured that tensions remained high in the North. Indeed the occasion of Moray's murder in February 1592 provided additional cause for scandal. The killing proved the culminating point of the long tussle between the two over land and fishing rights. Towards the end of 1589 Moray and his wife had taken legal action against the Gordon earl following increased levels of poaching on the Spey and a series of alleged raids that had been made on the Moray landholdings. By mid-1590 little had been done to follow up on these proceedings and in light of this Huntly had looked to gain an even greater hold on disputed property such as Spynie Palace.

It was from this point that Moray sought to build up alliances in order to

93 Cathcart, *Kinship and Clientage*, 159.
94 R. Grant, 'The Brig o' Dee Affair, the Sixth Earl of Huntly and the Politics of the Counter-Reformation', in Goodare and Lynch (eds), *Reign of James VI*, 93–94, 101–102.

challenge Huntly's dominance of the North. He managed to draw up a bond of mutual assistance with a number of different individuals, all of whom seem to have been discontented with the Gordon hegemony in some way. This was brought to pass in November 1590 and involved, amongst others, Grant of Freuchy, John Campbell of Cawdor, the earl of Atholl, Fraser of Lovat and Moray himself. The Mackintoshes and Clan Chattan also formed part of the Moray axis through a recent alliance they had made with Clan Grant.[95] In the face of this Huntly drew up a number of bonds of his own the following year. These were with Allan Cameron of Lochiel, a number of prominent Morayshire barons, and perhaps most importantly, with Clan Macpherson.[96] This went a long way to neutralising Moray's challenge, not least with the split it generated in the Clan Chattan confederacy. Confrontations did occur in the North as a result but essentially, as 1591 wore on, Moray was increasingly on the defensive. This situation was confirmed in October when the king engineered a temporary reconciliation between Huntly and the Mackintoshes and Grants.

Parallel to this, Moray's standing at the royal court also began to suffer. On the one hand his position was undermined by the death of his influential wife in November. On the other he became increasingly associated with the earl of Bothwell, an individual whom James VI regarded as a great danger by that time. In late December Bothwell even made an attempt to kill the chancellor, Sir John Maitland, and to seize the king, a situation that by implication did little to improve Moray's standing. Indeed, commissions were soon issued to Huntly and Lennox for the arrest of Bothwell and any who supported him. Huntly seems to have regarded this as the ideal opportunity finally to crush his northern rival and on 7 February 1592 a raid was conducted on the Doune family property of Donnibristle House on the north shore of the Firth of Forth, and Moray was killed. Whether this outcome was by accident or design is perhaps a moot point; either way the outrage that it generated remained palpable. Charges of conspiracy and murder were rife and even the king began to find himself implicated. But once again it was only due to the urgings of the Presbyterian clergy and the English that James saw fit to take any kind of action against the Gordon earl, and even then the punishment involved only a short term of confinement in Blackness Castle.[97]

Nevertheless, from then pressure mounted on Huntly and on the king. Two fresh revelations contributed towards this process. Firstly, in January 1593 the English ambassador, Robert Bowes, revealed that Huntly and the Catholic

95 Potter, *Bloodfeud*, 154–159.

96 See the transcriptions of these bonds in *Miscellany of the Spalding Club*, IV, 245–247.

97 Potter, *Bloodfeud*, 164–205. The Moray killing is also covered in some detail in E.D. Ives, *The Bonny Earl of Murray. The Man, the Murder, the Ballad* (East Linton, 1997), 37–41.

earls had once again been in correspondence with Spain. This time the matter involved the interception of several sheets of blank paper signed by Huntly, Errol and the Earl of Angus and attached with their respective seals. Again there was an implication that the earls had involved themselves in treasonous plotting with the Spaniards, perhaps with a view to facilitating an invasion of England via Scotland, or even to persuading James VI to convert to Catholicism.[98] The king came under renewed pressure to act against Huntly – something that he again initially sought to avoid. Even in November 1593 when he did eventually pass an Act against the Catholic earls calling for them to abjure their faith it appears that this was done primarily with a view to engineering their full pardon. But the earls failed to see that the tide was now finally flowing against them and by the deadline date of 1 February 1594 they had failed to comply.[99]

The second major revelation came in May 1594 and related back to the Moray killing of 1592. On 4 February 1592, just three days prior to the raid on Donnibristle House, John Campbell of Cawdor had been assassinated, seemingly the victim of a struggle for power then raging within Clan Campbell. Cawdor had manoeuvred himself into the position of sole guardian to the young seventh earl of Argyll, much to the chagrin of other key Campbell lairds, notably Archibald of Lochnell, Duncan of Glenorchy and James of Ardkinglas. As a result, upon discovery of his murder, it was initially suspected that one or more of these lairds must have been responsible. And a confession extracted from Ardkinglas on 21 May 1594 served to introduce a new level of conspiracy to the proceedings. Ardkinglas admitted that the Moray and Cawdor murders formed part of a wider design, one that had also included the projected assassination of Argyll and his only brother, John Campbell of Lundie. Through these acts certain conspirators, Huntly amongst them, would have looked to have made significant gains. The Campbell lairds would have risen in standing within the clan, and Lochnell, as next in line, would have gained the earldom. Huntly, for his part, would have rid himself of two of his key opponents in the North: Moray and Cawdor. If conspiracy it indeed was, then this last goal, at least, was certainly achieved.

Whether such a conspiracy actually existed or not is hard to say. There was no evidence at the time to back up Ardkinglas's confession, and this in itself had been offered under the threat of torture. It may well be that the Cawdor murder resulted from nothing more than a clan dispute, while the Moray killing may have just been the product of opportunism on Huntly's part.[100] It does

---

98 Potter, *Bloodfeud*, 205–207.
99 *Ibid.*, 207–210.
100 For the original postulation of the conspiracy theory, see D. Gregory, *The History of the Western Highlands and Isles of Scotland from A.D. 80 to A.D. 1493* (2nd edn, London, 1881), 244–254.

nevertheless remain intriguing that Huntly had in the recent past drawn up bonds with Lochnell and Glenorchy, two of the main Campbell protagonists in the conspiracy theory. True or not, the revelations certainly seem to have had an impact on Huntly and the Catholic earls. It is noticeable that just a few days after Ardkinglas's confession James VI moved to have them forfeited and declared traitors. Furthermore, the individual to whom a commission was given to apprehend the earls was none other than the earl of Argyll, a man no doubt anxious for some kind of redress in light of the conspiracy theory recently expounded.[101] Huntly's standing with the king would also not have been helped by reports that he was beginning to form closer bonds with the king's arch-rival, Bothwell.[102]

In the end Argyll marched an army towards the Gordon heartlands but it was intercepted by a Huntly-led force and defeated at the Battle of Glenlivet on 3 October 1594.[103] This forced the king into personally conducting a campaign in the North with the result that Strathbogie Castle was taken and the defences cast down. A similar fate awaited a number of other Catholic strongholds, notably Errol's chief seat at Slains. In the meantime the earls fled, Huntly to Sutherland and then eventually to Denmark. Many, however, remained unhappy that they were still being treated leniently. For example, although the earls had been forfeited, their property remained in the possession of their spouses. In addition, the man who replaced Huntly as a lieutenant of the North was his own brother-in-law, Ludovick Stewart, second duke of Lennox. On top of this, James never closed the door on the idea of reconciliation and negotiations were soon under way with a view to facilitating the earls' return. In Huntly's case, this was under the condition that he would publicly submit to the Kirk and admit his wrongdoing regarding the killing of the earl of Moray. This he remained willing to countenance and so in a ceremony in Aberdeen on 26 June 1597 both he and Errol formally subscribed to the Protestant faith.[104] Somewhat remarkably, then, Huntly had survived what undoubtedly had been a very trying decade, and was now in a position to re-establish himself within the mainstream of Scottish political life.[105]

---

101 Potter, *Bloodfeud*, 210–211.

102 M. Lee, *Great Britain's Solomon: James VI and I in his Three Kingdoms* (Urbana and Chicago, 1990), 76; A.R. MacDonald, *The Jacobean Kirk, 1567–1625: Sovereignty, Polity and Liturgy* (Aldershot, 1998), 57–58.

103 Marren, *Grampian Battlefields*, 128–137.

104 Potter, *Bloodfeud*, 220–225; A.R. MacDonald, 'James VI and the General Assembly, 1586–1618', in Goodare and Lynch (eds), *Reign of James VI*, 174–175.

105 Opinions have varied over the years as to the extent Huntly genuinely sought to help engineer violent counter-reformation in Scotland with the help of Spain. Ruth Grant has argued convincingly that Huntly's machinations were primarily aimed at countering rivals and manoeuvring himself into a position of even greater power. See Grant, 'Brig O' Dee Affair'.

The troubles of the 1590s had, however, caused much disruption across the North of Scotland, not least of all along the Highland fringes. Essentially, with the Moray bond of 1590 and the Huntly alliances of 1591, a situation unfolded where factional violence reached almost epidemic proportions. Clans such as the Mackintoshes and the Grants had begun to find their own reasons for opposing Huntly; not least there may have been a degree of trepidation over the extent of Huntly's power in the Badenoch area, particularly in light of his attempts to refortify Ruthven Castle.[106] The chiefs of these clans, Mackintosh of Dunnachton and Grant of Freuchy, may also have been aggrieved that Huntly had taken little action against the Macdonalds of Keppoch following raids upon their lands some years previously.[107] The Grants in particular had become further alienated from the House of Huntly following recent confrontations between adherents of the two kindreds.[108] From 1590, and especially with the death of Moray in 1592, the incidents proved more and more serious, with the two sides engaging in a series of tit-for-tat raids.[109] The process culminated at Glenlivet in 1594, a battle in which both the Mackintoshes and the Grants came out on Argyll's side.[110]

In light of the above, to what extent had Huntly's pre-eminent position in the North been undermined during the 1590s? It is clear that for much of the decade his hold over the area had been seriously challenged, first of all by Moray himself, and later by his allies. In response, Huntly had remained robust and for the most part retained the upper hand in the field. In particular he had been able to form an alliance of clans capable of seeing off the challenge at hand. It is also noteworthy that his traditional support base in the North-East remained firm. At Glenlivet Huntly fielded a highly motivated force comprising most of the Gordon cadet families as well as traditional allies, the Hays of Errol.[111] In terms of the military challenge, Huntly had remained more than able to hold his own.

Not only that, but by the turn of the century he had regained the allegiance of the Grants and the Mackintoshes.[112] Perhaps more importantly, the feuds between the Gordons and the houses of Argyll and Moray were also resolved by this time.[113] On the surface, then, it seemed that Huntly had managed to regain his position and had managed to heal a number of divisions, a fact that

106 Potter, *Bloodfeud*, 158; Macfarlane, *Genealogical Collections*, I, 252.
107 A. Macdonald and A. Macdonald, *The Clan Donald*, 3 vols (Inverness, 1896– 1904), I, 619–620.
108 Potter, *Bloodfeud*, 135, 158–159.
109 *Ibid.*, 204–205.
110 Fraser, *Chiefs of Grant*, I, 173; Cathcart, *Kinship and Clientage*, 173–178.
111 See Potter, *Bloodfeud*, 216–218; 'Balbithan MS', 10, 23, 33, 59; Bulloch, 'Abergeldie', 85; Lee, 'Coclarachie', 124.
112 Fraser, *Chiefs of Grant*, I, 175; Cathcart, *Kinship and Clientage*, 198.
113 Brown, *Bloodfeud in Scotland*, 171.

contemporary chronicler, Robert Gordon of Gordonstoun, deemed important. With reference to the situation as it stood in 1599 he concluded that 'the
ClanChattan, the Grants, the Forbesses, the Clancheinnzie [Mackenzies], the
Leslies, the Irvings, the Innesses, the Monroes, the Dumbars, and all the neighbouring tribes did willinglie submit themselues to the marquis of Huntly'.[114]

However, a number of underlying realities muddied the picture somewhat.
For example, although Huntly had managed to reach an accord with the
Mackintoshes and Clan Chattan, the relationship remained a strained one, not
least because the then chief, Lachlan Mackintosh, had aligned himself more
fully with the House of Argyll by that time. This move had been signposted in
1595 with the drawing up of a bond between Lachlan and Archibald Campbell,
seventh earl of Argyll. At this time the Mackintosh chief had also managed
to reconcile himself with the Macphersons, thus bringing them back into the
Clan Chattan fold, a move that markedly undermined Huntly's recently created
alliance network in the North. The increasing influence of the Campbells
in Mackintosh affairs was confirmed in 1608, when a new chief (also called
Lachlan) nominated Argyll as one of his guardians.[115]

To a certain degree an undermining of Gordon influence had also become
evident in the burgh of Aberdeen. Huntly's reported involvement in the Spanish
intrigues did little to bolster his position there and also seems to have affected
the prospects of his clients, the Menzies family. Their monopoly of the post
of provost was already being challenged by the late 1580s and in 1593 it was
finally overturned with the election of John Cheyne, a client of William Keith,
fifth earl Marischal.[116] The burgh had thus seemingly entered a new phase in its
history, one in which the House of Huntly would play a much less dominant
role. By contrast, Keith's standing in the town and in the North-East generally
was becoming ever more apparent. Not least amongst his achievements was
his founding of a new university in Aberdeen in 1593.[117] He was also recognised
as being one of the wealthiest individuals in Scotland at that time.[118] Huntly's
increasing concern at this was perhaps evident as early as February 1589 when
he sought to humble the earl Marischal by sponsoring a Mackintosh raid on
Keith land in the Mearns.[119]

114 Gordon and Gordon, *Genealogical History*, 231.
115 A. Cathcart, 'Crisis of Identity? Clan Chattan's Response to Government Policy in the Scottish
     Highlands, c.1580–1609', in Murdoch and Mackillop (eds), *Fighting for Identity*, 175, 179;
     Cathcart, *Kinship and Clientage*, 200.
116 M. Lynch and H.M. Dingwall, 'Elite Society in Town and Country', in Dennison, Ditchburn
     and Lynch (eds), *Aberdeen before 1800*, 190; White, 'The Menzies Era', 234–237.
117 D. Stevenson, *King's College, Aberdeen, 1560–1641: from Protestant Reformation to Covenanting
     Revolution* (Aberdeen, 1990), 37.
118 Brown, *Noble Society in Scotland*, 32.
119 Macfarlane, *Genealogical Collections*, I, 244–245.

On the surface, at least, Huntly's public renunciation of the Catholic faith in 1597 seemed indicative of relative decline. This involved not only his promise that he would faithfully reform his own personal beliefs, but that he would also take steps to ensure that all Jesuits, priests and excommunicated Catholics be banished from his household. In this, special mention was made of his uncle, the Jesuit priest, James Gordon.[120] The latter certainly expressed his shock and disappointment that Huntly and the other Catholic earls had given in to political pressure in this way, thus setting a 'miserable example', and that everywhere in Scotland Catholics now 'yielded to grief and terror'. Part and parcel with this he noted that 'a great change' had taken place in his nephew.[121]

However, as some contemporaries noted, Huntly had undoubtedly acted insincerely regarding his personal oath to the Kirk. Indeed, even when reproaching Huntly, Father James Gordon seemed well aware of this likelihood.[122] Certainly it seems likely that, ensconced once again in his palatial residences in the North, Huntly continued hearing mass and practising his old beliefs as before. For example, with the rebuilding of Strathbogie Castle many additions were made that left observers in little doubt as to his true confessional bent. One of the finest and most ostentatious of these was a magnificent and unique frontispiece installed over the main doorway, which was richly adorned with Catholic imagery. One section displayed the five wounds of Christ along with representations of St Mary and St John. Crowning the display was a circular panel depicting the risen Christ. The attached coda read 'I rise again with divine power'. Similarly, the addition of a giant exterior frieze proclaiming Huntly's name and that of his spouse perhaps also indicated a self-proclaimed return as 'Cock of the North'.[123]

Nevertheless, Father Gordon's comment regarding a 'change' in Huntly may well have contained more than just a grain of truth. Robert Gordon of Gordonstoun certainly dated a shift in Huntly's priorities to around this time. He stated: 'Thus the Marquis of Huntlie, having fortunatlie red himself out of his great troubles, resolved to leave at home, frie from [the] factions and vexations of the court. He gave himself wholly to policie, planting, and building.'[124] In other words, Huntly was looking to make a point of removing himself from the machinations of public affairs and concentrate instead on his local position and standing. In light of this, it is noticeable that he never occupied public office

120 *RPCS, 1592–99*, 329.
121 W.F. Leith (ed.), *Narratives of Scottish Catholics under Mary Stuart and James VI* (Edinburgh, 1885), 232 (Gordon to Aquaviva, 1 September 1597).
122 *Ibid.*, 232.
123 C. McKean, *The Scottish Chateau: the Country House in Renaissance Scotland* (Stroud, 2001), 216–218; C. Tabraham, *Huntly Castle* (rev'd edn, Edinburgh, 1995), 21–24.
124 Gordon and Gordon, *Genealogical History*, 231.

again, a fact that probably reflected a number of new realities, not least of all his own personal preference.[125] Having said this, it is true that Huntly had been reconciled to the central regime, a fact made only too clear by the award of the marquisate in 1599. It also seems that he managed to renew his friendship with the king. The Protestant minister, David Calderwood, noted that during the Parliament of 1600, 'the erle of Huntlie at this time [was] a great courteour with the King. They passed over the tyme with drinking and waughting'.[126] Such closeness was also confirmed in 1603 when Huntly accompanied Queen Anna to London at the personal request of the king.[127] But to what extent could this relationship continue now that the king had moved to England? At the very least the coming of the new world of the three Stuart kingdoms brought with it a tangible degree of uncertainty for the House of Huntly.

CONCLUSION

In conclusion it can be said that from at least the time of the royal household of Bruce, the Gordons of Huntly had steadily grown in power, particularly so in the North of the country. Moreover, from around the mid-fifteenth century their rise had been particularly meteoric, bringing as it did an earldom, numerous landholdings, wealth, fame and a firm hold over regional governance. The House of Huntly had further amplified this through the manipulation of kin networks and via alliance networks based on bonding and local association. The road had not always been a smooth one and there were occasions when the household had to take great care steering itself through the uncertain waters of political upheaval, particularly during the 1560s and 1570s. On top of this the Gordons had built up a number of animosities along the way, most evidently so with the family of Forbes and with the earls of Moray, and also to a certain extent with Clan Mackintosh.

The final decade of the century was particularly trying for the household. Political scandal dogged the sixth earl of Huntly for much of the period, so much so that his ultimate survival remains quite remarkable. This had been due to a number of factors, not least of all his friendship with James VI and the latter's need to retain a balanced approach to both Catholics and Protestants. Having said this, despite some recovery, and despite the award of a marquisate in 1599, the overall position of the House of Huntly had been shaken in a number of

125 The point regarding Huntly never being given public office again has been made in J. Goodare, 'Scottish Politics in the Reign of James VI', in Goodare and Lynch (eds), *Reign of James VI*, 39. Goodare emphasises the point that Huntly could not be trusted any more.

126 D. Calderwood, *The History of the Kirk of Scotland*, ed. T. Thomson, 8 vols (Edinburgh, 1842–49), VI, 100.

127 *Miscellany of the Spalding Club*, IV, 160–161 (James VI to Huntly, 8 April 1603).

ways. Perhaps most noticeable in this regard was a relative decline in Gordon influence in the burgh of Aberdeen and a seeming desire on the part of Huntly henceforth to distance himself from the uncertainties of public life. To what extent he would be able successfully to achieve this remained a debatable point. With the coming of the union of the three Stuart kingdoms many things must have seemed uncertain to contemporaries, not least how their overall position would be affected. This may have been a particularly pertinent question for the Scottish nobility, facing, as it did, potential marginalisation with the removal of the royal court to London. James VI had already shown signs of wishing to engineer tighter central regulation of his Scottish kingdom, something that potentially had profound implications for power-broking families such as the Gordons of Huntly.

TWO

Power-broking and Popery:
the House of Huntly, 1603–1625

INTRODUCTION

The regal union of 1603 was an epoch-making event in British history. Facilitated in the first instance by the 1503 marriage of the Stuart king, James IV, to the English princess, Margaret Tudor, this union of the three crowns of Scotland, England and Ireland saw the creation of a new, dynamic political entity – a Greater Britain, destined (so later Whig historians would seek to argue) to become the pre-eminent player on the global political stage. With this new Greater Britain came an equally new dimension in terms of both foreign and domestic policy. On the one hand the traditional 'auld' enemies, England and Scotland, no longer had a natural recourse to war over dynastic and foreign policy disputes – a factor that had kept the British Isles in turmoil for much of the preceding centuries. On the other hand, with the elevation of James VI of Scotland to the thrones of England and Ireland, a programme could be instigated to bring about closer union and greater uniformity in all things throughout his three kingdoms. In this James experienced mixed results. While, for example, he achieved success with the creation of a standard authorised text of the Bible, he completely failed in his attempt to bring about a full incorporating union of the Scottish and English parliaments into a single British body. In addition, wherever James did look to innovate and challenge the status quo, tensions would inevitably result.

In terms of Scottish affairs, key aspects of the king's 'Britannic' policy included the attempt to bring Scotland and England more into line in terms of Church government and liturgical practice, and the move to bring once peripheral areas such as the Western Highlands and the Borders under more effective central control. Similar policies had already been in evidence within a purely Scottish context in the years leading up to union. The Highlands had long been a thorn in the side of successive Scottish monarchs and by the 1590s James VI had begun to take more systematic action with a view to controlling and 'civilising' the area. He had moreover made moves towards undermining what, by the end of 1592, had become a purely Presbyterian form of Church governance. Having said that, the extent to which post-1603 policy was merely a continuation of old policy is open to question. Put simply, a new 'Britannic agenda' was now evident, not just in religious and frontier policy, but also with regard to foreign and colonial policy. In part this chapter will look to examine the position of the Gordons vis-à-vis such developments.

The House of Huntly remained a powerful presence in the North and could potentially provide useful support to a king seeking to retain or extend his influence in that part of the world and in the Highlands. Throughout this early 'Britannic' period James still looked to employ Huntly's services as a lieutenant in the North, while Huntly himself retained extensive local power in his own right via his sheriffships, baronies, networks and landholdings. However, James had also already made moves that appeared to suggest his desire was to establish a more professional, centralised administration, one that could potentially bring the traditional role of the Scottish nobility into question. In this chapter, this issue will be addressed with specific reference to the Gordons. Was there any relative decline in power at this early stage?

'CIVILISING' THE WESTERN SEABOARD

Royal attempts to gain more effective control of the Highlands had been ongoing for over a century. This was continued from the late 1580s with the additional Jacobean agenda of seeking to introduce the facets of a more 'civilised', Lowland-orientated way of life.[1] At one level this policy can be seen as part of the more general move towards the creation of a more orderly, 'civil' society across Scotland as a whole, one that included such aspects as the tighter regulation of royal finances and the eradication of feuding. On top of this, the Union of the Crowns brought with it new Britannic strategic concerns. Areas now deemed to be unruly and in need of 'civilising' included not only the Western Highlands and the border region between Scotland and England but also Ulster in the North-East of Ireland. Prior to 1603 these areas had been remote and had marked the boundaries of the realm – a wild buffer zone separating Scotland from English-administered areas. This no longer remained the case. They now contained key routes of communication within a new political entity encompassing three kingdoms. In addition, James also looked to areas such as the Highlands, and indeed Ulster, as being sources of more regular royal income. Given all this, three major strands emerged with regard to Jacobean

---

1 For examinations of this topic from a mainly Scottish perspective, see M. Lynch, 'James VI and the "Highland Problem", in Goodare and Lynch (eds), *Reign of James VI*, 208–227; J. Goodare, *State and Society in Early Modern Scotland* (Oxford, 1999), 256–285; J. Goodare and M. Lynch, 'The Scottish State and its Borderlands, 1567–1625', in Goodare and Lynch (eds), *Reign of James VI*, 186–207; Goodare, *Government of Scotland*, 220–245.

frontier policy: firmer policing of the border areas, the planting of Scots and English settlers in Ulster, and the imposition of more centralised control over the Highlands and Islands of Scotland.[2]

Regarding this last strand, three Highland clans were eventually targeted as part of the Crown's push towards a more 'civilised' Britain: the MacDonalds of Islay and Kintyre (essentially Clan Donald South), the MacIains of Ardna-murchan and the MacLeods of Lewis. In addition to this, the central Highland clan, the MacGregors, were outlawed completely.[3] As part of this push, James even sought to plant Lowland 'adventurers' along the western seaboard, most notably on the island of Lewis, which had been forfeited to the Crown in 1598.[4] As things turned out, this particular project proved to be problematic. Although a group of Lowland settlers did establish themselves in late 1599, they soon came under attack from Clan Leod. By 1601, after much skirmishing, the settlers were defeated and forced to leave. Another attempt was made in the summer of 1605 but this also failed. Nevertheless, by late 1607 a fresh colonisation attempt had been put in motion.[5]

From the outset, and up until 1607, Huntly's name was linked with these attempts to establish the Lewis colony. In July 1599 he and the duke of Lennox were granted a joint commission of lieutenancy and justiciary over the Highlands and Islands within the sheriffdom of Inverness, partly to ensure law and order throughout the region and partly to provide assistance to the upcoming expedi-tion of the Lewis settlers.[6] In June 1601 a similar commission was issued, this time with Huntly as sole lieutenant over what contemporaries referred to as the North Isles (essentially the modern-day Western Isles north of Coll); Lennox, meanwhile was granted the lieutenancy for the islands to the south – an area

2 Allan Macinnes has been a particularly keen exponent of the Britannic dimension in Stuart frontier policy. See, for example, A.I. Macinnes, 'Politically Reactionary Brits?; The Promotion of Anglo-Scottish Union, 1603–1707', in S.J. Connolly (ed.), *Kingdoms United? Great Britain and Ireland since 1500. Integration and Diversity* (Dublin, 1999), 44; Macinnes, *Clanship, Commerce and the House of Stuart*, 56–59; A.I. Macinnes, 'Regal Union for Britain, 1603–38', in Burgess (ed.), *New British History*, 38–45; A.I. Macinnes, 'Crown, Clans and Fine: the 'Civilizing' of Scottish Gaeldom, 1587–1638', *Northern Scotland*, vol. 13 (1993), 34; Macinnes, *British Revolu-tion*, 54–62. See, also, J.H. Ohlmeyer, '"Civilizinge of those Rude Partes": Colonization within Britain and Ireland, 1580s–1640s', in N. Canny (ed.), *The Origins of Empire. British Overseas Enterprise to the Close of the Seventeenth Century* (Oxford, 1998), 124–147.

3 A.I. Macinnes, 'Gaelic Culture in the Seventeenth Century – Polarization and Assimilation', in Ellis and Barber (eds), *Conquest and Union*, 165.

4 M. Lee, *Government by Pen. Scotland under James VI and I* (London, 1980), 10–11; Ohlmeyer, 'Civilizinge of those Rude Partes', 127.

5 Gregory, *History of the Western Highlands*, 290–316; J. Goodare, 'The Statutes of Iona in Context', *Scottish Historical Review*, vol. 77, 1, no. 203 (April 1998), 32–33.

6 *RPCS, 1599–1604*, 8–10.

increasingly regarded as being within the sphere of influence of the earls of Argyll.[7] Despite this, it appears that during these years the two nobles achieved very little and in practice the Lowland settlers were left to fend for themselves with little outside help.[8]

It is perhaps somewhat surprising that Huntly was subsequently given the opportunity to mount another expedition to the Western Isles, this time with a view to planting colonists of his own. This idea seems to have been originally proposed by King James himself, possibly as early as 1605.[9] Certainly by early March 1607 James was demanding of his Scottish Privy Council that they initiate negotiations with Huntly forthwith.[10] Discussions duly took place and over the course of mid-1607 a number of conditions were eventually arrived at. The main objective was for Huntly to extirpate a number of Highland chiefs and their clans, specifically the Captain of Clan Ranald with his clan, MacNeill of Barra with his clan, and what was termed 'the hole Clan Donnald in the North'. He was also called upon to assist the Lewis settlers should they require help either on that island or on Skye. Having achieved this he was then to plant men on the available islands, excluding Lewis, Harris and Skye. Special note was made that those planted should be 'civile people and [in] noway ather from Badyenauch or Locghaber men'. The occupied islands were then to be held in feu from the Crown and a yearly duty would be arranged.[11]

However, as things turned out, negotiations soon reached an impasse over the annual duty issue. Huntly expressed an unwillingness to go above a yearly amount of £400 Scots (£300 for Uist and £100 for the rest of the islands). This was far less than the £10,000 Scots sought by the lords of the Scottish Privy Council, a figure reportedly in proportion with that paid by the Lewis settlers. On top of this, the king continually failed to give any clear direction as to how much yearly duty he would be prepared to consider and in the end the whole deal fell through when the Privy Council began to instigate action against Huntly for religious non-conformity instead.[12]

---

7 *Ibid.*, 256; Gregory, *History of the Western Highlands*, 293–294.

8 Mooted expeditions in 1600 and 1602 also came to nothing. See *ibid.*, 292–293, 299.

9 *RPCS, 1604–7*, 92. James specifically declared such to be his intention in a letter to the Scottish Privy Council of December 1606. See *ibid.*, 504 (James VI to the Privy Council, 3 December 1606).

10 *Ibid.*, 511 (James VI to the Privy Council, 2 March 1607).

11 *Ibid.*, 340–342, 359–362, 524–525 (James VI to Privy Council, 20 May 1607). The islands forming part of the projected plantation included Uist, Eigg, Canna, Rum, Barra, Raasay and St Kilda.

12 *Ibid.*, 341, 359–342, 395–396, 523–524 (Privy Council to James VI, May 1607), 524–525 (James VI to Privy Council, 20 May 1607), 528–529 (Privy Council to James VI, 19 June 1607); *Highland Papers*, ed. J.R.N. Macphail, 4 vols (Edinburgh, 1914–34), III, 100–101 (Privy Council to James VI, 26 March 1607).

With Huntly sidelined, the Privy Council made little attempt to resurrect the idea of planting Lowlanders on these particular islands. The southern half of the Western Highlands and Islands had in the meantime been deemed the responsibility of the seventh earl of Argyll, and it was not until 1608 that the first successful full-scale military expedition was conducted along the western seaboard. Its commander, Andrew Stewart, Lord Ochiltree, operated with the distinct advantage of having English and Irish logistical assistance, and he proceeded to incarcerate a number of the main Highland chiefs. A further expedition was undertaken in 1609 by Andrew Knox, Bishop of the Isles, this time with a view to assessing how legislative reform could be instigated in the region. It was his findings that went on to form the basis of the famous Statutes of Iona, a new legalistic approach to 'civilising' the area. Meanwhile, the Lewis plantation scheme had once again run into serious opposition from the Macleods and in 1610 it was abandoned for good. Waiting to step into the gap was Kenneth Mackenzie, Lord Kintail, a man who had long coveted possession of Lewis, even to the extent of having covertly supported Macleod resistance to the settlers. He duly gained official government backing in July of that year, was formally granted the island, and by 1611 had succeeded in having the Macleod clan elite evicted.[13] A new major power was clearly on the rise in the North-West of the country.

Meanwhile, from 1607 the House of Huntly had had little direct involvement in the 'civilisation' project along the west coast. When the government did request that Huntly take action it invariably related to trouble emanating from those discontented clans who had originally been targeted, and only then if it looked as though the Gordon lordships of Badenoch and Lochaber would be directly affected. In 1615, for example, when certain branches of Clan Donald South broke out in rebellion, Huntly and his eldest son, George, earl of Enzie, were required to take action necessary to safeguarding their own boundaries and to apprehending certain named malcontents.[14] In the first instance this order related to Sir James MacDonald of the Islay branch of the clan, a key instigator of the rebellion, who had recently escaped from imprisonment in Edinburgh Castle. Upon discovery of this, commissions had duly been issued to Huntly and Patrick Murray, first earl of Tullibardine, in order for them to engineer his recapture should he try to reach the Western Isles via Atholl and/or

---

13 Macinnes, *Clanship, Commerce and the House of Stuart*, 60–61; Lee, *Government by Pen*, 77–81; Goodare, 'Statutes of Iona', 44–45.

14 For specific mention of the need to keep the rebels out of Lochaber, see *Highland Papers*, III, 250. During this period Huntly's eldest son was commonly known by two separate titles, Lord Gordon and the earl of Enzie. For the purposes of continuity and clarity he will henceforward be referred to by the latter title. For more detail on the rebellion, see Gregory, *History of the Western Highlands*, 347–390; Lee, *Government by Pen*, 138–144.

Lochaber. As it turned out, neither was successful in this and Sir James managed to make his escape.[15]

The Privy Council also sent out orders for the apprehension of two key accomplices in the successful MacDonald escape attempt, Allaster MacDonald of Keppoch, and his eldest son, Ranald. However, despite the issuing of a number of commissions to both Huntly and Enzie over the months that followed, little seems to have been done to follow this up with any degree of dispatch.[16] Indeed, as late as 1621 Ranald was reported still to be at large in Lochaber after a period of some six years 'on the run'. Once again, and despite another commission, Enzie appears to have taken little or no action.[17] Yet another instance, it would seem, of the House of Huntly proving less than useful in the government's drive towards the imposition of centrally-ordained law, order and 'civility'. What, then, were the reasons underlying the lukewarm attitude of the House of Huntly towards the 'civilisation' project along the western seaboard, and how was the overall standing of the family affected by their apparent inaction?

In the first instance it is worth reiterating that, as very little personal correspondence survives for the household during the first quarter of the seventeenth century, it is hard to gain a true appreciation of how the first marquess of Huntly or his son, the earl of Enzie, may have regarded the union of 1603, or if indeed they even appreciated that a new British agenda was in evidence regarding issues such as 'civility', law and order, and religion. There is the odd intriguing glimpse. In January 1602, for example, the Privy Council of Scotland made a request that Huntly, along with a number of other Highland landowners and chiefs, provide men for the purposes of aiding Elizabeth I of England against the rebels in Ireland, something that may well have made Huntly aware of the wider British context.[18] Meanwhile, some two years later, Huntly could be found impressing upon the king that certain members of the Scottish ministry were 'boith fasting and preaching maliciuslie aganis the union of the kingdomes', a statement that on the surface would seem to imply his own goodwill towards

15 *RPCS, 1613–16*, 733–735; Gregory, *History of the Western Highlands*, 367–368.
16 *RPCS, 1613–15*, 346–347, 405, 488, 577, 767, 771; *RPCS, 1616–19*, 293, 456, 460; Macdonald and Macdonald, *Clan Donald*, II, 624–625.
17 *RPCS, 1619–21*, 551–552; Gregory, *History of the Western Highlands*, 402–403. Incidentally, both Sir James MacDonald and Keppoch were eventually restored to the favour of James VI in 1621. It seems, also, that Ranald was pardoned, probably in 1622 while on a visit to London. See Gregory, *History*, 402; Macdonald and Macdonald, *Clan Donald*, II, 629–630. Sir Robert Gordon seems to have been alone in implying that Enzie achieved a degree of success in expeditions against Ranald. However, any urgency on the part of the former seems only to have been awakened by the thought of Mackintosh of Dunnachton succeeding with a similar commission. See Gordon and Gordon, *Genealogical History*, 357.
18 *RPCS, 1599–1604*, 343–344.

the idea of a Greater Britain.[19] On the other hand, he may just have been telling James what he thought he wanted to hear.

However, even when taking on board the idea that Huntly and Enzie may have been aware of and supportive of the king's British agenda, there were a number of overriding factors that limited the extent to which they could or would want to assist in the 'civilising' of the west coast. In the first instance there was Huntly's continued lack of conformity to the requirements and teachings of the Kirk, something that certainly began to restrict the extent to which he could serve as an agent of the Crown. Also of relevance was the fact that Huntly simply did not have the connections, the reach, or the base of operations to conduct a campaign much further west of his Highland lordships of Badenoch and Lochaber.[20] On at least one occasion he went to the extent of pointing this out to the king, stressing, in connection to the potential commission of 1607, that the task would be very difficult, particularly given that he had few allies in the area.[21] Indeed, on occasion it seems that the Gordon lords even had difficulty in securing support in the North-East. In April 1616, for example, the barons and the gentlemen of Elgin and Forres successfully petitioned the Privy Council to the effect that they would not have to lend any service to the earl of Enzie in connection with the Keppoch commission. They claimed that they were not used to serving in the Highlands and that Enzie's remit did not extend beyond the Gordon-held sheriffdoms.[22]

There is also the question of how little the Gordons stood to gain from the commissions of the period. First of all, the chief of Keppoch and his son had from time to time been of considerable use to Huntly. It is difficult to envisage either Huntly or Enzie having any complaints about the fact that Keppoch's clan was reported to be ravaging the lands of Mackintosh of Dunnachton during the mid-1610s.[23] As such it made little sense for the Gordons to expend too much effort in securing their capture. In the past Huntly had been very unwilling to take action against the MacDonalds of Keppoch and this had remained highly evident during the 1580s. Likewise, Huntly failed to exhibit Keppoch following calls for his arrest in 1604.[24] Meanwhile, as regards the Isles commission, Huntly certainly seems to have remained aware that, from a monetary point of view, it made little sense to agree to the feu-duty rates demanded by the government, particularly considering the fact that he would have to foot the bill for

19 *Letters and State Papers during the Reign of King James the Sixth*, 60–61 (Huntly to James VI, 10 December 1604).
20 This point owes its origins to a number of conversations with Dr Aonghas MacCoinnich.
21 *Highland Papers*, III, 101–102 (Huntly to James VI, 26 March 1607).
22 *RPCS, 1613–16*, 513.
23 Gordon and Gordon, *Genealogical History*, 357.
24 Macdonald and Macdonald, *Clan Donald*, II, 623.

the expedition. In fact, it seems that he was justified in thinking the annual duty figure of £10,000 Scots to be extortionate: the Lewis settlers were required to make an annual payment of only £1,000 Scots and 3,600 fish in return for their particular grant.[25]

What, though, were the consequences of all this for the Gordon lords? Firstly, it can be postulated that Huntly began to lose a degree of favour with the king, particularly as a result of his intransigence during the Isles discussions. Certainly, by mid-1607 it seems that James had become increasingly annoyed at the manner in which Huntly was holding out.[26] Indeed, as will be seen, this may have served to justify a situation whereby the king could quite happily allow proceedings against Huntly over his non-conformity to go forward.

Perhaps of more direct import was the extent to which potential dynastic rivals, such as the Campbells of Argyll and the Mackenzies of Kintail, rose in stature as a result of their more active involvement in the 'civilising' of the western seaboard. It seems clear that these two families were the main beneficiaries of the policy of expropriation, the Campbells in the South, and the Mackenzies in the North.[27] It was the growth of the Mackenzies, in particular, that potentially had the power to shatter the Gordon claim to hegemony over the North of the country. Although it is perhaps debatable as to what extent the Crown deliberately promoted the rise of the Mackenzies with a view to providing a counter-balance to the Gordon power-bloc, it is clear that this family had the connections and the ability to exploit their chances when these arose. Where Huntly remained unwilling and unable to campaign in the northern half of the Western Isles, Mackenzie of Kintail was prepared to take on the role. On top of this Kintail was able to take advantage of his ally and key connection within the government, the lord chancellor, Alexander Seton, first earl of Dunfermline. Rewards were soon forthcoming: Kintail was elevated to the peerage in 1610, and his son, Colin, was created earl of Seaforth in 1623.[28] The Campbells of Argyll, meanwhile, managed to retain their position in the south-western parts of the Highlands and Islands, and were the main beneficiaries of the expropriation of Clan Donald South.

25 Goodare, 'Statutes of Iona', 33.
26 Lee, *Government by Pen*, 76.
27 Macinnes, 'Gaelic Culture in the Seventeenth Century', 170.
28 Lynch, 'James VI and the "Highland Problem"', 225; A. MacCoinnich, '"His Spirit was Given only to Warre": Conflict and Identity on the Scottish Gàidhealtachd, c.1580–c.1630', in S. Murdoch and A. Mackillop (eds), *Fighting for Identity. Scottish Military Experience, c.1550–1900* (Leiden, 2002), 151–152. MacCoinnich postulates the idea of the Mackenzies perhaps having been promoted by James as a counterbalance to Gordon power. Kintail's rise was also attributable to the influence of the lord chancellor: Colin, the future earl of Seaforth, married one of Dunfermline's daughters in 1614.

MAINTAINING THE HIGHLAND LORDSHIPS

The onset of poor relations with the Camerons in Lochaber during the 1610s added significantly to the problems already exercising Gordon attention in the Highlands. The disputes that flared up with this clan traced their immediate origins to the acquisitive aspirations of Archibald Campbell, seventh earl of Argyll. He claimed to have rediscovered a century-old Campbell claim to the superiority of the lands of Allan Cameron of Lochiel and had instigated legal action with a view to having the latter removed.[29] Under pressure, Lochiel subsequently acknowledged Argyll's right in return for security of tenure, even though Huntly, as holder of the lordship of Lochaber, claimed superiority over the same lands. The latter, much offended at what he judged to be a direct challenge to his authority, demanded that Lochiel renounce the security given to him by Argyll, but to no avail. Even Lochiel's assurance of his continued personal loyalty did little to assuage the wrath of the marquess. Added to this, it seems to have been the case that Huntly was looking to secure increased control over Lochiel's lands anyway, and that the Argyll business may well have presented him with an opportunity to achieve this.[30]

At any rate, Huntly sought to take direct action against Lochiel, initially courting potential rivals of the latter within Clan Cameron itself, most notably the families of Erracht, Kinlochiel and Glen Nevis. Essentially, a number of individuals were offered Lochiel's lands in return for their acknowledgement of Gordon superiority. This being agreed, the earl of Enzie then proceeded to ensure that the new owners were installed in their holdings. This situation was short lived; within weeks Lochiel had rooted out and killed the leading pretenders and had repossessed the lands. In return the Privy Council granted a commission to Huntly and Enzie for the purpose of bringing Lochiel to heel. This was conveyed in December 1613 and by the end of the following year Lochiel had reportedly offered his submission and had been imprisoned in Inverness until such time as he gave Enzie surety for his future good behaviour. This was duly given.[31]

However, Gordon relations with Clan Cameron remained uneven. For a time

---

29 Gregory, *History of the Western Highlands*, 342. The claim apparently lay originally with the third earl of Argyll during the reign of James V.

30 See A. Mackenzie, *History of the Camerons; with Genealogies of the Principal Families of the Name* (Inverness, 1884), 79. A.M. Mackintosh, meanwhile, played down this particular aspect. See Mackintosh, *Mackintoshes*, 200.

31 Gordon and Gordon, *Genealogical History*, 287, 294-295; W. Fraser, *Memorials of the Earls of Haddington*, 2 vols (Edinburgh, 1888), II, 75-76 (James VI to Huntly, 18 October 1613); *RPCS, 1613-16*, 185-186, 189-191, 818-820; *Highland Papers*, III, 139-140; Gregory, *History of the Western Highlands*, 343-346.

there was some rapprochement. In July 1617 the Privy Council outlawed Lochiel for having opposed Mackintosh of Dunnachton's attempts to hold courts at Inverlochy in his capacity as heritable steward of Lochaber. This forced Lochiel into courting closer relations with the House of Huntly once again, and a deal was struck whereby Enzie was granted the lands of Mamore in Lochaber and Lochiel's son, John, would become his vassal and would pay an annual feu-duty. By this means Lochiel regained a degree of favour with the Gordons. It certainly remained the case that over the next few years Huntly and Enzie did very little to try to capture Lochiel when commissions were issued to them to that effect.[32] But this was not to last. By 1626 the Gordon lords and Clan Cameron were in dispute once again, this time over attempts on the part of Enzie to introduce improvements on his lands in Lochaber. An expedition was duly mounted against the clan, the results of which were recorded in vivid terms by Gordon of Gordounstoun:

> No former aige hath sein the lyk quyetnes ther, nor such obedience to the king's lawes in these remote pairts of this kingdome: which he [Enzie] broght to passe by the execution and death of some malefactors of the Clanchamron, at Inverlochie in Lochaber: a rare spectacle to sie any of the Clanchamerone hanged in these bounds.[33]

This is certainly a very intriguing and powerful reference and it is a pity that no other source seems to make mention of it. Sir Robert Gordon, given his close connections with the House of Huntly, cannot be said to be the most unbiased of commentators and so the extent to which Enzie conducted such a successful, all-powerful expedition can perhaps be questioned. The important point remains, however, that relations between the House of Huntly and the Camerons do seem to have reached something of an all-time low during this period.

Overshadowing all of this was the series of contemporaneous and interconnected disputes between the Gordon lords and the Mackintoshes. The first of these related to Enzie's attempts to raise a force for the purpose of marching against Lochiel in 1613. Essentially, upon being called by Enzie to provide men for the expedition, Lachlan Mackintosh of Dunnachton refused, citing as his chief reason his inability to act against Lochiel due to the conditions of a treaty that had been drawn up in 1598 over disputed lands of Glenluy and Locharkaig.

32 A. Cunningham, *The Loyal Clans* (Cambridge, 1932), 121, 124; Gregory, *History of the Western Highlands*, 397–398, 402–403; Mackenzie, *History of the Camerons*, 84–85; RPCS, *1619–22*, 402–404, 427–428, 502–503, 539–543, 586–587.
33 Gordon and Gordon, *Genealogical History*, 357.

In this, Dunnachton drew support from his father-in-law, John Grant of Freuchy, a man who did not favour the House of Huntly at the time.[34] In response, Enzie insisted that Mackintosh should observe the conditions set out in a bond of manrent of 1568 whereupon Mackintosh argued that this was no longer valid. Mackintosh also forbade members of his clan who were tenants of the earl of Moray from joining the expedition. Eventually, following a small skirmish that occurred between some Mackintoshes and one of Moray's agents, the latter and Enzie saw to it that Dunnachton was imprisoned in Edinburgh Castle. His time in prison was short, however, on account of the fact that he was much in favour at the royal court at the time. Indeed, he was eventually restored without having to find any kind of surety.[35]

Disputes also began to rage over matters relating to landholdings. In 1618 Enzie reportedly attempted to have a number of Mackintosh clansmen evicted from lands in the barony of Benchar, apparently with little success.[36] In that same year he took issue with Dunnachton over the teinds due on the latter's lands of Culloden, the tacks of which pertained to Enzie. Enzie complained to the king, stating that Dunnachton had been deliberately obstructive over the issue and had on one occasion prevented his agents from impounding corn from the said lands. It was further reported that Dunnachton had brought a number of Highland outlaws into his service, and had garrisoned them within the walls of Culloden House itself.[37] The property was also fortified at around the same time and all the corn was gathered to within shooting range of its walls.

Enzie clearly saw the need to make a show of force and in early November 1618 he marched upon Culloden at the head of a force of men.[38] Sources differ as to what happened next. Sir Robert Gordon asserted that the head of the garrison, Dunnachton's uncle, Duncan Mackintosh, yielded up the house and the corn in the face of Enzie's overwhelming superiority.[39] Meanwhile, the writer of the key Mackintosh source, the *Kinrara Manuscript*, provided a rather more detailed account. In this version it was related that, following a tense standoff,

34 Grant had also been a supporter of Argyll's attempt to gain more influence over Lochiel. See Fraser, *Chiefs of Grant*, I, 183.

35 Ibid., 356; Gregory, *History of the Western Highlands*, 397–398; Macfarlane, *Genealogical Collections*, I, 277–278; *RPCS, 1613–16*, 140–141.

36 Macfarlane, *Genealogical Collections*, I, 283; Mackintosh, *Mackintoshes*, 206–207.

37 *Letters and State Papers during the Reign of King James the Sixth*, 264–265.

38 Gordon and Gordon, *Genealogical History*, 357–359; Macfarlane, *Genealogical Collections*, I, 383–384. These two sources differed as to the size of the force fielded by Enzie. Sir Robert Gordon claimed that it consisted of 1,100 horsemen 'weill appointed and armed' and 600 Highlanders. The writer of the *Kinrara Manuscript* stated that Enzie had only 700 horse with him – still a good number.

39 Gordon and Gordon, *Genealogical History*, 359.

a few members of Enzie's party were allowed to check the house for Highland outlaws, and only then after much negotiation. This had seemingly been enough to satisfy Enzie's honour. Nevertheless the author remained scathing. He concluded that: 'Lord Gordon [Enzie] was pleased to proceed no further in his purpose of revenge; and so, having dismissed his army, he went home, carrying but small triumph and less glory, for even the teinds were not gathered.'[40] The difference in the two versions is intriguing, and presents the historian with the classic problem of which to give more credence to. Both are biased, perhaps more so Sir Robert Gordon's, given his own personal involvement. On the other hand, at least he is known to have been an eyewitness, and so it follows that his account must carry some weight. However, his portrayal of an easy Gordon triumph was perhaps coloured a bit too much by his personal leanings and by thoughts of the audience for whom his account was intended. Certainly, one of the later historians of the Mackintosh family, while presenting a synthesis of the Gordon and *Kinrara* accounts and pointing out the main differences, proceeded to favour the latter version.[41] Intriguingly, Enzie's own complaint, considered by the Privy Council on 1 December 1618, made no mention of the so-called 'Raid of Culloden'; it only highlighted events up to and including 21 September.[42] Having said all this, the key overall point is that relations between the House of Huntly and Mackintosh of Dunnachton remained tense.

Adding to the problem was Enzie's increasing resentment at Dunnachton's involvement in commissions against individuals such as Lochiel and Keppoch. In 1617 Dunnachton obtained a commission of fire and sword against Keppoch, largely it seems following on from Enzie's own lack of success in this regard. Dunnachton initially achieved little himself and had been set to try again, seeking this time to call on the services of clansmen who were tenants of the House of Huntly. Enzie could not tolerate this, and upon accusing Dunnachton of exceeding his powers, managed to have his own commission reinstated.[43]

Similar Mackintosh commissions against Lochiel also caused friction. In October 1618 Enzie could be found complaining to the Privy Council that Dunnachton was once again overstepping the remit of his commission and was assuming the full powers of a royal lieutenant. Particular offence had been caused by the fact that Dunnachton had been calling on the services of Gordon tenants within Badenoch and Lochaber.[44] Perhaps most worrying for the Gordon lords was the commission given jointly to Dunnachton, Kintail and Grant of

40 Macfarlane, *Genealogical Collections*, I, 284–285.
41 Mackintosh, *Mackintoshes*, 206–208.
42 *RPCS, 1616–19*, 478–480.
43 Mackintosh, *Mackintoshes*, 205–206; Gordon and Gordon, *Genealogical History*, 357.
44 *RPCS, 1616–19*, 456–457.

Freuchy in 1621 for the purpose of bringing Lochiel to justice. It specifically stipulated that both Huntly and Enzie should lend active aid and assistance in their capacity as sheriffs of Inverness.[45] Added to all this was the continuing resentment caused by Dunnachton's right to hold courts in Lochaber under the auspices of his hereditary stewardship.

The vehemence with which Enzie pursued a legal offensive against Dunnachton during much of 1619 proved an effective indicator of the level of the enmity. Essentially, the Privy Council upheld Enzie's assertion that Dunnachton had exceeded the terms of his commission against Lochiel. Moreover, upon his not appearing to answer the charge, they had denounced Dunnachton as a rebel.[46] Furthermore, on 30 March 1619, upon Enzie's complaint, a surety given in 1615 by the earl of Tullibardine and Grant of Freuchy for the good behaviour of Dunnachton was declared forfeit. Mackintosh and Grant incurred a penalty of £5,000 Scots, while on top of that Dunnachton was ordered to pay Enzie £2,500 Scots as well as to find caution for 5,000 merks Scots (£3,333 Scots) that he would remain in Edinburgh as long as was required.[47] According to the Lords of the Council, by June the sum due to Enzie from Dunnachton totalled a massive £10,500 Scots.[48] However, it appears that upon reaching a degree of reconciliation with Enzie later that year, it was agreed that part of that sum would be remitted. Despite that, it seems that Enzie managed to secure 'a good sum of money' from Dunnachton.[49]

All these episodes involving the Camerons and the Mackintoshes are revealing in a number of ways. In the first instance they indicate a willingness on the part of the Gordon lords to be much more proactive when their own interests were directly threatened and when they were operating more within the confines of their own Highland lordships. This was certainly made apparent by their actions against the Camerons in 1613 and in 1626, and through episodes such as the 'Raid of Culloden'. This remains in marked contrast with their attitude towards 'civilising' projects along the western seaboard. Having said this, it seems that they may well have seen limits to what could be effectively achieved by force of arms, particularly when Sir Robert Gordon's somewhat overly-triumphant accounts begin to be questioned. Enzie's grandiose 'Raid of Culloden' seems then to indicate the limitations of such an approach and perhaps by implication the increasing inability of the Gordon lords to force

45 Mackintosh, *Mackintoshes*, 209–210.
46 *RPCS, 1616–19*, 456–457.
47 *Ibid.*, 559. Given that this is a Scottish source, it has been assumed that pounds Scots is the monetary denomination being referred to.
48 *Ibid*, 585. See the previous note regarding the monetary denomination.
49 Gordon and Gordon, *Genealogical History*, 360.

their will in that part of the world. It has already been pointed out elsewhere that the Gordons ideally required Clan Chattan manpower in order to conduct operations in the Highlands. Indeed, the overall point regarding the Mackintoshes was that it was now arguably the case that the House of Huntly was no longer able to command the same degree of allegiance as it had during much of the previous century.[50] Meanwhile, worsening relations with Clan Cameron was something of a new and worrying trend for the House of Huntly.

Also noticeable was the extent to which other interested parties looked to involve themselves in the disputes of the time, whether it was as a result of family connections or through a simple desire to increase their own power and influence. Men like Kintail and the Grant of Freuchy could often be found taking the part of Mackintosh of Dunnachton, probably seeing this as an opportunity to undermine the standing of the House of Huntly in a part of the world where they themselves wanted to retain influence. More serious for the Gordon lords was the extent to which Argyll attempted to force his superiority over the lands of Lochiel. It was a sign of things to come.

LAW AND ORDER IN THE NORTHERN LOWLANDS

The Gordons also had to contend with feuds involving fellow members of the nobility. Most notable was the damaging dispute that broke out between the Gordons and the Hays of Errol in 1616. This was triggered by the murder of Adam Gordon, brother of Sir George Gordon of Gight, at the hands of Francis Hay, first cousin of the ninth earl of Errol. In response, Gight took the law into his own hands and apprehended Francis during a raid on the home of one of the Hays of Brunthill. Francis was then delivered to the sheriff-depute in Aberdeen, John Gordon of Clubbisgoull, and after what was in effect a rigged trial in front of a stacked jury, was duly executed. Not satisfied with this, Gight and his men went on to conduct another raid on the Brunthill family and inflicted a number of injuries. The earl of Errol, outraged at the manner in which his cousin had been executed and at the actions of Gight, sought recompense before the Justice Court in Edinburgh. The case was put that Gight had originally acted without a commission and that the sheriff-depute had acted beyond his remit. The marquess of Huntly sought to defend the positions of both his depute and his cousin, while at the same time trying to bring off a reconciliation with Errol. Errol was insisting on future exemption from Huntly's jurisdiction for himself, his family and tenants – a point that could not be conceded by the marquess. Eventually the feud was brought to a conclusion at the personal intervention of the king himself during his visit to Scotland of 1617. Both Gordon of Clubbisgoull and Gight were duly punished, the former with a spell of imprisonment and

50 This point has been made in Cathcart, 'Crisis of Identity?', 179–180.

the latter with a damages payment for his raids on the Hays of Brunthill. Even then, relations between Huntly and Errol remained frosty until 1627 when John Gordon, fifth son of the former, married Sophia Hay, fifth daughter of the latter.[51]

Gordon involvement in the messy affairs of the Sinclair House of Caithness also involved a degree of feud resolution. Around the year 1614 the lords of the Privy Council requested that Huntly help resolve a dispute between the fifth earl of Caithness and Sir Robert Gordon, something that Huntly eventually had to give up on, admitting that he had often engineered temporary reconciliations between the two in the past but that a final solution was impossible to bring off.[52] Tied up with this was the fact that there had recently been bad blood between Caithness and the earl of Enzie. The latter, as a confederate of Sir Robert Gordon, had taken his part in the dispute with Caithness. One night in June 1612 a scuffle broke out between the two parties in the middle of Edinburgh's High Street and both Enzie and Caithness were subsequently called before the Privy Council for the purpose of reconciliation.[53] Despite this, in the early 1620s, Enzie, as 'ane neutrall and indifferent nobleman', was given a joint commission with Sir Robert to resolve the troubles of the heavily indebted House of Caithness and capture the outlawed fifth earl of Caithness. The latter was suspected of the killing of one Thomas Lindsay, and had claimed to be unable to appear before the Privy Council for fear of falling foul of his creditors. Added to this was the difficulty that existed between the earl of Caithness and his equally indebted son, Lord Berriedale, over the inability of the former to secure the release of the latter from prison. These were murky waters and by 1623 Enzie had turned his attentions elsewhere, with little having been resolved in the far North. Eventually it was only through the sole efforts of Sir Robert Gordon that Caithness was pacified, a fact that did not go unobserved by the lords of the Privy Council. They even considered writing a letter to the king to point out the good service undertaken by Sir Robert, as well as the fact that Enzie had been unable to attend fully to matters on account of 'his owne adois'.[54]

Much can be taken from the examples of the Hay feud and the Caith-

---

51 Gordon and Gordon, *Genealogical History*, 340–342; Brown, *Bloodfeud in Scotland*, 74; *RPCS*, 1613-16, 496–502; *State Papers and Miscellaneous Correspondence of Thomas, Earl of Melros*, I, 257–258 (Binning to James VI, 21 August [1617]), I, 296 (Binning to James VI, 11 September [1617]), I, 297 (Dunfermline to James VI, 23 December 1617). For Errol's letters to the king thanking him for taking note of the case, see NLS, Denmilne Estate Papers, Adv. MSS 33.1.1, vol. VII, no. 22 (Errol to James VI, 20 June 1616); NLS, Adv. MSS 33.1.1, vol. VII, no. 24 (Errol to James VI, 13 August 1616).

52 Gordon and Gordon, *Genealogical History*, 295.

53 *Ibid.*, 286–287; *RPCS*, 1610-13, 422.

54 Gordon and Gordon, *Genealogical History*, 365–375, 377–380; *State Papers and Miscellaneous Correspondence of Thomas, Earl of Melros*, II, 409–411 (Privy Council to James VI, 28 June 1621); *RPCS*, 1619-22, 548; *RPCS*, 1622-25, 123–128, 391–392.

ness disputes. In the first instance they provide an indication of the range of continued Gordon involvement in local affairs, from the Lowlands of Buchan to the far North of the country. There were, however, limitations to this. Huntly, after all, admitted that he had been unable to resolve properly the earlier dispute between Sir Robert and Caithness. In addition, the earl of Enzie achieved little success with his interventions in the far North, something that stood in stark contrast to the efforts of the ubiquitous Sir Robert. On top of this, the outcome of the Hay feud can be seen as something of a rebuff for the Gordons, involving, as it did, the dressing down of both Gight and Huntly's own sheriff-depute of Aberdeen. The affair also brought with it other new uncertainties. Prior to 1616 the houses of Huntly and Errol had been in very close alliance, but this was beginning to show signs of crumbling. Whether this would last remained to be seen.

In terms of the wider context of bloodfeud regulation it can be seen that the examples do arguably reflect the tenor of the times. By the 1610s centrally ordained rules and regulations with regard to feuding had been formulated and ratified, and formed part of the important general trend towards the creation of what James VI would have looked on as being a more modern, 'civilised' and uniform society. The key breakthrough legislation regarding bloodfeud regulation was the 1598 'Act Anent Removing and Extinguishing of Deidlie Feuds'. This laid out clearly what action was required in particular cases. Feuds involving no killing could be resolved by a local power-broker and those involving killing on both sides could also be handled locally following initial referral to the Crown. The final type involved killing on one side. In this instance the aggrieved party was now required to take the case to court to be tried by professional lawyers. This was the main key change and implied a slow move away from the old fully decentralised system. On top of this the king reserved the right to intervene when he deemed necessary. A follow-up Act of 1604 extended the legislation further. This said that offended parties should now bring their case before the Privy Council, which would decide if the grievance was legitimate and would warn the parties against seeking any private retribution.[55]

What is important to point out is that the legislation was never designed to bring about a sudden end to the role of power-brokers like Huntly in feud regulation. What it was designed to remove was the internecine tit-for-tat disputes of the past and the abuse of local privilege.[56] As can be seen from the Caithness material there were still times when the mediation services of members of the House of Huntly were called upon. Meanwhile, what the Hay feud revealed was that men like Huntly and Errol do seem to have broadly followed the new

---

55 Wormald, 'Bloodfeud', 85–86; Brown, *Bloodfeud in Scotland*, 241–243.
56 Brown, *Bloodfeud in Scotland*, 245; Goodare, *State and Society in Early Modern Scotland*, 83.

regulations. This dispute was mutually submitted for arbitration and in the end was resolved by the king in person. The most important point was that neither of these nobles personally sought to escalate the violence. This in turn indicates that there was little resistance to the new regulations from Huntly and others. This was despite the fact that the regulations could be seen to be impinging on Huntly's traditional role as fount of all justice in the North. In the case of the Hay feud, where Huntly's justice may once have been the final word (given that he was the sheriff), this could now be more easily bypassed in certain cases. The fact that there was little resistance also lends support to the idea that the nobility sought largely to co-operate with the king in bringing about a less violent society.

Alongside this came a range of associated legislation, most notably that relating to gun control, the curbing of duels and private combat, and the regulation of noble retinues. Calvinist ideology, as espoused by the ministry of the Kirk, may have been influential in shaping ideas of what constituted a civil society.[57] The forming of private bands of association was also increasingly frowned upon. For example, in 1607 the Privy Council required that Huntly suppress a group known as the 'Society and Company of Boyes', who had banded together under the leadership of George Gordon of Gight, had taken oaths of mutual defence, and had proceeded to commit 'heir-schippes and utheris enormities' across the North-East.[58] Given that little was heard of the 'Boyes' after this time, it is probably safe to conclude that Huntly succeeded in this particular task.[59]

The drawing up of bonds of manrent and friendship was much less in evidence from around 1603. This was certainly true of the House of Huntly: only three bonds were drawn up in 1603 and virtually none after that.[60] The implications of this were perhaps not immediately obvious. It has been argued that, as the clientage associated with bonding was hereditary, old established alliances based on the system would not have died away overnight.[61] However, from the medium- to long-term point of view, die away they inevitably did. It has, for example, been seen how Mackintosh of Dunnachton denied the necessity of observing a bond of 1568. The traditional alliance between the Gordons

---

57 Brown, *Bloodfeud in Scotland*, 185–190, 246–252.
58 *Ancient Criminal Trials in Scotland*, ed. R. Pitcairn, 3 vols (Edinburgh, 1833), 581 (Privy Council to Huntly, 20 January 1607).
59 Allan Macinnes has speculated that the 'Society and Company of Boyis' was a confederacy of Catholic gentry 'intent on upholding Gordon hegemony in the North-East'. See A.I. Macinnes, 'Catholic Recusancy and the Penal Laws, 1603–1707', *Records of the Scottish Church History Society*, 23, part 1 (1987), 37. There may have been some truth in this, particularly given that Gight was the leader, and given that Huntly seems to have been slow in bringing the society to heel.
60 *Miscellany of the Spalding Club*, IV, 254–260.
61 Macinnes, 'Crown, Clans and Fine', 44.

and the Hays was also not as strong as it once had been. No new bonds were drawn up between the two households following the feud of 1616–17; another instance, then, of the slow but steady passing away of the old order of things in the North of Scotland.

All of this must be viewed within the context of a centralising tendency in Scottish government. Although the king appreciated the value of his nobles and their continuing role as agents of royal policy in the localities, he still looked to implement changes that would bind them more tightly to the central regime. As can be seen with regulations relating to feuds, this was largely to be achieved with the co-operation of the nobility rather than in the face of opposition. James VI and I did elevate a number of men to the peerage during the early seventeenth century, but he also looked to incorporate the traditional landed nobility into his vision of increased centralisation. The noble estate was strengthened as a whole by the injection of new blood.[62] In 1609, James did introduce a new administrative layer in the localities in the form of justices of the peace. However, he never seems to have any intention of undermining the traditional role of the sheriffs. Indeed, evidence would suggest that the sheriffs and JPs ended up operating in relative harmony. The latter developed a niche for themselves in dealing with very low-level offences such as vagrancy and in fixing local wages and prices.[63]

HUNTLY, THE CROWN AND THE KIRK

The move towards centralisation and increased professionalism in government coincided with the beginnings of royal policy to introduce changes in Church governance and in religious doctrine and worship. The king's desire to bring the Kirk under a greater degree of control predated the Union by a number of years. From around 1596 he had looked to take a more proactive role regarding Church policy, a decision well in keeping with his concurrent desire to exert a greater degree of control in other fields. By 1603 relations with the Kirk were becoming more strained. As had been the case in the past, many ministers continued to express their concern that not enough action was being taken against the Catholic nobles, Huntly being foremost amongst them. The king's prorogation of successive planned General Assemblies only added to tensions. The Kirk also retained grave misgivings that, upon becoming king of England, James would increasingly favour a full-blown Episcopalian church settlement. In this they were not far wrong.

---

62 Goodare, *Government of Scotland*, 5–6; Brown, 'Nobility of Jacobean Scotland', 72. This idea of the co-operation and incorporation of the old landed nobility has been underplayed in the work of Maurice Lee, who argued that the king sought to pursue a more openly combative agenda against his over-mighty subjects. See Lee, 'James VI and the Aristocracy'; Lee, *Great Britain's Solomon*, 198–202, 213–218.

63 Goodare, *Government of Scotland*, 203–205.

From December 1596, following an attempted pro-Presbyterian rising in Edinburgh, the king began a step by step process designed to undermine the Kirk's administrative autonomy while at the same time aiming to restore power to the Scottish bishops.[64] At the General Assembly of 1610 this process was largely completed with the transference of key remaining powers from the presbyteries to the bishops. Furthermore, the idea of episcopal succession was also restored with the consecration in London of three Scottish bishops at the hands of their English counterparts. Not satisfied with this, the king went even further in the following decade with the institution of the infamous Five Articles of Perth – a series of controversial reforms relating to church worship, designed to bring the Scottish Church more in line with its counterpart south of the border. Not without some difficulty, these were approved by the Perth General Assembly of 1618, ratified by the Privy Council that same year, and ratified again by the Scottish Parliament in 1621.[65]

The king's attitude towards Huntly during this lengthy process is notable. The Kirk remained vehement in its desire to pursue an anti-Catholic agenda, particularly against key suspect recusants like the marquess of Huntly. Recommendations made at a succession of General Assemblies stand testament to this, and on occasion it was even deemed fitting that Protestant ministers be placed in the houses of recusant nobles with a view to ensuring their conformity.[66]

---

64 For analysis of the events in Edinburgh in December 1596, see J. Goodare, 'The Attempted Scottish *Coup* of 1596', in J. Goodare and A.A. MacDonald (eds), *Sixteenth-Century Scotland: Essays in Honour of Michael Lynch* (Leiden, 2008), 311–336.

65 For studies of Kirk–Crown relations, see G. Donaldson, 'The Scottish Church, 1567–1625', in A.G.R. Smith (ed.), *The Reign of James VI and I* (London and Basingstoke, 1973), 40–56; D.G. Mullen, *Episcopacy in Scotland: the History of an Idea, 1560–1638* (Edinburgh, 1986); MacDonald, *Jacobean Kirk*; MacDonald, 'James VI and the General Assembly'; A.R. MacDonald, 'James VI and I, the Church of Scotland, and British Ecclesiastical Convergence', *Historical Journal*, vol. 48 (2005), 885–903; W.R. Foster, *The Church before the Covenants* (Edinburgh and London, 1975); J. Wormald, 'The Headaches of Monarchy: Kingship and the Kirk in the Early Seventeenth Century', in Goodare and MacDonald (eds), *Sixteenth-Century Scotland*, 365–393. For detailed examinations of the Five Articles of Perth, see I.B. Cowan, 'The Five Articles of Perth', in D. Shaw (ed.) *Reformation and Revolution* (Edinburgh, 1967), 160–177; P.H.R. Mackay, 'The Reception given to the Five Articles of Perth', *Records of the Scottish Church History Society*, vol. 19 (1977), 185–201; J.D. Ford, 'Conformity in Conscience: the Structure of the Perth Articles Debate in Scotland, 1618–1638', *Journal of Ecclesiastical History*, vol. 46 (1995), 256–277; L.A.M. Stewart, 'The Political Repercussions of the Five Articles of Perth: a Reassessment of James VI and I's Religious Policies in Scotland', *Sixteenth Century Journal*, vol. 38, no. 4 (2007), 1013–1036. For a detailed examination of the Parliament of 1621, see J. Goodare, 'The Scottish Parliament of 1621', *Historical Journal*, vol. 38, no. 1 (1995), 29–51. See also V.T. Wells, 'Constitutional Conflict after the Union of the Crowns: Contention and Continuity in the Parliaments of 1612 and 1621', in Brown and Mann (eds), *Parliament and Politics in Scotland*, 82–100.

66 Calderwood, *History of the Kirk of Scotland*, VI, 25–26, 113–116, 161–162; J. Row and J. Row, *The History of the Kirk of Scotland from the Year 1558 to August 1637 ... with a Continuation to July*

By 1604 the ministers of the Synod of Aberdeen had begun calling for a more concerted effort against Huntly. They also sought a forum, preferably a General Assembly, in which to 'lay opin their greeves' on the matter.[67] Indeed, over the course of the next two years James found himself increasingly having to come to Huntly's aid, usually by blocking attempts to have him excommunicated for non-conformity. At the same time the king also looked to defend his own prerogative by refusing to be pressurised by sections of the Kirk into calling a General Assembly.[68]

In the past James had made his distaste for an overbearing Presbyterian polity perfectly obvious. This alone served to lend him plenty reason for defending Huntly during the first half of the decade. Having said that, the king was a careful enough politician to ensure that, while making sure all charges against the marquess were dropped or deferred, he was at the same time seen to be reproachful of the latter's unenthusiastic backing of the Protestant faith. A letter from the king to the Privy Council of 1604 provides ample illustration of this tactic. In it James concluded:

> Although the said Marques [Huntly] his behaviour hath not bene such in our service as wee ought to extend any clemency or courtesie towardis him upon his owne deserte, yet … if that said Marques be contended to finde sufficient caution, or may be able to verifie that he offers to here conference, frequentis the sermons, obeyes the lawes anent the receipt of excommunicated persons and recusantis, and generallie satisfies in all other pointes of externall obedience the discipline of the Kirk, it is our pleasour that yee graint him suspension, and dischardge them [the Presbytery of Aberdeen] of any proceeding against him.[69]

The point regarding external obedience is a key one. Clearly James had no real problem with Huntly practising his faith as long as it was done discreetly.

To the ever-shrewd James, Huntly still served a purpose beyond that of mere

---

1639, ed. D. Laing (Edinburgh, 1842), 205–206, 209.

67 Calderwood, *History of the Kirk*, VI, 268. It is noteworthy that this provides a good example of the fact that early modern Aberdeen was clearly not as conservative a place as some historians once thought. See MacDonald, *Jacobean Kirk*, 105. For the view that the North was conservative, see G. Donaldson, 'Scotland's Conservative North in the Sixteenth and Seventeenth Centuries', *Transactions of the Royal Historical Society*, 5th series, vol. 16 (1966), 65–79.

68 *RPCS, 1604-7*, 19–20, 462, 468 (James VI to the Privy Council, 25 September 1604), (James VI to the Privy Council, 22 March 1605); J. Spottiswoode, *History of the Church of Scotland*, 3 vols (Edinburgh, 1847–51), III, 187–188; Calderwood, *History of the Kirk*, VI, 274; *Letters and State Papers during the Reign of King James the Sixth*, 60–61 (Huntly to James VI, 20 November 1604).

69 *RPCS, 1604-7*, 462 (James VI to the Privy Council, 25 September 1604).

friendship. He still remained a power in the North of Scotland and could be used by the king to counterbalance the Presbyterian threat. In September 1605, for example, following the unsanctioned meeting of the General Assembly at Aberdeen, James charged Huntly, as sheriff, to ensure 'that na sic assemblie or meiting of the ministerie salbe haldin or keipit within the same'.[70] In addition, Huntly still had his uses as a royal lieutenant and as a key landholding magnate in the North.

Despite all of this, as the decade progressed, Huntly did find himself under mounting pressure over his non-conformity and the king found himself increasingly unable or unwilling to help. By late 1607 proceedings were under way against Huntly and from May the following year the king had seemingly abandoned him to his fate. A warrant was duly issued for Huntly's confinement in Aberdeen. Meanwhile the other two key Catholic earls, Angus and Errol, were confined within the towns of Glasgow and Perth respectively.[71] At the General Assembly in July the Catholic earls were excommunicated.[72] Huntly was later transferred to Stirling Castle, while Errol was sent to Dumbarton Castle and Angus was given permission to leave the country.[73]

Two main reasons may be advocated as to why the king took action against Huntly at this time. Both can be linked to an overall agenda of seeking to 'civilise' and bring about uniformity across the three kingdoms. The first reason related to the attempt on the part of the Crown to involve Huntly in the subduing of the Western Isles. Put simply, as Huntly became more and more intransigent over the associated negotiations, there remained less reason for the king to keep supporting him. That said, the real reason why the king moved so readily against Huntly in 1608 probably owed more to the wider religious context. At the time James was seeking to re-establish the power of the Scottish bishops, while the Kirk as a body remained discontented over the fact that not enough was being done to deal with the non-conformity of high-profile Catholics. Many ministers were also still unhappy at the direction royal policy seemed to be taking and that a pre-arranged 'official' General Assembly had not been held since 1602. The key point here is that one was scheduled to take place in July 1608 and it was at this crucial juncture that the king decided to sanction action against Huntly, Errol and Angus. Ministerial obedience during this all-important assembly is what the king sought and this on the whole is what he got. The sacrifice of the three nobles had served to satisfy many within the Kirk. At the same time, atten-

70 *RPCS, 1604–7*, 123–125.

71 *RPCS, 1607–10*, xxx, 9, 490, 505–506 (James VI to the Privy Council, 2 February 1608), (James VI to the Privy Council, 13 May 1608).

72 *Ibid.*, 140.

73 *Ibid.*, 186, 537 (Privy Council to James VI, 8 November 1608).

tion was diverted away from James's ongoing pursuit of an Episcopalian settlement. Indeed, two years later this objective was largely achieved at the General Assembly of 1610.[74] The fact that the Penal Laws against Catholics had been codified and re-enacted in 1609 may also have aided the king in this regard.[75]

The importance of keeping Huntly, Errol and Angus confined throughout 1609 and 1610 was emphasised in three letters to the king of that period. The first, from George Home, earl of Dunbar and the bishops of Galloway and Orkney is undated but was probably sent to James either in late 1609 or early 1610. In it they pointed out that:

> Consulting togidder anent the best meanes for advancing your Hienes service at the ensuing Generall Assemblie, [we] thocht it most expedient that the Marqueise of Huntlie, and the uther two Earles confined, sould vpon no offeris or conditiounes be inlarged befoir the said Assemblie. We were bold to take suche resolutioune, knowing the greate contentment your Maiesteis directiounes anent ther confining hes givin vniuersallie to all sorte of your Hienes best subjects, in so muche that the hartis of all men ar inclined to quyetnes and obedience, and we do assuiredlie expect ane happie success of all thingis concerning your Maiesteis service.[76]

The other two letters, one from Archbishop Spottiswoode and the other from the members of the Court of High Commission in the Province of Moray (written in March and April 1610 respectively), echoed this view.[77] The king and chief advisors such as the earl of Dunbar had almost certainly used action against the Catholic nobles to help further the chances of restoring the power of the bishops. It is hardly coincidental that, following royal success at the General Assembly of 1610, Huntly and Errol soon found themselves at liberty.[78]

The Kirk continued to pursue Huntly for non-conformity in the decade that followed. Now the newly restored bishops had joined the calls for action to be

---

74 MacDonald, *Jacobean Kirk*, 141.

75 This was not a completely new move: the Penal Laws had already been partially re-enacted in 1604 and 1607. See Macinnes, 'Catholic Recusancy', 37.

76 *Original Letters relating to the Ecclesiastical Affairs of Scotland, chiefly written or addressed to his Majesty King James the Sixth after his Accession to the English Throne*, ed. B. Botfield, 2 vols (Edinburgh, 1851), I, 198–199 (Dunbar and bishops of Galloway and Orkney to James VI, [1609]).

77 *Ibid.*, I, 235–236, 243–244 (Spottiswoode to James VI, 12 March 1610), (Court of High Commission of St Andrews to James VI, 10 April 1610).

78 On 15 November 1610 James ordered that Huntly be released and on 15 January 1611 the Privy Council duly sent instruction to that effect. See *RPCS, 1610–13*, 585–586 (James VI to the Privy Council, 15 November 1610); HMC, *Report of the Manuscripts of the Earl of Mar and Kellie preserved at Alloa House* (London, 1904), 67.

taken. In October 1612 they informed the king of their fears that the marquess probably remained insincere in his promises to give satisfaction to the Kirk.[79] By 1614, the bishops were becoming ever more concerned that recusancy was on the rise in the North and as a result renewed attempts were made to have Huntly and Errol excommunicated.[80] In actual fact, support for Catholicism had stagnated by 1614. It would not be until around 1617 that Jesuit missionaries would begin to develop a coherent strategy for the reinvigoration of the faith in the Lowlands. Even then the change would only become noticeable within the bounds of the Gordons in the North-East and the Maxwells of Nithsdale in the South-West. The movement would remain small and would pose no serious threat to the political establishment. James, it could be argued, had grasped this as long ago as 1589. He never at any time seemed to doubt Huntly's personal loyalty. If Huntly had at any time in the past ever actually been seriously in league with Catholic powers such as Spain, those days were certainly long gone.[81]

Nevertheless, in 1616 the High Commission imprisoned Huntly following his refusal to subscribe to the Confession of Faith. Within a week, however, he had been released at the command of Chancellor Dunfermline. He then travelled to England where he received absolution from the archbishop of Canterbury. The bishops in Scotland thus had little choice but to follow suit and so at the General Assembly of 1616 Huntly was duly absolved.[82] His political rehabilitation was confirmed when he was readmitted to the ranks of the Privy Council in February 1617.[83]

The king had obviously reverted to a position of tolerance towards Huntly's recusancy. He had been able to use Huntly during the years 1608–10 and clearly saw that there was no advantage in allowing the Kirk to take any substantial action against him in the years that followed. James was still engaged in the process of introducing major religious changes, in particular the highly controversial Five Articles of Perth. However, following the reinstatement of the bishops he may have felt secure enough to pursue such reforms without having to rely on taking action against the Catholic nobles as a means by which to placate some of the more outspoken Scottish ministers. There is no evidence of such action being taken against Huntly at the time of the Perth General Assembly of 1618 and the

---

79 W. Fraser, *Memoirs of the Maxwells of Pollock*, 2 vols (Edinburgh, 1863), II, 63 (Scottish archbishops and bishops to James VI, 25 October 1612).

80 *Original Letters relating to the Ecclesiastical Affairs of Scotland*, I, 341–343 (Scottish archbishops and bishops to James VI, 23 June 1614).

81 Macinnes, 'Catholic Recusancy', 28–29, 35–36.

82 MacDonald *Jacobean Kirk*, 154; *Original Letters relating to the Ecclesiastical Affairs of Scotland*, II, 474–477 (James VI to the Archbishop of St Andrews, 1616), (Archbishop of Canterbury to the Archbishop of St Andrews, 23 July 1616).

83 *RPCS, 1616–19*, 48. The earl of Enzie had been admitted the previous year. See *RPCS, 1613–16*, 440.

Scottish Parliament of 1621.

AN UNCERTAIN FUTURE?

While religion remained the weak underbelly of the House of Huntly, the Gordon lords did at least retain their status as prominent landowners in the North of Scotland. Following his return to political favour in the late 1590s the first marquess of Huntly undertook a series of extensive building and repair works. A brand new mansion called Newhouse was built in Deeside at a place called Kandychyle (now Deecastle). Huntly also erected new houses at Aboyne and Plewlands in Moray, and oversaw the reworking of the castle of Ruthven in Badenoch. He repaired the family townhouses in Elgin and Old Aberdeen, and enlarged and redecorated Bog of Gight in the Enzie.[84] In 1618 the traveller John Taylor saw fit to describe the last residence as a 'sumptuous house'.[85] Arguably the most impressive were the repairs and improvements made to Strathbogie Castle. These had been a necessity in light of the reduction of the property by royal decree in 1594. Nevertheless, going on the evidence of the results, Huntly seems to have relished the opportunity. Of particular note were the oriel windows that enhanced the front façade, the intricately detailed stone fireplaces that dominated the lodging rooms of the marquess and his lady, the exterior frieze bearing the names of these two principal occupants, the belvedere that crowned the south-western tower, and the magnificent frontispiece that adorned the main entrance tower. A loggia along the south front is also dateable to the same period and would have overlooked what would then have been extensive gardens and grounds.[86] Likewise, in the early 1620s the earl of Enzie spent a significant amount of money on the repairs to the 'decayed and almost ruynous' Inverness Castle.[87]

By this time Huntly felt secure enough in his extensive holdings to apportion certain estates to his three surviving sons while keeping the bulk of his holdings entailed. His second son, Adam, was given the lordship of Auchindoun, while the third son, John, Viscount Melgum, was given the lands of Aboyne, Cromar, Gartly, and Plewlands, and the eldest son, Enzie, was given the lands in Strathdon.[88] At the time this concept of 'preferential partibility' remained

---

84 Gordon and Gordon, *Genealogical History*, 231; *Collections for a History of the Shires of Aberdeen and Banff*, ed. J. Robertson (Aberdeen, 1843), 640.

85 *Early Travellers in Scotland*, ed. P.H. Brown (Edinburgh, 1891), 125.

86 McKean, *Scottish Chateau*, 216–218; Tabraham, *Huntly Castle*, 21–24; D. Howard, *Scottish Architecture. Reformation to Restoration, 1560–1660* (Edinburgh, 1995), 65–66, 81; *The Statistical Account of Scotland, 1791–1799*, ed. Sir J. Sinclair, 20 vols (Wakefield, 1973–83), XV, 204.

87 Gordon and Gordon, *Genealogical History*, 209; *Report on the Manuscripts of the Earl of Mar and Kellie*, 117.

88 Gordon and Gordon, *Genealogical History*, 231.

one method by which the needs of younger sons could be accommodated with minimal impact on the integrity of the estate as a whole.[89]

These landholdings continued to provide the Gordon lords with a rich income. Rents varied in type depending on where individual holdings were placed geographically. In the largely arable Lowland parishes, such as those in the Strathbogie area, the lion's share of the rent would normally take the form of mixed payments in kind (usually grain) and money (maill). These would often be augmented by a number of smaller payments, also in kind, that reflected the specialities of individual holdings. Typically these comprised items such as poultry, lambs, peat, eggs, marts (cows already killed and salted for storage), wedders (sheep) and, in some cases, cloth. In more pastoral areas and in the Highlands, principal payments of money were more typical, although for the holdings in the Cabrach, payments in butter were also common. Meanwhile, for the holdings in Badenoch, labour services (ariage and bonnage) often also formed a major element in payment. Alongside this the Gordon lords rented out a number of mills (typically one to a parish), which the tenants were compelled to use. In certain parishes the Gordon lords also drew rent from alehouses.[90]

However, Gordon confidence and assertiveness in domestic affairs was not always a guarantee of success. This was made particularly apparent in relation to attempts on the part of the earl of Enzie to gain (or rather, resume by process of 'recognition') possession of lands held in feu of the House of Huntly by the Mackintosh lairds of Dunnachton (later of Torcastle). This formed part of the wider wrangles between the two households during this period and it was only with the monetary backing and combined political muscle of Colin, Lord Kintail (later earl of Seaforth), Sir John Grant of Freuchy and Sir Donald Mackay of Farr that Gordon designs on the Mackintosh lands were held in check.[91] In 1620 Enzie also made a failed attempt to secure a tack of the rents and casualties of Orkney and Shetland. This does not seem to have gone beyond being discussed by the lords of the Privy Council, many of whom no doubt shared the view of Thomas Erskine, first earl of Kellie, that 'whoesoever cume in that plaice, thaye have noe relatione to onye great man and speciallye to Huntlye, he being alreddye soe great in that north cuntrye'.[92]

89 Brown, *Noble Society in Scotland*, 37.
90 *Miscellany of the Spalding Club*, IV, 261–319; I. Whyte, *Agriculture and Society in Seventeenth-Century Scotland* (Edinburgh, 1979), 32–33, 35.
91 The various stages of the landholding wrangles between Enzie and the Mackintosh lairds up until the intervention of Kintail, Freuchy and Farr in 1623 can be followed in *The Mackintosh Muniments, 1442–1820, preserved in the Charter Room at Moy Hall, Inverness-shire*, ed. H. Paton (Edinburgh, 1903), 67, 72–73, 76, 81.
92 *State Papers and Miscellaneous Correspondence of Thomas, Earl of Melros*, ed. J. Maidment, 2

CONCLUSION

Overall, despite some continued security within the domestic sphere, it seems clear that by the early 1620s the House of Huntly was struggling to retain the level of influence it had enjoyed in the previous century. With regard to royal plans to 'civilise' the western seaboard the first marquess of Huntly seems to have been aware of his limitations and to have had little enthusiasm for the project from the outset. Probably overriding all was his belief that he had little to gain from it. This left a situation where the other major families, the Campbells of Argyll and the Mackenzies of Kintail, could seek to exploit the same chances and enhance their own standing and influence in that part of the world. Meanwhile, it was evident that, when their own interests were more directly threatened in the lordships of Badenoch and Lochaber, the Gordon lords remained much more proactive. This can be seen with their attempts to overawe the Camerons and the Mackintoshes. Having said that, it is questionable how successful they actually were in this. In short, a new level of defiance seemed to be rising in the lordships, one that could be manipulated by other interested parties such as Argyll, Kintail and Grant of Freuchy.

Elsewhere, many of the old facets of lordship remained largely intact and the Gordon lords were still involved in local arbitration and in the exercising of the law of the land. Some centrally ordained changes were, however, beginning to make themselves felt, particularly in relation to the regulation of feuds. In addition, the sudden demise of the practice of bonding was very noticeable. Already there were hints that some old associations and alliances were in decline. The key example here was the now frayed relationship between the Gordons and the Hays of Errol. On top of all this Huntly had to face the continued problem of his Catholicism. Essentially this compromised his chances of ever again becoming an influential force in the governance of the country and ensured that he remained on the defensive for much of the period. Indeed, he was reduced for a time to being a pawn in the increasingly complex manoeuvrings between the Crown and the Kirk. It remained to be seen what effect his recusancy would have during the upcoming reign of Charles I.

---

vols (Edinburgh, 1837), II, 365–366 (Privy Council to James VI, 20 July 1620); HMC, *Supplementary Report on the Manuscripts of the Earl of Mar and Kellie preserved at Alloa House, Clackmannanshire* (London, 1930), 101–102 (Kellie to Mar, 8 August 1620). Sir John Buchanan was eventually successful in becoming the royal tacksman for Orkney and Shetland. See *RPCS, 1619–22*, lviii–lix.

THREE

Religion, Fire and Sword: the House of Huntly, 1625–1637

INTRODUCTION

Upon his deathbed on the morning of 27 March 1625, Great Britain's self-appointed Solomon, King James VI and I, may have felt a degree of satisfaction at the manner in which his reign had been conducted. He may in these last moments have basked in the light of his own achievements, perhaps reflecting on the fact that he had helped bring about the successful and peaceful union of the two crowns of England and Scotland, or that he had overseen the creation of what would arguably become the most important text in the English language, the authorised King James version of the Bible, or that he had managed to reinstate the bishops north of the border. Any and all of the above certainly stand as testament to the fact that, in spite of the manner in which he has often been portrayed, James was a very remarkable man and a very gifted politician and ruler. It is without much doubt, then, that his son, Charles I, had a lot to live up to from the beginning. However, as history was to reveal, the latter's attempts at emulation would ultimately result in frustration and failure; indeed, his end would be a particularly bitter one – that of contemplating the executioner's block at Whitehall on a cold January day in 1649.[1]

It is perhaps understandable, then, that historians of Charles's reign have almost invariably sought, in the first instance, to explain this dramatic downfall. The landscape of historical debate has tended to become littered with a veritable 'canon' of familiar episodes, an anthology of 'lowlights', all gathered together with a view to charting the progress of royal decline. In a Scottish context there tends to be an emphasis on explaining the process whereby the reins of central government were taken over by the Covenanting regime. The familiar milestones in this instance include the unpopular revocation scheme, the dissatisfaction over absentee monarchy, the high-handed manner with which Charles conducted his belated visit of 1633, the attempts to push through uniformity with regard to the economy and administration, the unpopularity of

---

1 The date of the execution of Charles I was 22 January 1649.

his innovations in religion, the high-profile legal proceedings initiated against prominent dissenters, notably John Elphinstone, Lord Balmerino, and finally, the prayer book riots of 1637, the inception of the National Covenant and the civil wars that followed.[2]

While acknowledging that the above narratives and associated analyses are important and do stress the key trends, it should at the same time be pointed out that, obsessed as they are with linking into the overall narrative of central government, they arguably do not reveal the whole story. Scotland, despite Jacobean success in bringing about a degree of control, remained highly decentralised in many ways. The large aristocratic landholding households retained a level of power that, in European terms at least, was almost unparalleled. True, some families remained more in the ascendant than others: the extent to which the Huntly Gordons were going through a period of stagnation has already been made highly evident. Nevertheless, at the outset of the reign of Charles I much power did indeed remain locally based. What, then, was happening in such areas in the late 1620s and 1630s? How was each individual noble reacting to the revocation scheme? Were their sheriffships and other privileges in danger? Were they affected by an upsurge in religious persecution? Had violent feuding really been fully eradicated at a local level? Did any families enter into a period of further decline?

This chapter, then, will address such questions with reference to the House of Huntly. As will be seen, these years were very problematic for the Gordon lords, the family increasingly finding itself under pressure on questions such as religion, and regarding their heritable positions. In addition, as will be seen, levels of violence and disorder would reach alarming proportions during these years. Moreover, the old order of things would begin to be questioned, the spectre of fire and sword would ravage the land, and the most powerful magnate in the area, George Gordon, first marquess of Huntly, would find himself imprisoned in Edinburgh and on his deathbed soon thereafter.

---

2 See, for example, M. Lee, *The Road to Revolution: Scotland under Charles I, 1625–37* (Urbana and Chicago, 1985); Macinnes, *Charles I and the Making of the Covenanting Movement*, 49–213; Macinnes, *The British Revolution*, 74–110; D. Stevenson, *The Scottish Revolution, 1637–1644. The Triumph of the Covenanters* (paperback edn, Edinburgh, 2003); P. Donald, *An Uncounselled King. Charles I and the Scottish Troubles, 1637–1641* (Cambridge, 1990); Brown, *Kingdom or Province?*, 99–111; D.L. Smith, *A History of the Modern British Isles, 1603–1707. The Double Crown* (Oxford, 1998), 100–104; M Kishlansky, *A Monarchy Transformed. Britain, 1603–1714* (London, 1996), 130–133. For an in-depth examination of the king and the Scottish Parliament of 1633, see J.R. Young, 'Charles I and the 1633 Parliament', in Brown and Mann (eds), *Parliament and Politics in Scotland*, 101–137.

RELIGION, POLITICS AND THE SHERIFFSHIPS

For much of the 1620s, and indeed for the first couple of years following the accession of Charles I in 1625, the Catholic population of Scotland experienced a period of respite from the levels of persecution so well known to them in previous decades. In one of his annual letters to the superior general of his order, Scottish Jesuit Father John Leslie, even saw cause to note that although Scottish Catholicism had been in decline for some time, there had been something of a revival following the arrival of the influential priest, Father William Leslie, in 1617. Prior to this it had apparently been commonplace for Catholic nobility and gentry to attend 'heretical worship' for the sake of a show of conformity and this had naturally enough done the Catholic cause a disservice.[3] However, the revival, coupled with increased levels of toleration, certainly seemed to indicate that by 1628 things were beginning to look up. Another Scottish Jesuit, Father John Macbreck, even managed to make the slightly outrageous boast that he had personally been in contact with King James sometime prior to the latter's death and that this in itself had led to an end to the persecution.[4] In actual fact it seems more likely that the influence exerted by Charles's new Catholic bride, Queen Henrietta Maria, would have been somewhat more telling.[5]

But by early 1629 the climate had changed again and Catholics were seemingly being pursued with renewed vigour.[6] In north-east Scotland, Huntly, as most powerful regional magnate, was initially expected to provide active support for this new anti-Papist push. In his capacity as landlord and employer he had, in the first instance, to apprehend a number of named individuals and present them before the Lords of the Council. All of them were either Huntly's tenants or household men and had been excommunicated and outlawed for non-conformity and disobedience to the High Commission of the Kirk. The Privy Council also charged that he dismiss all such individuals from his service. In addition he would be required to carry out a similar task in his capacity as sheriff of Aberdeen and again an accompanying list of noted recusants was given. Meanwhile, as sheriff of both Aberdeen and Inverness, he would be expected to pursue and arrest a number of named Jesuits and seminary priests.[7]

3 W.F. Leith, *Memoirs of Scottish Catholics in the Seventeenth and Eighteenth Centuries*, 2 vols (London, 1909), I, 17–19 (Leslie to Vitelleschi, annual letter of 1628); P.F. Anson, *Underground Catholicism in Scotland* (Montrose, 1970), 25.

4 Leith, *Memoirs of Scottish Catholics*, I, 12 (Macbreck to Vitelleschi, 7 April 1628).

5 Anson, *Underground Catholicism*, 29.

6 *Ibid.*, 30; Lee, *Road to Revolution*, 63; Leith, *Memoirs of Scottish Catholics*, I, 15 (Leslie to Vitelleschi, annual letter of 1628).

7 *RPCS*, 1627–28, 496–507.

Huntly did little to further this agenda and in February 1629 the Privy Council confirmed a sentence of excommunication against him and outlawed him for failing to act.[8] Huntly simply reacted as he always had in such circumstances and sought a personal audience with his sovereign, Charles I, much to the disdain of the Lords of the Council in Scotland.[9] The writer Hamon L'Estrange later presented this incident in rather comic terms: Huntly had apparently come scurrying down to the royal court 'as fast as his old legs cold carry him [...] his cold countrey being grown too hot for him'.[10] Nevertheless Huntly's future intentions remained clear: he would not willingly pursue Catholics within his own bounds.

Charles and Huntly eventually arrived at a compromise intended to ensure the removal of the sentence of excommunication and outlawry. In return for the resignation of the sheriffships of Aberdeen and Inverness to the Crown, both Huntly and the earl of Enzie would no longer be required to apprehend recusants within those shires.[11] As part of this deal it was envisioned that on behalf of the House of Huntly, Enzie would receive a payment of £5,000 sterling (£60,000 Scots) as compensation for the loss.[12] The Council at this stage saw no reason to oppose the ruling and in November 1629, upon receipt of Huntly's personal admission of past misconduct, they allowed him to return home to Strathbogie in peace.[13]

However, calls soon resumed for Huntly to take action against recusants, this time solely in his capacity as a landlord. The solution this time was for Enzie to be given a specific commission to enforce the law regarding recusant activity – a man who, in the words of Charles I, 'may best performe that which his father should have done therein'.[14] The Council eventually agreed and permitted Huntly the freedom of his estates once again.[15] Although he would be called into question on a couple of occasions over the years that followed, generally speaking the king remained willing to come to his defence.[16] As such, religion

8 *RPCS,1629–30*, 28–30.
9 *Ibid.*, 78–79 (Privy Council to Charles I, 28 February 1629).
10 H. L'Estrange, *The Reign of King Charles: an History Faithfully and Impartially Delivered and Disposed into Annals* (London, 1655), 103.
11 *Stirlings Register*, I, 368 (Charles I to the Privy Council, 8 August 1629).
12 *CSPD, 1629–31*, 48 (Charles I to the Exchequer, 2 September 1629).
13 *RPCS, 1629–30*, 332–333.
14 *The Earl of Stirling's Register of Royal Letters relative to the Affairs of Scotland and Nova Scotia from 1615 to 1635*, ed. C. Rogers, 2 vols (Edinburgh, 1885), II, 413 (Charles I to the Chancellor, 4 January 1630).
15 *RPCS, 1629–30*, 552–553.
16 *Stirling's Register*, II, 657, 716 (Charles I to the Privy Council, 15 March 1633), (Charles I to the Archbishop of St Andrews, 24 January 1634); *RPCS, 1633-35*, 53–54.

would never be as big a problem for him as it had been on so many occasions in the past.

Some intriguing questions do remain with regard to religion and the withdrawal of the Gordon sheriffships in the late 1620s. Was there a hidden agenda of some kind? Who really gained from the outcome? Was the overall power of the House of Huntly affected in any way? To answer these it is necessary to examine the motives and actions of all the main interested parties in turn, starting with what could loosely be termed the Scottish political mainstream: essentially the clergy and the Lords of the Privy Council.

Firstly, to what extent was genuine anti-Catholicism the main reason for the renewed agenda of persecution? The Jesuit, Father John Leslie, certainly seemed to be in no doubt that this was the case. He noted that many Protestants had been incensed over claims by a fortune-teller named Walter Baird who in 1628 predicted that Catholicism would be fully restored in Scotland within three or four years. Following on from this, some Catholics had apparently composed a popular song suggesting that this would actually come to pass in the year 1630. Leslie also noted that the Thirty Years' War had not been going well for the Protestant side at the time and that there existed a genuine fear that Catholicism would reign triumphant in Europe once again.[17] In his view increased persecution was the result, and over the next few years he and other Catholic priests would go on to record the privations suffered by their Scottish co-religionists.[18]

Historians have now come to question the extent to which widespread persecution was really in evidence. Despite Jesuit complaints, actual persecution was sporadic and for the most part the Catholic nobility was left untouched.[19] It also appears that very few Catholics were actually prosecuted and that large areas of Scotland, notably the Highlands, were left virtually unaffected.[20] Having said that, it should be remembered that the initial call for action did originally emanate from the Kirk and the Privy Council; as such, although their directives were not always pursued with the intended amount of virulence by local agents such as Huntly, this should not obscure the fact that a simple *de facto* anti-Catholic agenda may have existed in the first place. The language used by such bodies at the time certainly remained highly sectarian in nature. Concerning Catholics the Privy Council saw fit to emphasise 'thair scandalous behaviour otherwayes

---

17 Leith, *Memoirs of Scottish Catholics*, I, 19–20 (Leslie to Vitelleschi, annual letter of 1628).

18 *Ibid.*, I, 21–135 (Leslie to Vitelleschi, annual letter of 1628), (Leslie to Vitelleschi, annual letter of 1629), (Leslie to Vitelleschi, 1 May 1629), (Valens to Vitelleschi, 16 June 1629), (Leslie to Vitelleschi, 8 June 1630), (Leslie to Vitelleschi, 1 September 1630), (Leslie to Vitelleschi, 1630), (Leslie to Vitelleschi, 13 June 1633).

19 Lee, *Road to Revolution*, 65.

20 Macinnes, 'Catholic Recusancy', 44.

to the offence of God, disgrace of the gospel and misregard of his Majesties auctoritie'. Meanwhile, of the Jesuits in particular, the Council thundered that in them lay the desire 'to poysoun and infect his Majesties good subjects throw the north pairts of this kingdom with thair hereticall opinions and to corrupt thame in thair alledgeance and obedience to his Majestie'; indeed, they were seen to be the 'most pernicious and wicked pests in this commoun weale'.[21]

For many, Huntly, as a notable Catholic, remained part of the same problem. In 1629 Thomas Hamilton, first earl of Haddington, intimated to William Graham, seventh earl of Menteith, that Huntly's going to royal court could not have any other effect but to embolden committed recusants in the North, and that ensuring Huntly and other Catholic nobles were kept in check would be 'an exercise worthie of the care of all noblemen at court professedlie inclined to our religion'.[22] Similarly, in December of that year, representatives of the dioceses of Aberdeen and Moray sent a petition to the king insisting that any immunity shown to Huntly and his wife would be a great encouragement to the Catholic cause.[23] Such individuals certainly remained committed to the pursuit of Huntly and his household over religion. As late as 1634 the king could be found acknowledging to the archbishop of St Andrews that complaints were still being made about Huntly but that he felt that the latter had given sufficient satisfaction and that he and his spouse presented no real danger.[24]

However, some may have been pursuing other agendas when they called for action against Huntly and his household. Father Leslie noted that around the same time John Erskine, earl of Mar, had been at loggerheads with Huntly over an old claim to some lands in the latter's possession. In this Mar could get no satisfaction and so, according to Leslie, he became an ardent supporter of action against Huntly and the Catholics.[25] Meanwhile, the bishops looked to foster anti-Catholic hysteria as a means by which to divert attention away from their lukewarm attitude towards the king's revocation scheme.[26] Alternatively, some in the establishment may have had what they regarded to be the good of the kingdom in mind. At the time the king's key advisor on Scottish affairs was the earl of Menteith. He argued that Huntly had too much power in the North and that his wings needed to be clipped in some way; the removal of the sheriffships

21 *RPCS, 1627–28*, 92–93.
22 Fraser, *Earls of Haddington*, II, 162–163 (Haddington to Menteith, [c.March 1629]), (Haddington to Menteith, 24 March [1629]).
23 *RPCS, 1629–30*, 373–376.
24 *Stirling's Register*, II, 716 (Charles I to the Archbishop of St Andrews, 24 January 1634).
25 Leith, *Memoirs of Scottish Catholics*, I, 28–29 (Leslie to Vitelleschi, annual letter of 1628); HMC, *Supplementary Report on the Manuscripts of the Earl of Mar and Kellie preserved at Alloa House, Clackmannanshire* (London, 1930), 252–253 (Mar to Huntly, 1 June 1630).
26 Macinnes, 'Catholic Recusancy', 41.

was one method by which this could be achieved. As a result, an anti-Catholic agenda had been pursued with this very much in mind.[27]

The king was certainly no rabid advocate of anti-Catholic purges; indeed, he remained prepared to ensure that Huntly did not suffer too much for his religion. Like his father, however, Charles would have preferred religious uniformity throughout his three kingdoms and therefore remained prepared to admonish Huntly when it seemed politically expedient to do so. Again like his father, he tended to favour the approach of ensuring that younger generations from Catholic households be educated elsewhere and be brought up to believe in the reformed faith. This can be seen as early as 1626 when Charles wrote to Alexander Livingston, second earl of Linlithgow, insisting that the latter's son be removed from Huntly's tutelage.[28] He also encouraged that the earl of Enzie's sons be brought up in a similar manner and that they be educated in a suitable institution – in this case King's College, Aberdeen.[29] Having said that, Charles did not seem to care how the females in such families were brought up or what their beliefs were.[30]

Nonetheless, the king did stand to further his own agenda through the acquisition of the Gordon sheriffships. The Privy Council detailed his associated gains as including 'all fees, dewteis, casualiteis, liberties, immunities and righteous pertinents thairof'.[31] Enzie, at least, remained well aware of what his family had lost, and upon making a complaint about the non-receipt of the promised payment of £5,000 sterling in 1637, he saw fit to point out that the king had benefited greatly from the proceeds of the said offices in the meantime.[32] However, it is important not to portray the House of Huntly as being some kind of special target in this regard. The surrender of the sheriffships was simply one aspect of a much wider revocation scheme, and, in the face of some very stiff opposition, Charles I looked to make gains anywhere he could.[33] Some have posited that the king may have instigated the campaign against Huntly and the Catholics solely with a view to getting his hands on the sheriffships.[34] But

27 Lee, *Road to Revolution*, 65.
28 *Stirling's Register*, I, 98–99 (Charles I to Linlithgow, 22 November 1626).
29 *Ibid.*, II, 599 (Charles I to Aboyne [Enzie], 14 June 1632). Enzie's eldest three sons, George, James (later Viscount Aboyne) and Lewis (later the third marquess of Huntly) all entered King's College in the 1630s. See *Roll of Alumni in Arts of the University and King's College of Aberdeen, 1596–1860*, ed. P.J. Anderson (Aberdeen, 1900), 11, 13.
30 *Stirling's Register*, I, 391 ('instructiones for the clairgie', 6 November 1629); W. Fraser, *The Red Book of Menteith*, 2 vols (Edinburgh, 1880), II, 107 (Alexander to Menteith, 12 January [1630]).
31 *RPCS, 1629–30*, 317–318.
32 *CSPD, 1636–37*, 340–341.
33 For the most comprehensive analysis of the revocation scheme, see Macinnes, *Charles I and the Making of the Covenanting Movement*, 49–101.
34 Lee, *Road to Revolution*, 64.

this overlooks the fact that the bishops, and not the king, had been among the main instigators of renewed Catholic persecution. It is arguably more likely that Charles acted opportunistically. Huntly came to him with a specific problem and Charles immediately saw a means by which to gain from it and to milk it for all it was worth. Once he had secured the sheriffships the king's attitude then returned to one of seeking to defend the House of Huntly in as far as was politically expedient. The fact that actions against Huntly had tailed off by the end of 1630 remains somewhat telling.

It is also worth examining the actions and attitude of Huntly and Enzie during this period. What kind of strategy did they employ, and was the House of Huntly really affected that much by the persecution and the removal of the two sheriffships? From the evidence available it seems fairly certain that, for the most part, Huntly remained steadfast in the Catholic faith, so much so that he was prepared to surrender the sheriffships rather than compromise this. He also remained prepared to harbour fellow Catholics on his lands and in his houses. In December 1629, for example, the Privy Council established that Dr William Leslie, 'ane profest and avowed traffiquing papist', had been living in Huntly's house in Elgin.[35] Some years later the king even saw fit to admonish Huntly for retaining practising Catholics in his household and for being 'a meanes to schelter others against our lawes'. The king, it has to be said, was more concerned about the public scandal this was beginning to cause than anything else. He stated to Huntly: 'We expected that yow would have bene more carefull that none of your familie or [those] under your command would have gevin any offence or contempt to the odours of the church and religion professed therin.'[36] In other words, it was better that matters be kept out of sight and thus out of the public eye. On occasion Huntly's resolve could be seen to waver slightly, but overall he remained personally unwilling to pursue Catholics in his territories.[37]

Enzie's position was somewhat different from that of his father. He had spent time at the court of King James VI and I and by 1628 had become a well-

---

35 *RPCS, 1629–30*, 369.

36 *Stirling's Register*, II, 748–749 (Charles I to Huntly, 13 May 1634).

37 Father Leslie alleged that, in an effort to satisfy the initial calls for action against Catholics, Huntly had been willing to countenance a situation whereby his deputies would have been given the task of tracking down recusants. That said, the thoroughness of such a search may have been open to doubt. See Leith, *Memoirs of Scottish Catholics*, I, 46 (Leslie to Vitelleschi, annual letter of 1629). In March 1633 Huntly had thought it expedient to exhibit a Catholic woman before the Privy Council. See *RPCS, 1633–35*, 50 (Privy Council to the Bishop of Aberdeen, 15 March 1633). This seems to have been an isolated incident and the king soon excused Huntly from having to apprehend any more Catholics due to his great age and again because the sheriffships of Inverness and Aberdeen were no longer in his hands. See *ibid.*, 53–54 (Charles I to the Privy Council, 15 March 1633).

established figure on the Scottish scene. He had been admitted to the Privy Council in 1616, and from this time his attendance had increased considerably.[38] Like his father, however, he had been initially unwilling to countenance any action against Catholics on Gordon lands; indeed, the sheriffships had originally been surrendered on the understanding that neither of them would have to pursue such an agenda.[39] According to Sir Robert Gordon of Gordonstoun, Enzie had a number of reasons for not wanting to take the anti-Catholic commission. Chief amongst these were that he did not wish to offend his parents and that he did not want his chances of securing a position in the French army to be compromised. However, in the end he found himself forced to accept, largely because it had become a matter of political expediency and because elements of the Privy Council had continued to insist that Huntly take action in his capacity as a landlord. Once he got the commission, Enzie seems to have been at pains to ensure that all sides in the affair be kept placated in as far as this was possible.[40] However, not all Catholics were happy. In a letter of December 1630 Charles I congratulated Enzie on the progress he had made but at the same time acknowledged that 'the displeasur and indignation of many great [Catholic] persones, both at home and abroad' had been incurred.[41]

It has been claimed that in terms of effective power and influence, Huntly and Enzie would have been little affected by the upheavals of the time, the sheriffships being only two of their many assets.[42] Compensation had been promised regarding their surrender, and it could be argued that the two new sheriffs, Sir Robert Gordon and Alexander Irvine of Drum, would have remained very pro-Gordon in sympathy.[43] But for such individuals the post was not a hereditary one as it had been for the Huntly Gordons. In 1630 a John Johnston became sheriff of Aberdeen while a year later John Forbes of Pitsligo replaced him. In the same year Thomas Fraser of Strichen replaced Sir Robert Gordon as sheriff of Inverness.[44] Essentially the posts would never become the monopoly of any

38 See *RPCS, 1622–25*, 110, 117, 119, 121; *RPCS, 1625–27*, 80, 90, 95, 344, 351, 361, 366, 373, 440, 448, 450, 454, 458, 459, 465, 466, 476, 482, 483, 485, 490, 491, 494, 495, 498, 500, 506, 508, 517, 519, 523, 525, 526, 529, 531, 537, 539, 545, 550, 556, 560, 565, 616, 617, 618, 620, 627, 631, 634; *RPCS, 1627–28*, 1, 3, 200, 209, 210, 225, 229, 231, 232, 245, 293, 305, 323; *RPCS, 1629–30*, 316, 372, 379, 383, 387, 392, 396, 401, 404, 545, 551, 552, 609, 613, 621; *RPCS, 1630–32*, 1, 4, 7, 14, 76, 80, 84, 85, 93, 130, 135, 137, 140, 178, 181, 187, 197, 209, 299, 310, 335, 351, 485, 489, 492, 496, 497, 498, 500, 506, 507, 510, 512, 578, 579, 580, 582, 584, 586, 587, 611.

39 *RPCS, 1629–30*, 33 (Charles I to the Privy Council, 8 August 1629).

40 Gordon and Gordon, *Genealogical History*, 411.

41 *Stirling's Register*, II, 492 (Charles I to Lord Gordon [Enzie], 17 December 1630).

42 Macinnes, *Catholic Recusancy*, 43; C. Hesketh, 'The Political Opposition to the Government of Charles I in Scotland' (unpublished PhD thesis, King's College, London, 1999), 198.

43 *RPCS, 1629–30*, 291.

44 Spalding, *Memorialls*, I, 21, 26.

one person or faction to the same extent again and certainly did not remain under the sole influence of the House of Huntly. Meanwhile, the payment of £5,000 sterling was not forthcoming, and for much of the following decade Enzie made frequent requests for it to be discharged to him.[45] It is recorded that in 1727 the payment had still not been received.[46] In itself the loss of the two sheriffships would have been an undoubted blow. Not only did they deliver a guaranteed source of income, they also provided the Gordon lords with a legitimate right to enforce the law there. Moreover, in a world where prestige and conspicuous power was of paramount importance, they remained an outlet that the House of Huntly could ill afford to lose.

THE MORAY LIEUTENANCY

Another factor that served to undermine the overall position of the Gordon lords during the late 1620s and early 1630s was the granting of a lieutenancy of the North to James Stewart, third earl of Moray. The extent to which past members of the House of Huntly held a virtual monopoly over these lieutenancies has already been discussed. Traditionally they had been the preserve of the Gordons – a situation that was generally only ever brought into question when the earls themselves were in temporary disgrace.

The immediate cause of this related to a breakdown in relations between Moray and the Clan Chattan in 1624. Two years previously Moray had evicted a number of his Mackintosh tenants from lands over which he held superiority. A grudge was nursed with the eventual result that a party of over 300 Mackintoshes mounted a series of raids within Moray's bounds. Initially, the latter managed to obtain a commission from James VI for the purpose of taking action against the raiders, and, although lacking in resources and manpower of his own, managed to engineer a split within the Clan Chattan ranks and thereby quell the insurrection.[47]

In the following year, however, Moray had still been seeking to take action against the insurgents and any who had supported them, and had managed to have the commission extended by Charles I to that of a lieutenancy covering all the sheriffdoms in the North – a measure that brought about a situation whereby Moray's remit now covered areas pertaining to the Marquess of Huntly.

---

45 *Stirling's Register*, II, 431, 541, 588 (Charles I to the Exchequer, 4 April 1630), (Charles I to the thesaurer and deputy, 30 June 1631), (Charles I to the chancellor, 21 April 1632); *CSPD, 1636–37*, 340–341 (Huntly [Enzie] to Windebank, 5 January 1637).

46 Gordon, *Family of Gordon*, II, 134–135. There seems to be no evidence that the sum was ever paid. See *Records of the Sheriff Court of Aberdeenshire*, II, 521–522.

47 Gordon and Gordon, *Genealogical History*, 391; Macfarlane, *Genealogical Notes*, 289–291; *More Culloden Papers*, ed. D. Warrand, 5 vols (Inverness, 1923–30), I, 10; Mackintosh, *Mackintoshes*, 217–219.

Whether this was actually some sort of move on the part of Charles I to begin to restrict the power of the Gordons in the North is something of a moot point. Sir Robert Gordon did make the claim that, even at this early stage, Moray had convinced Charles to make a move on the two Gordon sheriffships, and as a means to that end first of all giving him a lieutenancy of the North.[48] Moray certainly seems to have been in great favour at the royal court and it is tempting to read some kind of long-term planned attack on Gordon privileges into the above events.[49] But while it seems convincing enough that the lieutenancy may have been given to Moray with a view to curbing Gordon power specifically, the same argument cannot be so convincingly made concerning the sheriffships. As has been demonstrated, their revocation had formed part of a more general attack on noble privilege and moreover had been the product of a degree of opportunism on the part of the king. Having said this, whatever the reasons, the overall effect on the House of Huntly remained the same: that of a now steady sapping away of power, privilege and prestige.

By all reports Huntly was outraged that Moray had received the lieutenancy, a fact that the king himself acknowledged. The latter even wrote to all concerned, impressing upon them to keep the peace and to put the good of the country first. He also requested that Moray not extend his commission beyond dealing with Clan Chattan 'till we understand the nature of the differences betweene yow [Moray and Huntly] from our Counsall'.[50] Much discontent was also evident in the burgh of Inverness, where the provost, Duncan Forbes, saw fit to address a petition to the king complaining that Moray was being unreasonable and was extending his commission too far.[51] Huntly in turn took the opportunity to correspond with Forbes with a view to providing advice as to the best way of airing the grievances of the burgh and of bringing an end to Moray's activities.[52] In the end it was largely due to the Gordon lords that Moray's lieutenancy was not extended far beyond an expiry date of February 1632. According to Gordonstoun, Charles I had assured them that such would be the case at the time of the surrendering of the two sheriffships.[53] Indeed, it seems that Enzie reminded the king of this when Moray tried to get his lieutenancy renewed.[54]

---

48 Gordon and Gordon, *Genealogical History*, 392, 413.

49 *Culloden Papers*, ed. H.R. Duff (London, 1815), 2 (Sir William Alexander to the Bailiffs, Council and Committee of Inverness, 28 March 1626); Hesketh, 'Political Opposition', 198.

50 *Stirling's Register*, I, 67–68 (Charles I to Huntly, 28 July 1626), (Charles I to Moray, 28 July 1626), (Charles I to the Privy Council, 25 August 1626); Gordon and Gordon, *Genealogical History*, 392.

51 *Culloden Papers*, 1, 4 (Petition from Duncan Forbes, Provost of Inverness, in the name of the inhabitants of that town to Charles I, 1626).

52 *More Culloden Papers*, I, 12–13 (Huntly to Forbes, 1 February [1627]).

53 Gordon and Gordon, *Genealogical History*, 414.

54 Spalding, *Memorialls*, I, 30–31.

In terms of years, then, the Moray lieutenancy was actually quite short-lived. However, the overall effect it produced was arguably somewhat more profound. In the first instance it coincided with a period of much disorder in the North of Scotland. Sir Robert Gordon attributed this directly to the fact that Moray did not have the power or personal following needed to quell the depredations of the numerous outlaws, bandits and broken men that emerged at the time.[55] For the most part the outlaws tended to be broken men of the Clan Gregor or followers of the notorious James Grant of Carron, arguably the most famous and feared 'limmer' of the period.[56] For the Gordon lords the lieutenancy question only heightened the sense that the traditional outlets of legitimate power once so firmly in their grasp were beginning to erode. Moreover, the levels of disruption created on the Lowland peripheries at this time would begin to feed a sense that perhaps the Gordons were no longer able to exact the same degree of control that they once had.[57]

THE FIRE OF FRENDRAUGHT

This impression would be compounded as the decade progressed, particularly in light of the controversial fire at the castle of Frendraught, an occurrence that heralded a period of much strife for north-east Scotland. The fire, which took place during the night of 8–9 October 1630 remains one of the most tragic occurrences in the history of that part of Scotland. Its immediate result was the death of Huntly's fifth son, John, Viscount Melgum (and Aboyne), and of his kinsman, John Gordon, Laird of Rothiemay, and over the longer term it would instigate a bitter feud that would unleash much disorder. Eventually things would reach such a pitch that the central authorities would see no other option but to reprimand Huntly and imprison him for having failed to take effective action. Moreover, the incident would colour the politics of the North-East for many years to come.

One of the strands of the problem can be traced back to the bitter discord between James Crichton of Frendraught and William Gordon of Rothiemay

---

55 Gordon and Gordon, *Genealogical History*, 413; Hesketh, 'Political Opposition', 198.

56 A.G.M. MacGregor, *History of the Clan Gregor*, 2 vols (Edinburgh, 1898–1901), II, 36–44. It should be noted that Moray did manage to engineer the capture of Grant of Carron in 1630 through the services of a party of Mackintoshes. See *Stirling's Register*, II, 495 (Charles I to Moray, 7 January 1631), (Charles I to the Privy Council, 7 January 1631); Gordon and Gordon, *Genealogical History*, 416; Macfarlane, *Genealogical Notes*, I, 292. This seems to have been a very rare example of Moray effectively seeking to take control of the situation. Carron subsequently escaped from Edinburgh Castle in 1632 and returned to operating across north-east Scotland again. See Spalding, *Memorialls*, I, 29.

57 This idea of an erosion of Gordon power has been noted by Keith Brown. See Brown, *Kingdom or Province?*, 104.

over the rights to salmon fishing on some land the latter had sold to the former. After legal proceedings Frendraught had been found to be in the right and, unwilling to accept this, Rothiemay had proceeded to conduct raids into Crichton territory. However, following a subsequent skirmish, Rothiemay had died of his wounds and his son, John, had gone on to ally himself with James Grant of Carron in order to continue the raids. Nevertheless, Huntly managed to intervene and to reconcile the two sides, and, as part of the associated settlement, Frendraught reportedly paid a sum of 50,000 merks Scots (£33,333 Scots) to the aggrieved widow, Lady Rothiemay. This had apparently settled things for the meantime.[58]

Another strand to the problem harked back to a contemporaneous dispute between Frendraught and the Leslies of Pitcaple. Frendraught had obtained a commission to apprehend one John Meldrum of Reidhill, an ex-servitor of his who had stolen two of his horses. Meldrum took refuge with a brother-in-law, John Leslie of Pitcaple, and another skirmish followed. On this occasion Pitcaple was shot in the arm by one of the Crichton men and Huntly was again approached to bring about reconciliation. According to John Spalding, Pitcaple had been the one to approach Huntly first but the latter had favoured Frendraught over him. Pitcaple had apparently left highly displeased at the situation. Sir Robert Gordon's version was slightly different: it had been Frendraught who had made the initial approach but Pitcaple would not agree to anything. Either way the matter remained unresolved.[59]

For the purposes of safety and of keeping the peace Frendraught remained at Huntly's residence of Bog of Gight for a couple of days. Huntly then ordained that a small company of Gordon men escort the Crichton laird back to his home. Among the company were John, Viscount Melgum and John Gordon of Rothiemay. The journey itself passed without any trouble and upon reaching their destination Frendraught invited the Gordon party to stay the night in a free-standing tower located not far from the main castle. During the night, whether by accident or design, a fire broke out and Melgum, Rothiemay and most of the other Gordon men were burned to death.[60] The Huntly faction in their anger and grief claimed that foul play had been involved, and Lady Rothiemay in particular probably remained more incensed than most; this grisly death of her son on Crichton property following hard upon the death of her husband at Frendraught's hands.

Theories as to what happened have abounded over the years. The evidence remains confused, however, and it is unlikely that the mystery will ever be

---

58 Gordon and Gordon, *Genealogical History*, 416–419; Spalding, *Memorialls*, I, 13–14.
59 Gordon and Gordon, *Genealogical History*, 419–420; Spalding, *Memorialls*, I, 15–16.
60 Gordon and Gordon, *Genealogical History*, 420; Spalding, *Memorialls*, I, 17–18.

unravelled. Not least of all remains the problem of motive: who really had anything to gain from the fire?[61] The ubiquitous conspiracy theorist, Father John Leslie, suggested that the Scottish clergy instigated it as a means by which to bring about the demise of the Catholic, Melgum. Frendraught was noted as being malevolent and either a heretic or an atheist, and as such had been the ideal instrument to this end.[62] Another Catholic priest, Gilbert Blakhall, also remained convinced regarding both Frendraught's guilt and the anti-Papist agenda.[63] Some commentators even tried to link the Earl of Moray to the crime, claiming he wanted to get some kind of revenge for the death of his father at the hands of Huntly and the Gordons in 1592.[64] If this really was the case why had he waited so long? Huntly, at least, does not seem to have attached any credence to such rumours. Neither did he insist on any specific action against Lady Frendraught, who some believed to have been a prime suspect. A ballad entitled 'The Fire o' Frendraught' certainly posited the view that she had had a central involvement.[65] Sir Robert Gordon reflected that it was unlikely that Frendraught had been at fault. He had lost a great quantity of silver in the fire as well as a number of irreplaceable writs and charters. Gordonstoun went on to observe that many maintained that the fire had been an accident, while others thought that the discontented Leslie of Pitcaple might have been responsible.[66] The Crichtons certainly seemed to favour the latter option, particularly given the fracas with Meldrum of Reidhill. But in a sense the question of actual guilt is not the key factor. Rather more important is what the main protagonists thought and what they were prepared to do about the situation.

Frendraught, in lieu of a verdict of accidental death being acceptable to Huntly, encouraged that John Meldrum be apprehended and questioned as to his potential guilt. The Gordons remained convinced that the Crichtons had been responsible and sought the apprehension of one of Frendraught's household men, John Toschach, in the hope that he would provide the information

---

61 Mathew, *Scotland under Charles I*, 141–147. Mathew provides a competent overview of the incident and of the evidence and potential motives. Maurice Lee has also provided an overview of the incident. See Lee, *Road to Revolution*, 172–173. In general, though, the fire and its aftermath have been largely ignored by historians.

62 Leith, *Memoirs of Scottish Catholics*, I, 100–103 (Leslie to Vitelleschi, annual letter of 1630).

63 G. Blakhal, *A Brieffe Narration of the Services Done to Three Noble Ladyes*, ed. J. Stuart (Aberdeen, 1844), 124–125.

64 *CSPI, 1625–32*, 582 (Rawdon to Conway Jr, 24 October 1630).

65 For versions of the ballad, see Leith, *Memoirs of Scottish Catholics*, I, 110–113; Bulloch (ed.), *House of Gordon*, II, 70–72; *The Greig-Duncan Folk Song Collection*, eds P. Shuldham-Shaw, E.B. Lyle, P.A. Hall, E. Petrie, S. Douglas and K. Campbell, 8 vols (Aberdeen and Edinburgh, 1981–2002), II, 168–169; Spalding, *Memorialls*, I, 409–411.

66 Gordon and Gordon, *Genealogical History*, 420.

they required.[67] Commissions were issued by the Privy Council in November 1630 and both men were duly denounced, arrested and imprisoned.[68] Nevertheless, the overall case did not go well for Huntly and the Gordons. Frendraught was cleared of all charges of wrongdoing in July 1632 and proceeded to initiate legal action against Huntly and Enzie with a view to winning damages and expenses.[69] Furthermore, after nearly three years in prison, Meldrum was eventually found guilty of the offence and was executed in August 1633 – certainly not a result that placated the Gordons. The verdict itself had been based solely on the fact that Meldrum had admitted that he had been on bad terms with Frendraught at the time. No real confession of guilt was made and to all intents and purposes he died a scapegoat.[70] Indeed, it seems fairly certain that he had in fact been innocent. He had been tortured while in prison and had not confessed. Moreover, Frendraught seems to have remained of the opinion that the fire had been an accident; in June 1632, for example, he revealed to the Lords of the Privy Council that he saw little point in having Meldrum put to torture, 'being doubtful what may be the event of it'. At the same time he was willing to concur with the continuation of Meldrum's trial if other parties insisted on trying to pin down a culprit.[71]

The execution of Meldrum certainly did not satisfy Huntly, who argued that the investigation continue, particularly with a view to obtaining incriminating evidence from Toschach. Officially it was ordained that Meldrum could not have been alone in planning the fire and that his accomplices would have to be tracked down.[72] Unofficially, it seems that no one had really believed in his guilt; for Frendraught and for those who wanted to see an end to the matter, he had remained a convenient scapegoat; for Huntly the main quarry was Frendraught himself. Quite simply, the guilty verdict against Meldrum had most likely been a tragic miscarriage of justice. In the end, and despite the questioning of a number of witnesses, Huntly did not secure the outcome he desired. Toschach was kept in prison for just under four years, partly at Huntly's own expense,

---

67 Mathew, *Scotland under Charles I*, 144.
68 *RPCS, 1630–32*, 51–53, 58, 74; Gordon and Gordon, *Genealogical History*, 421; *Selected Justiciary Cases, 1624–1650*, eds S.A. Gillon and J.I. Irvine, 3 vols (Edinburgh, 1953–74), I, 151–153.
69 *RPCS, 1630–32*, 512.
70 Spalding, *Memorialls*, I, 42; Gordon and Gordon, *Genealogical History*, 467.
71 *RPCS, 1630–32*, 502. Frendraught had originally advocated the torture of Meldrum the year before. See *ibid.*, 205–206. It is uncertain whether Meldrum was actually tortured prior to September 1632, when the king is known to have authorised such a course of action. See Fraser, *Red Book of Menteith*, II, 44 (Charles I to Strathearn, 27 September 1632). In February 1631 Enzie and Lord Hay, the two main commissioners investigating the affair at the time, advocated that the torture of Meldrum and Toschach not go ahead until further evidence could be gathered. See *RPCS, 1630–32*, 136. Both no doubt wanted to ensure a watertight case against Frendraught.
72 *Stirling's Register*, II, 693–694 (Charles I to the Privy Council, 23 October 1633).

but did not provide any breakthrough evidence. Finally, in November 1634, the Privy Council authorised his release.[73]

THE HARRYING OF FRENDRAUGHT

In the absence of an acceptable legal settlement the situation in north-east Scotland descended into chaos and disorder as bands of Highlanders and Gordon adherents proceeded to conduct a series of raids on Frendraught's lands. Such raids had been in evidence as early as 1631. In April of that year the Privy Council ordained that an act of protection covering all of Frendraught's tenants be declared at every market place across the North-East. This was in response to a number of incursions that had been made by Highlanders and outlaws, who, as the Council saw it, used the situation as a pretext 'for a cover to thair thievish and unhappie trade of lyfe'.[74] Later that same year Frendraught complained about the damage caused to his lands by a number of the tenants and adherents of Huntly, Enzie and Lady Rothiemay, and Enzie became bound for their good behaviour in the future.[75] This seems to have helped calm the situation and there was no further widespread raiding of Frendraught's land until 1634.

From that point until the death of the first marquess of Huntly in June 1636 the depredations suffered by Frendraught became ever more regular. In January 1634 a party of MacGregors spoiled his grounds.[76] In September another party of unidentified Highlanders conducted a raid, and in October a force of around 600 Macgregor and Cameron men joined up with some Gordon lairds for the same purpose. In response Frendraught raised his own adherents, pursued some of the raiders as far as Glenfiddich and forced them to disperse. On this occasion

---

73 A number of different witnesses were either called or sought after. It was even suspected that the outlaw James Grant of Carron may have had some evidence or involvement. By mid-1632 Huntly was claiming that the justice deputes were obstructing his efforts to get Toschach tried properly but finally he himself recognised that the whole legal process was a lost cause and withdrew any financial provision for keeping Toschach in prison. See *RPCS, 1630–32*, 362, 588, 607–608; *RPCS, 1633–35*, 163, 175–176, 317, 325, 419–420, 652–653 (Huntly to Farquharson [c.27 July 1634]); Fraser, *Chiefs of Grant*, I, 231; Fraser, *Red Book of Menteith*, II, 44–45 (Charles I to Strathearn, 27 September 1632); *Stirling's Register*, II, 622–623 (Charles I to the Privy Council, 27 September 1632); Gordon, *Family of Gordon*, II, 140–141. For further in-depth detail on the legal proceedings against Meldrum and Toschach, see Spalding, *Memorialls*, I, 381–408; Aberdeen University Special Collections, MS 797, Trial of John Meldrum. From this point on the Gordons tried little in the way of further legal proceedings in an attempt to get satisfaction. In June 1638 Enzie (by then the second marquess of Huntly) did attempt to obtain a further trial of Frendraught but nothing seems to have gone ahead. See *A Diary of the Public Correspondence of Sir Thomas Hope of Craighall, 1633–1645*, ed. T. Thomson (Edinburgh, 1843), 73.
74 *RPCS, 1630–32*, 215–216.
75 *Ibid.*, 333–334.
76 Spalding, *Memorialls*, I, 45.

he captured three of the Gordon men and had them hanged at Frendraught Castle upon his return. This only inflamed matters and throughout November a group of around 40 Gordon horsemen and 60 men on foot conducted a series of violent raids on what was reportedly a daily basis. Cattle and sheep were stolen, corn was burned and fatalities occurred. According to Gilbert Gordon of Sallach, not even the goods and houses of ministers and churchmen were safe. Eventually Frendraught felt the need to flee to Edinburgh and report the situation to the Lords of the Council. Meanwhile, the Gordon raiders continued to oppress his lands, and marauding Highlanders, including the MacIains of Glencoe, continued to make incursions.[77]

In the face of all this Huntly seemed increasingly unwilling or unable to act, and both the king and the Privy Council grew ever more impatient. Numerous directives and commissions were issued to him with regard to dealing with the outlawed men and Huntly was twice imprisoned for having failed to do this. Indeed, on the latter occasion, the imprisonment resulted from his having allegedly orchestrated the raids.[78] Already an old man, it seems that the whole experience did little for his health and in June 1636 he died just after having been released from his second period of imprisonment in Edinburgh.[79]

But had Huntly really been guilty of having conspired with Highlanders and outlaws and of having orchestrated the Frendraught raids behind the scenes? Gilbert Gordon of Sallach certainly remained sure that this had been the case and John Spalding made the comment that 'it wes vehementlie suspectit that the Gordonis war the out hounderis of thir Hielanderis, [out] of verie malice aganis Frendracht for the fyre foirsaid'.[80] Certainly, upon reading the formal denunciation that subsequently led to Huntly's imprisonment, it is hard to conclude otherwise.

This denunciation was made by Adam Gordon, younger of Park, in 1635. He was the second son of the main leader of the Gordon raiders and had decided to give evidence before the Privy Council in Edinburgh. Firstly, he alleged that Huntly had conferred payments to him via James Gordon of Letterfourie and had encouraged him to carry out raids. In his defence Huntly stated that a payment had been made but that it 'war given to Adam out of pitie for suplieing of his neccessitie and estate'. Park replied that this was nonsense. He

77 *Ibid.*, I, 46–50; Gordon and Gordon, *Genealogical History*, 474–475; Macdonald and Macdonald, *Clan Donald*, II, 20.

78 *RPCS, 1633–35*, 407–408, 439–442, 445, 450, 495, 502, 512–513, 525, 521–524, 528–529; *RPCS, 1635–37*, 9–11, 16, 19, 88, 121–122, 211–212; Gordon and Gordon, *Genealogical History*, 478–479, 475–476; Spalding, *Memorialls*, I, 66; *Stirling's Register*, II, 814–815, 852 (Charles I to the Privy Council, 16 December 1634), (Charles I to the Privy Council, 15 May 1635).

79 Spalding, *Memorialls*, I, 71–72.

80 Gordon and Gordon, *Genealogical History*, 474; Spalding, *Memorialls*, I, 46.

also accused Huntly of having made a similar approach to George Gordon of Logiealtoun and claimed that the latter had been promised the assistance of a number of Highlanders. To this charge Letterfourie could apparently make little denial. Similarly, Macdonald of Keppoch had allegedly been approached but had refused to take any action against Frendraught without a specific warrant. The lack of such a warrant had also initially been a problem for the tutor of Cameron of Glen Nevis, who nevertheless proceeded to lead his Highlanders in a raid on the assurance from Donald Farquharson (one of Huntly's bailies), that one would be obtained. Park went on to state that the raiders had also apparently been able to store stolen goods within the bounds of Strathbogie Castle and that Huntly had not been averse to them using a house in the nearby hamlet of Torrisoule. Huntly was also denounced for having failed to fulfil his commission regarding the capture of the raiders.[81]

It should be stressed that some care must be taken when considering the above denunciation. Sallach stated that Huntly had been pursuing Gordon, younger of Park, at the time as part of his commission and that the latter, by giving his evidence, had been looking to obtain his own pardon.[82] Spalding noted that this Adam Gordon and a number of the other Gordon raiders had actually been chased out of the country upon Huntly's orders some time in May. Sallach recorded that during this action Adam's elder brother, James, was killed and that his severed head had been subsequently sent to Edinburgh. Of those captured a number were hanged. Whether Adam had come back to reveal the truth or to take his revenge is a moot point; at any rate he secured a remission for himself on account of his revelations.[83]

Although Huntly had begun to take more strenuous action against the raiders by mid-1635, this does not necessarily negate the idea that he had originally encouraged them prior to this. His first period of imprisonment had ended in May of that year and it is from this point that he seems to have begun to act in earnest. The action against the Gordons of Park is a case in point. It is also recorded that Huntly presented George Gordon of Auchterless and his son, Adam, before the Privy Council in June, whereupon they obliged themselves not to leave Edinburgh 'till they be releeved, under the pane of ane thowsand punds'.[84]

81 NLS, Antique Papers, MS 1915, ff. 25–32. Another memorial exists in the same bound volume linking Huntly's name with that of James Grant of Carron and a party of Macgregors who lived in Strathavon and Delnabo. See *ibid.*, ff. 33–34. This would seem to refer to the period prior to the fire when Carron had been operating in support of Gordon of Rothiemay. If Carron had been raiding Frendraught's lands in 1634–35, Spalding and Sallach would surely have noted the fact.
82 Gordon and Gordon, *Genealogical History*, 478.
83 *Ibid.*, 476; Spalding, *Memorialls*, I, 62, 64.
84 *RPCS, 1635–37*, 28.

Prior to May 1635 his attempts at apprehending the raiders had been half-hearted and he may well just have been presenting a front to keep the Privy Council off his back. He did arrest Adam Gordon, elder of Park, sometime in late 1634 or early 1635 but the latter soon managed to 'escape' from Auchindoun Castle after being, as Sallach put it, 'negligentlie looked to'. At other times Huntly complained about not having an appropriate warrant and about the fact that many of the outlaws were not his tenants or servants.[85] He also made the claim that he was too old and weak to take action and that he would need the return of Enzie from France before anything constructive could be done.[86] This was plainly nonsense. The expedition of May 1635 against the Gordons of Park had been undertaken by his third son, Adam of Auchindoun, in conjunction with James Gordon of Letterfourie.[87] On the balance of evidence, then, it would seem that he had indeed originally given at least some encouragement to the raiders oppressing Frendraught's lands. It is, after all, notable that such widespread raiding did not really commence until late 1634, just as Huntly's attempts at haranguing Frendraught by legal means were beginning to come to naught. He had then briefly attempted to return to the old ways of rule by force and intimidation and had been humbled as a result.

In terms of overall effect, the Frendraught affair and its aftermath were revealing in two main ways. In the first instance it provided further indication that there had been a shift in how feuding was regulated and in the extent to which private violence was tolerated. Huntly had, for the most part, continued to show a willingness to follow the guidelines as set out in the legislation of the late sixteenth and early seventeenth centuries. As such, while he could still be seen to act as intermediary regarding less serious disputes such as those between Frendraught and Gordon of Rothiemay, and Frendraught and Leslie of Pitcaple, he also remained willing for the Frendraught affair to be investigated by the Privy Council. True, it is likely that at a later stage he covertly encouraged intimidation of Frendraught and widespread raiding of his lands, but at the same time he had to appear to the eyes of the government to be outraged at, and innocent of such acts. Gone were the days when he could happily apply strong-arm tactics and find that little of any consequence would be done to require him to answer for it. Such actions were simply not acceptable any more and for the most part Huntly realised this and was prepared to be seen to adapt himself to the new situation. This was especially noticeable through his willingness to appear before the Privy Council when required and also to countenance imprisonment.

85 Gordon and Gordon, *Genealogical History*, 475.
86 Ibid., 477; Spalding, *Memorialls*, I, 60; *CSPD, 1623–25*, 143; NAS, GD 406/1/324 (Huntly to Hamilton, 7 March 1635).
87 Spalding, *Memorialls*, I, 62.

In the end, though, what it again indicated was something of a fundamental truth about Huntly's attitude to accepted authority and hierarchy, a truth that had arguably been in evidence throughout his career. This was that invariably he in the end adhered to the wishes of what was acceptable to him as the ultimate authority in the land, whether the monarch or the Privy Council. In that sense Huntly was a very conservative man, aware of his own place within a hierarchical system, and unwilling to buck too much against it. As a result, as powers and privileges were slowly taken away from him over the years, there was little natural inclination on his part to resist.

However, what the Frendraught affair and the troubles of the 1630s also indicated was that violence and feuding had not been fully brought under control in the north-east Lowlands by the time of the death of James VI.[88] The particular venom with which the Gordons of Rothiemay and the Gordons of Park sought vengeance following the Frendraught fire certainly stands as stark testament to this. For them, at least, the legal proceedings in Edinburgh did little to suggest that justice had been done, and they had subsequently wreaked havoc across north-east Scotland as a result. It was not until Huntly (under pressure from the Privy Council) had belatedly sought to enforce law and order that the widespread violence was largely assuaged. True, by the 1630s Lowland Scotland was well on the way to becoming a less violent society, but it is arguable that, for the North-East at least, it was not until after the Civil Wars that a more fulsome and lasting reduction became noticeable.

A final striking aspect of the Frendraught affair was the extent to which it brought out some strains and tensions within the Gordon 'conglomerate' itself. The ruthlessness with which Huntly dealt with the Gordons of Park provides an ideal illustration of this. This branch of the Gordon family, along with their close relatives, the Gordons of Rothiemay, were plainly something of a law unto themselves and became a liability to Huntly as the decade wore on, regardless of whether he had covertly encouraged them beforehand.[89] And Adam Gordon, younger of Park, certainly seems to have had few qualms about providing the Privy Council with information that would see the imprisonment of his chief.

The affair also opened up a rift between Huntly and John, thirteenth earl of Sutherland. The problem was that Sutherland was brother-in-law to Frendraught and refused fully to condemn him in respect of the Frendraught fire. In January 1632 Sutherland paid a visit to Bog of Gight but was reportedly treated to a very

---

88 This was in contrast to the situation in other Lowland areas of Scotland. See Brown, *Bloodfeud in Scotland*, 184–265.

89 For the relationship between the Gordons of Park and Gordons of Rothiemay, see 'Balbithan MS', 36.

cold welcome by Huntly and the two parted on bad terms.[90] Clearly, given all of the above, Huntly did not enjoy blanket support from the Gordon cadets through the period of these troubles, and what active support there was could clearly backfire on him from time to time. It was an indication that the 'Gordon conglomerate' was no longer as united an entity as it had been in past decades.[91]

SHOULDERING THE BURDEN

Huntly's successor, Enzie, had very little direct involvement in the Frendraught troubles. This was largely due to the fact that for much of the period he was in France serving in the army of Louis XIII. The idea of Enzie raising a company of 100 soldiers for French service had been mooted as early as 1624 but it was not until the early years of the 1630s that this had finally been put into motion. He and his troops landed in France sometime in mid-1633 from where they were dispatched to fight under the command of the Marshal of France, Jacques-Nompar de Caumont, duc de la Force in Lorraine, and later in Alsace and Germany.[92] Gilbert Gordon of Sallach noted that Enzie's soldiers 'did behave themselves valiantlie, and were always set upon the hardest and most difficult interpryses'. He also recorded that Enzie's eldest son, George, was wounded in the thigh during the storming of the town of Spire.[93]

Enzie was still in France when the first marquess of Huntly passed away at Dundee in June 1636. He also missed the lavish funeral that took place in Elgin in August. In October he travelled from France to England accompanied by his wife, his two eldest sons, George (now Lord Gordon) and James, Viscount Aboyne, and his eldest daughter, Ann. An infant son and daughter, the twins Henry and Catherine, were left in France under the care of a distant kinsman, the physician William Davidson. The five other children, Lewis, Charles, Henrietta, Jean and Mary had been left in Scotland under the care of their grandparents during Enzie's years of military campaigning. Enzie finally arrived in Strathbogie in June 1637 to take up his position and title as second marquess of Huntly.[94]

90 Spalding, *Memorialls*, I, 27–28.
91 This would thus question the extent to which Hesketh is correct in her assertion that all Gordon cadets rallied to the support of their chief up until his death in 1636. See Hesketh, 'Political Opposition', 201. Indeed, the Gordons of Park had played a major part in bringing about his inglorious demise.
92 Gordon, *Family of Gordon*, II, 611, 628–629, (Patent from Louis XIII to Enzie, 9 April 1624), (Louis XIII to Enzie, 3 February 1633), (Louis XIII to Enzie, 19 October 1633). I have to thank Thomas Brochard for providing translations of these letters.
93 Gordon and Gordon, *Genealogical History*, 460.
94 Spalding, *Memorialls*, I, 71–76. For more detail on William Davidson, see J. Small, 'Notice of William Davidson, M.D', *Proceedings of the Society of Antiquaries of Scotland*, vol. 10 (1875),

What he inherited was a household clearly going through a marked period of crisis. This was reflected in the domestic sphere where former Gordon confidence was no longer so readily apparent. In Badenoch the Mackintoshes succeeded in asserting their position at the expense of that of the first marquess. By February 1635 the young William Mackintosh of Torcastle was of age to be confirmed in the possession of the feued lands held of the House of Huntly, thus putting to an end Gordon hopes of gaining full control over them.[95] Moreover, the following year the first marquess sold his lands and barony of Melgund in Angus to Henry Maule of Dunbar, something of a surprise given that he acquired these as recently as 1630 and had put time and effort into improving the associated castle and its grounds.[96] Clearly, the first marquess had been presented with some reason to get hold of ready cash at this juncture and it may be that, given his position of political weakness at the tail end of the Frendraught troubles, he was feeling the squeeze from opportunistic creditors. That marquess also sought to finance his way of life through the wadsetting (mortgaging) of some of his landholdings.[97] Indeed, whereas examples of land recorded as being wadsetted in the rental sheet of 1600 are quite rare, it can be seen that by the late 1640s, in the parish of Rhynie/Essie alone, over one-third of the properties were under wadset.[98]

By the 1630s the Gordons of Huntly had also failed realise the full commercial potential of their lands to the same extent as their chief rivals, the Campbells of Argyll and the Mackenzies of Seaforth. The earls of Seaforth had been particularly industrious in their endeavours to develop the coastal burgh of Stornaway as a major fishing station over the first half of the seventeenth century.[99] The Gordons did not seek to develop a similar window on the sea. Admittedly, their holdings did not hug the coastline as much as did those of other northeast families such as the Keiths, but they did own the lands of Enzie along the Moray Firth. Burghs of barony existed at Fochabers and Ruthven in Badenoch, but these were geared towards the traditional agricultural economy. Perhaps

265–280, J. Reid, *William Davidson of Aberdeen: the First British Professor of Chemistry* (Aberdeen, 1951).

95 *Mackintosh Muniments*, 84, 87.

96 *RGSS, 1634–51*, 182; Spalding, *Memorialls*, I, 58.

97 See, for example, the Huntly lands recorded as remaining under wadset in the sheriffdom of Aberdeen in 1633 in *Miscellany of the Spalding Club*, III, 121–124, 126–128, 130–132. Wadsetting was a common practice adopted by many landlords during this period. See Brown, *Noble Society in Scotland*, 93.

98 *Miscellany of the Spalding Club*, IV, 261–319; NAS, TE 5/37. To single out the Rhynie lands alone, five out of the nine recorded properties were wadsetted.

99 A. MacCoinnich, 'Native and Stranger: Lewis and the Fishing of the Isles, c.1610–c.1638' (unpublished paper delivered at the Research Institute of Irish and Scottish Studies, 8 March 2004).

most tellingly, while the Seaforth earls were energetically looking to develop Stornoway, Gordon attempts to set up a successful burgh of barony at Inverlochy in Lochaber remained stagnant. Originally, the idea of erecting what was to be named Gordonsburgh had been mooted from 1597 as part of the Jacobean drive to 'civilise' the Highlands and Islands. The creation of Stornoway had also formed part of this, as had the creation of Campbeltown on Argyll's lands in Kintyre.[100] However, that the site of Inverlochy had remained undeveloped by the 1650s was apparent in the correspondence of Cromwellian officers stationed there at the time. It was made clear to them that Inverlochy was 'a most commodious haven for shippes and a place abounding with many casualties as woodes, fishing and other commodities' but that a burgh had not yet been erected there. It was recommended that this be put in hand forthwith as 'the only way for civilising thes places and curbing the insolency of the savage and lawles Hylanders and bringing them under odedience to the law'.[101]

To a limited degree the Gordon lords did look to exploit woodland resources and river fishing. A number of estates of the House of Huntly were richly blessed with extensive forests and salmon-filled rivers, and the occasional reference does emerge to suggest that at least some commercial advantage was taken of this. It is recorded that around the year 1637 the second marquess authorised three men of the surname Macinnes to transport timber out of Lochaber.[102] Indeed, during the 1650s Cromwellian officers saw fit to note the commercial possibilities of such trade in that part of the world.[103] Afforested regions along the rivers Dee and Spey may also have been exploited by the Gordons but, unfortunately, there appears to be virtually nothing to prove this.[104]

Overall there was little to alleviate the great burden now being taken on by the second marquess of Huntly, as Enzie now became known. Another major problem was the extensive debts that had been accrued by him and his father over the years. The first marquess had done much to account for this through his building works, as had the second marquess during his time spent at Court and abroad, and through his pursuit of the lifestyle expected of a high-ranking Scottish noble.[105] The chronicler James Gordon of Rothiemay noted that in 1638

---

100 *APS, 1593–1625*, 139.
101 *More Culloden Papers*, I, 126.
102 *Mackintosh Muniments*, 91.
103 *More Culloden Papers*, I, 126–127.
104 Army reports of 1652 made plain that timber could be transported down these two rivers. This could imply that such had already been at least attempted by the Gordon lords. See *CSPD, 1651–52*, 103–104 (Sandelands to Lilburne, 14 January 1652).
105 *Letters and State Papers during the Reign of King James the Sixth*, 177 (Enzie to James VI and I, [1609]); HMC, *Tenth Report, Appendix, part IV, The Manuscripts of the Earl of Westmorland, Captain Stewart, Lord Strafford, Lord Muncaster and others* (London, 1885), 390 (Herbert to

the total amount of debt being shouldered by the second marquess amounted to as much as £100,000 sterling, a staggering amount even by contemporary standards.[106] To say the least the affairs of the household were in a worrying condition.

CONCLUSION

The first ten years of the reign of Charles I had clearly been very trying ones for the Gordon lords. The first marquess of Huntly's Catholicism had remained a major problem and continued to compromise his chances of being a player in Scottish politics, whether at a national or regional level. In particular it brought into question his ability to continue as sheriff of the shires of Aberdeen and Inverness, a situation that was only partially alleviated by the Protestantism of the earl of Enzie. He at least managed to help broker deals whereby his father would not have to pursue Catholics for non-conformity. However, it seems that neither of them ever received the payment of £5,000 that had been promised in return for giving up the sheriffships. On top of this, the associated loss of power and prestige remained a bitter blow to Gordon aspirations and presents a real indication that in relative terms their power was truly beginning to be compromised.

In terms of the wider political situation, it can be seen that Charles I could opportunistically benefit from the Gordon position and happily receive the sheriffships as part of his ailing attempts to revoke various powers from the localities. At the same time, other central power-brokers could also seek to exploit Huntly's weakness, whether out of animosity, self-interest or a need to divert attention away from their own lack of commitment to the revocation scheme. Compounding the negative effect of the loss of the sheriffships was the granting of a lieutenancy of the North to the earl of Moray, another sign that Gordon power was beginning to be eclipsed in that part of the world. This in itself helped bring about much discontent and disruption in the North, with many people (Huntly foremost among them) being very displeased at Moray's elevation. On top of this, the latter's apparent inability to perform adequately in this role coincided with a period of much disorder across the North as outlaws and broken men rampaged along the Lowland fringes.

This situation became further entrenched with the Frendraught fire of 1630, a disaster that sparked an extended legal battle between Huntly and Crichton of Frendraught and a bitter Gordon–Crichton feud that would eventually result in

---

Calvert, 27 December 1623); Spalding, *Memorialls*, II, 91; Brown, *Noble Society in Scotland*, 92–109.

106 Gordon, *History of Scots Affairs*, I, 49–50. Gordon of Rothiemay was well placed to be an authority on this. His father, Robert Gordon of Straloch, was a key confidant and adviser to the second marquess of Huntly during the late 1630s and 1640s.

Huntly's imprisonment in Edinburgh. In the main the feud was something that was openly pursued by the Gordon cadet families of Park and Rothiemay, with only covert support from the marquess himself. This, then, while indicating that violence and feuding had not been fully eradicated from Lowland Scotland, at least showed that Huntly felt he had to be seen by the outside world to conform to what was regarded to be civilised and law-abiding conduct of the time. With this in mind it seems clear that, in his old age, Huntly was paying more heed to the government's requirements than he had in past decades. The Frendraught affair also had the side-effect of teasing out animosities within the Gordon conglomerate as cadet branches such as the Gordons of Park and the Gordons of Sutherland began to feel a degree of alienation from the Huntly line. Enzie's willingness to accept a commission against northern Catholics may also have helped contribute towards this process. All in all, the House of Huntly was clearly under pressure with the result that the second marquess would be ill prepared to meet any new challenges that might come along. Little did he know in 1637 that he would soon be faced with the greatest challenge of his life.

FOUR

The Bishops' Wars, 1638–1641

INTRODUCTION

With the disruptions of the first half of the 1630s still fresh in the memory, the House of Huntly had little time to recover prior to the onset of the Scottish Revolution of the years 1637 to 1641. Indeed, from the inception of the National Covenant of 1638 the family became deeply involved in Royalist attempts to defend the prerogative of Charles I and to oppose all those who would seek to implement sweeping and revolutionary changes with regard to how the kingdom was governed. This key period of Scottish history has been well studied in recent years, increasingly so with a view to linking it in with the wider Britannic, European and even transatlantic contexts. The Scottish Revolution did indeed have a profound impact on the other Stuart kingdoms and so it is only right that a number of historians, in their macro-studies of the period, have looked to highlight this. However, despite the flurry of recent publications, many fruitful avenues of research remain untapped, particularly in terms of in-depth regional studies. The Gordons of Huntly, although arguably in the middle of a slow relative decline, were still an important regional family with the potential to contribute greatly on a wider national level. This chapter will show that through the pursuit of a micro-study centred mainly on the Gordons and the North of Scotland, much light can be shed on the bigger picture.

Of course, as history was to reveal, the cause of Charles I ultimately proved a futile one in Scotland, with the result that by 1641 he was forced to accept a series of radical changes in the way the country was governed. The extent to which the House of Huntly played a meaningful role during these crucial years and to which it contributed effectively towards the Royalist cause is a question of great import. Moreover, it is crucial that an assessment is made of the family's standing in light of this Royalist defeat, and of how the rigours of war contributed to an overall relative decline in fortunes.

HUNTLY AND THE ROYALIST CAUSE

For the most part, the direct causes of the Civil Wars can be traced to the late 1620s and the onset of what can be termed the prerogative rule of Charles I. Essentially this was characterised by a style of government that was uniformly non-consensual and prerogative-driven across all three of his kingdoms. Increasing discontent soon became apparent in all the Stuart dominions, but it was undoubtedly in Scotland that this was at its most marked. Commencing with the highly unpopular revocation scheme of the late 1620s, opposition to the rule of Charles I steadily grew, particularly in relation to his increasing over-management of Scottish political life, damaging economic policies, renewed elevation of the bishops to positions of temporal power, and his desire to institute controversial liturgical changes, most notably as advocated in the deeply unpopular Scottish prayer book of 1637.

It was this last innovation that was to prove the main catalyst for the revolutionary process in Scotland. From July of that year anti-prayer book riots in Edinburgh and Glasgow heralded a wave of discontent and by February 1638 the National Covenant had been drawn up – a document of a wide-enough appeal to encapsulate the views of a broad stratum of society, from discontented members of the nobility to the scandalised grass-roots ministry of the Kirk. While on one level it reiterated an anti-Catholic stance in terms of religion, it also sought to bind the king into a constitutional contract and, through that, to sanction a right to resist should it be deemed that he had become tyrannical and was undermining the country's interests. The attack on the king's prerogative remained plain, and was one that he failed to counter over the years that followed. Indeed, from as early as the Glasgow General Assembly of November–December 1638 the Covenanters were beginning to take control, promulgating, as they did, the removal of all the offices and trappings of Episcopalian church governance.[1]

From the outset, George Gordon, second marquess of Huntly, remained a steadfast exponent of the Royalist cause. A good deal of detail can be pieced together to gain an appreciation of his character and beliefs, and why he took the side of the king. The year of his birth has hitherto not been established with any degree of certainty. On the grounds that the marriage of his parents took place in 1588, past estimates have ranged between the years 1590 and 1592.[2] A

---

1 For analysis of the prerogative rule within a British context, see R. Cust, *Charles I: a Political Life* (Harlow, 2005), 31–243; Macinnes, *British Revolution*, 74–110. For Scotland in particular, see Stevenson, *Scottish Revolution*, 15–87; Lee, *Road to Revolution*; Macinnes, *Charles I and the Making of the Covenanting Movement*, 49–182; Hesketh, 'Political Opposition'; Young, 'Charles I and the 1633 Parliament', 101–137.

2 Mathew, *Scotland under Charles I*, 149; David Stevenson, 'Gordon, George, second marquess of Huntly (*c*.1590–1649)', *ODNB*, http://www.oxforddnb.com, accessed 27 August 2009.

definite date remains impossible to arrive at, but from the scant contemporary evidence available it would seem that 1590 is the more likely of the options. It is a matter of record that in this year one Robert Grant baptised a child of the Earl of Huntly at the family residence of Bog of Gight.[3] While uncertainty remains as to whether or not this child and the future second marquess were one and the same, it is fair to assert that they probably were.

Little remains on record to cast light on his early upbringing as the earl of Enzie. What is certain is that he was soon joined by a cohort of younger siblings: four brothers and four sisters. Next to nothing is known about two of the brothers, Laurence and Francis, other than that the latter reportedly died in Germany in 1620, perhaps as a casualty of the Thirty Years' War. Another brother, Adam of Auchindoun, later died unmarried and childless. The final brother, John, went on to marry Sophia Hay, fifth daughter of Francis, ninth earl of Erroll. In 1627 he gained the titles of Viscount Melgum and Lord Aboyne but soon after met an unfortunate end, a victim of a fire at the castle of Frendraught in 1630. Enzie's eldest sister, Ann, was contracted in marriage to James, third earl of Moray in 1607 as part of the effort to assuage the feud between the two families. His sister Elizabeth's marriage was to Alexander, Lord Livingston (later second earl of Linlithgow), but she died in childbirth in 1616. Another sister, Mary, married William, eleventh earl of Angus (later created marquess of Douglas). She died in 1674. The last sister, Jean, married Claud, Lord Strabane, a notable Scottish planter in Ireland. Following his death in 1638 she married Sir Phelim O'Neill, one of the leaders of the insurgents during the 1641 Irish rebellion.[4] The year 1607 saw Enzie's own marriage to Anne Campbell, second daughter of Archibald, seventh earl of Argyll, a match that signalled the end of the feud which had developed between the Campbells and Gordons during the troubles of the 1590s.[5]

Given the Catholic background of his family, it is perhaps understandable that in the past some historians have assumed that the second marquess had been of the same confessional bent.[6] In reality, however, his religious convictions were more complex. Gordon of Rothiemay noted that he had spent some of his teenage years at the English court of James VI and I for the express purpose of ensuring that he 'might one day be as usefull for the promovall of the reformed relligione as his father had been hurtfull theretoo.'[7] While there he certainly

3 *RPCS, 1545–1625*, 373.
4 Paul, *Scots Peerage*, IV, 544–545; *ibid.*, I, 100.
5 *Ibid.*, IV, 546.
6 Macinnes, *Charles I and the Making of the Covenanting Movement*, 131, 193; Ohlmeyer, *Civil War and Restoration*, 78; D. Scott, *Politics and War in the Three Stuart Kingdoms, 1637–49* (Basingstoke and New York, 2004), 17.
7 Gordon, *History of Scots Affairs*, I, 48–49. The available evidence suggests that the future second marquess departed south to Court sometime during the early months of 1608. See *Letters and*

found great favour with the king's heir, Henry, and was in personal attendance at the crowning of the latter as Prince of Wales at Westminster on 4 June 1610. The previous day, along with a number of other young nobles, the king had honoured the young Gordon lord by making him a knight of the Bath.[8] The nature of this experience at Court was by no means unique. By the early seventeenth century it had become common practice on the part of the monarch to ensure that young nobles, particularly those from Catholic households, were 'adequately educated for future royal service'.[9] It was also to the king's advantage that nobles were reared to espouse the Episcopalian form of Protestantism, and that values such as loyalty and conformity were indoctrinated early. This can be seen as part of an ongoing process later developed by Charles I, who, as Edward Hyde, earl of Clarendon, pointed out, tried to 'unite his three kingdoms in one form of God's worship and in a uniformity in their public devotions'.[10]

Despite this experience of being carefully moulded at Court some later commentators held the opinion that the second marquess had in fact been Catholic. On the whole, however, such testimony does not stand up to close scrutiny. In his history of the Gordon family dating from 1691 David Burnet claimed that the marquess only made an exterior show of Protestant conformity in order to protect himself during the 1640s when the Covenanting regime was in power in Scotland.[11] This, however, does not explain why he had adhered to Protestantism prior to that. It was also the case that Burnet intended his account to be read at the exiled court of the Catholic James VII and II with a view to boosting the then flagging Jacobite credentials of George, first duke of Gordon, himself a Catholic. Burnet's history was thus by no means a document without bias. In 1628 Father John Leslie made a claim much like Burnet's, noting that the future second marquess 'was a Catholic by conviction, though not venturing openly to avow his opinions'.[12] Clearly Leslie hoped that the Gordon lord would

---

　　State Papers during the Reign of King James the Sixth, 122–124 (Huntly to James VI, 6 February [1608]), (same to same, 26 February [1608]). It is recorded that he returned to Scotland in the summer of 1612. See Gordon and Gordon, *Genealogical History*, 286–287.

8　Gordon and Gordon, *Genealogical History*, 261–262; Anon., *The Order and Solemnitie of the Creation of the High and Mightie Prince Henrie, eldest Sonne to our sacred Soueraigne, Prince of Wales, Duke of Cornewall, Earle of Chester, &c. As it was celebrated in the Parliament House, on Munday the fourth of Iunne last past. Together with the Ceremonies of the Knights of the Bath, and other matters of speciall regard, incident to the same. Whereunto is annexed the Royall Maske, presented by the Queene and her Ladies, on Wednesday at night following* (London, 1610).

9　Brown, *Noble Society in Scotland*, 183.

10　[Hyde], Edward, earl of Clarendon, *The History of the Rebellion and Civil Wars in England begun in the Year 1641...*, ed. W.D. Macray, 6 vols (Oxford, 1888), I, 111.

11　Aberdeen University Special Collections, MS 658, The Pourtrait of True Loyalty exposed in the Family of Gordon by D. Burnet, ff. 473–474, 673.

12　Leith (ed.) *Memoirs of Scottish Catholics*, I, 27 (Leslie to Vitelleschi, 1628).

at some point be persuaded to convert to the faith of his father. A similar assertion made in 1639 by the Venetian ambassador that the second marquess had
become 'suspect as a professing Catholic' can be regarded as nothing more than
an ill-informed rumour of the type that was fairly common at the time.[13]

Rather more intriguing was a set of instructions from 1642, addressed from
a Roman Catholic prelate to his agent travelling in Ireland and Scotland which
stated that a letter had been sent from the second marquess and a number of
other Scottish nobles to the Spanish ambassador, Cárdenas, to 'communicate
with Father Heugh Sempil [a Scot in Spanish service] for the transmission of
the things requisite for the performance of divine worship as in the past year
1641, and to continue his good offices for the conservation and augmentation
of the Roman Catholic religion in Scotland'.[14] However, this instruction seems
to have been more a product of Cárdenas's enthusiasm to build up contacts and
networks based on outdated intelligence as to how things stood in the traditional Catholic households of Scotland. If the second marquess ever sent a letter
on the matter then it would remain a very strange and uncharacteristic anomaly.

A much more convincing case can be made to attest to the fact that from the
time of his youth and early manhood as the earl of Enzie, right through to his
later years, the second marquess of Huntly remained a Protestant. His sojourn
at Court clearly had an impact. In a letter written as early as 1609 he assured
the king of his conformity, of which he would 'giue ane constant proofe to my
verie last breath'. This, he added, was despite what his father, the first marquess,
might think on the matter.[15] Enzie's adherence to the reformed faith went on
to become a commonly accepted fact. In 1629 a visitor to Scotland pointed out
that the heirs of the three greatest Catholics in Scotland were all Protestants
– the sons in question being the future second marquess of Huntly, the future
marquess of Argyll and the future third marquess of Hamilton.[16] A few years
later the traveller and writer William Lithgow saw fit to include the earl of Enzie
in a list of the Protestant nobles of Scotland.[17] There is also the testimony of
Gilbert Blakhal, a Catholic priest who put together a very detailed chronicle of
his services on behalf of a number of female members of the House of Huntly
during the 1630s and 1640s. At no point in his narrative did he make reference

13 *CSPV, 1636–39*, 539, (Giustinian to the Doge and Senate, 13 May 1639).
14 *CSPD, 1641–43*, 305.
15 *Letters and State Papers during the Reign of King James the Sixth*, 177 (Lord Gordon [Enzie] to
    James VI, [1609]).
16 HMC, Thirteenth Report, Appendix, part VII, *The Manuscripts of the Earl of Lonsdale* (London,
    1893), 83.
17 William Lithgow, *Scotland's welcome to her native sonne, and soveraigne lord, King Charles*
    (Edinburgh, 1633).

to the second marquess being Catholic.[18] If such had been the case then Blakhal would surely have made mention of it. Perhaps the most telling evidence comes from the records of the commissions of the General Assemblies of Scotland for 1647. In this year it was recorded that a number of ministers of the Kirk were denounced for having engaged in acts of worship with the second marquess.[19] The latter had recently been excommunicated, not for recusancy, but for his unrepentant Royalism. Moreover, during his army's occupation of Aberdeen in 1644, the second marquess also made a point of regularly attending the local church services.[20] It would seem that the his Protestantism may have involved something more than just outward conformity. It is also noteworthy that following the conversion of his third daughter, Jean, to Protestantism in 1640, he made a point of writing her a letter congratulating her on the matter.[21]

However, the picture is further complicated by the fact that a number of commentators recorded that the second marquess remained somewhat cold to organised religion as a whole. The staunch Covenanting minister, Robert Baillie, described him as 'that feeble, effeminate foolish athiest', while the Catholic priest, Father Robert Gall – who witnessed the execution of the second marquess in 1649 –testified that 'Huntley dyed, as he had lived, more atheist than Christianlike'.[22] Added to this was the keen interest the marquess had in astrology, a fact attested to by French ambassador, Jean de Montereul in 1647.[23] He was even known to favour a motto that translated from Latin as 'I will leave it to the heavenly powers themselves to decide', a fatalistic sentiment that seems to have suited his personality quite well and certainly linked in with his astrological leanings.[24] Gilbert Burnet went so far as to say that this pursuit of astrology remained nothing less than Huntly's ruin. 'He was a naturally gallant man,' wrote Burnet, 'but the stars had so subdued him that he made a poor figure the whole course of the [civil] wars.'[25]

18 Blakhal, *Breiffe Narration*.
19 *The Records of the Commissions of the General Assemblies of the Church of Scotland holden in Edinburgh the Years 1646 and 1647*, eds A.F. Mitchell and J. Christie (Edinburgh, 1892), 241–246, 253, 255, 260.
20 Spalding, *Memorialls*, II, 341, 349, 351.
21 Fraser, *Earls of Haddinton*, II, 181.
22 *The Letters and Journals of Robert Baillie, Principal of the University of Glasgow, 1637–1662*, ed. D. Laing, 3 vols (Edinburgh, 1841–42), II, 164 (Baillie to Spang, 12 April 1644); Leith, *Memoirs of Scottish Catholics*, II, 49–50 (Gall to Leslie, July 1649).
23 *The Diplomatic Correspondence of Jean de Montereul and the Brothers de Bellièvre, French Ambassadors in England and Scotland, 1645–48*, ed. J.G. Fotheringham, 2 vols (Edinburgh, 1898–99), II, 347 (Montereul to Mazarin, 7 December 1647).
24 *Letters of Sir Robert Moray to the Earl of Kincardine*, ed. D. Stevenson (Ashgate, 2007), 140 (Moray to Kincardine, 12 February 1658).
25 G. Burnet, *History of my own Time*, ed. O. Airy, 2 vols (Oxford, 1897), I, 63. For more detail on astrology and its impact on the early modern mind, see K. Thomas, *Religion and the*

But on the balance of evidence it seems safe to conclude that the second marquess did demonstrate a clear public conformity to the Protestant faith as professed by James VI and I and Charles I. Indeed, going on the General Assembly records and church attendance evidence mentioned earlier, this may have extended to encompassing a personal belief also. That he was also keenly interested in astrology is little in doubt, although to claim that he was wholly atheistic is going too far. Meanwhile, there arguably remains little to sustain the view that he was Catholic, either publicly or privately. That is not to say that he did not remain tolerant of those around him who professed that particular faith. After all, his parents were Catholic, as were his siblings. There is evidence, for example, that during the mid-1640s one of his younger sisters, Lady Strabane, turned the Gordon castle of Lesmore into what was reportedly a haven for Catholic worship.[26] Around the same time Huntly also remained content, after much urging from the priest, Gilbert Blakhal, for one of his nieces, Lady Henrietta Gordon, to be escorted to France where she would be brought up as a Catholic. Huntly's initial truculence over the matter had resulted from the fact that such practice was against the law at the time.[27] In addition, in April 1639, upon submitting to a Covenanting army, he negotiated to ensure that Catholics amongst his followers would not be treated harshly.[28]

His Protestantism aside, Huntly's formative years at Court also ensured that in the eyes of some he had become, to a certain extent, anglicised. In his summation of Huntly's life and character the chronicler Patrick Gordon of Ruthven certainly found much to bemoan about this. In his view, Huntly's key failings were the product of his time in England, particularly his tendency to remain cold and distant towards his followers. This 'proud show of affecting steat', Gordon of Ruthven continued, had not naturally been in Huntly's character:

> He was knowen to be both affable, courteous, and sociable befor he was called to court; [but] his breiding in Ingland, the habit and longe custom he gott there, owercam and whollie changed his naturall inclinatione, so as it was the Inglish breiding, and not his naturall inclinatione, that had imped and ingrassed this error.[29]

Decline of Magic. Studies in Popular Beliefs in Sixteenth- and Seventeenth-Century England (Harmondsworth, 1973), 355–458; P. Curry, *Prophecy and Power. Astrology in Early Modern England* (Oxford, 1989); A. Geneva, *Astrology and the Seventeenth Century Mind. William Lilly and the Language of the Stars* (Manchester, 1995); R. Gillespie, *Devoted People: Belief and Religion in Early Modern Ireland* (Manchester and New York, 1997), 127–147.

26 Leith, *Memoirs of Scottish Catholics*, I, 258–259; *Extracts from the Presbytery Book of Strathbogie, A.D. 1631–1654*, ed. J. Stuart (Aberdeen, 1843), 47.

27 D. Stevenson, *King or Covenant? Voices from Civil War* (East Linton, 1996), 59.

28 Gordon, *History of Scots Affairs*, II, 231–232

29 Gordon, *Britane's Distemper*, 230.

The English manners of the period were strongly influenced by stoicism, a philosophy that manifested itself in the suppression of emotion and the maintenance of a distanced demeanour. The second marquess, then, was very much of this cast.[30]

Research has shown that his was an exceptional case in Scottish aristocratic life during the seventeenth century. Although there is some evidence to suggest that there may have been a general trend among some to seek to emulate the expensive lifestyle of the English court, on the whole Scottish nobles remained largely immune to the adoption of English manners. For reasons of expense and distance the majority spent little time at court and so anglicisation was minimal. Even a sense of 'Britishness' remained underdeveloped.[31] The second marquess had actually belonged to a select, privileged elite group that James VI and I had sought to mould into ideal, conformist Jacobean courtiers and subjects. Somewhat unusual in his upbringing, Huntly may have had more of a sense of 'Britishness' than most of his Scottish contemporaries, but as has been seen, this also attracted the ire of observers like Gordon of Ruthven, concerned at the consequences of his having 'gone native' during his time in England.

Gordon of Ruthven further criticised Huntly for his 'self will and obstinate opinione', which made him cairlesse of counsell'. Indeed, it was from this that most of his faults reportedly emanated:

> He was both constant and reall in his friendship to whom he professed it; nor could anie threatnings or fair persuasions be able to alter or change him; but if fortoune frouned, or the world went against him, he was in this onlie lyke other noblemen, not aboue them. Seruice don, and not to doe, was forgotten, and old seruants, for whom there was no use, most be brusht or rubt off as spots from cloathes; so as this falt, if it may be tearmed a falt, was truelie a noble one, for it attendeth allwayes on nobilitie; and yit the hard constructione which was mad of this did more harm to himselfe then to those castaways, for it did, by little and little, insensiblie alienate the hearts of his followers.

This distanced demeanour 'gott him but an outward and constreaned obedience' but eventually resulted in him losing the active support of some of his followers

30 D. Stevenson, 'English Devil of Keeping State: Elite Manners and the Downfall of Charles I in Scotland', in R. Mason and N. Macdougall (eds), *People and Power in Scotland: Essays in Honour of T.C. Smout* (Edinburgh, 1992), 127–133.

31 K.M. Brown, 'Aristocratic Finances and the Origins of the Scottish Revolution', *English Historical Review*, vol. 104, no. 410 (Jan. 1989), 47–48, 63–64; K.M. Brown, 'Origins of a British Aristocracy: Integration and its Limitations before the Treaty of Union', in Ellis and Barber (eds), *Conquest and Union*, 223, 248; Brown, 'Scottish Aristocracy, Anglicization and the Court', 544–550.

in the long run.[32] An illuminating testimony to his coldness was provided by Gilbert Blakhal, and concerned Huntly's treatment of his sister-in-law, Lady Aboyne, prior to the approach of Montrose's Covenanting army in 1639. Since she was a widow, she requested that the marquess provide her with arms in order to defend her home. Huntly, Blakhal noted, 'scorned her demand, saying, ladies were not ordeaned for feighting, and send her non, neither for herself nor for her tenantes'. Luckily, the resourceful Blakhal had been on hand to obtain weapons and ammunition for her in nearby Aberdeen.[33]

To what extent Gordon of Ruthven presented a balanced portrayal is hard to say. He may himself have been one of the unfortunate 'castaways' referred to in his text, with the result that he could have harboured a grudge that eventually found an outlet in his writing. However, it remains a fact that his chronicle was written primarily with the objective of defending the conduct of Huntly and the Gordons during the Civil Wars. In particular he praised the marquess for his loyalty to the king. Ruthven pointed out that he would not attempt to clear Huntly of all his faults, and that he would 'in keeping the trueth als neir as my knowledge or intelligence can lead me, strive to vindicate him from the hatred and vnplacable malice of his enemies'.[34]

Yet it is important not to portray Huntly solely in a negative light as having been a cold and forbidding character. There was certainly more to him than just the attitude and trappings of an anglicised frequenter of the Stuart court. In 1618, the traveller and poet John Taylor made the important and enlightening observation that during the whole month of August, nobles such as the earls of Moray, Mar and Enzie would go on extended hunting trips in the hills and wilds and while doing so would 'conforme themselves to the habite of the Highland-men' complete with tartan hose, kilts and plaids. Later in his journey, Taylor also stayed with Enzie in the family's chief Highland stronghold of Ruthven in Badenoch, from where they would regularly set out in pursuit of local game.[35] Further to that, in 1629 other travellers related how Enzie was 'esteemed the ablest man of body in the kingdom, and will familiarly go in the mountains after the deer eighty miles a day'.[36] Such testimony certainly adds other elements to the profile of the second marquess. He was clearly at home within a 'Highland' context as well as a 'Lowland' one, and it begs the question of what the Stuart kings would have thought of this had they known. The facets

32 Gordon, *Britane's Distemper*, 229–230.
33 Blakhal, *Breiffe Narration*, 78.
34 Gordon, *Britane's Distemper*, 12. The main target of Gordon of Ruthven's ire was George Wishart's biography of James Graham, first marquess of Montrose, which had been published in Paris in 1647.
35 *Early Travellers in Scotland*, 120–121, 123.
36 HMC., Thirteenth Report, 83.

of Highland identity may well have been regarded by James VI and his son as being 'uncivilised', but, as far as Huntly was concerned, they clearly were not. The marquess was also held in high enough regard by the Gaelic bard, Iain Lom, to warrant the writing of two laments on the subject of his capture by the forces of the Covenanting regime and his subsequent execution.[37]

These same poems also serve to suggest that Huntly was a well-cultured individual. Fine music, Spanish wine and the game of chess were all recorded as having been enjoyed in the Gordon household.[38] His love of fine landscaping was evident, as was his appreciation of the fine arts.[39] Indeed, while in prison in 1648 the he took to translating pieces of literature, a work known as *Cassandra* being the one he was concentrating on at the time.[40] Whether this meant that he was naturally more disposed to the peaceful pursuits of learning and contemplation as opposed to those of a more martial nature is unclear. Gordon of Ruthven certainly bemoaned the fact that for Huntly:

> The contemplative facultie did so farre exceed the active … which mad the following furth of the externall act becom more slowe and lasie, through want of a constant and satled resolutione, and thus growing cold, it died befor it gott the lyf of rectified approbatione.[41]

This view presents something of a contrast to what is known of Huntly's exploits in his younger days. His expeditions against the Mackintoshes and Camerons in the 1610s and 1620s seem to suggest a man unafraid to take assertive action. His period in the service of Louis XIII also seems to point to a young lord more than willing to pursue the noble art of war in foreign climes. At any rate, the 'contemplative' and 'active' faculties did not necessarily have to be mutually exclusive. In the words of one noted historian of the Scottish nobility: 'a noble education was intended to produce men proficient in the necessary skills of war and government but also possessing a good, rounded understanding of the arts, sciences and languages'.[42] However, it may be that with age, and in light of his experience of armed service on the continent, the marquess developed a greater awareness of the terrible waste of war. In the aftermath of the First Bishops' War, he saw fit to commit the following to writing on the subject of civil conflict:

---

37 *Orain Iain Luim. Songs of John MacDonald, Bard of Keppoch*, ed. A.M. MacKenzie (Edinburgh, 1964), 44–55. The laments were entitled 'The Capture of the Marquis of Huntly' and 'A Lament for the Marquis of Huntly'.

38 *Ibid.*, 48–49.

39 *Ibid.*, 44–45; Gordon, *Britane's Distemper*, 13.

40 *Diplomatic Correspondence of Jean de Montereul*, II, 446 (Montereul to Mazarin, 4 April 1648).

41 Gordon, *Britane's Distemper*, 230.

42 Brown, *Noble Society in Scotland*, 203.

I foresee with horrour the miseryes, that will attend it; firing of Houses, wasting of Goods, ffamine, Ruine of Townes, & Citties, & the unjust Liberty, which we ambitiously usurpe, lost in an instant, & forever. Wife, Children, & Bloud, man by Nature holdeth deare: if we pitty not our selues, let us not forgett them we hold dearer.[43]

The death of Huntly's wife, Anne Campbell, in June 1638 may also have contributed to his adopting a more circumspect attitude at this time. The marriage was evidently a very successful one, spawning no fewer than ten children, five boys and five girls. The burial of the marchioness was suitably lavish, the scene being recorded for posterity by the chronicler John Spalding:

At hir lifting the toune of Abirdein causit schoot there haill ordinance for ane good nicht. Scho is convoyit with multitudes of people in magnifick honorabill maner, haueing hir corpis careit upone the berares of ane coache be six barronis, and led be horssis under ane murning pale. The croun, with hir armes and armes of hir four bransches wes careit, and thus wes scho convoyit to Sanct John the Evangelistis Iyll, or bischop Lichtoun's Iyll, on the north side of Maucher churche, and thair bureit with gryte murning and lamentatioun.

Spalding further noted that on the morning after the burial Huntly travelled to Strathbogie Castle in a state of 'heiche melanchollie'.[44]

Whatever the state of his mind following his wife's death, Huntly's devotion to the Royalist cause was plainly evident. Shortly afterwards the Covenanters made an approach to him, offering to defray all of his considerable debts if he would join their side. According to the testimony of Gordon of Ruthven, the marquess flatly refused, pointing out that 'as his hous had risen by kinges, and had stand for their fidelitie and seruice to kinges, so he was resolued to stand or fall with this king as his present lord and soueraine'.[45] Prior to this incident the Covenanters had been under the mistaken impression that Huntly may have had sympathy for what they had to say.[46] The following year, while in Covenanting custody, he stood by this resolution not to take their side. On this occasion he made the reply:

43 Lambeth Palace Library, MS 3472, Fairhurst Papers, f. 260v.
44 Spalding, *Memorialls*, I, 90–91.
45 Gordon, *Britane's Distemper*, 13–14; Gordon of Rothiemay also recorded this incident. See Gordon, *History of Scots Affairs*, I, 48–50.
46 *Letters and Journals of Robert Baillie*, I, 82–83, 193 (Baillie to Spang, 5 April [1638]), (same to same, 28 September 1639).

Wheras you offer libertie, upon condition of my entring into your Covenant, I am not so bad a merchant as to buy it with the losses of my conscience, fidelity and honour, which in so doing I should make account to be wholly perisht. I have already given my faith to my prince, upon whose head this crowne by all law of nature and nations is justly fallen, and will not falsifie that faith by joining with any in a pretence of religion, which my owne judgement cannot excuse from rebellion.

He continued by denying the right of the Covenanters to resist their king:

For it is well knowne that in the primitive church no armes were held lawfull, being lifted by subjects against their lawfull prince, though the whole frame of Christianitie was then in question.

He ended with a flourish:

For my owne part, I am in your power, and resolv'd not to leave that foule title of traitour as an inheritance upon my posterity. You may take my head from my shoulders, but not my heart from my soveraigne.[47]

From this it can be seen that Huntly's Royalism was based on two central tenets: firstly his rejection of the Covenanting claim that it was the duty of a subject to take up arms against any one (including the king) who obstructed or undermined what they deemed to be the true reformed faith and the good of the country. This debate on rights of resistance was a common one throughout early modern Europe.[48] Secondly Huntly's words highlighted his desire not to bring his honour into question by deserting his sovereign. In this he held common cause with many of his contemporaries amongst the nobility and gentry of England who in 1642 would rally to the standard of Charles I. The concept of honour was central to the lives of most members of the aristocracy in the three Stuart kingdoms. For Royalists it manifested itself in a loyalty and obedience to the king that took precedence over any other beliefs or political preferences they might harbour. The sovereign was regarded as being the fount of all honour and as such must be given due service.[49]

---

47 [Gordon, G., second marquess of Huntly], *The Marquesse of Huntley his reply to certaine noblemen, gentlemen, and ministers, Covenanters of Scotland: sent from their associates, to signifie unto him, that it behoved him either to assist their designes, or be carried to prison in the Castle of Edinburgh: the 20 of April 1639* (London, 1640).

48 For a useful overview, see J.P. Sommerville, 'Absolutism and Royalism', in J.H. Burns and M. Goldie (eds), *The Cambridge History of Political Thought, 1450–1700* (Cambridge, 1991), 347–373.

49 J.G. Marston, 'Gentry, Honor and Royalism in Early Stuart England', *Journal of British* Studies, vol. 13 (1973), 22; P.R. Newman, 'The King's Servants: Conscience, Principle, and Sacrifice in Armed Royalism', in J. Morrill, P. Slack and D. Woolf (eds), *Public Duty and Private Conscience in Seventeenth-Century England* (Oxford, 1993), 227; P.R. Newman, *The Old Service: Royalist*

THE FIRST BISHOPS' WAR

As early as June 1638 Huntly was involved in discussions on how best to counter the Covenanting threat, and from October was highly active in obtaining subscriptions to what became known as the King's Covenant, which essentially was a set of concessions that curtailed some of the recent innovations in religion while at the same time reasserting overall royal authority. In promoting the King's Covenant Huntly achieved some success in Aberdeen and in areas where his influence was strong; indeed he could still be found gathering in names into the early months of 1639.[50] The Royalist cause in the North-East was also aided by the presence of a group of influential academics and ministers known as 'The Aberdeen Doctors' who from mid-1638 became involved in a public debate with the Covenanters in defence of the royal prerogative and against the idea of resisting the monarch.[51] However, almost everywhere else in Scotland the King's Covenant was not a success, and by the time of the Glasgow Assembly the Covenanters had moved the debate on to seeking the removal of the bishops altogether.[52]

Regimental Colonels and the Civil War, 1642-46 (Manchester, 1993), 20–30. Gerald Aylmer concluded that concepts of honour and loyalty were more important for the majority of Royalists than the force and validity of any other arguments. See G.E. Aylmer, 'Collective Mentalities in Mid-Seventeenth-Century England: Royalist Attitudes', *Transactions of the Royal Historical Society*, 5th series, vol. 37 (1987), 1–30. For discussion of the concept of honour more generally, see M. James, *Society, Politics and Culture: Studies in Early Modern England* (Cambridge, 1986), 308–415. For an examination of noble honour within a military context in Ireland, see J. Ohlmeyer, 'The Baronial Context of the Irish Civil Wars', in J. Adamson (ed.), *The English Civil War: Conflict and Contexts, 1640–49* (Basingstoke, 2009), 122–124.

50 Spalding, *Memorialls*, I, 89, 112; Row and Row, *History of the Kirk*, 500–501; NAS, GD 406/1/449 (Huntly to Hamilton, 11 October 1638); NAS, GD 406/1/450 (Huntly to Hamilton [1638]); NAS, GD 406/1/456/2 (Huntly to [Hamilton], 2 November [1638]); NAS, GD 406/1/460 (Huntly to [Hamilton], 7 November [1638]); NAS, GD 406/1/461 (Huntly to Hamilton, 10 November 1638); NAS, GD 406/1/463 ([Hamilton] to Huntly, 14 November 1638); NAS, GD 406/1/753 (Huntly to Hamilton, 7 February 1639). In the King's Covenant Charles reiterated adherence to the Negative Confession of 1581, which had been a denunciation of all the tenets deemed to be associated with Roman Catholic worship. The Negative Confession had also formed the centrepiece of the opening section of the National Covenant. In terms of religious worship and Church governance he committed himself to withdrawing the prayer book and the Five Articles of Perth, and to dispensing with the Court of High Commission. See Spalding, *Memorialls*, I, 106.

51 Spalding, *Memorialls*, I, 95–100; Stevenson, *Scottish Revolution*, 86, 91, 101–102; M. Bennett, *The Civil Wars Experienced. Britain and Ireland, 1638–1661* (London, 2000), 1–8; G.D. Henderson, *The Burning Bush. Studies in Scottish Church History* (Edinburgh, 1957), 75–93; J.D. Ogilvie, *The Aberdeen Doctors and the National Covenant* (Edinburgh, 1921); Stevenson, *King's College*, 105–116; D. Stewart, 'The "Aberdeen Doctors" and the Covenanters', *Records of the Scottish Church History Society*, vol. 22 (1986), 35–44; B. McLennan, 'Presbyterianism Challenged: a Study of Catholicism and Episcopacy in the North-East of Scotland, 1560–1650' (unpublished PhD thesis, University of Aberdeen, 1977), 223–358.

52 Macinnes, *British Revolution*, 117–119.

The king soon fixed upon the idea that military force would be necessary in order to regain his authority, and with this in mind an ambitious multi-pronged assault was planned. While he would march northwards to the border at the head of an English army, Randal MacDonnell, second earl of Antrim, would invade the West of Scotland with an Irish force, while James, third marquess of Hamilton, would land a seaborne army at Aberdeen with the hope of linking up with a force under the command of Huntly. On top of this, Hamilton was designated the overall commander of the royal forces in Scotland and it was intended that everything would be co-ordinated through him.[53]

However, before this plan could be put into operation Huntly came under increasing pressure from the Covenanters in the North. But for reasons that will be duly outlined, he remained unwilling to fall to arms. On 7 February a Covenanting raiding party captured the castle of Inverness in the face of an attempt by Huntly to re-equip and regarrison it for the king.[54] A week later Huntly marched on Turriff with a view to overawing a Covenanting delegation that had gathered there, but when the prominently-placed local kirkyard was defended against him Huntly declined to fall to arms. Similarly, on 30 March, at the approach of a Covenanting army under the command of James Graham, fifth earl (later first marquess) of Montrose, Huntly saw fit to retreat and give up Aberdeen rather than stand and fight. Moreover, some days later he negotiated a cease-fire with Montrose at Inverurie and signed an oath acknowledging his submission. Despite this, a majority in the Covenanting high command deemed that it was unsafe to leave him at large and so on 13 April, after having been lured into carrying out discussions in Aberdeen, Huntly and his eldest son, Lord Gordon, were captured and interned in Edinburgh Castle.[55]

By this time the grand Royalist plan had not been progressing well on other fronts. Antrim had been unsuccessful in his attempt to raise an Irish army and at the same time the king was also experiencing similar problems. Royal attempts to gain aid on the Continent also fell on stony ground, particularly in comparison to Covenanting success in this regard. Particularly crucial were the arms and munitions that the Covenanters were able to import, as well as the veterans who returned from service in countries such as Sweden to serve in their armies.[56] Meanwhile, Hamilton and his seaborne force had been held

---

53 B. Robertson, 'The House of Huntly and the First Bishops' War', *Northern Scotland*, vol. 24 (2004), 1–2.

54 Spalding, *Memorialls*, I, 135–136.

55 Robertson, 'The House of Huntly and the First Bishops' War', 3.

56 C.M. Hibbard, *Charles I and the Popish Plot* (Chapel Hill, 1983), 104–107; A. Grosjean, 'General Alexander Leslie, the Scottish Covenanters and the Riksråd Debates, 1638–1640', in A.I. Macinnes, T. Riis and F. Pedersen (eds), *Ships, Guns and Bibles in the North Sea and Baltic States, c.1350–c.1700* (East Linton, 2000), 115–138; S. Murdoch, 'Scotland, Scandinavia and the Bishops'

up in the port of Yarmouth and had been unable to provide timely assistance to Huntly and his Royalists. Despite this, there was a rising of some of the Gordon-affiliated north-east lairds in early May which resulted in a victory over local Covenanting forces at Turriff on the 14th of that month and the subsequent recapture of Aberdeen. This being short-lived, the burgh was back in Covenanting hands by the time Huntly's second son, James, Lord Aboyne, freshly granted a royal lieutenancy, landed to regalvanise the Royalist North-East into action in early June. As things turned out this merely resulted in two defeats in the field, the first at Megray Hill near Stonehaven on 15 June and the second at the two-day battle of Bridge of Dee just outside Aberdeen from 18 to 19 June. In fact, the result of the latter remained somewhat academic given that the king, then with his army at the Scottish border, had by that time begun negotiating peace terms with the Covenanters. The Pacification of Berwick that resulted from this formally brought the First Bishops' War to a close, technically delivering a draw to both sides, but in real terms buying valuable breathing space for the Covenanters.[57] It also brought the release of Huntly and Lord Gordon from their captivity on 22 June.[58]

EXPLAINING ROYALIST DEFEAT

For some contemporaries the Gordon performance had been a lacklustre one. Thomas, earl of Arundel, noted how many in English Royalist circles were blaming Huntly personally for not taking sterner action against the northern

---

Wars, 1638–40', in A.I. Macinnes and J. Ohlmeyer (eds), *The Stuart Kingdoms in the Seventeenth Century: Awkward Neighbours* (Dublin, 2001), 113–134; S. Murdoch, *Britain, Denmark-Norway and the House of Stuart, 1603–1660* (East Linton, 2003), 92–109; A. Grosjean, *An Unofficial Alliance: Scotland and Sweden, 1569–1654* (Leiden, 2003), 165–190; D. Worthington, *Scots in Habsburg Service, 1618–1648* (Leiden, 2004), 104–30.

57 Robertson, 'The House of Huntly and the First Bishops' War', 5, 8, 11. Aboyne had actually gone south to Newcastle in person to obtain a commission and official support from the king. For coverage of the king's campaign in the First Bishops' War, see M.C. Fissel, *The Bishops' Wars. Charles I's Campaigns against Scotland, 1638–1640* (Cambridge, 1994), 3–39. For Antrim's attempts at raising an Irish force, see A. Clarke, 'The Earl of Antrim and the First Bishops' War', *Irish Sword*, vol. 6, no. 23 (1963), 108–115; Ohlmeyer, *Civil War and Restoration*, 77–99. For the marquess of Hamilton and the war, see J. Scally, 'Counsel in Crisis: James, Third Marquis of Hamilton and the Bishops' Wars, 1638–1640', in Young (ed.), *Celtic Dimensions*, 20–25. For detailed analysis of the working relationship between Charles and his chief Scottish counsellors from the onset of the troubles, See Donald, *Uncounselled King*, 1–171.

58 *Diary of Sir Archibald Johnston Lord Wariston, 1639*, ed. G.M. Paul (Edinburgh, 1896), 96. Another contemporary stalwart for the National Covenant, Henry Guthry, dated this to 23 June. See H. Guthry, *Memoirs … containing an Impartial Relation of the Affairs of Scotland, Civil and Ecclesiastical from the Year 1637 to the Death of King Charles I* (2nd edn, Glasgow, 1747), 60. As the latter was a memoir written after the events, the diary of Wariston can probably be taken as being more accurate.

Covenanters at an earlier time. Meanwhile, while stationed as part of the king's army in York in early April, Sir Edmund Verney deplored the fact that Aberdeen had been given up 'without soe much as a bluddy nose'.[59] The Covenanting minister, Robert Baillie, also saw occasion to deride Huntly's performance. In particular he drew attention to the latter's 'cowardish feare'.[60]

However, as something of a counterbalance to such views, it can be demonstrated that the Gordon lords had had a number of difficulties to contend with during the course of the conflict. For example, Huntly's war effort suffered from a lack of experienced, quality troops and officers, and from the fact that neither Aberdeen nor his own castles was particularly defensible in light of the standards of warfare of the time.[61] His crippling debt also restricted the length of time he could afford to keep an army in the field.[62] On top of this, neither Hamilton nor the king provided Huntly with any clear warrant or idea of when, or if, they wanted him to take offensive action. With this in mind it seems that Huntly concluded that the best course would be to seek a temporary accommodation with the Covenanters and sign what was in actuality a very short and vaguely-worded oath of submission.[63] Huntly may even have been thinking tactically when he made his submission, hoping it would leave him free from Covenanting aggression and place him in a position to await the expected arrival of Hamilton and his seaborne army.[64]

The Gordon risings of May and June also suffered from a lack of clear overall strategic co-ordination on the part of Hamilton and the king. The Gordon-affiliated lairds were never provided with adequate support or even a suitable warrant following the skirmish at Turriff in May. Similarly, while Aboyne remained committed to bringing the Covenanters to battle the following month, he received little in the way of support. By that time it seems that Hamilton, beset by his own problems, was becoming increasingly unsure of his position

---

59 *CSPD, 1639*, 14–15 (Arundel to Windebank, 4 April 1639); *Letters and Papers of the Verney Family down to the End of the Year 1639*, ed. J. Bruce (London, 1880), 212–213 (E. Verney to R. Verney, [about 4 April 1639]).

60 *Letters and Journals of Robert Baillie*, I, 196–197 (Baillie to Spang, 28 September 1639). For the typical line adopted by later historians, particularly the biographers of Montrose, see Reid, *Campaigns of Montrose*, 12; Hastings, *Montrose*, 81.

61 Robertson, 'The House of Huntly and the First Bishops' War', 5–6. With the idea of urban indefensibility in mind, Charles Carlton has calculated that, during the years 1639 to 1646, the burghs of Aberdeen changed hands nineteen times. See C. Carlton, 'Civilians', in J. Kenyon and J. Ohlmeyer (eds), *The Civil Wars. A Military History of England, Scotland, and Ireland, 1638–1660* (Oxford, 1998), 295.

62 Robertson, 'The House of Huntly and the First Bishops' War', 3.

63 *Ibid*, 5, 7. For a copy of the oath, see BL, Sloane 650, f. 90, The Marquess Huntlies Oath to the Covenanters.

64 Robertson, 'The House of Huntly and the First Bishops' War', 7.

and, like the king, was suffering from a lack of desire to fall to arms. As such, while Aboyne faced up to Montrose's Covenanting army at the Bridge of Dee, negotiations were already under way on the border with a view to bringing the First Bishops' War to a conclusion.[65] The Gordon risings of May and June also suffered from a lack of clear overall leadership on the ground.[66] In addition, it may have been the case that, in his own mind, Huntly felt a degree of uncertainty over whether to fall to arms, a state possibly compounded by his belief in astrology and by what he may have read into some notable natural portents of the time.[67] Moreover, given his cold and uninspiring character, Huntly was perhaps not best suited to command.[68]

The progress of the Royalist cause in the North was also impeded by the extent of the support enjoyed by the Covenanters in the region. Although it remains likely that the views of the Aberdeen Doctors were reflective of those of the majority of the citizens of that burgh, on closer inspection it is noticeable that a number of key individuals were sympathetic to the National Covenant, especially so within the ranks of the town council. This particular body had been faction-ridden for much of the 1630s and even as early as 1633 had included individuals such as the bailie, Patrick Leslie, who had shown a willingness to take a stand against the king.[69] Following that, a sizable Leslie-aligned faction had grown up within the council and remained a prominent presence by 1638. Granted, the council had, as a body, decided to reject the National Covenant, both in March and in July, but by August it appears that pro-Covenant sympathies were on the increase.[70]

In mid-August 1638 Robert Johnstone, the then provost, and two bailies reported to Huntly that six or seven council members had already subscribed

65 *Ibid.*, 8–9. The thoughts and actions of the king and Hamilton can be followed in G. Burnet, *The Memoirs of the Lives and Actions of James and William, Dukes of Hamilton and Castle-Herald* (Oxford, 1852), 150–174; *The Hamilton Papers: being Selections from Original Letters in the Possession of his Grace the Duke of Hamilton and Brandon, relating to the Years 1638–1650*, ed. S.R. Gardiner (London, 1880), 68–91.

66 Robertson, 'The House of Huntly and the First Bishops' War', 9–10. In May the Royalist lairds, lacking a clear overall commander, decided on the joint leadership of Sir George Ogilvie of Banff and Sir John Gordon of Haddo, with Colonel William Johnstone advising on military matters. In June Aboyne was beset by the conflicting councils of Johnstone and a military aide given to him by Hamilton, Colonel William Gunn.

67 *Ibid.*, 2–3, 6–7; with regard to astrology and its likely effects on Huntly, Gordon of Rothiemay's account of a blood-red sun seen shining a few days prior to the Covenanting occupation of Aberdeen in late March 1639 remains compelling. See Gordon, *History of Scots Affairs*, II, 223–224.

68 Robertson, 'The House of Huntly and the First Bishops' War', 3.

69 G. Desbrisay, '"The Civill Warrs did Overrun All": Aberdeen, 1630–1690', in Dennison, Ditchburn and Lynch (eds), *Aberdeen before 1800*, 240–241.

70 *Ibid.*, 241–245; D. Stevenson, 'The Burghs and the Scottish Revolution', in Lynch (ed.), *Early Modern Town in Scotland*, 167–171, 174–178.

the National Covenant and that most of the others were also that way inclined.[71] Moreover, the following month they related that at the recent council elections 'be pluralitie of wrytes' a number of known Covenanters had been chosen to be councillors.[72] Meanwhile, writing to Hamilton on the subject, Huntly noted that 'a most factious Covenanter', the aforementioned Patrick Leslie, had been the front runner for the post of provost but that a mob of 'the commons' had gathered in the street outside to protest this, 'and so [Leslie] wes contented to be but one of that councell'.[73] The election of magistrates had then gone ahead, three of those elected being Covenanters. Alexander Jaffray was elected provost, himself soon to become a signatory of the National Covenant.[74] True, with the inception of the King's Covenant it appears that, through encouraging subscriptions within Aberdeen, Huntly did manage to blunt pro-National Covenant sympathy somewhat. However, in effect, the council remained very divided, one manifestation of this being an initial reluctance to put Aberdeen on a defence footing in early 1639.[75]

It should also be noted that not all of the academics and ministers of the burghs and their immediate environs were pro-Royalist. In June 1638 Dr William Johnston, professor of Mathematics, subscribed the National Covenant, as did John Lundie, the grammarian of King's College, the following month.[76] Also in July, a number of local ministers subscribed, namely David Lindsay of Belhelvie, Andrew Melvin of Banchory-Devenick, Thomas Melvill of Dyce, Walter Anderson of Kinellar, William Robertson of Footdee, Robert Reid of Banchory-Trinity and Dr William Guild, the last, lamented Huntly, 'to the great discontent of all his fellow-brethren in Aberdeen'.[77] Lindsay, Guild and Lundie

---

71 NAS, GD 406/1/669 (Johnstone, Gray and Morrison to Huntly, 16 August 1638).

72 NAS, GD 406/1/447 (Johnstone, Gray and Morrison to [Huntly?], 27 September 1638).

73 NAS, GD 406/1/757 (Huntly to [Hamilton], 29 September [1638]).

74 NAS, GD 406/1/447 (Johnstone, Gray and Morrison to [Huntly?], 27 September 1638); Aberdeen City Council Archives, Council Register, LII (1), ff. 401–417; Desbrisay, 'Civill Warrs', 245.

75 Desbrisay, 'Civill Warrs', 246, 248. In most of the other burghs a clear-cut majority emerged in favour of the National Covenant. For Edinburgh, see Stewart, *Urban Politics*, 226–261. For Glasgow, see A.I. Macinnes, 'Covenanting, Revolution and Municipal Enterprise', in Wormald (ed.), *Scotland Revisited*, 97–106. For Perth, Dundee and Montrose, all towns lying north of the Tay, see *The Chronicle of Perth; a Register of Remarkable Occurences chiefly connected with that City, from the Year 1210 to 1668*, ed. J. Maidment (Edinburgh, 1831), 36; Dundee City Archives, Council Minutes, vol. IV, 1613–1653, ff. 131–131v; Forfar, Angus Archives, 58:352.1, Montrose Town Council Minute Book, 1621–1639, f. 167.

76 Desbrisay, 'Civill Warrs', 244; Row and Row, *History of the Kirk*, 494.

77 Spalding, *Memorialls*, I, 92–94; NAS GD 406/1/764 (Huntly to Hamilton, 7 August [1638]). Guild had been one of the seven original Aberdeen Doctors. See Stevenson, *King's College*, 110. For more on David Lindsay of Belhelvie, see A. Grosjean and S. Murdoch, *Belhelvie: a Millennium of History* (Belhelvie, 2000), 26–27.

went on to attend the General Assembly of 1638 as the three representatives for the Presbytery of Aberdeen.[78] Andrew Cant of Pitsligo was also another influential local minister with strong Covenanting sympathies.[79] With regard to the citizens of Aberdeen, it is hard to determine how many supported each side, or indeed, who attempted to straddle the fence. But it seems clear that, although there was probably more Royalist support than Covenanting, there was a noticeable division in opinion and, as such, the traditional idea of Aberdeen being staunchly and unequivocally Royalist is misleading.[80] Perhaps the starkest illustration of this is the fact that, in January 1639, Huntly felt the need to move from his house in Old Aberdeen to lodgings in New Aberdeen where he could be more easily watched over by his friends.[81] John Spalding noted that, this being done, 'thair wes aucht gentilmen appointit to watche his lodging on the night, thair tyme about, and fyre and candill still burning ilk night within the houss'.[82] Clearly he felt that Aberdeen was not quite Royalist enough for his safety to be guaranteed.

Elsewhere in the North-East it appears that the National Covenant was well subscribed to, notably so in Buchan, Mar, the Mearns and the Garioch. Spalding noted how 'multitudes' adhered to the Covenanting delegation that passed through these districts in late July and early August 1638, 'who subscrivit all'.[83] Many key north-east lairds were also strongly for the Covenant, something that would have had a strong bearing on the loyalties of the local populace. These included Alexander, Master of Forbes, Andrew, second Lord Fraser, James Crichton of Frendraught, Thomas Fraser of Strichen and representing the young earl of Errol and young Lord Pitsligo respectively, William Hay of Delgaty and Alexander Forbes of Boyndlie.[84] Collectively this brought out the

78 R King, *The Covenanters in the North; or Sketches of the Rise and Progress, North of the Grampians, of the Great Religious and Social Movement of which the Covenant of 1638 was the Symbol* (Aberdeen, 1846), 395.

79 Andrew Cant, David Dickson and key architect of the National Covenant, Alexander Henderson, were the three Covenanting ministers who came to Aberdeen in July 1638 as part of a commission to gain subscriptions there and in the surrounding area. Following their sermons within the close of the New Aberdeen town house of the earl Marischal on 22 July, the various local ministers mentioned were moved to subscribe the National Covenant. See Spalding, *Memorialls*, I, 91–92.

80 Desbrisay has correctly noted that the Episcopalian and Royalist influence in Aberdeen has been overplayed in past scholarly and popular historical works and that things were less clear-cut during the Covenanting Revolution. See Desbrisay, 'Civill Warrs', 240, 247.

81 *Ibid.*, 248.

82 Spalding, *Memorialls*, I, 131, 134.

83 *Ibid.*, I, 94.

84 Gordon, *Britane's Distemper*, 18; Spalding, *Memorialls*, I, 112–113, 133, 136, 153; NAS, GD 406/1/412 (Huntly to Hamilton, 18 January [1639]); NAS GD 406/1/758 (Huntly to Hamilton, 7 March [1639]). Huntly reported that staunch Covenanter, John Lyon, second earl of Kinghorn, also remained a leading influence over the followers of the earl of Errol. See NAS, GD 406/1/751

families of Hay, Fraser, Forbes and Crichton against the Gordons, the Forbes and Crichtons arguably influenced more by a desire to oppose their old enemies than solely by zeal for the Covenanting cause.[85] Perhaps most influential and powerful of all was William Keith, sixth earl Marischal, a noble whose loyalties were obscure for many months but who, by late March 1639, was firmly in the Covenanting camp.[86] As it turned out, he proved the cornerstone of their efforts in the North-East, providing important opposition to the Royalist risings of May and June 1639 as well as a watchful presence for much of 1640.[87]

West of the River Spey and over much of the far North the National Covenant was widely subscribed to, notably so in the burghs of Inverness, Forres and Elgin and the surrounding districts.[88] A number of the peers and lairds of the area also declared their support, among them Hugh Fraser, seventh Lord Lovat, James Stewart, fourth earl of Moray, James Grant, seventh laird of Freuchy, and John Gordon, thirteenth earl of Sutherland.[89] George Mackenzie, second earl of Seaforth, remained much more equivocal but eventually declared for the Covenant, probably more out of self-interest than for any other reason. His clansmen formed the nucleus of the Covenanting force that captured Inverness Castle in February 1639.[90] Meanwhile, from the Mearns southward into Angus, Perthshire and Fife, support for the Covenant was also thick on the ground,

---

(Huntly to Hamilton, 3 February 1639). Somewhat less staunch, but nevertheless still Covenanting in sympathy were Sir Thomas Burnet of Leys and his brother James Burnet of Craigmyle. See J. Allardyce, *The Family of Burnett of Leys with Collateral Branches* (Aberdeen, 1901), 45, 49.

85   Robertson, 'The House of Huntly and the First Bishops' War', 4.

86   He accompanied the army that occupied the burghs of Aberdeen on 30 March 1639. See Spalding, *Memorialls*, I, 513. Huntly's increasing suspicions with regard to the earl Marischal can be traced in some of his letters to Hamilton of early 1639. See NAS, GD 406/1/751 (Huntly to Hamilton, 3 February 1639); NAS, GD 406/1/755 (Huntly to Hamilton, 17 February 1639); NAS, GD 406/1/759 (Huntly to [Hamilton], 9 March 1639).

87   Spalding, *Memorialls*, I, 190–193, 202–212, 252–253, 266–269, 272–316.

88   NAS, GD 406/1/764 (Huntly to Hamilton, 7 August [1638]); NAS, GD 406/1/449 (Huntly to Hamilton, 11 October 1638); Spalding, *Memorialls*, I, 88; J. Leslie, earl of Rothes, *A Relation of Proceedings concerning the Affairs of the Kirk of Scotland from August 1637 to July 1638*, ed. J. Nairne (Edinburgh, 1830), 107–109.

89   E.M. Furgol, 'The Northern Covenanter Clans, 1639–1651', *Northern Scotland*, vol. 7 (1987), 124, 126, 128; Fraser, *Chiefs of Grant*, I, 245–253; Fraser, *Sutherland Book*, I, 227–230. The Royalist-leaning earl of Caithness noted in a letter to Huntly that there was great difficulty in keeping communications open with him by land due to the opposition of the earl of Sutherland. See NAS, GD 406/1/789 (Caithness to Huntly, 30 February 1639).

90   E.M. Furgol has observed that Seaforth sought the capture of Inverness because he feared that if the Royalists had triumphed in the North he would have to answer for having signed the National Covenant. See E.M. Furgol, *A Regimental History of the Covenanting Armies, 1639–1651* (Edinburgh, 1990), 36. According to Huntly, Seaforth had reportedly remained safely ensconced in Lewis while his clansmen carried out the action at Inverness. See NAS, GD 406/1/756 (Huntly to Hamilton, 25 February [1639]).

notable being John Lyon, second earl of Kinghorn, John, Lord Erskine, James, Lord Carnegie, David, Lord Elcho and Montrose himself.[91]

Huntly did retain a support base of his own which included cadet families such as the Gordons of Haddo, Gight and Newton. Outside of that he secured the allegiance of the Ogilvies of Findlater and Banff, the Irvines of Drum and Fedderate, and a number of other local lairds.[92] But support for the Royalist cause in the North-East was by no means overwhelming, and was certainly not as extensive as Huntly thought it was going to be.[93] Perhaps most noticeable was the fact that the Hays of Erroll were now occupying a separate political camp from the Gordons, something that would have seemed unthinkable in the 1590s.

In terms of Highlanders it seemed that Huntly could count on obtaining a little manpower from some of the Badenoch and Lochaber clans, most notably the Macphersons, and the MacDonalds of Keppoch.[94] The Camerons, though not in favour of the Covenant, still resented Huntly for past punishments inflicted upon them and thus could not be relied upon for support.[95] Meanwhile, the Mackintoshes remained split in their loyalties, the sickly chief, William, being Royalist in sympathy, while a number of his lairds looked more favourably on the Covenant.[96] The rest of Clan Donald, while well affected towards the Royalist cause, did little of any consequence prior to 1644, perhaps due to the fact that they felt under pressure from the Covenanting Campbells to the South.[97] A number of MacDonald and other West Highland chiefs did engage in plotting with the earl of Antrim during 1638 and 1639 but nothing resulted from this.[98] The main areas providing Highland levies for the Gordon armies

91 Spalding, *Memorialls*, I, 153–154.

92 *Ibid.*, I, 137, 265, 283; NAS, GD 406/1/456/1 (Huntly to Hamilton, 5 November [1638]); NAS, GD 406/1/460 (Huntly to [Hamilton], 7 November [1638]); NAS, GD 406/1/461 (Huntly to Hamilton, 10 November [1638]); NAS, GD 406/837 (Gentlemen of Aberdeen to Hamilton, 21 May 1639); J.F. Leslie, *The Irvines of Drum and Collateral Branches* (Aberdeen, 1909), 84–85.

93 He wrote to Hamilton on at least two occasions with the news that most of the population of the shires of Aberdeen and Banff was well affected. See NAS, GD 406/1/456/2 (Huntly to [Hamilton], 2 November [1638]); NAS, GD 406/1/449 (Huntly to Hamilton, 11 November 1638). The majority may by early 1639 have been well affected in Banffshire, but certainly not in Aberdeenshire.

94 Furgol, 'Northern Highland Covenanter Clans', 129; Macfarlane, *Genealogical Collections*, I, 306. In October 1638 Huntly guaranteed to Hamilton that he could raise 500 men from Badenoch and Lochaber. See NAS, GD 406/1/449 (Huntly to Hamilton, 11 October 1638).

95 Gordon, *History of Scots Affairs*, III, 163–164.

96 Furgol, 'Northern Highland Covenanter Clans', 127–128; Macfarlane, *Genealogical Collections*, I, 304, 306.

97 Furgol, 'Northern Highland Covenanter Clans', 120; NAS, GD 406/1/462 (Huntly to Hamilton, 10 November 1638); NAS, GD 406/1/412 (Huntly to Hamilton, 18 January [1639]).

98 D. Stevenson, *Scottish Covenanters and Irish Confederates: Scottish-Irish Relations in the Mid-Seventeenth Century* (Belfast, 1981), 22–32.

were Strathavon, Strathdee, Glen Muick and Glen Tanar.[99] Huntly also looked
to recruit bands of outlaws, most notably those pertaining to the notorious John
Dugar (a Macgregor), and James Grant of Carron. In February 1639 he even
wrote to Hamilton stating that 'if his Ma[jes]tie hould it fitt to grant a protection
to James Grantt, and to all who beere the name of Clangregoure, it will certainlye
muche trouble the other partye heere'.[100] A remission was duly granted to Grant
of Carron, and both he and Dugar served in Huntly's forces in 1639.[101]

   Royalist prospects elsewhere were bleaker. In the far North well-affected
nobles such as Donald Mackay, Lord Reay and George Sinclair, fifth earl of Caithness, with his son, William, Lord Berriedale, were hemmed in by the powerful
earl of Sutherland to the South, and could achieve little. Lord Berriedale's son,
John, master of Berriedale, was also an energetic Covenanter who did much to
frustrate the efforts of his father and grandfather.[102] Sir Robert Gordon reportedly favoured the Royalist cause but evidently could make little ground with his
nephew, Sutherland.[103] In Moray there seems to have been little Royalist support,
with the result that the bishop of the diocese and the Royalist-leaning ministers
were left somewhat exposed, the former eventually retreating to the safety of his
castle at Spynie.[104] Southwards into Angus and Perthshire, committed support
remained sporadic and invariably restricted to individuals who could field little
in the way of substantial manpower. For example, the party that landed in the
North-East with Aboyne in early June 1639 included the earl of Tullibardine but
virtually no common soldiery.[105] Meanwhile, the Royalist James, Lord Ogilvy,
was able to do little in the First Bishops' War other than write to Hamilton and

99 Gordon, *Britane's Distemper*, 20; Gordon, *History of Scots Affairs*, II, 261; Spalding, *Memorialls*,
    I, 205.
100 NAS, GD 406/1/756 (Huntly to Hamilton, 25 February [1639]).
101 Spalding, *Memorialls*, I, 169, 205; Gordon and Gordon, *Genealogical History*, 496; HMC,
    Eleventh Report, Appendix, part VI, *The Manuscripts of the Duke of Hamilton* (London, 1887),
    108 (Rothes to Hamilton, 27 June 1639).
102 NAS, GD 406/1/441 (Copies of letters from Hamilton to Caithness and Berriedale, 20
    September 1638); NAS, GD 406/1/462 (Huntly to Hamilton, 10 October 1638); NAS, GD
    406/1/8224, (Huntly to [Hamilton], 7 December [1638]); NAS, GD 406/1/412 (Huntly to
    Hamilton, 18 January [1639]); NAS, GD 406/1/786 (Berriedale to Huntly, 9 February 1639);
    NAS, GD 406/1/787 (Berriedale to Huntly, 23 February 1639); NLS, Wodrow Manuscripts,
    Wod.Qu.CVI (Master of Berriedale to Berriedale, [1638]); Gordon and Gordon, *Genealogical
    History*, 490.
103 NAS, GD 406/1/8224 (Huntly to [Hamilton], 7 December [1638]).
104 NAS, GD 406/1/1794 (Huntly to [Hamilton], 16 October [1638]); Spalding, *Memorialls*, I,
    142–143.
105 Spalding, *Memorialls*, I, 199; Row, *History of the Kirk*, 518; *Historical Notices of St Anthony's
    Monastery, Leith and Rehearsal of Events which occurred in the North of Scotland from 1635
    to 1645 in Relation to the National Covenant*, ed. C. Rogers (London, 1877), 47; NAS GD
    248/46/2/64 (Innes to Ballindalloch, younger, 8 June 1639).

the king about the need for swift assistance to be sent to Aberdeen.[106] The Angus Royalists, like others elsewhere, lacked the necessary arms to be able to counter covenanting operations.[107]

Concerning the intellectual case for Royalism, the stand taken by the Aberdeen Doctors had been of some use in bolstering the king's position and making it known that not all Scots were in total agreement with the Covenanters. This group comprised Robert Baron, Alexander Scroggie, William Leslie, James Sibbald and Alexander Ross, all academics, under the leadership of John Forbes of Corse, son of Patrick Forbes, late bishop of Aberdeen. In their 'paper war of pamphlets' they expanded on the argument previously made by Bishop Forbes himself (with regard to the Five Articles of Perth) that recent liturgical innovations concerned minor details of worship consisting of matters indifferent. Such elements were not essential to the reformed Church, but at the same time there existed no reason to outlaw their use. The key was that the lawful prince, Charles I, had championed what were deemed to be minor innovations, and as such the Doctors were prepared to bolster his position, oppose the idea of resistance by force of arms, and seek, for the good of the kingdom and, more widely, the Protestant faith, to get the Covenanters to back down. They adopted a similar argument regarding Episcopalianism and countered the Covenanting claim that bishops had been one of the intended targets in the Negative Confession. They further advocated the need for Protestants to be united in the theological essentials so that the battle could be won against the real enemy – Roman Catholicism.[108]

However, there was a limit to the extent to which they could actively maintain their position, particularly in the face of increasing intimidation from local Covenanters. In fact, on at least a couple of occasions in 1638, the leader, Forbes of Corse, showed definite signs of wavering. He felt obliged, for example, to retract an initial version of his tract *A Peaceable Warning to the Subjects in Scotland* due to complaints from certain Covenanters that some of

106 NAS, GD 406/1/1056 (Ogilvy to Hamilton, 23 May 1639); NAS, GD 406/1/781 (Ogilvy to Charles I, 24 May 1639); NAS, GD 406/1/782 (Ogilvy to Hamilton, 26 May 1639). Lord Ogilvy's father, James, first earl of Airlie had gone south to serve in the king's army by this time. See W. Wilson, *The House of Airlie*, 2 vols (London, 1924), I, 210.

107 NAS GD 406/1/780 (Ogilvy (first earl of Airlie from April 1639) to Hamilton, 10 March 1639). Much of the Lowland nobility had become demilitarised by this time. See Goodare, 'Nobility and the Absolutist State', 180.

108 Spalding, *Memorialls*, I, 95–97; Stevenson, *Scottish Revolution*, 102; Stevenson, *King's College*, 80, 106–107; Macinnes, *British Revolution*, 117. For more on the life and work of Bishop Patrick Forbes, see Stevenson, *King's College*, 61–93; W.G.S. Snow, *The Times, Life and Thought of Patrick Forbes, Bishop of Aberdeen, 1618–1635* (London, 1952).

the contents were slanderous.[109] And according to Huntly, Corse came very close to subscribing the National Covenant at the same time as William Guild did.[110] He and the other Doctors also showed little willingness to attend the 1638 General Assembly, supplicating on one occasion that 'we can doe lit[t]le or no good, and may receave much evill'.[111] Indeed, despite the urgings of the king that they should attend, the Presbytery of Aberdeen was eventually represented by the Covenanters Guild, Lindsay and Lundie.[112] The Doctors also showed little desire to stand their ground in Aberdeen on the approach of the Covenanting army in March 1639. For his part Forbes of Corse elected to hide out in Buchan until danger had passed.[113] By comparison, the Covenanting intelligentsia, irrespective of whether they won the intellectual case or not, remained much more resolute and willing to advocate decisive action. In them the Doctors were seeking to persuade people who were simply not open to argument.[114] True, the Doctors were amongst the few who remained prepared to take any kind of outspoken stand, but it was one that soon evaporated when pressure started to mount. It is important not to overplay their significance.

The King's Covenant, although designed to bolster and shore up the Royalist cause, actually caused damage in its own right. Through his concessions Charles I actually ended up undermining the stance taken by the Aberdeen Doctors and others on his behalf. The king's reassertion of the Negative Confession would also have done little to inspire confidence and bolster morale among Catholics in the North-East, many of whom made up a sizeable proportion of Huntly's followers. A degree of Royalist demoralisation may well have been the result, something that the cold, aloof Huntly would have found hard to combat.[115]

The Gordon lords certainly remained aware of the odds ranged against them, both within and outwith the North-East. Given the roll-call of individuals and families adhering to the National Covenant it is hardly surprising that in March 1639 Huntly wrote to Hamilton:

109 NAS, GD 406/1/416 (Forbes of Corse to Huntly, 4 May 1638); NAS, GD 406/1/639 (Forbes of Corse to Huntly, 20 July 1638); NAS, GD 406/1/432 (Forbes of Corse to Burnet of Leys, 3 August 1638); NAS, GD 406/1/434 (Forbes of Corse to Huntly, 7 August 1638).

110 NAS, GD 406/1/764 (Huntly to Hamilton, 7 August [1638]).

111 NAS, GD 406/1/446 (Supplication of the ministers and professors of Aberdeen to Huntly, 5 October 1638).

112 NAS, GD 406/1/457 (Forbes of Corse to Huntly, 6 November 1638).

113 Spalding, *Memorialls*, I, 151; Aberdeen University Special Collections, MS 635, A Diary or Spritiwall Exercises Written by Dr John Forbes of Corse and Copied from his Own Manuscript. Anno Dom 1687 and 1690, 173.

114 Ogilvie, *The Aberdeen Doctors and the National Covenant*, 11; Stewart, 'The "Aberdeen Doctors"', 42.

115 Robertson, 'The House of Huntly and the First Bishops' War', 4.

George Gordon, sixth earl and first marquess of Huntly (1562–1636), and his wife, Henrietta Stewart
.1642). Sketched by Charles Fitzpatrick Sharpe after an original painting by George Jamesone.
ottish National Portrait Gallery.

George Gordon, second marquess of Huntly (c.1590–1649). By George Jamesone. Reproduced with the permission of the Trustees of the Goodwood Collection.

ne Campbell, second marchioness of Huntly (d.1638). By George Jamesone. Reproduced with the permission
the Trustees of the Goodwood Collection.

George Gordon, second marquess of Huntly (c.1590–1649). By Anthony van Dyck and Studio. Reproduced with the permission of the Trustees of the 9th Duke of Buccleuch's Chattels Fund.

George, lord Gordon (d.1645). Attributed to David Scougall. In the collection of Lennoxlove House Limited, Haddington © 2010.

Right. George Gordon, fourth marquess of Huntly and first duke of Gordon, by Schuneman. Collection unknown, image recorded in Scottish National Portrait Gallery reference section.

Below. Bog o' Gight (Gordon Castle). By John Slezar. First published in the 1719 edition of his *Theatrum Scotiae* in which it was mistakenly referred to as 'The Castle of Inverero'. Reproduced by permission of the Trustees of the National Library of Scotland.

Strathbogie Castle (now known as Huntly Castle). Photograph by Edda Frankot.

The inscriptions of George Gordon, first marquess of Huntly, and his wife, Henrietta Stewart, as they appear on the south façade of Strathbogie Castle (Huntly Castle). Photograph by Edda Frankot.

Right. The elaborate frontispiece at Strathbogie Castle (Huntly Castle). Photograph by Edda Frankot.

Below. One of the fireplaces at Strathbogie Castle (Huntly Castle). The medallion portraits depict George Gordon, first marquess of Huntly, and his wife, Henrietta Stewart. Photograph by Edda Frankot.

It wilbe a hard game for us to play, against so many adversaryes, nor (in my opinion) will they come but so strong as not to be resisted heere, and in that case his majesty may endanger the loss of his partye heere.[116]

Just under a month earlier he had alerted Hamilton of the need for Royalist supporters in Angus and the Mearns to try to prevent any substantial forces marching against him from the South.[117] Little seems to have been done. Indeed, it is probable that in late March Huntly's army was outnumbered by at least two to one.[118] Given all of this, the timely arrival of the seaborne force under the command of Hamilton was imperative. It never came, thus leaving Gordon of Ruthven to lament that, had additional forces been made available, Huntly could have 'made himself maister of all the North'.[119] Regardless of the outcome, Huntly cannot be faulted for the manner in which he energetically sought to bolster the king's position, both through promotion of the King's Covenant and through maintaining regular correspondence with key individuals, notably the marquess of Hamilton.[120] However, as events proved, such correspondence in itself was no guarantee of success, nor could it necessarily guarantee widespread support. The earl of Rothes noted how most of the northern nobility subscribed to the National Covenant despite individually having received letters from Huntly entreating them not to.[121]That said, and despite all the problems, north-east Scotland arguably remained the one area where the Royalists managed to make a credible stand. It was a front where Hamilton and the king should have looked to develop more energetically. This was particularly the case from May 1639 when Hamilton's fleet in the Firth of Forth remained within easy sailing distance of the Royalist lairds of the North-East, and of the army of Lord Aboyne. A contemporary chronicler noted that:

In all probability, if Duke Hamilton had had orders to land in that harbour [Aberdeen], fortify the town, and join the Gordons in that northern country, where without doubt, the most considerable strength of the Kingdom lies, he would have given the Covenanters a great deal of

---

116 NAS, GD 406/1/762 (Huntly to [Hamilton], 17 March 1639).
117 NAS, GD 406/1/756 (Huntly to Hamilton, 25 February [1639]).
118 Robertson, 'The House of Huntly and the First Bishops' War', 4–5.
119 Gordon, *Britane's Distemper*, 15.
120 Scally, 'The Political Career of James, Third Marquis and Duke of Hamilton', 256. Indeed, the extent of Huntly's correspondence was made clear in a letter to Hamilton of July 1638. In it Huntly stated that he had sent letters to individuals in Caithness, Sutherland, Inverness, Ross, Moray, Banff and Aberdeen. See NAS, GD 406/1/426 (Huntly to Hamilton, 13 July 1638).
121 Leslie, *Relation of Proceedings*, 105–106. All in all, evidence suggests that it is too simplistic to say that northern Scotland was wholly conservative during the entirety of the sixteenth and seventeenth centuries.

uneasiness; and by that powerful diversion had obliged them to keep in the heart of the kingdom, the army which Lesly marched to the Borders.[122]

The Covenanting minister Robert Baillie also remained well aware of the danger presented by the Gordons and their supporters in the North.[123]

COMPLETING THE REVOLUTION

Following the Pacification of Berwick, the Covenanters looked to consolidate and proceed with the Revolution. In response the king planned for another military campaign and, in order to secure English funding, convened what became known as the Short Parliament in April 1640. Although this body failed to vote him the required supply, Charles sought to make war on the Covenanters anyway, thus bringing about the Second Bishops' War – a short, sharp conflict which resulted in humiliating defeat for the Royalist forces and the Scottish occupation of northern England. The king was then forced into calling another English Parliament (The Long Parliament) in order to obtain money to pay off the Scots. This provided English malcontents with a platform from which to follow the Covenanting example and mount a challenge to his prerogative rule, a process that would eventually result in the outbreak of civil war in England. Meanwhile, back in Scotland the Covenanters had, by July 1640, consolidated their grip and had reconstituted their centralised co-ordinating committee for the parliamentary peers, lairds and burgesses as the Committee of Estates. They had also abolished the clerical estate from Parliament, increased the voting power of the lairds, made the signing of the National Covenant compulsory for all those seeking public office, and succeeded in instituting a triennial Act ordaining the holding of regular Parliaments.[124]

Little could be mounted in the way of resistance by this stage. For the Gordons of Huntly the strains of the First Bishops' War had evidently taken their toll, with the result that the family remained relatively muted for the remainder of the Covenanting Revolution. Huntly was present at the Scottish Parliament that commenced in September 1639 and was one of the Lords of the Articles as well as part of a faction coordinated by John Stewart, first earl of Traquair, which

---

122 D.R. de Muscry, *The History of the Troubles of Great Britain*, trans. J. Ogilvie (London, 1735), 48.
123 *Letters and Journals of Robert Baillie*, I, 204–205 (Baillie to Spang, 28 September 1639).
124 J.R. Young, *The Scottish Parliament, 1639–1661. A Political and Constitutional Analysis* (Edinburgh, 1996), 20–24; Young, 'The Scottish Parliament and the Covenanting Movement', 164–184; J.R. Young, 'The Scottish Parliament and the Covenanting Heritage of Constitutional Reform', in Macinnes and Ohlmeyer (eds), *The Stuart Kingdoms in the Seventeenth Century*, 228; Macinnes, *British Revolution*, 125–141; Brown and Mann, 'Parliament and Politics in Scotland', 22; J. Scally, 'The Rise and Fall of the Covenanter Parliaments, 1639–51', in Brown and Mann (eds), *Parliament and Politics in Scotland*, 140.

sought to halt the revolutionary process and defend the prerogative of the king.[125] But over the course of 1640, and for much of 1641, Huntly removed himself to London, while in the North-East any hopes that the Gordons would rise again remained unfulfilled.[126] Meanwhile, during the course of 1640, Covenanting armies managed to overawe those areas that remained Royalist in sympathy, the North-East being thoroughly subdued by Colonel Robert Monro over the summer months, and the castle of Strathbogie occupied.[127]

It was not until late August 1641 that Huntly returned to Scotland, travelling to Edinburgh to attend the king at the Parliament of that year. However, due to the fact that he had not subscribed the National Covenant, he found himself amongst those unable to sit.[128] The king, in an attempt to inculcate a Royalist foothold in Parliament, had consented to the idea of some of his supporters (a group that can be termed the 'pragmatic Royalists') subscribing to the Covenant, but this gained him little ground. Moreover, the political fallout following a reported attempted assassination of Hamilton and Argyll known as 'The Incident', left him increasingly compromised, and pushed the pragmatic Royalists closer to the Covenanters. In addition, wavering moderate Covenanters such as Montrose, who were concerned at the direction the Revolution was taking, had by this time been outmanoeuvred and sidelined by the 'Radical Mainstream' led by Argyll. With this as the backdrop, the Scottish Estates thus gained a commitment from Charles that state officials, including privy councillors, would thereafter only be chosen with their consent.[129] As a result Charles failed get things his own way when he put forward his nominations for membership of the Privy Council. Indeed, Huntly found himself amongst seven other Royalist nobles who were denied posts as councillors.[130] The Royalist cause now dormant in Scotland, and with news of rebellion in Ireland, Charles had little option but to return to England. Huntly, meanwhile, made the journey home to his own estates, finally arriving in Strathbogie on 7 January 1642.[131]

His decision to remain in London for so long in 1640 and 1641 is an intriguing one and little evidence survives to attest to what he did during this period or why he went there in the first place. John Spalding had little else to say other

---

125 *Aberdeen Council Letters*, ed. L.B. Taylor, 4 vols (London, 1942–54), II, 135 (Jaffray to [New] Aberdeen Council, 2 September 1639); J. Balfour, *Historical Works*, ed. J. Haig, 4 vols (London, 1824–25), II, 360; *APS, 1625–1641*, 249–252.

126 Huntly left Edinburgh for London on 26 November 1639. See Spalding, *Memorialls*, I, 240.

127 Gordon, *History of Scots Affairs*, III, 210–211.

128 Spalding, *Memorialls*, II, 64.

129 Macinnes, *British Revolution*, 136–141.

130 *RPCS, 1638–43*, 480–481; *Historical Works of Sir James Balfour*, III, 66; Young, *Scottish Parliament*, 39–40

131 Spalding, *Memorialls*, II, 86–91.

than that Huntly went south to be with the king, Huntly's two eldest sons, Lords Gordon and Aboyne, being there already.[132] Gordon of Rothiemay had nothing to add to this and Gordon of Ruthven had nothing to say on the matter whatsoever.[133] A number of explanations could be suggested. Huntly may have been seeking to be of use in some kind of advisory capacity and his attendance at Court may have been suggested by the king to provide counsel and to act as a contact to certain individuals in Scotland. That said, there remains little evidence of this outside of a letter of July 1640, in which Huntly entreated Robert Maxwell, first earl of Nithsdale, to remain steadfast in the face of the siege of his castle of Caerlaverock, and some letters to Thomas Hamilton, second earl of Haddington, seeking refutation of rumours that the latter had become a staunch Covenanter.[134]

Probably much more pertinent as a reason was the need for Huntly to remove himself to England to escape the attention of his creditors. While there, he could obtain a royal warrant for protection from imprisonment, something that he had found increasingly hard to secure in Scotland.[135] Connected to this, he may also have sought a degree of protection from the increasingly overbearing attentions of his brother-in-law, Argyll, a man whose acquisitiveness was perhaps only matched by his zeal for the National Covenant, and who by then had designs on enhancing his own power at the expense of the House of Huntly.

Having said all this, being present at Court with all its cliques and intrigues was sometimes not the safest option either, particularly given the political instability of the time. Throughout 1639 and 1640 many covert dealings were afoot in relation to foreign affairs. In particular, the king and many at Court had grave suspicions that the Covenanters were involved in plotting with the French, an idea that Spanish agents were keen to encourage.[136] Such suspicions reached their height some days prior to the commencement of the Short Parliament when four Covenanting commissioners were detained in connection with a draft letter, apparently intended for the French court, which sought to justify their recourse to arms against the king. The leading commissioner, John Campbell, Lord Loudoun (a kinsman of Argyll), was imprisoned for two months in the

---

132 *Ibid.*, I, 240.

133 Gordon, *History of Scots Affairs*, III, 159; Gordon, *Britane's Distemper*, 29–35.

134 Fraser, *Book of Carlaverock*, II, 134 (Huntly to Nithsdale, 19 July [1640]); Fraser, *Earls of Haddington*, II, 180, 183–184 (Huntly to Haddington, 2 March 1640), (Huntly to Haddington, 27 March [1640]), (Huntly to Haddington, 27 May 1640). Haddington replied stressing that the only reason he had signed the National Covenant was that it had been a requirement for all privy councillors and that the king himself had sanctioned it. See Fraser, *Earls of Haddington*, II, 181 (Haddington to Huntly, 16 March 1640).

135 *RPCS, 1638–43*, 122.

136 Hibbard, *Charles I and the Popish Plot*, 113–164.

Tower of London as a result.[137] Even Huntly was not above suspicion, with the result that he saw fit to publish his reply to the Covenanters of the previous year in which he had refused to join them in opposing Charles I.

With Huntly in London, the Royalist strongholds had been easier prey for the Covenanting forces of Monro. Working in conjunction with the earl Marischal, he had little trouble in cowing the Royalist families of the area.[138] Marischal also managed to persuade Huntly's mother, Henrietta Stewart, to surrender the keys to Strathbogie and to make a payment of 'fyftie golden angellis' to Monro in lieu of a horse that the latter had requested. She resided in Bog of Gight at the time and seems to have offered no resistance to such requests, something that saved that particular residence and its outlying lands from any widespread plundering. The Gordon castle of Auchindoun also submitted with little trouble.[139] Meanwhile, Strathbogie Castle was occupied and the immediate Gordon hinterland was plundered for livestock, horses and meal. A number of trees were also cut down for the soldiers to build into huts for their own quartering. Perhaps most notable was the damage done to the unique Strathbogie frontispiece, the imagery, 'which looked somewhat popish and superstitiouse lycke', being hewn off by a James Wallace, one of Monro's captains of foot.[140]

FALLOUT AND CONSEQUENCES

Huntly's efforts on behalf of the king certainly did little to alleviate his state of indebtedness. On top of this, as the Covenanting Revolution progressed, little option remained open to him and his family other than to keep on borrowing. Over the latter half of 1639, for example, Huntly obtained loans totalling 3,000 merks Scots (£2,000 Scots) from a John Burdoune.[141] Furthermore, in January 1640, he and his two eldest sons borrowed a further 20,000 merks Scots (£13,333 Scots) from an Edinburgh burgess, John Rhind, and his son, David.[142] According to Argyll, by 1640 the family had gone on to run up debts totalling something

---

137 Macinnes, *British Revolution*, 132.

138 Spalding, *Memorialls*, I, 280–290, 293–296.

139 *Ibid.*, I, 297–300.

140 *Ibid.*, I, 297–299, 305; *CSPD, 1640–41*, 53 (Drummond to Hay, 12 September 1640); Gordon, *History of Scots Affairs*, III, 211. Wallace's action pre-empted (by a matter of days) an ordinance of the 1640 General Assembly that stipulated that all Catholic imagery should be destroyed. See *Records of the Kirk of Scotland containing the Acts and Proceedings of the General Assemblies, from the Year 1638 downwards, as authenticated by the Clerks of Assembly; with Notes and Historical Illustrations*, ed. A. Peterkin (Edinburgh, 1843), 279.

141 *APS, 1648– 60*, 325.

142 NAS, GD 44/14/10/1. This source does not actually stipulate if the figure was in sterling or Scots. Given that this is a Scottish source, it has been assumed that the denomination referred to was Scots.

in the region of one million merks Scots (£666,667 Scots).[143] On top of this, from mid-1639 Huntly also began to find himself increasingly under pressure from past creditors.[144] One of his leading creditors was the wealthy merchant and financier to the Covenanting cause, William Dick of Braid, a man who was owed 72,000 merks Scots (£48,000 Scots) by 1640.[145] Furthermore, in October 1641 Huntly even found himself pursued by a kinsman, Sir James Gordon of Lesmore, who was owed 26,000 merks Scots (£17,333 Scots) – a sure sign that as far as money was concerned, blood ties within the extended Gordon family apparently counted for little.[146] A month later he was also being pursued by Gilbert Kirkwood of Pilrig for a loan of £35,526 Scots dating from August 1630 (as well as the £3,052 Scots per annum interest due on it).[147] With this worsening situation came the need to try either to save money or to raise it elsewhere. For example, in November 1639, just prior to leaving for London, Huntly gave up his Edinburgh townhouse on the Canongate and discharged all of the associated servants.[148] In addition, it is recorded that, around the time of the 1639 Parliament, Huntly sold his Moray lands of Plewlands, Ogston and Belormy to Sir Robert Gordon, lands that in 1642 were amalgamated to create the barony of Gordonstoun.[149]

This was nothing compared to the actions of Huntly's brother-in-law, Argyll, during this period. The finances of the former being in the state they were, it was agreed that Argyll would become chief cautioner for the tochers (dowries) required for the marriages of Huntly's three eldest daughters. The amounts concerned were reportedly 40,000 merks Scots (£26,667 Scots) for the marriage of Lady Ann Gordon to James, Lord Drummond (later third earl of Perth), another 40,000 merks Scots for the marriage of Lady Henrietta Gordon to George, Lord Seton (eldest son of the third earl of Winton), and 30,000

---

143 Anon., *The Last Proceedings of the Parliament in Scotland, against the Marquesse of Argyle. Together, with the speech and defence of the said Marquesse, in vindication of himself from the aspersions of his having a hand in the deaths of His late Majesty, James Duke Hamilton, Marquesse Huntley, Marquesse of Montros. And of his dealing with the English after Worcester Fight* (London, 1661). This figure worked out at around £55,560 sterling (£666,720 Scots). See J. Willcock, *The Great Marquess: Life and Times of Archibald, Eighth Earl, and First (and only) Marquess of Argyll (1607–1661)* (Edinburgh and London, 1903), 226.

144 *RPCS, 1638–43*, 122.

145 NAS, GD 44/14/7/6. In 1639 Dick of Braid reportedly lent £130,000 Scots to help fund the Covenanting cause. See M. Lynch, 'The Scottish Early Modern Burgh', in Wormald (ed.), *Scotland Revisited*, 73.

146 *Records of the Sheriff Court of Aberdeenshire*, II, 484. Given that this is a Scottish source, it has been assumed that the denomination referred to was Scots.

147 *Ibid.*, II, 485. See the previous footnote regarding the monetary denomination.

148 Spalding, *Memorialls*, I, 240.

149 Gordon and Gordon, *Genealogical History*, 497, 510; Fraser, *Sutherland Book*, I, 202; *RGSS, 1634–51*, 428.

merks Scots (£20,000 Scots) for the marriage of Lady Jean Gordon to Thomas, second earl of Haddington. David Carnegie, first earl of Southesk, was a fellow cautioner for the Drummond match.[150] The first two marriages took place in late 1639 just prior to Huntly's departure for London, and the third in January 1640.[151] Indeed, Argyll, with the help of his half-brother James Campbell, Lord Kintyre, and with the full blessing of Huntly, took care of all negotiations and arrangements for the Haddington match – such was his growing influence over the family.[152] In return for Argyll's and Southesk's involvement as cautioners it was stipulated that Huntly would wadset (mortgage) the Highland lordships of Badenoch and Lochaber to them.[153] In effect, this meant that Huntly would become indebted to Argyll and Southesk and had granted away the said lands until everything could be repaid.

With this in mind, a real Machiavellian streak became apparent in Argyll with regard to his activities in Badenoch and Lochaber in 1640. In June of that year the Committee of Estates provided him with a commission to campaign in Atholl, the Braes of Angus, the Braes of Mar, Badenoch, Lochaber and Rannoch, ostensibly to subdue all those not yet well affected towards the National Covenant. This was duly undertaken with much zeal and resulted in widespread plundering, destruction and in the burning of two Royalist strongholds, the castle of the Angus Ogilvys at Forther, and the house of MacDonald of Keppoch. The chief Ogilvy seat at Airlie was also ransacked and its defences were reduced.[154] But what the commission in effect allowed Argyll to do was to pursue what was deemed to be the public good while at the same time advancing his own private interests. This remained particularly true for Badenoch and Lochaber where he could devastate the land and cause rents to fall, thus increasing the financial

---

150 W. Fraser, *History of the Carnegies, Earls of Southesk, and their Kindred*, 2 vols (Edinburgh, 1867), I, 142.

151 Spalding, *Memorialls*, I, 240, 245; *Aberdeen Council Letters*, II, 165–166 (Jaffray to [the Provost of Aberdeen], 17 January 1640). Although Spalding did not stipulate if the figures were in sterling or Scots, it has been assumed that the denomination being referred to was Scots.

152 Fraser, *Earls of Haddington*, II, 173–176, 179 (Argyll to Haddington, 28 November [1639]), (Kintyre to Haddington, 13 December [1639]), (Argyll to Haddington, 13 December [1639]), (Argyll to Haddington, 25 December [1639]), (Huntly to Haddington, 28 January [1640]); WSRO, The Montrose Letters, Goodwood/1431/14 (Huntly to Kintyre, 28 December [1639]); WSRO, Goodwood/1431/16 (Huntly to Argyll, 13 January [1640]).

153 NAS, Breadalbane Collection, GD 112/39/79/10 (Argyll to Campbell of Glenfalloch, 29 May 1640; Spalding, *Memorialls*, I, 240; Gordon, *History of Scots Affairs*, III, 163. Although Spalding and Rothiemay make no mention of Southesk's involvement, it is clear from the *Register of the Great Seal* that he was indeed a cautioner for the Drummond tocher and did receive rights in Badenoch and Lochaber. See *RGSS, 1634–51*, 350–351.

154 NAS, GD 406/1/1143 (Lord Ogilvy to Charles I, 1 August 1640); NLS, Campbell of Inverawe Papers, MS 1672, ff. 4–8; Balfour, *Historical Works*, II, 380; Guthry, *Memoirs*, 76; Spalding, *Memorialls*, I, 271, 291–292; Stevenson, *Scottish Revolution*, 197.

distress of the House of Huntly and, through that, decreasing the likelihood of Huntly being able to pay off his debts.[155] Furthermore, as Gordon of Rothiemay noted, Argyll could also look to increase his influence in the area by exploiting the poor relations that existed between the House of Huntly and Clan Cameron; 'therfor he worought upon ther humors, and by them first worm'd himselfe into thes places'.[156]

The extent to which Huntly initially felt beholden to Argyll in late-1639 is uncertain. Surviving personal correspondence between the two is scanty, but the contents of one particular letter from late December 1639 would seem to suggest that Huntly wanted to portray himself as more sympathetic to some of the aims of the National Covenant than he had in the past. In it Huntly intimated:

> For anything I know, our countrey affaires will goe according to our owne carriages in the prosecution of them, for certainlye the King hath no intention to corrupt our religion, nor infringe our libertyss, and therefore if our demandes shall proue to be moderate on the one side I am confident that his Ma[jes]tie wilbe gracious on the other, whiche (in my opinion) is the most secure way for us towards both satisfaction and peace.[157]

Of course with such moderate words Huntly may just have been seeking to avoid antagonising his brother-in-law in any way. He would have been aware of the power that Argyll held over him and so any apparent friendliness was almost certainly little more than a front.

Meanwhile, Argyll certainly made a lasting impression on his nephew, George, Lord Gordon. In April 1641 he persuaded him to subscribe the National Covenant, no doubt convincing him that it would be the best course for securing the future wellbeing of the House of Huntly. Lord Gordon duly gave assurances of his future loyalty to both the Committee of the General Assembly and the Committee of Estates before travelling back to the North-East to gain subscriptions from his supporters there.[158] In such a manner, Argyll had not only looked to gain some hold of the lordships of Badenoch and Lochaber during this period, he had also intended to increase his influence within the House of Huntly in a much more fundamental manner through adopting the role of the 'caring' uncle.

As it turned out, divisions within the House of Huntly were not necessarily all of Argyll's making. In early 1641 Huntly's third son, Lewis, absconded to the

155 Macinnes, *Clanship, Commerce and the House of Stuart*, 97.
156 Gordon, *History of Scots Affairs*, III, 163.
157 WSRO, Goodwood/1431/15 (Huntly to Argyll, 28 December [1639]).
158 Spalding, *Memorialls*, II, 3, 12–13.

Netherlands following an argument with his father and, as Spalding related, 'unwyslie and unhappellie convoyit privatlie with him his fatheris haill jewellis in ane littill cabinet'.[159] Indeed, as has been seen, such division remained reflective of the developing situation within the extended family at the time. The actions of James Gordon of Lesmore in his pursuit of loans certainly seemed to indicate that individual interests could sometimes take precedence over the wider interest of the House of Huntly. The earl of Sutherland's enthusiastic adherence to the National Covenant also stood in stark contrast to the Royalism of the second marquess of Huntly. Despite some efforts by Sir Robert Gordon to ensure Sutherland's loyalty to the House of Huntly, the 'Gordon conglomerate' was evidently no longer the united powerhouse it once had been.[160] On top of this the wider alliance that had once encompassed the House of Errol now also lay in tatters. In its place came a new level of bitterness between the two households, something that was apparent in the 1639 Parliament when a complaint was lodged on behalf of the young earl of Errol that Huntly's followers had plundered his town house in Turriff.[161] It was certainly all a far cry from 1594 when the Hays had stood shoulder to shoulder with the Gordons on the eve of the Battle of Glenlivet.

CONCLUSION

The House of Huntly had an important role to play during the Scottish Revolution, particularly so in the build-up to, and during the First Bishops' War. But for a number of reasons the family was not successful in opposing the Covenanters in north-east Scotland at that time. Factors such as the inexperience of Huntly's men and the indefensibility of Aberdeen left the Gordons in a poor position from the start. Moreover, for most of the war, leaders such as Huntly and Royalist lairds lacked a suitable remit to allow them to assert themselves to their fullest capacity. Compounding this was the fact that the marquess of Hamilton and the king failed to provide a strong consistent lead as to how they wanted the Covenanters to be dealt with – a prime illustration of this being the decision to open peace negotiations with the Covenanters on the border at precisely the same time that Aboyne was seeking to defend the approach to Aberdeen. In addition, Royalist operations at a local level were bedevilled by the lack of a fully effective command structure.

159 *Ibid.*, II, 6.
160 Around the year 1620 Sir Robert Gordon had written a letter of advice to his nephew, the young earl of Sutherland, advising him, amongst other things, to follow Huntly as his chief. He also added 'let a Gordone's querrell be your own, so farr as he hath right and equitie on his syde'. See Fraser, *Sutherland Book*, II, 358. Evidently, when it came to the National Covenant, Sutherland felt that Huntly was no longer on the right side.
161 Spalding, *Memorialls*, II, 229.

Overriding all of this was the fact that the Gordons were eventually simply outnumbered in the North-East. The king did enjoy significant support there, mainly in the Gordon heartlands and to a certain extent in Aberdeen, but the Covenanters secured widespread support too. On top of this, when also taking into account the situation west of the Spey and south of the Dee, it can be seen that the scales definitely tipped in favour of the latter. Meanwhile, what Royalist support there was was often half-hearted, particularly in areas such as the Mearns and Angus where it was vital that well-affected nobles do their best to oppose Covenanting forces that were looking to march northwards against Huntly. Similarly, while the Aberdeen Doctors did initially take an intellectual stand in favour of the king, they proved very reluctant to stand by their convictions when the pressure started to mount. The arrival of the promised seaborne force under the command of Hamilton was seen as essential. It never arrived, and the North-East remained an underdeveloped front despite the fact that, all other problems aside, it remained the one area where local Royalists made any kind of credible stand.

From this point onwards the Gordon lords remained limited in what they could do for the king. Huntly's time in London did provide him with some scope to serve Charles in an advisory capacity, but on the whole he had probably gone there to escape his creditors, and to a certain extent, the attentions of his acquisitive brother-in-law, Argyll. Meanwhile, in the North-East, much of Huntly's land was left open to the ravages of the Covenanting army of Monro. All this did little to help the already precarious financial situation of the household. Indeed, Huntly's financial embarrassment afforded the earl of Argyll the opportunity to exert his influence over the family by acting as a cautioner for the tochers of Huntly's three eldest daughters. Through that, he then managed to secure for himself a share of Huntly's wadsetted Highland lordships of Badenoch and Lochaber. All in all it had been a devastating period for the House of Huntly and one from which it would require much time to recover.

FIVE

The Wars of the Stuart Kingdoms, 1642–1660

INTRODUCTION

By 1642 the revolutionary process in Scotland had gone on to act like a trigger, providing an incendiary example to the discontented in the other two Stuart kingdoms, Ireland and England. The series of wars that erupted across these kingdoms as a result had profound implications for their overall political framework, and instigated a process that eventually saw the execution of Charles I, the rise of the Cromwellian regime, and the dominance of what can be called the 'Gothic' dynamic within British and Irish politics – that is to say, a situation where English interests came to dominate, whether military, political, confessional or commercial.[1] Indeed, it could perhaps be argued that during the course of the 1650s this 'Gothic' ideal morphed into something much more exclusive – a Cromwellian dynamic, at once dictatorial, godly and self-righteous. During this process not only did the Royalist cause become eclipsed, but also that of the Covenanters, a situation that resulted in the Gordons of Huntly twice being on the losing side – firstly as supporters of Charles I and secondly as part of the Scottish patriotic accommodation designed to oppose Cromwell on behalf of Charles II. As such, the Gordons of Huntly became just as embroiled in the affairs of the time as they had been during the Covenanting Revolution, once again at great cost to their overall position.

WAR AND PEACE

Between 1640 and 1642 things had moved fast in the three Stuart kingdoms. The Covenanting military campaign in England did much to facilitate a situation whereby English malcontents had felt ever more confident in airing their grievances regarding the prerogative rule of the king. From there the situation had

---

1 Allan Macinnes has identified three other main formulations within the Stuart kingdoms during the period: the Britannic, the Scottish and the Irish. The first encompassed the imperial pretensions of the Stuart monarchs, the second the confederal approach of the Covenanters, the third the more associative ideas encapsulated in what would become the Irish confederacy. See, Macinnes, *British Revolution*, 8–24.

steadily deteriorated and in October 1642 war broke out between Charles I and the English Parliament. On top of all this, in October 1641 Irish Catholics instigated rebellion in Ulster with a view to getting their own political and confessional grievances addressed. This quickly spread to other areas of the kingdom and brought about a need on the part of the Covenanters, the king and the English Parliament to respond. Indeed, in April 1642 an English-funded Scottish army was deployed to Ireland. The Irish Catholics, already hotly engaged with Protestant forces there, soon succeeded in co-ordinating their efforts following the formation of a confederacy, the supreme council of which was to be based in the Leinster town of Kilkenny. With this consolidation, bitter civil war looked set to continue for some time to come.[2]

Meanwhile, the situation in Scotland remained relatively peaceful. Indeed, for indebted nobles like Huntly there was some opportunity throughout 1642 and early 1643 to lead a quieter, less public life in an attempt to stabilise the position of their respective families. Gordon of Ruthven noted that, during this time, the marquess 'liued at home in a retyred way, as if he had beene carelesse how the world went'.[3] This requirement for stability and renewal was made all too plain in an agreement arrived at between Huntly and his two eldest sons during the first half of 1642. According to Spalding's account, the burden on the household was seen at the time to be 'grevous', particularly given that rents were no longer being received from the lordships of Badenoch and Lochaber. As such, it was decided that 'for the payment of his debt and provisioun of his barnes' Huntly should renounce his estate in favour of Lord Gordon, with the proviso that he would receive an annual sum of 10,000 merks Scots (£6,667 Scots) and would retain the use of Strathbogie Castle and the town house in Old Aberdeen. Lord Gordon was to maintain everything else. Lord Gordon was also to receive an annual sum of 6,000 merks Scots (£4,000 Scots), while his brother Aboyne was to have the annual sum of 5,000 merks Scots (£3,333 Scots).[4]

Having said this, it remains somewhat unclear as to how all this was to benefit the family in practice. It seems likely, though, that being particularly in favour

---

2 For more detail on these developments, see Russell, *Fall of the British Monarchies*, 90–524; A. Hughes, *The Causes of the English Civil War* (Basingstoke and London, 1991), 166–182; J. Adamson, *The Noble Revolt: the Overthrow of Charles I* (London, 2007); A. Clarke, *The Old English in Ireland, 1625–42* (paperback edn, Dublin, 2000), 125–234; M. Ó Siochrú, *Confederate Ireland, 1642–1649. A Constitutional and Political Analysis* (Dublin, 1999), 11–54; Canny, *Making Ireland British*, 461–550; R. Armstrong, *Protestant War. The 'British' of Ireland and the Wars of the Three Kingdoms* (Manchester and New York, 2005), 14–68; M. Bennett, *The Civil Wars in Britain and Ireland, 1638–1651* (Oxford, 1997), 69–141; Scott, *Politics and War*, 25–54; Macinnes, *British Revolution*, 133–148.

3 Gordon, *Britane's Distemper*, 47.

4 Spalding, *Memorialls*, II, 91, 207–208. Again, it has been assumed that Spalding was referring to merks Scots.

with the government, Lord Gordon may have felt strong enough to seek to take control of the situation. In this he may have retained the blessing of his uncle, Argyll. The continued closeness of the working relationship between the two certainly remained apparent in a letter of February 1643 in which Lord Gordon stated that he was busily collecting rents at Inverlochy for Argyll's interest as well as his own.[5] It is even possible that Argyll may well have been a driving force behind the whole design. In the end, though, Huntly did little to honour the agreement, thus rendering the whole matter somewhat academic. In practice he retained control of his remaining lands.[6]

Meanwhile, it seems that Huntly remained comfortable enough with the new Covenanting regime to be prepared to become involved in regional and local affairs. For example, in May 1642 he and Lord Gordon were to be found at a justice court in Elgin taking part in discussions over how best to deal with the disruption caused by bands of outlawed MacGregors. Moreover, in January 1643 Huntly was chosen to be chancellor of King's College, Aberdeen – the institution to which he had sent his fourth son, Charles, the previous month. He also continued to mediate in local disputes, notably in that between Gordon of Gight and his mother in July 1642.[7]

Further to retaining a peaceful lifestyle Huntly also sought to occupy himself in planting and building, something that he may have deemed quite necessary in light of the damage done by Monro's soldiers.[8] During a visit to Strathbogie in the summer of 1643, the priest Gilbert Blakhal, commented that:

> He [Huntly] was so much taken up with his newe buildings, from four hours in the morning until eight at night, standing by his masons, urging their diligences, and directing and judging their worke, that he had scarce tyme to eate or sleep, much less to wreat.[9]

All this would have done little to alleviate his financial burdens, a situation only compounded by the fact that past creditors continued to hound him. In February 1642 an Isobel Robertson, widow of Aberdeen burgess Henry Buchan, pursued a claim against him at the Sheriff Court regarding a loan of 21,000 merks Scots (£14,000 Scots) that dated from 1630.[10] Things got so bad that, by April 1643, Huntly had been outlawed for failing to pay some of his debts. These

---

5 Inveraray Castle Archives, bundle 7/143 (Lord Gordon to Argyll, 22 [February] 1643).

6 Spalding, *Memorialls*, II, 92.

7 *Ibid.*, II, 142, 175, 216, 252–253.

8 Gordon, *Britane's Distemper*, 47.

9 Blakhal, *Breiffe Narration*, 170.

10 *Records of the Sheriff Court of Aberdeenshire*, III, 4. It has been assumed that the figure was in merks Scots.

had apparently accrued from as early as 1617 and included, in one instance, money due to a London clothmaker named Avary Ridge. Moreover, upon his failure to repay the debts, Huntly's lands and goods were forfeited to the Crown, a situation that forced the king into making a show of gifting them to James Stewart, duke of Lennox and Richmond, an Anglo-Scottish Royalist, and a kinsman on Huntly's mother's side.[11] This may well have been a means of protecting the Gordon estates from the continuing machinations of Argyll as much as anything else.[12]

Huntly's position was more seriously compromised in mid-1643 when he and Aboyne were linked to a controversial Royalist plot in England. The revelations came following the capture of the earl of Antrim by the Covenanters in May. Antrim and his servants were questioned over the contents of a series of incriminating letters and the full scale of the plot was unearthed and publicised. Essentially, the key conspirators, Antrim, Nithsdale, Airlie, Aboyne and the earl of Newcastle, had hatched a plan that called for a pan-British and Irish solution to the king's problems. This involved the brokering of a truce between the Royalists and the Irish Confederates who would then unite their efforts with a view to defeating the Covenanting expeditionary force in Ulster. This accomplished, they would then invade Scotland and link up with prominent Royalist nobles there, among them Huntly and Aboyne. At the same time a separate force under Nithsdale and Newcastle would mount an invasion from the North of England, while along the Forth–Clyde axis, Hamilton and other Royalist-inclined individuals would rise up.[13]

The extent to which Aboyne was involved in the plot was certainly made apparent in the letters, two of which were addressed from him to Antrim.[14] Huntly's complicity remained less clear, his name only cropping up in a letter from Nithsdale to Antrim in a manner that did not specify whether he had been party to the plot.[15] He may well have had some knowledge of it, particularly given that he retained a keen interest in how the Civil War was progressing in England and knew that Aboyne had been in York with Antrim and others during this period.[16] In view of this, it is unfortunate that no correspondence

---

11 NAS, GD 44/55/1/34–35.

12 Huntly did benefit from the death of his mother, Henrietta Stewart, when he succeeded to the lands of the Bog of Gight previously granted to her in liferent. She died in France in September 1642. See Spalding, *Memorialls*, II, 185. As can be seen, however, this only went some way to relieving the overall burden.

13 Ohlmeyer, *Civil War and Restoration*, 117–119, 121–122.

14 BL, Add. 28937, f. 40 (Aboyne to Antrim, 3 May 1643), (Aboyne to Antrim, 8 May 1643).

15 *Ibid.*, (Nithsdale to Antrim, 8 May 1643).

16 Spalding, *Memorialls*, II, 234–235; *Miscellany of the Spalding Club*, I, 14 (Huntly to Straloch, 31 March [1643]).

appears to have survived between Huntly and Aboyne during the latter's time in England. If such had ever existed (and although it seems likely, there is no way of truly knowing), it would no doubt have proved very revealing in this matter.

Meanwhile, Huntly's actions following the exposure of the plot remain interesting. With suspicions falling on the king and queen over what was popularly being portrayed as a popish plot, he became one of those instructed to have a proclamation distributed and broadcast disclaiming royal involvement. But at the same time, over several days in early June, he also entered into a series of discussions with Montrose, Lord Ogilvy and a number of other Royalist-inclined lairds.[17] Robert Baillie remained in no doubt that this had involved anti-Covenanting plotting. He related that Montrose had persuaded Huntly and Ogilvy to subscribe a bond pledging to lend their support to a new Royalist campaign in Scotland. The earl Marischal, who had also been present, resolutely refused to follow suit, and went on to persuade Huntly into withdrawing his support as well. This, Baillie concluded, 'in the great providence of God, seems to have marred the designe'. But he did ruefully add that indebted nobles like Montrose, Huntly, Antrim, Nithsdale and the rest had much to gain from seeking disturbance in the kingdom and that 'publick commotions are their privat subsistance'.[18] In light of Huntly's financial situation at the time, this was perhaps a fair assessment. Whatever the overall motive, it certainly seems that from mid-1643 Huntly was once again beginning to consider the need to take action on behalf of the king. The affair also provided an indication of the vehemence with which Montrose was beginning to expound the Royalist cause.

At a Britannic level the Antrim Plot hastened moves between the Covenanters and the English Parliament to conclude negotiations for the formation of a confederative union for mutual defence.[19] This Solemn League and Covenant was approved by the two parties on 17 August, the first article of which enshrined a mutual commitment to preserve the true religion as expounded in the Church of Scotland, and reform religion in England and Ireland 'according to the Word of God, and the example of the best Reformed Churches'. It also required that they endeavour to engineer confessional unity across all three kingdoms. The third article called for the need to 'preserve the Rights and Privileges of the Parliaments', while at the same time defending the king's person and authority 'in the preservation and defence of the true Religion'.[20] Overall it was very much

---

17 Anon., *Declaration of the Lords of his Majesties Privie Councell and Commissioners for conserving the Articles of the Treatie: for the Information of his Majesties Good Subjects of this Kingdome* (Edinburgh, 1643); Spalding, *Memorialls*, II, 250–253.

18 *Letters and Journals of Robert Baillie*, II, 74. (Baillie to Spang, 26 July 1643).

19 Ohlmeyer, *Civil War and Restoration*, 123; Macinnes, *British Revolution*, 148–150.

20 Stevenson, *Scottish Revolution*, 285–286. The extracts are taken from *Scottish Historical Documents*, ed. G. Donaldson (corrected edn, Glasgow, 1974), 208–209.

a Covenanting agenda and indicated that the Scots were controlling the political agenda at this stage.[21] Alongside this came an accompanying agreement for the raising of a Scottish army of 20,000 men for the purpose of intervening in the English Civil War on the side of the Parliamentarians.[22]

All this had profound implications for the House of Huntly. Aboyne found himself outlawed for his part in the Antrim Plot and by December 1643 was to be found back at the royal court in Oxford.[23] Meanwhile, Lord Gordon – no doubt with Argyll's advice – decided to subscribe the Solemn League and Covenant, and along with the earl Marischal became actively involved in raising men for the Scottish army.[24] This was facilitated by the formal division of Banff-shire, Aberdeenshire and the Mearns between the two nobles, something that left Marischal unsatisfied with his share of territory, and Lord Forbes highly offended that he had been passed over altogether.[25] In effect, Lord Gordon became one of the two leading Covenanters in the North-East, a situation that according to Gordon of Ruthven had been facilitated by his overall desire to preserve the position of his family.[26]

But Huntly remained incensed at the action of his eldest son and would have little to do with him, despite the mediations of the likes of Robert Gordon of Straloch and Alexander Irvine of Drum. As Spalding noted, 'it wes this last covenant [the Solemn League] the Marques wes offendit at, quilk his sone had subscrivit'. All that Huntly would consent to was that the town house in Old Aberdeen would be made available to Lord Gordon as a residence.[27] For his part Lord Gordon remained open to reconciliation and tried his best to ensure that his father would not be denounced for his failure to subscribe to the Solemn League.[28] Despite this, the Convention of Estates did outlaw Huntly for failing to appear before them. They also refused to countenance his pleas that he was much indebted and could not afford to reside any length of time in the capital. He even offered to go to France with fifty gentlemen to serve in the French army

---

21 Young, *Scottish Parliament*, 63–82; Scott, *Politics and War*, 65–66; Macinnes, *British Revolution*, 150.

22 Stevenson, *Scottish Revolution*, 287.

23 *Selected Justiciary Cases*, III, 573–574; *Letters and Journals of Robert Bailiie*, II, 116 (Baillie to Spang, 7 December [1643]).

24 Gordon, *Britane's Distemper*, 46; Spalding, *Memorialls*, II, 320–321; Anon., *An Act of the Convention of Estates for putting the Kingdome into a posture of defence, for strengthening the Armie and providing of Armes and Ammunition to the Kingdome* (Edinburgh, 1644). In contrast to the situation with the National Covenant, the vast majority of the citizens of Aberdeen subscribed the Solemn League without too much trouble. See Spalding, *Memorialls*, II, 288–289.

25 Spalding, *Memorialls*, II, 280, 289–290; Furgol, *Regimental History*, 145.

26 P. Gordon, *Britanes Distemper*, 46.

27 Spalding, *Memorialls*, II, 290.

28 *Miscellany of the Spalding Club*, I, 28 (Lord Gordon to Straloch, 6 September [1643]).

but this was likewise rejected. Instead, the Estates continued to hound Huntly. According to Spalding he became 'so abusit by the tirranny of thir new cum Estaites, as he could nather get peace nor rest'. Finally, on 6 February 1644 the sheriff of Banff, Abercromby of Birkinbog, went to Bog of Gight with a commission to apprehend the marquess. Huntly refused to be taken and Abercromby was left with little option other than to write this up in a report. In addition, Huntly forbade all of his friends, followers, tenants or servants to comply with any order emanating from the Estates.[29] Everything seemed to be building towards a showdown.

THE SCOTTISH CIVIL WAR (PHASE ONE), MARCH 1644–SEPTEMBER 1645

This came with Huntly's decision to rise up in arms against the Covenanting regime in March 1644. Partly this may have been a response to the increasing pressure being placed upon him following the promulgation of the Solemn League and Covenant. However, there were additional factors. In the first instance, initial acts of aggression against the Covenanters were not made by Huntly himself but by a number of the more enthusiastic Royalist lairds, chief amongst them being Sir John Gordon of Haddo. On 19 March Haddo led a raid on Aberdeen and succeeded in capturing a number of prominent local Covenanters including Alexander Jaffray and the then lord provost, Patrick Leslie.[30] Although displeased at this being undertaken without his permission, Huntly nevertheless felt compelled to issue a public declaration justifying the action. He also subsequently took to the field himself and by 27 March Aberdeen had been occupied.[31]

In the second instance, it also seems clear that the rising was designed to coincide with Royalist offensives elsewhere. In the Western Isles, an Antrim-sponsored Irish force under the command of islesman Alasdair MacColla looked to make inroads into the territory of the Campbells. Meanwhile, in the South, Montrose planned to march towards Huntly from the English border.[32] On 1 February the king had drawn up commissions for Huntly and Montrose,

---

29 Spalding, *Memorialls*, II, 268–269, 301–302, 306, 320.

30 *Ibid.*, 324–325; Gordon, *Britane's Distemper*, 48; D. Stevenson, *Revolution and Counter Revolution in Scotland, 1644–1651* (paperback edn, Edinburgh, 2003), 5; *Extracts from the Council Register of the Burgh of Aberdeen, 1643–1747*, ed. J. Stuart (Edinburgh, 1872), 17; *Diary of Alexander Jaffray, Provost of Aberdeen*, ed. J. Barclay (3rd edn, Aberdeen, 1856), 48.

31 Stevenson, *Revolution and Counter Revolution*, 5; Spalding, *Memorialls*, II, 329–331.

32 Reid, *Campaigns of Montrose*, 41; D. Scott, *Politics and War*, 80–81. The Venetian secretary in England was certainly of the opinion that MacColla had originally planned to link up with Huntly and his north-east Royalists. See, *CSPV, 1643–47*, 128 (Agostini to the doge and Senate, 9 August 1644).

evidently with a view to mounting a new multi-pronged offensive. Montrose was designated lieutenant-general of all Scottish forces under the ultimate command of Prince Maurice as lieutenant-governor and captain-general, and in the latter's absence was to assume the full powers of command.[33] Huntly, meanwhile, was made lieutenant of all royal forces raised between Caithness and 'the Mounth' and of any that were brought within these bounds. Nevertheless, he was to remain under the overall command of the lieutenant-general.[34] According to Gordon of Ruthven, it was the timely arrival of news of this commission, along with news that Montrose, Aboyne and others were planning to launch an attack towards Dumfries that ultimately persuaded Huntly to take up arms.[35]

In the end, Huntly achieved little in the North-East. The town of Montrose was briefly occupied by a small force under the command of the Irvine of Drum's son, Alexander, but apart from that no attempt was made to engage the Covenanters. Huntly's apparent lack of fortitude was only highlighted by the fact that many under his command urged a more dynamic plan of action. When this proved fruitless, a degree of insubordination set in. The raid on Montrose, for example, remained largely the initiative of the same group of Royalist lairds who had conducted the earlier raid on Aberdeen. In addition, the experienced soldier, Colonel Nathaniel Gordon saw fit to leave Huntly's service after being castigated for impounding some herring from a Danish ship without orders. Furthermore, by the end of April desertions had become widespread.[36] Eventually, with the approach of a stronger Covenanting force from the South under the command of Argyll, and with the offensives of MacColla and Montrose seemingly coming to naught, Huntly decided to disband, thus leaving the Covenanters free rein to subdue the area once again. He subsequently took ship to Strathnaver in the far North of Scotland in early May and was to remain there until October 1645, safely ensconced in the house of Lord Reay at Tongue.[37] All the key Royalists involved in the rising found themselves excommunicated for

33 NAS, Montrose MSS, GD 220/3/126.

34 NAS, GD 44/13/5/8.

35 Gordon, *Britane's Distemper*, 49–50. David Stevenson and John Young have both noted that the multi-pronged Royalist plan of early 1644 was wildly overambitious in its scope and in the time schedule envisaged. See Stevenson, *Highland Warrior*, 104; J. Young, 'Invasions: Scotland and Ireland, 1641–1691', in P. Lenihan (ed.), *Conquest and Resistance. War in Seventeenth-Century Ireland* (Leiden, 2001), 65.

36 Spalding, *Memorialls*, II, 337–338, 341, 347, 351.

37 Stevenson, *Revolution and Counter Revolution*, 5–7; E. Furgol, 'The Civil Wars in Scotland', in Kenyon and Ohlmeyer (eds), *Civil Wars*, 51, 53; Gordon, *Britane's Distemper*, 53; *CSPD, 1644*, 138 (Committee of Both Kingdoms to Manchester, 27 April 1644); Gordon, *Family of Gordon*, II, 404–405; Spalding, *Memorialls*, II, 353–381.

their trouble.[38] In addition, Huntly found himself with a price of £12,000 Scots on his head for his apprehension, dead or alive.[39]

Huntly's inaction and the failure of the other Royalist offensives aside, the Gordon rising also suffered from the fact that the household continued to be split in its loyalties.[40] Throughout his father's campaign, Lord Gordon seemingly remained rooted to the Covenanting side. It seems clear that he saw this as the best course of action for his household, as well as for 'the trew interest off the poor cuntrye in generall and everye particular man in particulare'.[41] Having said this, he remained unwilling to engage his father in the field – and this despite his lofty position within the local Covenanting hierarchy. In the immediate aftermath of the Aberdeen raid, for example, he removed himself to Moray, apparently for the purpose of avoiding direct confrontation.[42] Apart from some blocking actions, his forces also had little involvement in the Covenanting campaign against the Royalist army of Montrose and Alasdair MacColla.[43] Following the failure of his campaign in the early months of 1644, MacColla had once again landed on the west coast of Scotland in early July, this time with another Antrim-sponsored force of around 2,000 men.[44] His credibility as a political figurehead being limited, MacColla had been lucky enough to link up with Montrose at Blair Atholl and the two had proceeded to march towards the North-East, defeating a Covenanting army at Tibbermore (1 September) on the way.[45] A second victory had followed at Justice Mills on the outskirts of Aberdeen on 13 September, and, after taking the burgh, the Royalists proceeded

38 *Records of Old Aberdeen, 1157–1903*, ed. A.M. Munro, 2 vols (Aberdeen, 1899–1909), II, 18; *A Diary of the Public Correspondence of Sir Thomas Hope*, 204–205.

39 *APS, 1643–47*, 402–408; NAS, GD 44/55/1/40. Despite the reward no attempt appears to have been made on the part of the Estates to capture Huntly while he was in Strathnaver. The earl of Sutherland saw fit to bemoan: 'It is no wonder that the M[aste]r of Reay doth giwe no obedience to the Esteats ordours, when in despyt of them he doth keipe ane open table to the Marquss of Huntly.' See W. Fraser, *Memorials of the Family of Wemyss of Wemyss*, 3 vols (Edinburgh, 1888), III, 90 (Sutherland to Elcho, 14 August 1644).

40 Williams, *Montrose*, 134; C.V. Wedgwood, *The King's War, 1641–1647* (London, 1958), 276.

41 *Miscellany of the Spalding Club*, I, 32 (Lord Gordon to Straloch, 18 March 1644).

42 Spalding, *Memorialls*, II, 329.

43 Reid, *Campaigns of Montrose*, 49, 71.

44 In addition to this Scottish expeditionary force, Antrim had also planned to raise a 10,000-man force for the purpose of fighting the Parliamentarians in England. See Ohlmeyer, *Civil War and Restoration*, 129–130. From the point of view of the Confederates in Ireland the Scottish expeditionary force formed part of a wider design to draw elements of the Covenanting army away from Ireland. See J. Ohlmeyer, 'The Civil Wars in Ireland', in Kenyon and Ohlmeyer (eds), *Civil Wars*, 87. In the end this was only partially successful. See J.S. Wheeler, *The Irish and British Wars, 1637–1654: Triumph, Tragedy and Failure* (London, 2002), 101.

45 Macinnes, *British Revolution*, 176–177; S. Reid, *Auldearn, 1645. The Marquis of Montrose's Scottish Campaign* (Oxford, 2003), 19–23.

to march along the fringes of the north-east Highlands foraging, plundering and recruiting as they went. In pursuit was a force under the command of the marquess of Argyll.[46]

Lord Gordon was not present on the Covenanting side at Justice Mills and the Gordons were represented there by nothing more than a small cavalry squadron under the command of Lord Lewis Gordon.[47] After a period in French military service, Lewis had gone on to fight on the Royalist side in the English Civil War, being present at the First Battle of Newbury in September 1643. While journeying to Scotland through northern England he had then, like Lord Gordon, fallen under the influence of his uncle, Argyll, and, in return for the latter's assistance, had evidently given satisfaction as to his new found loyalty to the Covenanting cause. Gordon of Ruthven stated that, at the time, this had merely been a pragmatic move on the part of Lewis and that he remained in a state of 'longeing till gratious Heaven might offer him the occasion whereby he might doe his king and countray seruice, and helpe his father to recouer his looses'.[48] The extent to which this was actually so at the time is certainly open to question, particularly considering that Gordon of Ruthven was writing with the benefit of hindsight and at a time when Lewis himself was seeking to expand his credentials as loyal servant to the Stuart kings in the late 1640s and early 1650s. Whatever the truth of the matter, it certainly remains the case that both he and Lord Gordon were soon to be found switching to the Royalist camp.

To what extent Lord Gordon was beginning to have doubts over the Covenanting cause prior to Montrose's Scottish campaign is hard to say. A number of factors seem to have eventually contributed towards his decision. Firstly, relations between him and other leading north-east Covenanters were by no means good. This situation seems to have come to a head when, with Montrose marching towards Aberdeen, Lords Forbes, Fraser and Crichton refused to attend Lord Gordon's summons to rendezvous at Kildrummy. Lord Gordon had recently been made lieutenant-general of the North, a situation that hereditary enemies such as these had found impossible to countenance. Furthermore, the Committee of War at Aberdeen subsequently conferred the rank onto Lord Forbes, something that left Lord Gordon nursing a deep resentment at the manner in which his honour had been slighted.[49] Secondly, he grew increasingly unhappy at the way in which Argyll was conducting the pursuit of Montrose and the Royalists. Argyll seems to have taken the opportunity to lay waste to as much Gordon territory as possible, undoubtedly with a view to

46 S. Reid, *Auldearn, 1645*, 23–33; Spalding, *Memorialls*, II, 414–415, 419, 423, 426, 434.
47 Marren, *Grampian Battlefields*, 159.
48 Gordon, *Britane's Distemper*, 84–85.
49 Spalding, *Memorialls*, II, 399–400; Gordon, *Britane's Distemper*, 79–80.

leaving the family even further at his mercy. Lands and areas affected included Strathbogie, Strathavon, Auchindoun, Aboyne, the Enzie and the Highland lordships of Badenoch and Lochaber. Lord Gordon may also have resented the fact that, during the same period, Argyll conferred the governorship of Inverness on Sir Mungo Campbell of Lawers rather than on him.[50]

It would thus have come as no surprise that, when the tide began to turn against Argyll militarily, Lord Gordon found it politic and in his family's best interests to change sides. Over the winter of 1644–1645 Montrose and MacColla had mounted a devastating campaign into the heart of Campbell territory, proving that, although it may have been a 'far cry to Lochawe', it was certainly not beyond the reaches of a determined enemy. To cap it all, Argyll had been overwhelmingly defeated at the Battle of Inverlochy on 2 February 1645, thus leaving Clan Campbell in a crippled state and increasing the chances of an overall Royalist victory in Scotland.[51] Lord Gordon duly joined the Royalist side on 19 February. Lewis Gordon followed his brother's example and switched sides at around the same time.[52]

But divisions continued to remain apparent within the House of Huntly. Crucially, the second marquess remained unwilling to forgive his eldest son for his past adherence to the Covenant. In March 1645 he took pains to write to Lewis insisting that he have nothing to do with Lord Gordon, 'for he hath so prejudiced his majesties service and neglectit me that I am resolved to tak notice of it'. He also authorised Lewis to take command of the Gordon contingent and others who owed loyalty to the House of Huntly.[53] Nevertheless, Montrose continued to favour Lord Gordon, with the result that for much of 1645 Gordon recruits were not as plentiful as they might have been, many of that name no doubt wishing to avoid offending Huntly by adhering to the banner of his estranged eldest son.[54] Matters were only complicated by the arrival of the second son, Lord Aboyne, from England in late April.[55] According to Gordon of Ruthven, Huntly much preferred the latter to the former anyway, something that evidently bred a degree of jealousy between the two. Ruthven further commented that:

> The eyes of that great and numerous family of Gordon wer fixed upon thes two; upon Aboyne, because of his great worth, and because the father seimed to prefer him; upon the elder, as having by birth the precedence, and

50 Gordon, *Britane's Distemper*, 86–88; Spalding, *Memorialls*, II, 417–432.
51 Reid, *Auldearn*, 33–35.
52 Spalding, *Memorialls*, II, 447–448.
53 NAS, GD 248/46/4/5 (2 letters of Huntly to Lewis Gordon, 7 March 1645).
54 Stevenson, *Revolution and Counter Revolution*, 22–23.
55 Spalding, *Memorialls*, II, 469.

by his many and incomparable pairts, but chiefly that he was so curteous, gentle, and affable, nowayes reserved nor keeping distance, and this gott him a great following, even when his father strove for the contrarie.

Gordon of Ruthven added that: 'both these noble youths, being admirable in their kind, did divyd the wholl name betwixt them'.[56]

Such divisions, while preventing overwhelming Gordon support, did not prevent the household from rendering good service to the Royalist cause throughout much of 1645. Gordon formations played a vital part in Montrose's three additional victories of that year. These were at Auldearn (9 May), Alford (2 July) and Kilsyth (15 August).[57] Especially crucial was the cavalry element that the Gordon lords brought with them – a vital addition if extended campaigning in the Lowlands was to be considered.[58] Although generally standing at little over 200 in number during this period, the Gordon horse was evidently a very effective and well-motivated fighting unit. Gaelic chronicler, Niall MacMhiurich, for example, referred to the Gordon cavalry as being excellent and well equipped.[59] The unit performed particularly well at the battles of Auldearn and Alford, making well-timed and effective cavalry charges on both occasions. Aboyne reputedly captured no fewer than five enemy colours at Auldearn.[60]

However, coming in for special praise from all quarters was Lord Gordon, particularly following his untimely death at the Battle of Alford. George Wishart concluded that this 'seemed to eclipse all the glory of victory'.[61] Similarly, chronicler James Fraser recorded that:

The brave lord Gordon fell in this battell, to the great greefe of all that knew him, his death being universally bemoaned and bewailed, even of his enemies as well as friends.[62]

A Covenanting ballad seemed to confirm this view, stating, 'in Scotland there was not a match to that man where he lay'.[63] The Gaelic commentators Niall MacMhiurich, and Iain Lom, also extolled the virtues of the dead lord, while a

---

56 Gordon, *Britane's Distemper*, 117–118.

57 See Reid, *Auldearn*, 41–84.

58 Stevenson, *Highland Warrior*, 166.

59 *Reliquiae Celticae. Texts, Papers and Studies in Gaelic Literature and Philology left by the late Rev. Alexander Cameron*, eds A. MacBain and J. Kennedy, 2 vols (Inverness, 1892–94), II, 192–193.

60 Gordon, *Britane's Distemper*, 122–126, 129–130.

61 G. Wishart, *Memoirs of the Most Renowned James Graham, Marquis of Montrose* (Edinburgh, 1819), 151.

62 J. Fraser, *Chronicles of the Frasers. The Wardlaw Manuscript entitled 'polichronicon seu policratica temporum, or, the True Genealogy of the Frasers', 916–1674*, ed. W. Mackay (Edinburgh, 1905), 299.

63 *The Thistle of Scotland. A Selection of Ancient Ballads with Notes*, ed. A. Laing (Aberdeen, 1823), 70.

Royalist pamphleteer described him as 'a brave gentleman, who lived faithfully, and died valiantly, in his Majesties service'.[64]

However, the Gordon contribution remains somewhat underplayed in histories of the Civil Wars. Up until around the mid-twentieth century the historiography almost unanimously tended to present Montrose as the great military genius, almost single-handedly planning and executing an impressive series of victories against the Covenanters.[65] In this, writers took the lead from George Wishart's hagiographic biography and from the series of pamphlets that circulated at the time of the campaigns.[66] Through all this the tendency was to subordinate the individual importance of leaders such as MacColla and the Gordon lords (with the partial exception of Lord Gordon).[67] Some more recent biographers did attempt a more rounded portrayal of Montrose but in the main they still tended to overplay his tactical gifts.[68] Latterly there has rightly been more of a move towards highlighting Montrose's faults as well as his gifts. In particular it has been noted that, for all his flair, Montrose did frequently tend to be caught short by the enemy due to poor reconnaissance.[69] Alongside this, some historians have increasingly come to recognise and champion MacColla's contribution to the Royalist victories, particularly at Auldearn.[70] Indeed, the

64 *Reliquiae Celticae*, 190–191; *Orain Iain Luim*, 32–33; Anon., *The copie of a letter showing the true relation of the late and happie victorie received by the marques of Montrose against Generall lieuetenant Baylie, and others of the rebels, at Alfoord, the second of Julie, 1645* (1645), 7–8.

65 In particular, writers tended to single out Auldearn as being the great pre-planned victory. See de Muscry, *The History of the Troubles of Great Britain*, 206; M. Napier, *Memoirs of the Marquis of Montrose*, 2 vols (Edinburgh, 1856), II, 501–505; Buchan, *Montrose*, 245–250. Particularly influential in this regard was the account of Samuel R. Gardiner. See S.R. Gardiner, *History of the Great Civil War, 1642–1649*, 4 vols (London, 1893), II, 222–227.

66 Wishart, *Memoirs*; Anon., *A true relation of the happy successe of his maiesties forces in Scotland under the conduct of the Lord James Marquisse of Montrose his excellencie, against the rebels there. Also, causes of a solemne fast and humiliation kept by the rebels in that Kingdom* (Edinburgh, 1644); Anon., *The copie of a letter … Alfoord*; Anon., *The true relation of the late and happie victorie obtained by the marques of Montrose his excellencie, his majesties lieuetenant, and Generall Governor of the kingdom of Scotland: against General Lieuetenant Baylie, and others of the rebels, at Kilsyth, 15 August 1645* (1645).

67 John Buchan, for example, tended to be particularly disparaging about the leadership skills and tactical ability of Alasdair MacColla. See Buchan, *Montrose*, 180–181, 277.

68 Again, in the main, the tendency was towards overemphasising the extent to which Montrose orchestrated the victory at Auldearn. See C.V. Wedgwood, *Montrose* (London, 1952), 96–97; Williams, *Montrose*, 239–245; Hastings, *Montrose*, 249–254.

69 For example, see Cowan, *Montrose*, 170, 198, 201–205. Most authors now tend to point out that Montrose was indeed frequently caught on the hop, particularly at Auldearn. See Reid, *Campaigns of Montrose*, 99–101, 112–118; Williams, *Heather and the Gale*, 150; Reid, *Auldearn*, 31–33, 35–67; T. Royle, *Civil War. The Wars of the Three Kingdoms, 1638–1660* (London, 2004), 344–345.

70 The breakthrough work in this regard was David Stevenson's seminal biography of MacColla, originally published in 1980. In particular his chapter on the Battle of Auldearn remains a masterpiece of revisionist writing. See Stevenson, *Highland Warrior*, 166–194. For Allan

increasing tendency seems to be to refer to the joint victories of Montrose and MacColla as opposed to them solely being attributable to the former.[71]

Although a step in the right direction, this arguably does not go far enough. To comprehend fully the Royalist campaigns in Scotland a more nuanced understanding is needed as to the nature of the force that marched under Montrose's banner. In essence (and despite the terms of Montrose's commission), it remained more in the nature of a confederation of allies, with the bulk of the manpower being provided by the Irish brigades, the Gordons and some of the Highland clans. To see the Royalist army as some kind of professional outfit, and the likes of MacColla, Lord Gordon and Aboyne as being junior officers wholly deferential to Montrose, is to misunderstand the nature of this force, while opening up the danger of wallowing in anachronisms.[72] When all was said and done, the men of the Irish brigade owed their immediate allegiance to MacColla, while those in the Gordon formations owed their loyalty to Huntly's sons.[73] This being the case, the Royalist victories are probably best viewed as largely being the result of the collaborative efforts of the main leaders, including Montrose, and to the excellence of the units under their command. A close reading of Ruthven's account certainly provides the strong impression that, when battle was joined, the victories largely resulted from individual initiatives taken in the field and from the steadiness of the Royalist troops, rather than from some great master plan. This remained particularly true at both Auldearn and Alford, and was arguably the case at Kilsyth as well.[74]

Macinnes, MacColla remains the more successful of the two Royalist commanders. See Macinnes, *British Revolution*, 177–178. See also J.M. Hill, *Celtic Warfare, 1595–1763* (Edinburgh, 1986), 55; P. Lenihan, '"Celtic" Warfare in the 1640s', in J.R. Young (ed.), *Celtic Dimensions*, 129; Young, 'Invasions', 67–69.

71 Scott, *Politics and War*, 80; Macinnes, *British Revolution*, 176–177; Ó Siochrú, *Confederate Ireland*, 69; P. Lenihan, 'Confederate Military Strategy, 1643–7', in M. Ó Siochrú (ed.), *Kingdoms in Crisis. Ireland in the late 1640s. Essays in Honour of Dónal Cregan* (Dublin, 2000), 163; P. Lenihan, *Confederate Catholics at War, 1641–49* (Cork, 2001), 83; Young, 'Invasions', 66. Stuart Reid has introduced a note of caution to all this. In his view, apart from at Tibbermore, it is probably inaccurate to suggest that MacColla remained an architect of Montrose's victories. He asserts that, from Justice Mills onwards, Montrose was the main tactician. See Reid, *Campaigns of Montrose*, 175–176. However, this arguably does not go far enough in acknowledging the contribution of MacColla and the Gordons.

72 These points have largely been appreciated by Stuart Reid and David Stevenson. See Reid, *Campaigns of Montrose*, 174; D. Stevenson, 'Montrose and Dundee', in L. Maclean (ed.), *The Seventeenth Century in the Highlands* (Inverness, 1986), 142. In connection with all this, the issue of 'desertion' will be dealt with presently.

73 With this in mind, Stuart Reid is correct to question Wishart's assertion that the Gordon rank and file had a great love for Montrose over and above all others. See Reid, *Campaigns of Montrose*, 74.

74 Gordon, *Britane's Distemper*, 123–126, 129–131; Reid, *Campaigns of Montrose*, 176. Cowan has stated that Alford was very much a Gordon victory. See Cowan, *Montrose*, 211.

The reputation of the Gordons, and of Aboyne and Lewis Gordon in particular, was certainly not aided by the light in which Wishart presented some of their actions. Seen as particularly damning were the occasions when the Gordons chose to absent themselves temporarily from the Royalist army. In Wishart's view this, when it occurred, amounted to nothing less than dereliction of duty. Accompanying this was the view that both Aboyne and Lord Lewis were inconstant, fickle and unreliable and that they remained largely responsible for these 'desertions'. On occasion, Aboyne's efforts in raising recruits also came in for some sharp criticism. In contrast to this, Lord Gordon was revealed to be ever constant and a paragon of virtue, frequently having to undo the damage done by his younger siblings.[75]

Most heinous, in Wishart's view, was the decision by most of the Highlanders and by MacColla and Aboyne to leave Montrose in early September 1645, Aboyne taking all of the Gordon manpower with him.[76] The Royalist army was undoubtedly left seriously weakened by this, with the result that Montrose soon found himself heavily defeated at Philiphaugh (13 September) by a Covenanting force under the command of Lieutenant-General David Leslie.[77] For his part, MacColla departed with a view to continuing a campaign along the western seaboard, thus fulfilling the main thrust of Antrim's original commission.[78] Meanwhile, several explanations have been mooted with regard to Aboyne's decision to leave. Some of Montrose's biographers have emphasised his jealousy and impetuous ill temper, something that seemingly stemmed from the fact that Montrose failed to make due mention of his contribution in dispatches to the king, as well as from the knowledge that James, Lord Ogilvy, was apparently being favoured over him. Aboyne was also reportedly angered by the manner in which pamphleteers were underplaying the Gordon contribution and at the warm reception Montrose was giving to the fair-weather Royalists who flocked to his banner after the Battle of Kilsyth.[79]

However, while acknowledging all of these factors, Gordon of Ruthven maintained that, no matter how offended, Aboyne 'would not for this desert the service of the prince [Charles I]'. For Gordon of Ruthven the main reason behind Aboyne's departure remained that he received a letter from his father

---

75 Wishart, *Memoirs*, 62, 97–98, 116, 120, 128, 141–143, 160.

76 *Ibid.*, 190–192.

77 Reid, *Auldearn*, 85–88.

78 Macinnes, *British Revolution*, 177. Macinnes notes that the departure of MacColla and the Highlanders proved a great loss to Montrose. He fails, however, to give due attention to the departure of the Gordons.

79 Napier, *Memoirs of Montrose*, II, 143–144; Williams, *Montrose*, 284–285; Buchan, *Montrose*, 281–282.

requesting his return.[80] Given this was the case, it is a pity that the letter itself does not seem to have survived, particularly in view of the fact that Huntly's reasons for ordering the recall of his son remain unrecorded. Nevertheless, it seems probable that, as Huntly had his heart set on returning to his north-east estates at this time, he may have desired that Aboyne and the fighting men of the household be there at his side, particularly given that traditional enemies such as the Forbeses and the Frasers still retained the potential to cause him problems.

The Marquess of Argyll also sought to maintain pressure on the House of Huntly at this time. He had begun to buy up Huntly's debts with a view to laying claim to the entire Gordon estate with the result that the Gordon lords were left in little doubt of the continued precarious state of their finances. In a letter to Aboyne of the time, Lord Ogilvy warned:

> Argyll leaves no winds unfurled to sow dissentione among you, and draw
> your lordship aff, and hath ordered a friend of yours to wreitt to that effect
> to you and your father.[81]

Although Huntly and Aboyne never deserted the Royalist cause, it may certainly have been the case that financial restraints and the associated need to defend the Gordon landholdings may have prompted a rethink in the family's strategy. If nothing else, Argyll may have provided a reminder of this requirement. All things considered, it seems that Aboyne, like MacColla, left Montrose to address priorities that were more important to him and his family at the time. This only reflected the occasions earlier on in the campaign when, far from deserting like some kind of ill-disciplined rabble, the majority of the Gordon lairds and gentlemen occasionally saw a need to return home to defend their lands and families from the encroachments of local Covenanting agitators.[82] Throughout, it must be remembered that they were not professional soldiers in the modern sense of the term and they should be judged accordingly.

---

80 Gordon, *Britane's Distemper*, 83.
81 *Memorials of Montrose and his Times*, ed. M. Napier, 2 vols (Edinburgh, 1848), II, 234–236 (Ogilvie to Aboyne, [September 1645]).
82 Stevenson, *Highland Warrior*, 169. Without a fully centralised command structure, the effective co-ordination of a confederate army such as that operating in Scotland in 1644 and 1645 was always going to end up being a problem. Comparisons can perhaps be drawn with the Irish Confederacy in this regard. See Macinnes, *British Revolution*, 174, 181.

THE SCOTTISH CIVIL WAR (PHASE TWO), SEPTEMBER 1645–DECEMBER 1647

The defeat at Philiphaugh did not spell the end of Royalist attempts to regain Scotland for the king. Alasdair MacColla carried on the campaign along the western seaboard, while in the North Montrose and the Gordons continued to look to make inroads against the Covenanters. However, the chances of overall success were compromised by the poor working relationship between Montrose and the recently-returned Huntly. Again George Wishart sought to highlight instances where, as he saw it, the malicious Huntly tried to inhibit the noble efforts of the heroic Montrose. It was claimed that such obstructionism dated as far back as 1644. For example, it was pointed out that during the period immediately following the sack of Aberdeen, Huntly deliberately thwarted Montrose's plans to recruit amongst the Gordons by issuing an order that his followers were not to join.[83] A later historian of the Gordon family refuted this allegation stating that as Huntly had been in Strathnaver at the time, it was improbable that news of Montrose's victories would have reached him so soon, and doubly unlikely that orders would have made their way back to be circulated amongst the Gordon lairds.[84] It seems more likely that, as Lord Gordon still adhered to the Covenant at the time, most Gordons would have seen little reason to join Montrose's army. Wishart also accused Huntly of maliciously preventing Aboyne and the Gordon horse and foot from marching southwards in support of Montrose over the weeks that followed the defeat at Philiphaugh.[85] However, as Gordon of Ruthven asserted, the real reason for this was that Huntly wanted the North-East to be secure from the potential incursions of the Covenanters. At that time a force under the command of Colonel John Middleton was operating

---

83 Wishart, *Memoirs*, 93.

84 Gordon, *Family of Gordon*, II, 442. Writing in 1661, one John Reynolds backed up Wishart's assertion of obstructionism by publishing the transcript of a letter supposedly addressed to Montrose from some unnamed followers of Huntly, claiming that the latter 'hath withheld us all, forbidding even with threats all with whom he hath power to have any thing to do with your Lordship, or to assist you either with their power or counsel'. See J. Reynolds, *Blood for Blood: or Murthers revenged. Briefly, yet lively set forth in thirty tragical histories. To which are added five more, being the sad product of our own times. Viz. K. Charles the Martyr. Montrose and Argyle, Overbury and Turner, Sonds and his two sons, Knight and Butler. With a short appendix to the present age* (Oxford, 1661), 325. No original copy of this letter seems to have survived; and given its highly uncertain provenance and questionable tone and contents, it was most likely a fabrication. Mark Napier later wrongly dated this already questionable letter to October 1645. See *Memorials of Montrose*, II, 240.

85 Wishart, *Memoirs*, 211–219; According to Reynolds, Montrose sent a stern letter to Huntly on this occasion berating him for not coming to his aid. A transcription of the letter was included. It also remains of highly questionable provenance and should not be relied upon as a true source. See Reynolds, *Blood for Blood*, 327–328.

in that area with a view to bringing the Gordons to heel.[86]

That said, there was probably little natural desire on the part of Huntly to go out of his way to lend any help to Montrose. There were reasons for this. During the First Bishops' War Montrose had been one of those responsible for Huntly's capture at Aberdeen. Moreover, this had been achieved in the face of a guarantee of safe conduct given to Huntly so that he could visit the burgh.[87] Although Montrose had probably been innocent of deliberately having misled Huntly (the latter's capture being insisted upon more vociferously by others), the likelihood remains that Huntly never forgave Montrose for what happened.[88] The considerable age gap between the two may also have led to difficulties in building any kind of natural bond or affinity.[89] In addition, Huntly may have been envious of the glory that Montrose had garnered for himself during his campaigns. Moreover, it is probable that he would have looked down on this recently elevated marquess as being a lesser nobleman, not in the same league as a magnate like himself.[90] He may have been further alienated by a degree of brash arrogance on the part of Montrose.[91]

Despite their differences, a meeting did eventually take place between the two at Bog of Gight in December 1645. The main topic of discussion was how best to continue the Royalist campaign in the North. George Wishart and Gordon of Ruthven remain the only two sources as to what was actually agreed. What seems certain is that a two-pronged advance towards Inverness was decided upon, with Huntly to march along the coast via Moray, and Montrose to march further inland via Strathspey. Technically, Montrose was acknowledged as the overall commander but Huntly was to be consulted on all matters. Meanwhile, Huntly would in practice be given free rein to act independently, Montrose only coming to his assistance if required. Once the North was reduced to obedience, it was then envisaged that a combined force would march southwards for the purpose of retaking Scotland for the king. The accounts do, however, differ on a technicality; that of the speed at which this march on Inverness was to be undertaken. Wishart maintained that an immediate advance was agreed upon while Gordon of Ruthven insisted that it was intended that Huntly would spend time reducing Moray first.[92] It seems clear that, in spite of the rank conferred by

---

86 Gordon, *Britane's Distemper*, 162–167. The withdrawal of the Gordons on this occasion left Montrose unable to mount an offensive towards his desired target of Glasgow.

87 *Ibid.*, 16; Gordon, *History of Scots Affairs*, II, 232–233.

88 Wedgwood, *Montrose*, 37; Hastings, *Montrose*, 306.

89 Montrose's year of birth has been placed at around 1612, which made him a good twenty years younger than Huntly. See Napier, *Memoirs*, I, 1; Williams, *Montrose*, 3.

90 Wishart, *Memoirs*, 211; Hastings, *Montrose*, 306.

91 Gordon and Gordon, *Genealogical History*, 531.

92 Wishart, *Memoirs*, 231–232; Gordon, *Britane's Distemper*, 168–172.

his commission, Montrose sought to gain Huntly's assistance through persuasion and compromise.[93] In turn, Huntly felt satisfied that he would be able to exercise his own lieutenancy without interference. Whatever the full nature of the agreement, it appears that, initially at least, Montrose did countenance Huntly's desire to be consulted in all things. Indeed, in the series of letters that he wrote to the latter in the weeks that followed Montrose adopted a tone very much in keeping with the arrangement.[94]

During the first two months of 1646 Huntly certainly seems to have worked hard to satisfy the terms of his commission of lieutenancy, corresponding with individuals such as Seaforth and Lord Reay in an attempt to secure their support for the king, and taking and laying siege to a number of castles in Moray.[95] Claims that Huntly trifled his time away doing this solely in an attempt to enrich his own family out of the spoils are arguably unfair.[96] Indeed, it seems that, upon securing the submission of strongholds, Huntly would sometimes merely seek assurances that the besieged would henceforward remain well disposed to the king. A bond would then normally be sought guaranteeing a cash payment to Huntly if this was reneged upon. In return the latter would look to spare the castle or house in question from plunder.[97] This is not to say that Huntly did not also look to improve his own situation when such a chance presented itself. For example, on taking the castle of Burgie he obtained the discharge of a debt he owed to the occupant, Robert Dunbar.[98] The Gordon formations also caused widespread damage to the lands of prominent Covenanters, as well as to the countryside of Moray more generally. During the siege of Lethin, Huntly's men burned the house, barns and land of Francis Brody of Ballivat, and plundered his stocks of cattle, horses and sheep.[99] Many of the inhabitants of Elgin also

93 Aberdeen University Special Collections, MS 658, 498–500.
94 See *Memorials of Montrose*, II, 260–268 (Montrose to Huntly, 23 December 1645), (same to same, 29 December 1645), (same to same, 31 December 1645), (same to same, 10 January 1646), (same to same, 12 January 1646), (same to same, 25 January 1646), (same to same, 1 February 1646), (same to same, 6 February 1646), (same to same, 18 February 1646), (same to same, 20 February 1646).
95 NAS, Reay MSS, GD 84/2/202 (Huntly to Lord Reay, 21 February 1646); Gordon, *Britane's Distemper*, 173–174; Gordon and Gordon, *Genealogical History*, 530.
96 Claims of this nature were originally made by Wishart. See Wishart, *Memoirs*, 249–250.
97 This is certainly what happened with regard to Alexander Brodie of Lethin, the agreement between him and Huntly being drawn up on 23 February 1646. See NAS, GD 44/14/4/11; Gordon, *Britane's Distemper*, 177–179; *The Diary of Alexander Brodie of Brodie, 1652–1680 and of his Son, James Brodie of Brodie, 1680–1685 consisting of Extracts from the existing Manuscript, and a Republication of the Volume printed at Edinburgh in the Year 1740*, ed. D. Laing (Aberdeen, 1863), lxix–lxx (Brodie to Douglas, 10 March 1646).
98 Upon Dunbar's supplication, the Committee of Estates revoked this discharge in 1647. See *APS*, *1643–47*, 784.
99 *APS, 1648–60*, 214. The lands of Lethin were also burned during this time. See *ibid.*, 303–304.

suffered from widespread plundering.[100] Meanwhile, during his occupation of Rothes, Lewis Gordon reportedly spread much terror in the surrounding area.[101]

But Montrose remained unhappy about the length of time Huntly had spent in Moray. Lethin Castle withstood a lengthy siege and, as Montrose saw it, little progress was made towards securing the main target of Inverness. Tensions caused by this difference of opinion over strategy were only increased by moves on the part of Montrose to assert his overall leadership in a more proactive manner. Huntly was displeased on finding out that Montrose had been in communication with Seaforth, thus interfering in areas that he regarded as being within the remit of his lieutenancy alone.[102] In addition, when a Captain Darcy arrived in the Moray Firth with a boatload of ammunition towards the end of March, Montrose instructed that under no circumstances was he to commune with Huntly.[103] Some rumours even circulated amongst the Gordons that Montrose may have been secretly encouraging Grant of Ballindalloch to continue holding out against them in the Castle of Spynie.[104] Gordon of Ruthven got to the heart of the matter when he stated:

> Jealousie and privat interest, prompt by a streame of ambition in both, made the sinceritie of both there intentions doubtfull [to] the aither, so as the one was ever readie to make construction on the others meaneing.

Despite the exchange of many messages between the two, the situation became increasingly fraught.[105]

The final impasse came with Huntly's decision to return across the Spey to defend his lands and his tenants following the arrival of Covenanting reinforcements in the North-East, firstly under the command of an officer named Barclay, and latterly under Major-General John Middleton. Both Huntly and Aboyne requested that Montrose join them in an advance back towards Aberdeen, but the last remained adamant that Inverness should be captured first.[106] Indeed, as if seeking to underline the increasingly volatile relationship, both Montrose

100 *Ibid.*, 264–265, 457–458. In 1646 a set of depositions was drawn up in which the citizens of Elgin detailed their losses suffered during that and the previous year. See J. Barrett and A. Mitchell, *Elgin's Love-Gift: Civil War in Scotland and the Depositions of 1646* (Chichester, 2007) for a transcription of this important document and for accompanying analysis.

101 Fraser, *Chronicles of Frasers*, 313.

102 Gordon, *Britane's Distemper*, 174.

103 Gordon and Gordon, *Genealogical History*, 532.

104 Gordon, *Britane's Distemper*, 174–175.

105 *Ibid.*, 175.

106 *Ibid.*, 175–178; *Memorials of Montrose*, II, 272–274 (Montrose to Aboyne, 15 March 1646), (Aboyne to Montrose, 15 March 1646).

and Huntly independently approached the Grants in an attempt to gain recruits for their own forces.[107] Finally, with the two quarrelling Royalist factions thus divided, Middleton managed to take advantage of the situation and successfully crossed the Spey with little opposition. He then proceeded to march swiftly on Inverness and force Montrose to raise his siege on 9 May. Montrose's army melted away before him, leaving little option other than to take to the hills.[108]

With Middleton gone, Huntly set his sights on Aberdeen and successfully stormed the burgh on 14 May.[109] His occupation was short-lived, however, most of his Highland foot deciding in time-honoured fashion to return home with their spoils. When Middleton once more approached, Huntly retreated to Strathbogie via Deeside.[110] By this time news must have been circulating that the king had surrendered his person to the Covenanting army at Newark on 5 May. His forces in England all but defeated, Charles had then issued an order for his commanders in Scotland to disband. Huntly duly did so on 3 June.[111] Montrose remained more reluctant but eventually followed suit. Being one of those denied a pardon, he subsequently sailed for continental exile in early September.[112]

Despite disbanding in line with the king's instructions, Huntly did not take the opportunity to reconcile himself fully to the Covenanting regime. Although a pardon remained a possibility, he would not accept the charge that he had in any way been in rebellion. He also courted censure by keeping some of his men in arms.[113] His continued defiance became something of an issue for the Covenanters and in mid-September 1646 he even had to write a letter to the king assuring him that he had disbanded.[114] The Committee of Estates then dispatched Middleton north in order to gain Huntly's formal submission. The

107 Fraser, *Chiefs of Grant*, II, 77–80 (Montrose to Grant, 22 April 1646), (Huntly to Grant, 22 April 1646), (Montrose to Grant, 6 May 1646); NAS, GD 248/68/5/14.

108 Gordon and Gordon, *Genealogical History*, 532; Gordon, *Britane's Distemper*, 184–187. A request by Montrose for Huntly to prevent Middleton crossing the Spey seems to have arrived too late for him to do much about it. See WSRO, Goodwood/1431/12 (Montrose to Huntly, 7 May 1646).

109 This remains one of the neglected battles of the Civil Wars. The fullest contemporary account remains that of Gordon of Ruthven. See Gordon, *Britane's Distemper*, 187–189. John Spalding also included a detailed rendition. That part of his 'Trubles' manuscript now lost, sections of his account survive in Gordon, *Family of Gordon*, II, 511–512.

110 Gordon and Gordon, *Genealogical History*, 533; Gordon, *Family of Gordon*, II, 513.

111 NAS, GD 44/13/4/15.

112 NAS, GD 84/2/204 (Montrose to [Lord Reay], 4 June [1646]); Cowan, *Montrose*, 249–251.

113 Drum Castle Archives, Irvine of Drum Papers, bundle 20, item 5 (Middleton to Huntly, 24 July 1646), (Huntly to Middleton, 1 August 1646); Leslie, *Irvines of Drum*, 115.

114 NAS, GD 406/1/2020 (Huntly to Charles I, 17 September 1646). Huntly's assuredness of his position was also reflected in a warrant of protection that he provided for Lord Reay and his son on 30 September. He stated that they had faithfully adhered to the king's service under his command as lieutenant of the North. See NAS, GD 84/2/205.

latter refused to countenance this and little was done in the immediate term to try to bring him to heel.[115] Writing from exile in France, Queen Henrietta Maria and Charles, Prince of Wales, even saw fit to congratulate both Huntly and Aboyne on their continued loyalty.[116]

By December 1646 the Gordon lords had become involved in a new scheme designed to further the interests of the king. At that time Charles remained a captive of the Covenanters at Newcastle where he busily prevaricated with them as well as with the English Parliamentarians over terms of settlement. Meanwhile, he remained open to other initiatives. One proposal reportedly involved Charles making an escape to Scotland in order to shelter with the Gordons. From there he could then look to continue a Britannic-wide civil war in concert with the likes of MacColla on the western seaboard and James Butler, twelfth earl of Ormond, in Ireland. The main champions of this idea remained the French ambassadors, the brothers de Bellièvre, and it was on their initiative that a messenger was sent to Huntly to discuss the plan. Evidently of the opinion that the king must be in full agreement with all this, Huntly drew together another army of around 2,000 men and occupied the coastal burgh of Banff. It was thought that the king could easily arrive at this location by sea. However, as the latter actually remained less than enamoured with the scheme, it was never put into practice. Huntly nevertheless stayed in Banff all that winter, his efforts ultimately being in vain.[117]

Finally, in March 1647, with the news that David Leslie was marching against him with a force of around 6,000 men, Huntly retreated to the Highlands.[118] Leslie subsequently had little trouble in taking the Gordon strongholds lying in his path.[119] The exact footsteps of Huntly and Aboyne over the months that followed remain quite hard to pinpoint with any degree of certainty. The first

---

115 Gordon and Gordon, *Genealogical History*, 535–536.

116 NAS, GD 406/1/2257 (Prince Charles to Aboyne, 16 October 1646), (Henrietta Maria to Aboyne, 18 October 1646).

117 Gordon and Gordon, *Genealogical History*, 536; Gordon, *Britane's Distemper*, 196; *Diplomatic Correspondence of Jean de Montereul*, I, 372–376 (Bellièvre to Brienne, 24 December 1646).

118 Gordon, *Britane's Distemper*, 197. In March another two letters were sent to Aboyne by the queen and Prince Charles. Once again they encouraged the Gordon lords to remain loyal to the cause of the king. See NAS, GD 406/1/2257 (Prince Charles to Aboyne, 21 February 1647), (Henrietta Maria to Aboyne, 4 [March] 1647).

119 These included Strathbogie, Lesmore, Bog of Gight, Wardhouse, Auchindoun and the stronghold on Loch Kinnord. See *The Journal of Thomas Cuningham of Campvere, 1640–1654*, ed. E.J. Courthope (Edinburgh, 1928), 153. At Strathbogie, Wardhouse and Lesmore, Leslie acted with particular ruthlessness against Irish members of the respective garrisons. In each case they were rounded up and hanged. See *A Collection of the State Papers of John Thurloe, Esq; Secretary first to the Council of State, and afterwards to the Protectors, Oliver and Richard Cromwell*, ed. T. Birch, 7 vols (London, 1742), II, 89 (Leslie to the Committee of Estates, 27 March 1647); Gordon, *Family of Gordon*, II, 530.

stop seems to have been Ruthven Castle in Badenoch, a location where a decision was probably taken to disband most of the remaining Gordon troops.[120] Some attempts were made to try to engineer a link-up with MacColla, but for the most part Huntly and Aboyne had their work cut out just to remain out of the clutches of the Covenanters.[121] By late April Ruthven Castle had been taken by a force under the command of Middleton, and Huntly and Aboyne had escaped into Lochaber with around 100 followers.[122] Middleton followed and, with the assistance of a group of Camerons, surprised the Gordon party and scattered them. A rearguard of around 40 of the best Gordon men allowed both Huntly and Aboyne to make their escape, whereupon the two decided to split up and flee by different routes.[123]

Huntly made for Strathavon and somewhere on route was reportedly betrayed by a Donald Guharrig (alias 'Durk'). On this occasion most of his remaining men were either killed or captured while he and a few others managed to make another escape.[124] Finally, in either late November or early December 1647, a Covenanting search party under the command of Lieutenant-Colonel James Menzies captured Huntly at Delnabo in Strathavon. Once again his location had been betrayed to the enemy. Indeed, according to James Fraser, the informant had been one of Huntly's trusted friends, Alexander Innes of Condraught.[125] Huntly subsequently found himself incarcerated in Edinburgh.[126] Meanwhile,

---

120 *Diplomatic Correspondence of Jean de Montereul*, II, 65–72 (Montereul to Mazarin, 23 March 1647); Gordon, *Britane's Distemper*, 199–200.

121 In his letters to Cardinal Mazarin, the French ambassador to Scotland, Jean de Montereul, referred on a number of occasions to the idea of a link-up between the Gordons and MacColla. See *Diplomatic Correspondence of Jean de Montereul*, II, 64–65, 75–84, 95, 120, 126–127 (Montereul to Mazarin, 16 March 1647), (same to same, 30 March 1647), (same to same, 6 April 1647), (same to same, 27 April 1647), (same to same, 4 May 1647). Aboyne also alluded to this possibility as late as May 1647. See NLS, Miscellaneous Papers, MS 2207, f. 2 (Aboyne to an unnamed recipient, 25 May 1647). In mid-1647 there was a possibility that MacColla could have been reinforced by a new 5,000-strong Irish expeditionary force. See Stevenson, *Highland Warrior*, 231.

122 *Diplomatic Correspondence of Jean de Montereul*, II, 116–117, 152 (Montereul to Mazarin, 20 April 1647), (Montereul to Mazarin, 1 June 1647).

123 Gordon, *Britane's Distemper*, 200.

124 *Diplomatic Correspondence of Jean de Montereul*, II, 203 (Montereul to Mazarin, 20 July 1647).

125 Gordon and Gordon, *Genealogical History*, 537; *Diplomatic Correspondence of Jean de Montereul*, II, 346 (Montereul to Mazarin, 7 December 1647); Gordon, *Family of Gordon*, II, 545; Fraser, *Chronicle of the Frasers*, 334. The fact that Huntly had been informed upon was made perfectly clear in written instructions that Middleton issued to Menzies. Middleton knew for sure that Huntly was at Delnabo at the time. See NLS, Saltoun Papers, MS 16747, f. 99 (Middleton to Menzies, 10 November 1647). Menzies, nevertheless, subsequently collected the reward of £10,000 Scots for the capture. See NAS, GD 44/55/1/40.

126 *Diplomatic Correspondence of Jean de Montereul*, II, 362 (Montereul to Mazarin, 28 December 1647).

the whereabouts of Aboyne remained uncertain. One story circulated that he had died sometime in December of dysentery. However, this seems to have been no more than a fabrication designed to aid him in his escape.[127] Gilbert Gordon of Sallach maintained that he actually died in exile in Paris in 1649.[128] Whatever the truth of the matter, Royalist resistance in the North had been snuffed out for the time being. This paralleled the situation on the western seaboard where, by late June, David Leslie had successfully ejected MacColla's expeditionary force.[129]

In light of all of the above it can be seen that, by concentrating on the contribution of the House of Huntly, a fresh perspective can be gained on this much neglected second phase of the Civil Wars in Scotland. After all, any in-depth analysis of the Royalist campaigns after September 1646 quite understandably remained outside the remit of Montrose's many biographers. Important work was subsequently done on MacColla that did much to ensure more detailed coverage of the campaigns of 1646 and 1647. However, relatively little had been written in any detail on the Gordons. Some scholars of the British and Irish Civil Wars still tend to assert that the Royalist cause in Scotland was all but crushed with the defeat of Montrose at Philiphaugh in September 1645.[130] Such a conclusion introduces the danger of indulging in a deterministic reading that ignores the fact that, at the time, a Royalist renewal in Scotland remained a possibility. Both Henrietta Maria and Prince Charles were aware of the continued importance of the Gordons, and, for some at least, the idea of the king escaping to Banff in late 1646 was an option. Moreover, there was still the chance that the Gordons could once again unite with Irish forces under the command of MacColla. Throughout mid-1646 an Antrim-proposed plan was mooted with a view to mounting a renewed and freshly-reinforced Scottish campaign.[131] A similar scheme was also under consideration in mid-1647.[132] There would of course have been serious implications for the situation elsewhere had either of them come to fruition. For this reason alone the House of Huntly warrants serious consideration. And at any rate, in order to understand fully the wars in Scotland and why the Royalists lost, it is essential that due attention be devoted to understanding the strained relationship between the Gordons and the marquess of Montrose.

---

127 *Ibid.*, 359 (Montereul to Mazarin, 21 December 1647).
128 Gordon and Gordon, *Genealogical History*, 545.
129 Stevenson, *Highland Warrior*, 232–245.
130 See in particular Scott, *Politics and War*, 110; Macinnes, *British Revolution*, 178. Many authors make either little or no reference to the efforts of MacColla and the Gordons for the period beyond mid-1646. See Bennett, *Civil Wars in Britain and Ireland*; A. Woolrych, *Britain in Revolution, 1625–1660* (Oxford, 2002); Royle, *Civil War*.
131 Ohlmeyer, *Civil War and Restoration*, 176–177.
132 Stevenson, *Highland Warrior*, 231.

Moreover, this needs to be accompanied with well-rounded analysis, free from the shackles of any kind of hero worship of the latter.

THE PATRIOTIC ACCOMMODATION

With Huntly imprisoned and Aboyne in exile, leadership of the household fell to the third son, Lord Lewis Gordon. Having argued with his father over money, he had not taken part in the rising of December 1646 and thus, with Argyll's help, the possibility remained for him to reconcile himself to the regime in 1647. In June of that year he was even given permission to raise a regiment for military service in Spain. However, this plan was compromised that same month with the news that he had maintained communications with known Royalists. Excommunicated and imprisoned for a time, it seems that he was then allowed to go into exile in the Netherlands where he remained for much of 1648.[133]

Meanwhile, after years of warfare, matters began to come to a head in the three Stuart kingdoms. By February 1649 the radical Kirk Party had taken control of the reigns of Scottish government and had passed the Act of Classes – legislation designed to exclude Royalists and the more conservative Covenanters from office. Meanwhile, in England a political faction that broadly encompassed the Independents, Oliver Cromwell and the New Model Army had manoeuvred itself into power. On 26 January Charles I was executed at Whitehall and England saw the institution of a republic and the elevation of Cromwell to a position as foremost authority in the land. The Scottish reaction to the regicide was one of outrage, and within a month a decision had been taken by the Kirk Party to declare Charles, Prince of Wales, as king, not just of Scotland, but of Great Britain and Ireland as a whole. This had Britannic implications and guaranteed a hostile response from the fledgling Cromwellian regime. But firstly Cromwell decided on the need to subjugate Ireland. He duly embarked on a bloody campaign with the result that, by the time of his return to England in May 1650, this goal had largely been achieved.[134]

---

133 *Diplomatic Correspondence of Jean de Montereul*, II, 2–3, 50, 95, 120, 126–127, 141–142, 152, 165–169 (Montereul to Mazarin, 9 February 1647), (same to same, 9 March 1647), (same to same, 6 April 1647), (same to same, 27 April 1647), (same to same, 4 May 1647), (same to same, 11 May 1647), (same to same, 1 June 1647), (same to same, 15 June 1647); *APS, 1643–47*, 717; *Collection of State papers of John Thurloe*, II, 89 (Leslie to Committee of Estates, 27 March 1647); Gordon, *Britane's Distemper*, 200; Gordon and Gordon, *Genealogical History*, 537; *The Records of the Commissions of the General Assemblies of the Church of Scotland holden in Edinburgh the Years 1648 and 1649*, eds A.F. Mitchell and J. Christie (Edinburgh, 1896), 414.

134 Macinnes, *British Revolution*, 184–190; J.S. Wheeler, *Cromwell in Ireland* (Dublin, 1999); M. Ó Siochrú, *God's Executioner: Oliver Cromwell and the Conquest of Ireland* (London, 2008), 77–133.

During this time Lewis Gordon had returned to Scotland and had become involved in renewed Royalist plotting. He took part in the ill-co-ordinated and poorly-supported Pluscardine Rising of February–May 1649, but this produced little other than a pretext for the government to execute the second marquess of Huntly. This was in spite of the fact that he had been in prison for many months and had had nothing to do with the affair.[135] He was beheaded in Edinburgh on 22 March 1649.[136] The following year Lewis also formed part of the abortive Royalist coup known as 'the Start'. This attempted rising was very much a reactionary effort. On 24 June 1650 Charles II had landed on Scottish soil and, since that time, had been increasingly unhappy at the requirements being placed upon him by the Kirk Party. Cromwell had also invaded Scotland in July and had gone on to trounce the much-purged Scottish army at Dunbar (3 September). It had thus seemed to Charles that his continued adherence to the Kirk Party was not necessarily the best route into power. However, having arranged that Lewis and other key Royalists would rise on 3 October and that he would join them in the field, the king got cold feet and the whole thing was called off.[137]

Nevertheless, with increasing divisions opening up in the Kirk Party over issues such as the ideal relationship between the Estates and the king, and with Cromwell's army making significant military inroads, moves were gradually made to bring Lewis Gordon and the other Royalist nobles back into the political fold. On 20 October 1650 Lewis, the now Royalist Middleton and a number of others had signed what has become known as the 'Northern Band' – essentially an agreement to remain in arms until the authorities accepted that they did not intend to cause division and that they were in favour of the Solemn League. The Kirk Party duly issued an act of indemnity with the result that on 4 November the Royalists formally disbanded at Strathbogie.[138] From January 1651 a process was initiated to relax Lewis from his sentence of excommunication, while in March the title of marquess of Huntly was restored to him and the sentence of forfeiture lifted.[139] Following on from this, June saw the repeal of the

135 Gordon and Gordon, *Genealogical History*, 548–549; Stevenson, *Revolution and Counter Revolution*, 121–124.

136 *Extracts from the Records of the Burgh of Edinburgh, 1642–1655*, ed. M. Wood (Edinburgh, 1931), 192.

137 Stevenson, *Revolution and Counter Revolution*, 141–154; J.D. Grainger, *Cromwell against the Scots. The last Anglo-Scottish War, 1650–1652* (East Linton, 1997), 61–62.

138 Stevenson, *Revolution and Counter Revolution*, 155; Furgol, *Regimental History*, 378. The 'Northern Band' was also circulated in pamphlet format: Anon., *The Declaration and Engagement of the Marquesse of Huntley, the Earle of Atholl, Generall Midletou, and many of the nobility of Scotland that have lately taken up arms for the defence of his Maiesties person and just authority* (1650).

139 *The Records of the Commissions of the General Assemblies of the Church of Scotland holden in Edinburgh in 1650, in St Andrews and Dundee in 1651 and in Edinburgh in 1652*, ed. J. Christie

Act of Classes and the entry of the new, third marquess of Huntly and a number of others as members of the Committee of Estates.[140] He was also subsequently put in charge of all the forces raised in the shires of Aberdeen and Banff and was instructed by the king to bring them up to the main Scottish army.[141]

But Huntly seems to have achieved little. He never managed to reinforce the Scottish army in the South and, when the king marched to England in the ill-fated campaign that ended with defeat at the Battle of Worcester (3 September), Huntly failed to engage the Cromwellian forces that had been left in Scotland.[142] Following this, the final conquest of the North remained only a matter of time. On 28 September most of the members of the Committee of Estates were captured at Alyth in Angus, thus leaving only a few isolated pockets of resistance. In the North-East Huntly and the earl of Balcarres did hold out for a time but could make little headway against the enemy.[143] By 21 November Huntly had submitted to the Cromwellian forces of Colonel Overton on condition that his properties would not be garrisoned and that he and his followers would be protected in their person and estates. Overton also undertook to do his utmost to petition that the Gordon land would remain free of taxation.[144]

By the end of May 1652 Scotland had been fully subdued by Cromwell's forces, and little resistance was mounted against his regime for the remainder

---

(Edinburgh, 1909), 242–247, 272–273; NAS, GD 44/13/3/2; *APS, 1648–60*, 648, 652; Gordon and Gordon, *Genealogical History*, 559.

140 Young, *Scottish Parliament*, 285–286, 289.

141 NAS, GD 44/55/1/42–43; NAS, GD 44/55/1/44, ff. 70–71; Gordon and Gordon, *Genealogical History*, 560.

142 Furgol, *Regimental History*, 378. Furgol adds that Huntly's inability to bring up reinforcements may in part have been due to the slow response of burghs such as New Aberdeen. However, the diarist John Nicoll maintained that Huntly made no great effort to raise men for the king and instead spent his time 'poking up in his pockettis such moneyis as sould haif furneist the sodgeris'. See *A Diary of Public Transactions and other Occurrences chiefly in Scotland from January 1650 to June 1667 by John Nicoll*, ed. D. Laing (Edinburgh, 1836), 49. Meanwhile, writing in late October, William Clark insinuated that both Huntly and Alexander Lindsay, first earl of Balcarres, were levying money for horses but were keeping the proceeds for themselves. See *Scotland and the Commonwealth, 1651–53*, ed. C.H. Firth (Edinburgh, 1895), 335 (Clark to the Speaker, 23 October 1651). To what extent both of these stories merely contained scandalous hearsay is hard to accertain. Nevertheless, they do give an impression of how some regarded the third marquess of Huntly.

143 Stevenson, *Revolution and Counter Revolution*, 173–176; F.D. Dow, *Cromwellian Scotland, 1651–1660* (Edinburgh, 1979), 11–18; Grainger, *Cromwell against the Scots*, 164–172; *The Blairs Papers, 1603–1660*, ed. M.V. Hay (London and Edinburgh, 1929), 38, 43 (Gall to [Leslie], 10 November 1651), (Gall to Leslie, 24 November 1651).

144 Gordon and Gordon, *Genealogical History*, 561; *Letters from Roundhead Officers written from Scotland and chiefly addressed to Captain Adam Baynes, July 1650 – June 1660*, ed. J.Y. Akerman (Edinburgh, 1856), 39 (R. Baynes to A. Baynes, 20 November 1651); NAS, Dalhousie MSS, GD 45/1/120.

of the decade apart from the chaotic Glencairn Rising of 1653–54.[145] Committed Gordon involvement in this new Royalist upsurge remained minimal. For his part, Huntly was at pains to remain on amicable terms with the English and in late September 1653 he could be found giving surety to keep the peace. Indeed, in a letter to Gordon of Straloch he stressed that his good depended on such a course.[146] He remained in no position to indulge in Royalist adventurism. By late 1653 he was also in very poor health and by 18 December reports were circulating that he had died in his house of Bog of Gight.[147] Huntly's younger brother, Lord Charles Gordon, did join the Glencairn Rising in January 1654, no doubt bolstered in this decision by news that, if restored to the throne, Charles II would look to convey upon him the title of Lord Aboyne.[148] However, by late March Argyll had persuaded him of the need to return to a peaceable state. In a letter to Colonel Lilburne Argyll pointed out that he had met with his nephew and had promised him an interest in part of the Gordon estate should he lay down arms.[149] That Lord Charles had consented to this course of action was made clear in a letter he sent to Gordon of Straloch the following year. That it was addressed from Aboyne Castle probably provides some indication of the part of the Huntly estate to which Argyll had been referring.[150] With this marked display of self-interest Gordon support for the Royalist cause had limped into dormancy.

---

145 The last Scottish stronghold, Dunnottar Castle, surrendered in May 1652. See Stevenson, *Revolution and Counter Revolution*, 176. For an overview of the Glencairn Rising, see Macinnes, *British Revolution*, 203. For full coverage of the Cromwellian period in Scotland, see Dow, *Cromwellian Scotland*; R. Scott Spurlock, *Cromwell and Scotland: Conquest and Religion, 1650–1660* (Edinburgh, 2007).

146 *Scotland and the Commonwealth*, 193 (Lilburne to Cromwell, 11 August 1653); *Miscellany of the Spalding Club*, I, 18 (Huntly to Straloch, 26 September 1653). In a letter to General Middleton, Sir Edward Hyde bemoaned the fact that Huntly seemed to be striving to gain credit with the Cromwellian regime. See *Calendar of the Clarendon State Papers preserved in the Bodleian Library*, eds O. Ogle, W.H. Bliss, W.D. Macray and F.J. Routledge, 5 vols (Oxford, 1872–1970), II, 296 (Hyde to Middleton, 25 December 1653).

147 *The Spottiswoode Miscellany: a Collection of Original Papers and Tracts illustrative chiefly of the Civil War and Ecclesiastical History of Scotland*, ed. J. Maidment, 2 vols (Edinburgh, 1845), II, 150.

148 *Military Memoirs of the Great Civil War, being the Military Memoirs of John Gwynne; and an Account of the Earl of Glencairn's Expedition, as General of his Majesty's Forces, in the Highlands of Scotland, in the Years 1653 and 1654 by a Person who was Eye and Ear Witness to every Transaction, with an Appendix*, ed. W. Scott (Edinburgh, 1822), 228; *Scotland and the Protectorate. Letters and Papers relating to the Military Government of Scotland from January 1654 to June 1659*, ed. C.H. Firth (Edinburgh, 1899), 13 (Lilburne to Lambert, 7 January 1654), 30.

149 *Scotland and the Protectorate*, 60 (Argyll to Lilburne, 25 March 1654).

150 *Miscellany of the Spalding Club*, I, 37–38 (Charles Gordon to Straloch, 15 April 1655).

THE SINEWS OF WAR

The commitment of the family to the Royalist cause over the course of the 1640s and early 1650s had nonetheless continued to exact a heavy toll on the Gordon lords. Not only had it resulted in military defeat and much devastation to their landholdings, it had also brought with it the deaths of the second marquess of Huntly and his three eldest sons, George, Lord Gordon, James, Lord Aboyne and Lewis, third marquess of Huntly. Moreover, although the Civil Wars had provided the Gordons with a new commission of lieutenancy for the North, this had been tempered by the fact that Huntly had been placed under the higher authority of Montrose. The need to furnish an army for the conflict also continued to exhaust Gordon funds and added to the overall problem of burgeoning debt. Meanwhile, with Huntly's forfeiture came a situation whereby rival nobles could seek to feather their own nests at his expense. For example, in February 1646 the earl Marischal gained the right of superiority to the lands of Torterston and Ravenscraig near Peterhead – lands that would now be held directly from the king instead of from Huntly.[151] Similarly, in March 1647 Sir John Grant of Ballindalloch obtained superiority to the lands of Morinsh, again previously held from Huntly.[152]

But by far the most fundamental problem for the household was the increased influence being exerted by the marquess of Argyll. The manner in which he worked on the sympathies and loyalties of the children of the second marquess of Huntly has already been demonstrated. It also appears that by the mid-1640s Argyll had persuaded Lochiel and many of Clan Cameron of the benefits of ignoring Gordon calls for them to take up arms for the Royalists.[153] While probably never affiliating themselves fully to the Covenanting side, many Camerons continued to nurse an enmity towards Huntly that eventually resulted in their aiding of Middleton when the former was on the run in 1647.[154] Accompanying such ploys had been the continued wasting of Gordon territory during the 1644 campaign against Montrose. Like his Highland campaign of 1640, the main motive of this seems to have been to reduce the productivity of

---

151 *APS, 1643–47*, 564–565.
152 *Ibid.*, 721.
153 WSRO, Goodwood/1431/18–19 (Huntly to Cameron, 3 April 1644), (Lochiel to Campbell, 20 June 1644).
154 Conversely, some Cameron men saw no problem in joining Huntly's ranks during his Moray campaign of 1646. In depositions drawn up in Elgin in that year, it is recorded that 100 of Clan Cameron took part in the occupation of that burgh. See Barrett and Mitchell, 'Elgin's Love-gift', 50. In light of this it would seem that, for many of these clansmen, the desire to reap profit from the fortunes of war remained a primary motive for lending their support to any one side. The telling point remains that, when the chance presented itself, many of their number were perfectly willing to aid in the capture of the second marquess of Huntly.

Huntly's lands thus making it harder for him to recover from his debt-ridden state.[155]

For much of the 1640s Argyll also looked to secure a legal claim over the entire Gordon estate by buying up as many of Huntly's debts as he could. In November 1641, for example, he provided surety for a sum of £700 sterling (£8,400 Scots) due to a Mrs Mary Wakefield of London. As early as August 1642 he received legal title to the estate under the Great Seal. However, complications initially arose from the fact that debts of £5,580 sterling (£66,960 Scots) owed to an Andrew Benson and £8,327 sterling (£99,924 Scots) owed to William Dick of Braid remained unpaid. As such, Argyll was unable to gain full benefit from the Huntly landholdings at that stage.[156] But in 1648 he managed to buy up these two debts and began looking to take control of the Gordon rents and properties, all of the time maintaining that he was acting in the best interests of the family.[157]

With Lewis Gordon active on the Royalist side in the North for periods during 1649 and 1650, it is unclear to what extent Argyll retained undisputed control over the Gordon lands and rents. Evidence remains scanty for this period but it seems to be the case that upon the arrival of Charles II in Scotland, he did at least have garrisons in both Bog of Gight and Strathbogie Castle.[158] How the restoration of Lewis and the lifting of the Huntly forfeiture affected the situation is also somewhat unclear. Presumably because the estate still remained heavily in debt to Argyll, nothing fundamentally would have changed. But with the English occupation of Scotland came policies designed to undermine the traditional Scottish landed elite. This was done through encouraging creditors to pursue their claims on heavily indebted individuals. John Stewart, first earl of Traquair, became the most spectacular casualty of this policy; by the middle of the decade he was ruined. Huntly also came under pressure from his creditors at this time.[159] This seems to have provided Argyll with the final impetus to gain control of his nephew's estate. Indeed, by June 1653 he had obtained a bond from Lewis acknowledging the family debt and giving him the right to sell as

---

155 Having said this, the fact that Badenoch and Lochaber remained in the war zone from 1644 to 1647 made it virtually impossible for Argyll to realise any significant levels of rent. See *APS, 1643-7*, 786–787; Macinnes, *Clanship, Commerce and the House of Stuart*, 107–108; Inveraray Castle Archives, bundle 8/190.

156 *RGSS, 1634–51*, 450; Inveraray Castle Archives, bundle 173/9.

157 Gordon, *Family of Gordon*, II, 547–548; Aberdeen Special Collections, MS 658, 520–521; Inveraray Castle Archives, bundle 173/9; *Miscellany of the Spalding Club*, I, 21–22 (Argyll to Straloch, 20 February 1650); Anon., *The Last Proceedings of the Parliament in Scotland against the Marquesse of Argyle*, 7–8.

158 *CSPD, 1650*, 266 (Ayton to Nicholas, 1 August 1650).

159 Menarry, 'Debt and the Scottish Landed Elite, 23–29. The English policy on debt soon changed upon the realisation that it was driving many nobles to join the Glencairn Rebellion.

much of the estate as was necessary to meet it. Most importantly, Argyll was also confirmed as having full legal title to the Gordon lands.[160]

To say that the latter had had to use strong-arm tactics in order to bring this agreement off is something of an understatement. An initial English-mediated meeting between the two had not gone as Argyll had hoped. As a result he took out legal processes to pursue Lewis for debt so that troops from the Cromwellian garrisons might apprehend him. Lewis had taken to the hills to avoid this and a second meeting was subsequently organised with Argyll in order that a mutually agreed settlement could be arrived at. This was scheduled to take place at Finlarig Castle in Breadalbane upon the understanding that the parties would be accompanied by no more than eighty men each. By all reports Argyll had gone against the terms of this agreement by stationing hundreds of armed men within the immediate vicinity of Finlarig. As a result Lewis had felt compelled, for his own safety and that of his party, to agree with all that Argyll advocated. His death had followed only a few months thereafter, reportedly from a dropsy brought on by the many nights he had recently spent out of doors while on the run.[161]

In March 1654 Argyll met with representatives of the Gordon interest for the purpose of discussing matters relating to the management of the estate.[162] This in turn presented the opportunity for some of these men to get what they could out of the overall settlement. Lord Charles Gordon seems to have secured himself in Aboyne Castle at this juncture. Gordon of Buckie also laid claim to some lands in recompense for a sum owed to him by the Huntly lords.[163] Decisions were also taken as to who would administer the Gordon estates on Argyll's behalf. In the Enzie area this was to be Robert Innes, younger of that ilk, and for Strath-bogie, Sir Thomas Gordon of Park.[164] Not that collecting the rents proved an easy business; Innes seems to have experienced a number of problems, and at one point even requested of Argyll that a party of troops be made available for his use to that end.[165] It should also be remembered that Argyll had his own financial burdens to shoulder. He remained considerably in debt following his

---

160 Aberdeen Special Collections, MS 658, 520–521; Inveraray Castle Archives, bundle 173/9. The band acknowledged that Lewis was in debt to Argyll to a sum in the vicinity of £28,000 sterling (£336,000 Scots). See Inveraray Castle Archives, bundle 67/no. 1. Argyll's title to the estate was formally confirmed by Sasine in July 1655. See NAS, GD 44/14/2/3.

161 At least four first-hand accounts were later made of the Finlarig meeting. See NAS, GD 44/14/1/1–3; *Miscellany of the Spalding Club*, IV, 166–167.

162 WSRO, Goodwood/1431/20 (Hamilton to Argyll, 6 January 1655); *Ane Account of the Familie of Innes compiled by Duncan Forbes of Culloden, 1698*, ed. C. Innes (Aberdeen, 1864), 183.

163 *Ane Account of the Familie of Innes*, 181–182 (Argyll to Innes, younger of that ilk, 23 October 1656).

164 *Scotland and the Protectorate*, 60–61 (Argyll to Lilburne, 25 March 1654).

165 *Ane Account of the Familie of Innes*, 174–176 (Innes, younger to Argyll, 29 September 1654).

involvement in the Civil Wars and now shouldered a commitment to pay off Huntly's debts, albeit with income gained from Gordon rents.[166] In 1657, for example, he was obliged to pay money due to the hospital in Aberdeen.[167]

It was perhaps due to the privations being suffered by leading members of the House of Huntly that they now looked for solace through a newly invigorated religious piety. They turned not to the Kirk, but to the Church of Rome. The third marquess of Huntly had embraced the Catholic faith by the time of his death in late 1653, as had his brother Charles by the middle years of the decade.[168] It is from the time of their conversion that the Gordons of Huntly can legitimately be described as a Catholic household again. The widow of the third marquess, Mary Grant, also became an enthusiastic convert and saw to it that the young fourth marquess was brought up in the same faith. Until 1656 she provided shelter for the prefect-apostolic of the non-Gaelic speaking areas of Scotland, William Ballantyne, who was able to use Bog of Gight as his base of operations.[169] This remained a far cry from the heady days of the first marquess's dealings with Spain, but it can, at least, be presented as an attempt, albeit small scale, to promote Catholicism in north-east Scotland. Nevertheless, the Kirk contained the situation fairly effectively. The activities of Mary Grant and Lord Charles Gordon were monitored carefully, so much so that in 1658 the former was excommunicated for her 'obstinacie in poperie'.[170] Her Catholicism will certainly have done little to recommend her case to the marquess of Argyll. Indeed, in a letter of March 1655 he sought to make plain to her that nothing more could be made available in the way of additional funds to assist with her upkeep.[171] At the time she was living in the family's Elgin town house,

---

166 By 1660 Argyll's personal debts stood at £360,000 Scots. See Macinnes, *Clanship, Commerce and the House of Stuart*, 112.

167 *Aberdeen Council Letters*, III, 165–167, 298–299 (Instructions of Council of [New] Aberdeen to Jaffray, 1 May 1650), (Argyll to Council of [New] Aberdeen, 16 October 1657), (Instructions from Magistrates of Aberdeen to Mollysoun, 19 October 1657). Argyll offered to make the payment with goods garnered from the lands of Strathbogie. See *ibid.*, II, 273.

168 *The Blairs Papers*, 55 (Anderson to Gordon, 24 January 1654), 212–213 (Macbreck to an unnamed recipient in Rome, 28 January 1656).

169 Anson, *Underground Catholicism*, 55, 60; F.A. MacDonald, *Missions to the Gaels: Reformation and Counter-Reformation in Ulster and the Highlands and Islands of Scotland, 1560-1760* (Edinburgh, 2006), 141.

170 *Extracts from the Records of the Synod of Moray*, ed. W. Cramond (Elgin, 1906), 114, 118–119, 125; *Selections from the Records of the Kirk Session, Presbytery and Synod of Aberdeen*, ed. J. Stuart (Aberdeen, 1846), 243, 258. See, also, *The Records of Elgin, 1234-1800*, eds W. Cramond and S. Ree, 2 vols (Aberdeen, 1903–8), II, 369.

171 *Ane Account of the Familie of Innes*, 179–80 (Argyll to Lady Huntly, 2 March 1655). In her letter to Argyll, Lady Huntly sought to make no bones about her desperate condition: 'I heave lived all this winter without fyr exceipt sum littill I got for munie which with greit defeicultie could serve for the kitching.' See NAS, GD 90/2/82 (Lady Huntly to Argyll, 27 January 1655).

struggling to make ends meet on an annual maintenance payment that had been fixed following the death of her husband. She also had four young children to support: George, fourth marquess of Huntly and his sisters, Anne, Mary and Jean.[172] The Gordons had indeed fallen on hard times.

CONCLUSION

For the House of Huntly the years 1642 to 1660 were as eventful as they were costly. At the outset, the second marquess of Huntly had recognised that his reduced estate was overburdened by debt and that there was a need for rapid recovery. Throughout 1642 and the first half of 1643 he seemed content to remain at peace and even to participate in meetings on local affairs. Having said this, the attentions of past creditors continued to be a problem and Huntly himself did little to alleviate this by commissioning new building work at Strathbogie. On top of this, the political situation elsewhere in the three kingdoms once again began to cast a shadow over the affairs of the household. Aboyne's highly publicised role in the Antrim Plot brought suspicions that the household was becoming involved in renewed Royalist agitation, while the promulgation of the Solemn League and Covenant only compounded divisions that existed between Huntly and his eldest son, Lord Gordon. While the latter renewed his commitment to a Covenanting solution, Huntly moved ever further towards the view that the Royalist cause should be renewed in Scotland.

The failure of the Huntly rising of early 1644 only highlighted the continuing splits in the Gordon household, and these in turn continued to be exploited to the full by Argyll. However, the latter's wasting of Gordon lands during his pursuit of Montrose and MacColla helped convince Lord Gordon of the need to change sides in early 1645. Continued divisions within the household meant that support for Montrose was never as overwhelming as it might otherwise have been, but nevertheless the Gordon horse and foot made a key contribution to the Royalist war effort in Scotland. This has arguably not been fully recognised in the historiography of the Civil Wars. In connection with this it could be advocated that a more nuanced understanding is needed of the nature of the force that marched under Montrose's banner. In practice it was much more of a confederation of allies, and the victories themselves were collaborative efforts rather than the product of the grand designs of either Montrose or MacColla. In the end the Gordon troops owed their immediate allegiance to Huntly and his sons, who in turn had their own military priorities to meet.

Following Montrose's defeat at Philiphaugh, the Royalist war effort in the North of Scotland was hampered by his poor working relationship with Huntly.

---

172 Fraser, *Chronicle of the Frasers*, 439; Gordon, *Family of Gordon*, II, 580.

Despite this, the Covenanters did not fully extinguish the threat posed by these two, as well as by MacColla, until late 1647. This fact has previously not been fully appreciated by the many historians who seek to argue that the war was all but over by October 1645. During 1646 and 1647 the Gordons conducted two campaigns and at the time the chance remained that they might once again link up with the Irish brigades under the command of MacColla. Additionally, in late 1646 the possibility existed that the king might make an escape to the North-East to continue pursuing his war aims from there. However, when all was said and done, such active participation in the Civil Wars ended up being very costly for the House of Huntly, bringing, as it did, defeat, forfeiture, the death of Lord Gordon in battle, and the eventual execution of the second marquess of Huntly in 1649.

Under the leadership of Lord Lewis, the Gordons continued to be involved in the affairs of the nation, following the death of Charles I, firstly as Royalists in support of Charles II and then as part of the patriotic accommodation that sought in vain to oppose the Cromwellian conquest of the early 1650s. However, Lewis also remained increasingly at the mercy of Argyll, who by this time had successfully bought up most of the debts of the Huntly estate and was seeking to push his claim to gain full legal title to the lands. This proved the culminating point of Argyll's long-pursued strategy to use all available means to increase his influence over the family. The process was finally completed with the humiliating agreement foisted on Lewis at Finlarig in June 1653 and his death some six months later. Following this, Lady Huntly and her four small children remained in relative poverty for the remainder of the decade. Little did they realise that deliverance for themselves as well as for the Scottish nation was only a few short years away.

SIX

Restoration and Revolution, 1660–1690

INTRODUCTION

With the restoration of the Stuart monarchy in 1660 came another fundamental reordering of politics within the three kingdoms. The death of Oliver Cromwell in September 1658 had facilitated the rapid collapse of his regime and as a replacement many power-brokers had seen the return of Charles II as being the best means by which to promote stability and thus avoid the possibility of a descent into renewed internecine civil war. With this came the chance for those with Royalist credentials to reassert their position within the body politic, whether at a national or a local level. Indeed, for families like the Gordons of Huntly the whole turn of events must have appeared as something of a godsend following the grim years of the preceding two decades. The House of Huntly had demonstrated a remarkable and often enthusiastic adherence to the cause of the Stuart kings, and now came the reward of the restoration of much of what they had lost in the way of landholdings since the beginning of the Civil Wars. In addition, the stability provided by Charles's reign also gave the Gordon lords an opportunity to consolidate this new-found position of favour.[1] Indeed, in 1684 Charles II elevated George, fourth marquess of Huntly, to the rank of duke of Gordon. Furthermore, from the accession of the Catholic James VII and II in 1685, it appeared that the family might once again be elevated into the first rank in terms of political power. All this was soon to be brought into question

---

1 While it was the case that northern Scotland experienced a time of stability during the Restoration period it should nevertheless be remembered that significant levels of unrest became apparent in other areas of the country, particularly in the South-West where opposition to the Episcopalian Church settlement and arbitrary government was at its most pronounced. This unrest, and its impact at a wider Britannic level, has been admirably examined in T. Harris, *Restoration. Charles II and his Kingdoms* (London, 2005), 85–135, 329–376. The Restoration period in Scotland has traditionally been much less studied in comparison with the first half of the seventeenth century. A number of historians are now beginning to address this imbalance. See, in particular, C. Jackson, *Restoration Scotland, 1660–1690: Royalist Politics, Religion and Ideas* (Woodbridge, 2003) and G.H. MacIntosh, *The Scottish Parliament under Charles II, 1660–1685* (Edinburgh, 2007).

with the increasing unpopularity of that monarch and the onset of a new period of revolution following the landing in England of the Dutch pretender to the throne, William of Orange. The ultimate victory of the latter brought with it another period of uncertainty for the Gordons of Huntly, after having associated themselves with the Stuart cause once again.

RESTORING THE ESTATES

Given the deep and bitter divisions that were so evident during the Covenanting period, the Restoration in Scotland remained a relatively trouble-free process. Many ex-Covenanters such as Middleton and John Maitland, second earl of Lauderdale, began vying for powerful governmental positions and, across the board, Scottish Parliamentarians appeared anxious to demonstrate renewed loyalty to their monarch. The reconstitution of the Lords of the Articles also ensured that a royal agenda would once again begin to take precedence in governmental affairs. Under the guidance of this body the king's prerogative was reasserted with regard to the calling of Parliament and the choosing of ministers and privy councillors. The domain of foreign affairs was also to be retained under his sole direction. Meanwhile, the Act Rescissory repealed all legislation that had been passed since 1633, a measure that succeeded in washing away the controversial reforms of Charles I and the Covenanting regime since that time. Moreover, a full-blown Episcopalian Church settlement was re-established over the latter half of 1661, those in authority doubtless regarding the return of the bishops as being the best means of retaining some control over the Kirk.[2]

This is not to say that Scottish politics during these years were not tinged with a degree of factionalism. From the outset a notable rivalry was apparent between the Scottish secretary, Lauderdale, and the king's commissioner in the Scottish Parliament, Middleton, something that occasioned much political manoeuvring on both their parts in order to secure bases of power. But underhand attempts by Middleton to get Lauderdale thrown out of public office led to nothing less than his own political demise in 1663, Charles II being less than amused at what he perceived to be an impertinent attempt to dictate who should be suitable for royal service. This left Lauderdale in a commanding position within the Scottish political world and ideally placed to build up a support network based on patronage. He also succeeded in consolidating what has been termed an 'inner core' of supporters on the Privy Council, a grouping

---

2 See R. Lee, 'Retreat from Revolution: the Scottish Parliament and the Restored Monarchy, 1661–1663', in Young (ed.), *Celtic Dimensions*, 186–195; Brown, *Kingdom or Province?*, 148–149; MacIntosh, *Scottish Parliament under Charles II*, 1–35.

that included John Hay, second earl of Tweeddale, and, for a time, John Leslie, seventh earl of Rothes.[3]

As acknowledged supporters of the Stuart dynasty, the Gordon lords looked to regain lost ground within this new political world. In 1660 Lord Charles Gordon submitted a petition on behalf of himself and his nephew, the young marquess of Huntly, pointing out the poor financial position of the family and asking that some form of financial redress be considered.[4] The following year Lady Huntly followed this up with a request that she be settled with a jointure equivalent to the amount granted to her by her husband, the third marquess, and that her son and three daughters be provided with aliments suitable to their noble position and that some effort be made to offset the debts they had incurred while attempting to maintain the status of their birth over the previous decade. She also hoped that one of the family's properties could now be made available to herself and her children.[5] In light of this petition it is likely that she and her family did at least gain temporary benefit from an Act of Parliament of July 1661 which granted Royalist households six years grace from having to meet whatever debts they had built up.[6]

Much more spectacular were the gains made by the family following the forfeiture and execution of the marquess of Argyll in May 1661. Although in the main Charles II had looked to reconcile himself with most of those who had opposed him and his father in the past, there remained certain key individuals for whom no pardon would be made available. Argyll was found guilty of having complied with the Cromwellian regimes throughout the 1650s and his fate was sealed.[7] What this brought to the House of Huntly was the sudden windfall of the return of all the estates that had fallen into Argyll's hands during the 1640s and 1650s. The household would also not be held liable for all the debts that Argyll and his heir, Lord Lorne, had bought up and built up on the lands in the meantime, a situation that left the latter under considerable

---

3 MacIntosh, *Scottish Parliament under Charles II*, 36–56; Brown, *Kingdom or Province?*, 146–147; R. Lee, 'Government and Politics in Scotland, 1661–1681' (unpublished PhD thesis, University of Glasgow, 1995), 57–67; G.H. MacIntosh, 'Arise King John: Commissioner Lauderdale and Parliament in the Restoration Era', in Brown and Mann (eds), *Parliament and Politics in Scotland*, 163–183.

4 BL, Add. 23114, f. 20.

5 BL, Add. 23116, f. 98.

6 Lee, 'Retreat from Revolution', 196. Lady Huntly provides a good contemporary example of a strong aristocratic woman acting in a very proactive manner on behalf of her family. She was by no means the only example of this in Restoration Scotland. See A. McSeveney, 'Non-Conforming Presbyterian Women in Restoration Scotland: 1660–1679' (unpublished PhD thesis, University of Strathclyde, 2005).

7 Donaldson, *Scotland, James V–James VII*, 361; Brown, *Kingdom or Province?*, 147–148.

financial duress.[8] Although Lorne was restored to the earldom of Argyll in
1663, the situation regarding the Huntly estates and associated debts remained
the same.[9] The Argyll lords could be found seeking to pursue their claim to
have this situation reversed without success well into the eighteenth century.[10]

But with the restoration of the estates came a fundamental change in circumstances for the House of Huntly – that of the division of the landholdings
between the fourth marquess and his uncle, Lord Charles. The rise of the
latter had commenced in September 1660 with his elevation to the peerage as
earl of Aboyne, lord of Strathavon and Glenlivet.[11] Following on from this, a
charter of 14 April 1662 granted him and his heirs holdings that included the
lands and lordships of Aboyne, Glen Tanar, Glen Muick, Cabrach, the forest
of Blackwater, the lands, lordship and barony of Strathavon and the towns and
forests of Glenlivet. The charter concluded with the proviso that the grant of
these lands was subject to the restriction that they not exceed the annual value
of £400 sterling (£4,800 Scots) and that any lands granted in excess of that
value were to be returned to the marquess of Huntly free of any debt.[12] Another
charter of the same date set out the myriad of lands and privileges that were to
be conveyed back to the marquess of Huntly. It also stipulated that an annual
sum of £500 sterling (£6,000 Scots) be made available to the widowed Lady
Huntly for her upkeep and that provisions be made for the maintenance of
the young Huntly's three sisters and his uncle, Lord Henry, the latter having
recently arrived in Scotland from Poland.[13] These latter amounts were to be

---

8 Bulloch, *First Duke of Gordon*, 5; *A Supplement to Burnet's History of My Own Time derived
   from his Original Memoirs, his Autobiography, his Letters to Admiral Herbert and his Private
   Meditations all hitherto unpublished*, ed. H.C. Foxcroft (Oxford, 1902), 6; Inveraray Castle
   Archives, bundle 173/9; NAS, GD 44/55/1/46, ff.73–75; *APS, 1661–9*, 102; A. Cunningham, *The
   Loyal Clans* (Cambridge, 1932), 313.

9 *Supplement to Burnet's History of My Own Time*, 83–84; Hopkins, *Glencoe*, 40.

10 *RPCS, 1669–72*, 97; *Leven and Melville Papers. Letters and State Papers chiefly addressed to
   George, Earl of Melville, Secretary of State for Scotland, 1689–1691, from the Originals in possession of the Earl of Leven and Melville*, ed. W.L. Melville (Edinburgh, 1843), 374–375 (Argyll to
   William III and II, 20 January 1690), (Argyll to Melville, 20 January 1690); *The Argyle Papers*,
   ed. J. Maidment (Edinburgh, 1834), 14; Inveraray Castle Archives, bundle 173/9; *APS, 1696–1701*,
   228–230, 232, 244, 252; *Seafield Correspondence from 1685 to 1708*, ed. J. Grant (Edinburgh, 1912),
   318 (Seafield to Carstairs, 1 January 1701); *CSPD, 1700–2*, 196 (William III and II to Queensberry,
   10 January 1701), (William III and II to Argyll, 10 January 1701); Hopkins, *Glencoe*, 466–467;
   Inveraray Castle Archives, bundle 67/no.1 (Campbell to Argyll, 1 January 1720).

11 *RGSS, 1660–68*, 3.

12 *Ibid.*, 113–114. The figure of £40 sterling recorded in this extract appears to be a misprint.

13 For detail on Lord Henry's time in Poland, as well as that of his sister, Catherine, see B.
   Robertson, 'The Gordons of Huntly: a Scottish Noble Household and its European Connections, 1603–1688', in D. Worthington (ed.), *British and Irish Emigrants and Exiles in Europe,
   1603–1688* (Leiden, 2010), 184, 189–190.

dependent on an up-to-date assessment of the value of the Huntly estate.[14]

Aboyne had no doubt been able to exploit royal promises made to him during the Glencairn Rising in order to help secure his earldom and the associated lands. Evidence also points towards the likelihood that he affiliated himself with the earl of Middleton at the time. In a letter to Gordon of Straloch of April 1661 he could be found referring to Middleton's nemesis, Lauderdale, as 'a constant and inueterat enemie to our familie'.[15] Moreover, in 1662 Middleton became tutor to the marquess of Huntly and donator of his ward,[16] a situation with which Lady Huntly seems to have been less than enamoured. Indeed, by March 1664 she found need to petition the king that she was experiencing trouble securing regular and full payments of money from both Aboyne and Middleton. This was despite the fact that it had been agreed by Middleton and a number of representatives of the family that she should receive her jointure, some money for the payment of debts and an annual payment for the maintenance of her three daughters. In addition, the young Huntly was to have received enough 'that he should want for nothing that was necessarie'.[17] She followed this up a month later in a letter to Lauderdale stating that she was still having trouble securing her money and that the representatives of the household 'will be loth to say annie thing for me that can offend my lord Midilltoun and my lord Aboyne'. She hoped that Lauderdale would be able to secure the payment for her and, for good measure, got her daughters, Anne and Mary, to send identical requests to that effect.[18]

From the early part of 1664 such letters to Lauderdale became more frequent, both from Lady Huntly and from the marquess of Huntly himself. For the most part they sought to ask continued favours of Lauderdale while at the same time expressing extreme gratitude for everything that he had done on their behalf.[19]

---

14 *RGSS,1660–68*, 114–116.

15 *Miscellany of the Spalding Club*, I, 39–40 (Aboyne to Straloch, 6 April 1661). This was probably in reference to Lauderdale's attempts of that period to secure a settlement for Lord Lorne. For some detail on this support for Lorne, see Hopkins, *Glencoe*, 39–40.

16 NAS, GD 44/13/3/3.

17 BL, Add. 23121, f. 61.

18 BL, Add. 23122, ff. 3–8 (Lady Huntly to Lauderdale, 10 April 1664), (Anne Gordon to Lauderdale, 10 April [1664]), (Mary Gordon to Lauderdale, 10 April [1664]).

19 BL, Add. 23121, ff. 19–22, 57–58 (Huntly to Lauderdale, 16 January 1664), (Lady Huntly to Lauderdale, 16 January 1664), (Lady Huntly to Lauderdale, 1 March 1664); BL, Add. 23122, ff. 35–36, 80–81, 130–131, 157–158 (Huntly to Lauderdale, 30 May 1664), (Lady Huntly to Lauderdale, 30 May 1664), (Huntly to Lauderdale, 4 July 1664), (Lady Huntly to Lauderdale, 30 August 1664), (Huntly to Lauderdale, 20 September 1664); BL, Add. 23123, ff. 182–185, 272–275 (Lady Huntly to Lauderdale, 12 September 1665), (Huntly to Lauderdale, 12 September 1665), (Huntly to Lauderdale, 30 December 1665), (Lady Huntly to Lauderdale, 31 December 1665); BL, Add. 23124, ff. 24–25, 46–47, 55–56 (Huntly to Lauderdale, 22 January 1666), (Lady Huntly

All this reflected the fact that the Scottish secretary was indeed becoming the major political force in the land and that, by contrast, Middleton's star was now on the wane. The letters also demonstrated a desire on the part of Huntly and his mother to rein in the overpowering influence of Aboyne. This viewpoint was certainly reflected in a letter that Huntly sent to the earl of Tweeddale in June 1667 questioning the friendly demeanour and true intentions of his uncle.[20] It was also reflected in the decision by Huntly, upon approaching the age of fourteen in mid-1664, to choose a number of individuals to act as curators for what he deemed to be the better management of his estate. This grouping comprised Lady Huntly, Lauderdale and powerful allies such as Tweeddale and Rothes.[21] It also included Sir James Baird of Auchmedden, a man whom Huntly was to leave in charge of his affairs in the North-East during periods spent on the Continent during the 1660s and early 1670s.[22]

Despite the interventions of Lauderdale and the curators, and notwithstanding the relatively speedy securing of Lady Huntly's jointure payment, the progress towards a final settlement of the affairs of the household proved to be a convoluted one.[23] In the first instance a disagreement between Huntly and his curators on the one hand, and his uncle, Lord Henry, on the other as to the true value of the estate, led to a lengthy delay in ascertaining what monetary portions should be allotted to the latter and to Huntly's sisters. Lord Henry went to the length of having his own private valuation carried out and was even prepared at one point to travel to the royal court at Oxford to plead his case.[24]

to Lauderdale, 3 February 1666), (Huntly to Lauderdale, 12 February 1666); BL, Add. 23125, ff. 94–95, 140–141 (Huntly to Lauderdale, 26 September 1666), (Lady Huntly to Lauderdale, 8 November 1666); BL, Add. 23128, f. 206 (Huntly to [Lauderdale], 3 December 1667); NLS, Yester Papers, MS 7004, f. 32 (Huntly to [Lauderdale], 16 April 1670); NLS, Yester Papers, MS 7005, ff. 6–7 (Huntly to Lauderdale, 5 February 1671). Lauderdale's efforts on behalf of the family did not go unnoticed or unappreciated by others outside the immediate family circle. See, for example, Edinburgh University Special Collections, Rothes Correspondence, La.iv.38, f. 19 (Rothes to Lauderdale, 24 May [no year]).

20 NLS, Yester Papers, MS 7003, ff. 50–51 (Huntly to Tweeddale, 18 June 1667).

21 BL, Add. 23122, ff. 80–81, 130–131 (Huntly to Lauderdale, 4 July 1664), (Lady Huntly to Lauderdale, 30 August 1664); BL, Add. 23123, ff. 178–179 (Huntly's curators to Lauderdale, 9 September 1665); BL, Add. 23124, ff. 34–35 (Huntly's curators to Lauderdale, 25 January 1666).

22 Baird, *Genealogical Collections*, 83–84 (Huntly to Auchmedden, 30 October 1664 [1669?]), (Huntly to Auchmedden, 30 July 1670). It is likely that part of the date of the first letter was wrongly transcribed by Baird.

23 BL, Add. 23122, f. 36 (Lady Huntly to Lauderdale, 30 May 1664).

24 Bulloch, *Polish 'Marquises of Huntly'*, 9–14, including transcriptions of letters: (Henry Gordon to [Lauderdale?], [n.d.]), (Henry Gordon to Lauderdale, 27 February 1665), (Henry Gordon to Lauderdale, 18 March 1665), (Henry Gordon to Charles II, 18 November 1665); BL, Add. 23123, ff. 184–185 (Huntly to Lauderdale, 12 September 1665); *RPCS, 1661–64*, 615–616 (Charles II to the Privy Council, 14 October 1664); Edinburgh University Special Collections, La.iv.38, f. 332

It was not until March 1667 that the king decided to follow the recommendations of Huntly's curators that Henry should be granted an annuity of 5,000 merks Scots (£3,333 Scots).[25] It was subsequently decided that this would be raised out of rents on a number of lands in the vicinity of Grange, Drumdelgie and Ruthven.[26] The king also eventually followed the recommendations with regard to the annuities for Anne, Mary and Jean, who were granted £18,000, £14,000 and £10,000 Scots respectively.[27]

A final settlement between Huntly and Aboyne over the division of land took even longer to conclude. From 1664 Huntly and his curators looked to assert that the lands granted to Aboyne did indeed amount to a yearly value of over £400 sterling and upon the king's instructions a formal valuation of the true worth of the estate was authorised.[28] However, this process was hampered by what was reportedly obstructionism on the part of Aboyne and some of those who held portions of his land by wadset. For example, in January 1665 Huntly reported to the Privy Council that he was having trouble getting access to some properties and papers held by Aboyne that would assist in the settlement of the estate affairs.[29] In August 1666 the Privy Council had to send specific charges to several non-compliant wadsetters for them to reveal the value of the lands they occupied.[30] Huntly also became concerned about the fact that Aboyne was cutting down sections of forests, selling the wood and redeeming wadsets on lands.[31] The fact that Huntly embarked on a lengthy tour of Europe in the late 1660s and early 1670s further lengthened the revaluation process. According to Huntly, it also presented Aboyne with the opportunity to continue trying to work things to his best advantage.[32] Finally, in August 1672 a decision was arrived at whereby Aboyne was required to renounce lands in favour of his nephew, in keeping with what had been stipulated in 1662 concerning the figure of £400 sterling. Huntly regained Strathavon, Glenlivet, Cabrach and the forest of Blackwater, 'all lyeing contigue to the said marquis his estate, and at a great

(Rothes to Lauderdale, 6 March [no year]); NAS, GD 44/55/1/47–48 (Charles II to Huntly's curators, 30 October 1665), (Charles II to Rothes, 21 December 1665); BL, Add. 23123, ff. 178–179 (Huntly's curators to Lauderdale, 9 September 1665); BL, Add. 23124, ff. 34–35 (Huntly's curators to Lauderdale, 25 January 1666).

25 Bulloch, *Polish 'Marquises of Huntly'*, 14; BL, Add. 23123, ff. 178–179 (Huntly's curators to Lauderdale, 9 September 1665).

26 NLS, MS 7003, ff. 48–49 (Huntly to Tweeddale, 27 May 1667); Bulloch, *Polish 'Marquises of Huntly'*, 14–15; *RPCS, 1665–69*, 302–305.

27 *RPCS, 1665–69*, 269–271 (Charles II to the Privy Council, 21 March 1667).

28 *RPCS, 1661–64*, 615–616 (Charles II to the Privy Council, 14 October 1664).

29 *RPCS, 1665–69*, 9–10.

30 *Ibid.*, 185–186.

31 NLS, MS 7003, ff. 24–25 (Lady Huntly to Tweeddale, 21 July 1666); *RPCS, 1665–69*, 190.

32 *RPCS, 1669–72*, 564; NLS, MS 7005, ff. 6–7 (Huntly to Lauderdale, 5 February 1671).

distance from the Earle of Aboyne', as well as the lands of Glen Tanar and Glen Muick on the south side of the River Dee. This left Aboyne with the lands directly appertaining to the title of his earldom on the north side of that same river.[33]

On balance it is certainly arguable that by the mid-1670s the marquess of Huntly had done well for himself, particularly when it is remembered how low the fortunes of the family had stood prior to 1660. Argyll's hold of the Gordon landholdings had been overturned and the weight of debt built up by him on the estate had been negated by the settlement of 1662. For a time this settlement had also brought about a drastic and fundamental division of the landhold-ings between the newly elevated earl of Aboyne and his nephew, the fourth marquess of Huntly; however, as has been seen, in 1672 much of the land was returned to the latter, leaving the estate not too dissimilar in terms of terri-tory to how it stood prior to the Civil Wars. But the creation of a new earldom out of the Aboyne lands was in itself a fundamental change in circumstances, bringing as it did a permanent alienation of the associated landholdings to this newly created noble household. By contrast Huntly's other uncle, Lord Henry, received relatively little, particularly when the value of his annuity is compared with the sums allotted to Anne, Mary and Jean. He died in Drumdelgic in 1675, and, unlike Aboyne, did not spawn a lineage of his own.[34]

What the dealings of the 1660s and 1670s also revealed was the remarkable bitterness that was generated within the family as a result. Huntly's increasing feelings of antipathy towards Aboyne were made plain on several occasions. The relationship between Huntly and Lord Henry also remained bitter. In one of his letters to Lauderdale Huntly could be found referring to the 'extrauagant pretensions' of the latter.[35] At the same time Henry found cause to express much disappointment at the manner in which he had been received by his family, stating that he had been better treated among foreigners than by his relations in Scotland.[36] But he remained luckier than some. In May 1664 his twin sister, Catherine, wrote from Warsaw hinting that she too would be obliged to receive the benefits of her birth into the noble House of Huntly.[37] Nothing seems to have been followed up on her behalf. One-time guardian of the twins, William Davidson, also wrote a letter pleading that he had expended much money on their upbringing and education in France and Poland since their birth and had received nothing from the family in return. He also pointed out that, as well as lending money to the second marquess of Huntly, he had also been forced

33 BL, Add. 23135, ff. 193–195 ('Report anent Huntly, 1672').
34 Bulloch, *Polish 'Marquises of Huntly'*, 15.
35 BL, Add. 23123, ff. 184–185 (Huntly to Lauderdale, 12 September 1665).
36 Bulloch, *Polish 'Marquises of Huntly'*, 12–13 (Lord Henry Gordon to Lauderdale, 18 March 1665).
37 *Ibid.*, 10–11 (Catherine, Countess Morztyn to [Lauderdale?], May 1664).

to provide a sum to pay for the funeral of James, Lord Aboyne, following the latter's death while in exile in France. In light of all this he hoped that the household in Scotland would see fit to compensate him for his trouble.[38] Again there is no evidence that anything was forthcoming on this score.

The restoration of the Gordon lands appears to have injected new life into the House of Huntly. Indeed, the evidence would suggest that from the late 1660s the fourth marquess was in a strong enough financial position to regain control of much of the land that had been wadsetted by his grandfather and great-grandfather. This fact seems clear when a comparison is drawn between the respective land valuations made for Aberdeenshire in the years 1667 and 1674. These valuations were assembled parish by parish for tax assessment purposes and were based on the rental value of each property as of the year 1656. As the decades went by, these fixed values bore little relation to the real worth of the land and it was rather through changing the tax rates that rises in value were accounted for. As such, given the fixed level of overall valuation figures, this system proves highly useful when looking to gain an indication of how nobles such as Huntly were faring over the decades in terms of lands held within a given parish.[39]

Between 1667 and 1674 it can be seen that the Huntly share of the valuations increased markedly in each of the parishes of the Presbytery of Strathbogie. Huntly had therefore more or less succeeded in gaining full control of properties that had, in all probability, previously been wadsetted. In Dunbennan the Huntly share of the valuation rose from £1,100 to £1,610 out of the total parish valuation of £1,610; in Kinnoir it rose from £500 to £1,260 out of a total of £1,260; in Ruthven/Botary it rose from £959 to £3,160 out of a total of £3,160; in Gartly it rose from £620 to £1,040 out of a total of £1,040; in Drumdelgie it rose from £425 to £650 out of a total of £650; in Rhynie/Essie it rose from £775 to £1,437 out of a total of £1,702; and in Glass it rose from zero to £1,800 out of a total of £1,800.[40] To a certain extent this shift is also apparent when comparing rental sheets of the Strathavon/Glenlivet holdings from 1680 and 1683, where there is some reduction in wadsetted (and even feued) properties and a resultant increase in some rental values. For example, whereas the properties of Achriachan and Wester Campdal were jointly feued for an annual figure of just over £47 in 1680,

38 NLS, Miscellaneous Manuscripts, MS 2955, f. 29–29v (Davidson to [Lauderdale], 21 April 1667).
39 R. Callander, 'The Pattern of Land Ownership in Aberdeenshire in the Seventeenth and Eighteenth Centuries', in D. Stevenson (ed.), *From Lairds to Louns. Country and Burgh Life in Aberdeen, 1600–1800* (Aberdeen, 1986), 1.
40 *The Valuation of the County of Aberdeen for the Year 1667*, eds A. and H. Tayler (Aberdeen, 1933), 30–31; Aberdeen City Council Archives, 1/15/1, Valuation Book of the County of Aberdeen made in the year 1674. The figures have been rounded down where necessary to ignore shillings and pence.

by 1683 they were apparently no longer held in feu but were being rented out for just over £65 each. Similarly, where in 1680 Nevie was held in wadset for the annual figure of £40, by 1683 it was realising £60. Not everything, however, changed. The property of Delnabo was still feued out for £46 a year in 1683 and although Lettoch no longer seemed to be wadsetted, it was realising the same rent as it had been in 1680.[41]

Evidence would also suggest that the fourth marquess of Huntly was less of a spendthrift than his immediate forebears. This seems to have been particularly the case with regard to building works. It is telling that Strathbogie Castle saw no further reconstruction or repair work following the execution of the second marquess in 1649 and, as the century wore on, Bog of Gight (Gordon Castle) increasingly became the main residence of the family. Whereas in the past the Gordon lords had seen fit to maintain a number of palatial residences, by the 1680s Gordon Castle had essentially become the sole pride and joy of the family. The fourth marquess had evidently recognised a need to retain a more modest number of holdings. Also noteworthy is a contract drawn up in 1682 whereby the fourth marquess undertook to provide a tocher of 15,000 merks Scots for his sister Jean's marriage to James, fourth earl of Dunfermline.[42] This sum simply does not compare with the higher figures that had been agreed by the second marquess for his three daughters thus indicating that the fourth marquess did indeed recognise the benefits of a degree of comparative austerity. He did, however, indulge himself in other areas. A number of references from the early 1680s attest to his keen interest in horse racing.[43] Horses were an expensive commodity and remained a key indicator of noble status.[44] It was recorded that in 1689 Huntly had twelve horses for his own personal use at Bog of Gight, one of them being valued at what seems to have been regarded as a remarkable price of 100 guineas.[45]

NATIONAL AND REGIONAL POLITICS

Although the recovery of the Gordon titles and lands had certainly been spectacular, this, however, did not see a corresponding rise in the fourth marquess of Huntly as a major political figure. Indeed, he did not even begin to approach the stature of his forebears in this regard. The early family historian, William Gordon, put this down to Huntly being precluded from public appointments

---

41 For the rental sheets, see V. Gaffney, *The Lordship of Strathavon. Tomintoul under the Gordons* (Aberdeen, 1960), 191–192.
42 NAS, GD44/13/11/2.
43 *The Annals of Banff*, ed. W. Cramond, 2 vols (Aberdeen, 1891–93), I, 160, 163.
44 Brown, *Noble Society in Scotland*, 213.
45 NAS, GD44/14/3/8.

on account of his Catholicism.[46] Given that Huntly barely registers on any of the records of state during this period, Gordon's assertion certainly seems to remain highly valid. But there was more to the matter than Huntly simply being Catholic. Although at a governmental level it was true that the Penal Laws were promulgated on five occasions during the Restoration period (1661, 1670, 1673, 1679 and 1681), usually this was in response to a need either to assuage public fears or to mirror policy south of the border. In reality the official position towards Scottish recusants was relatively relaxed. As such, although the laws brought with them the stipulation that no Catholic could hold civil or military office, in practice this was never applied uniformly across the board. For example, some Catholics attended a number of parliamentary sessions.[47] But the key, as Huntly correctly identified in a later memoir, was a willingness on the part of such men to sign oaths of allegiance putting king and country before religious affiliation and obligation, something that he remained unwilling to do. As he saw it, he 'lost great hopes of advancement' on account of his devotion to his faith.[48] Even during the period from 1679 to 1681 when the king's Catholic brother, James Duke of York, headed the Scottish administration it still proved problematic for Huntly to be shown much favour.[49] As late as 1683, opposition remained to the idea of him even being given a regiment to command.[50]

The fact that Huntly was still an adolescent in the 1660s and spent the early years of the 1670s travelling and campaigning as a soldier in Europe will have done little to improve his chances of making an immediate impact at home. Part of his education was conducted at the University of St Andrews during the years 1665 and 1666, under much protest on his part it has to be said.[51] His grand tour of Europe reportedly took in locations across Italy as well as in Austria, Hungary, Bohemia and Germany. An extract still exists from a diary detailing the cities, towns and fortifications visited by Huntly during the central European leg of his journey.[52] By June 1673 he was serving in the French army and was present at the siege of Maastricht. The following year he took part in the Burgundy

46 Gordon, *Family of Gordon*, II, 582.
47 Macinnes, 'Catholic Recusancy', 54–56; Anson, *Underground Catholicism*, 77. The most notable Catholic attendees were the earls of Nithsdale and Aboyne.
48 WSRO, Goodwood/1428, Incomplete memoir of the First Duke of Gordon, ff. 7, 16.
49 Hopkins, *Glencoe*, 68. For the York administration in Scotland, see MacIntosh, *Scottish Parliament under Charles II*, 179–211.
50 *Miscellany of the Scottish History Society*, 11 vols (Edinburgh, 1893–1990), XI, 185 (Claverhouse to Aberdeen, 1 March 1683).
51 BL, Add. 23123, ff. 274–275 (Lady Huntly to Lauderdale, 31 December 1665); Bulloch, *First Duke of Gordon*, 9–10.
52 Bulloch, *First Duke of Gordon*, 19; Gordon, *Family of Gordon*, II, 581; NLS, MS 7004, f. 32 (Huntly to [Lauderdale], 16 April 1670); NAS, Airlie MSS, GD 16/34/194 (Mouat to Airlie, 2 September 1668); NAS, GD 44/55/1/79–95; Robertson, 'Gordons of Huntly', 188–189.

campaign, and over the winter of 1674–75 he served under Marshal Turenne. In the summer of 1675 he campaigned in the army of the Prince of Orange in Flanders.[53] This desire to gain some experience of the noble art of war remained a common one for young aristocrats during the seventeenth century.[54] At least all this provided him with a rounded education. A contemporary, John Macky, described the marquess as a man well bred and knowledgeable of the *Belles Lettres*.[55] Huntly's interest in the acquisition of the latest books from France was certainly made plain in a number of his letters.[56] His marriage, in 1676, was to Elizabeth Howard, second daughter of Henry, Duke of Norfolk.[57]

By comparison, the first earl of Aboyne remained in a better position and was more willing to consider any action that might help him attain positions of power. Unlike his nephew, he did demonstrate a willingness to countenance signing oaths of allegiance and he drew benefits as a result. During the 1660s and 1670s he could be found attending a number of parliamentary sessions.[58] Moreover, in 1676 he was admitted a member of the Privy Council, something that brought with it an annual pension for life of £200 sterling (£2,400 Scots).[59] In accepting this, Aboyne put his past antipathy towards Lauderdale behind him and became an eager, if junior, member of the latter's power-sharing clique.[60] Over the course of the next three or so years he became a regular attendee at Council meetings and gained appointment to a number of public committees.[61] He also

53　Robertson, 'Gordons of Huntly', 184. For an overview of these campaigns, see J.A. Lynn, *The French Wars, 1667–1714: the Sun King at War* (Oxford, 2002), 40–44.

54　M. Glozier, *Scottish Soldiers in France in the Reign of the Sun King: Nursery of Men of Honour* (Leiden, 2004), 69, 86, 97.

55　Macky, *Memoirs of the Secret Services … during the Reigns of King William, Queen Anne and George I* (London, 1733), 195.

56　Scottish Catholic Archives, Blairs Letters, BL1/47/15 (Huntly to Burnett, 3 July [1677]); Scottish Catholic Archives, BL1/69/10 (Huntly to Barclay, 17 February [1681]).

57　Bulloch, *First Duke of Gordon*, 109.

58　*APS, 1661–69*, 3, 368, 446; *APS, 1670–86*, 3, 55. These were the second and third sessions of the first parliament of Charles II and the second and third sessions of the second parliament of Charles II.

59　*RPCS, 1673–76*, 545; *RPCS, 1676–78*, 6; *CSPD, 1675–76*, 546; *CSPD, 1676–77*, 222–223. In his memoir, Huntly made specific mention of Aboyne being one of the Catholics who was prepared to take the oaths. See WSRO, Goodwood/1428, f. 7.

60　Lee, 'Government and Politics in Scotland', 85–86. This was during a period when Lauderdale was coming under increasing pressure from political rivals and needed to inject new blood into his support network. See *ibid.*, 85; J. Buckroyd, *Church and State in Scotland, 1660–1681* (Edinburgh, 1980), 106.

61　*RPCS, 1673–76*, 547, 577, 590, 595; *RPCS, 1676–78*, 1, 3–6, 14–15, 17, 97, 105, 115, 122, 126, 133, 156, 166, 168, 177, 183, 188, 197, 199, 206, 213, 232, 237, 239, 250–251, 265, 270–271, 279–280, 283, 285–286, 291, 296, 327–328, 332–335, 337, 339, 347, 387, 389, 395, 400–401, 406, 413, 418, 425, 438, 444–446, 454–455, 459, 467, 470, 474, 476, 480–481, 491; *RPCS, 1678–80*, 263, 269–271, 278, 280, 293, 299, 301, 306, 344–345, 371, 374, 407–410.

managed to secure a number of influential positions in the North of Scotland, from that of a justice of the peace for the shires of Aberdeen and Banff to a commissioner for excise and supply and for the militia.[62] He also remained open to using violence and intimidation as a means by which to achieve dominance over his environs.[63] It was reputed that with this end in mind he often employed the services of Patrick Roy Macgregor, one of the most notorious Highland outlaws of the day.[64] Although never a major politician, he had, if nothing else, proved to be one of the great survivors of the mid-seventeenth century and on approaching death in March 1681 he may well have reflected on the relative comfort and security of his position in comparison with how things had stood during the 1640s and 1650s.[65]

Like Aboyne, Huntly also looked to become involved in local politics upon his return to Scotland. He seems to have been at pains to ensure that, while he was debarred from making an impact on the national stage, he made his mark at a regional level. This manifested itself in a number of ways. In the first instance he used his position as an influential magnate to help those he considered 'loyal persons' to be elevated and elected to positions of power in the shires of Aberdeen and Banff.[66] At times this involved the almost flagrant use of various forms of coercion. For example, during the 1681 election of commissioners for Banffshire, a number of complaints were lodged against him on account of the manner in which he attempted to interfere in matters, influencing (and by implication, intimidating) a number of the barons into voting in a certain way.[67] Through this he looked to ensure the elevation of individuals who would be suitably loyal to the power-brokers in Edinburgh, a fact that was made plain in a letter written to him by George Mackenzie in March 1685. Mackenzie intimated that:

> Those chiefly intrusted by his Majestie heer think the elections of commissioners for the ensueing Parliament very secure by your Grace's influence in all the shyres influenced by yow or your friends.[68]

62 *Records of the County of Banff, 1660–1770. One Hundred Years of County Government*, ed. J. Grant (Aberdeen, 1922), 60; *RPCS, 1661–64*, 675; *RPCS, 1665–69*, 284, 382–383; *RPCS, 1673–76*, 89–90, 587; *RPCS, 1678–80*, 220–221, 440–441; *CSPD, 1676–77*, 134–136; *APS, 1661–69*, 507–508, 543.

63 *RPCS, 1661–64*, 586–587.

64 A.I. Macinnes, 'Repression and Conciliation: the Highland Dimension, 1660–1688', *Scottish Historical Review*, vol. 65, no. 180 (Oct. 1986), 172. James Fraser described Macgregor as 'a vile Scithian rude outlaw' and referred to him being under the protection of 'the wicked lord Aboin Gordon'. See Fraser, *Chronicles of the Frasers*, 486–487.

65 For the month and year of Aboyne's death, see Bulloch, *Earls of Aboyne*, 12.

66 Huntly made this very point in his memoir. See WSRO, Goodwood/1428, f. 7.

67 *Records of the County of Banff*, 47–48.

68 NAS, GD 44/55/1/66 (Mackenzie to [Duke of Gordon], 10 March 1685).

Somewhat more oblique, but telling nevertheless, was a diary entry of Alexander Brodie of Brodie which stated that in June 1678 'Huntli carried al in Aberdeen'. Indeed, Brodie added with some sorrow that:

> This is the frame and constitution of our land. They that are great will cari all with them; not what's right, but what they will.[69]

Some years later Brodie's son and successor, James, also saw fit to comment on Huntly's techniques of persuasion. Evidently scandalised by the latter's methods, he commented that 'the Lord keip me from snares and temptations'.[70] Not only that, but from the 1680s Huntly also reportedly tried to utilise his increasing currency in governmental circles to influence regional politics. For example, Sir John Lauder of Fountainhall alleged that, in 1684, Huntly managed to sway the king's decision in relation to the election of a sheriff-depute of Aberdeenshire.[71] Huntly also succeeded in securing a number of local administrative positions. In 1670 and 1678 he was designated one of the commissioners of supply for the shire of Banff, while in 1677 he was appointed a commissioner of excise for Aberdeenshire.[72] In 1671 he was also appointed a justice of the peace for Aberdeenshire.[73] At a regional level, influential opportunities remained open to Catholic nobles.[74]

Evidence also points to Huntly working hard to retain or rebuild meaningful links with some of the Gordon cadet families. This was particularly the case with the Gordons of Sutherland. By the 1670s there had been some talk of that family changing their surname to Sutherland, something that no doubt would have further distanced them from the House of Huntly. However, from the early 1680s relations between the two households began to improve. In November 1682 Huntly and the heir to the Sutherland earldom, John, Lord Strathnaver (later the fifteenth earl), drew up a bond of amity promising mutual friendship and assistance. At the same time Strathnaver obliged himself and his heirs to

---

69 *Diary of Alexander Brodie of Brodie*, 401.
70 *Ibid.*, 492. For an examination of aspects of political management in Scotland during the reigns of Charles II and James VII, see A.J. Mann, '"James VII, King of the Articles": Political Management and Parliamentary Failure', in Brown and Mann (eds), *Parliament and Politics in Scotland*, 184–207.
71 *Historical Notices of Scotish Affairs selected from the Manuscripts of Sir John Lauder of Fountainhall, Bart., one of the Senators of the College of Justice, 1661–1688*, ed. D. Laing, 2 vols (Edinburgh, 1848), II, 569.
72 *Records of the County of Banff*, 146; *APS, 1670–86*, 221–227; *RPCS, 1676–78*, 186.
73 *RPCS, 1669–72*, 704.
74 Huntly did refuse to take the Test Oath of 1681. See WSRO, Goodwood/1428, f. 8. However, this proved only a temporary barrier to his advancement during the 1680s; his elevation to the rank of duke of Gordon in 1684 stands testament to this.

retain the surname of Gordon.[75] Close contacts were also maintained with the family of Gordonstoun during this period, a fact attested to by the correspondence that survives between Huntly and members of that family.[76] The fact that other Gordon lairds, such as Lesmore, Knockespock, Cocklarachy and Artloch, were employed as bailies to Huntly also points towards the idea of Huntly building and retaining a support network based on kinship.[77]

However, not all cadet families were closely allied to the main Huntly line. It has already been seen how the relationship between Huntly and Aboyne deteriorated during the 1660s and early 1670s. The second case in point was that of the Gordons of Haddo. From the time of his joining the ranks of the Privy Council in 1678, the political star of Sir George Gordon of Haddo had risen startlingly. This culminated with his elevation to the peerage as earl of Aberdeen and to the position of lord chancellor of Scotland in 1682.[78] This left Haddo in a position where he could assume a dominant role and seek to do favours for Huntly, instead of the other way around.[79] Huntly later described how the newly elevated earl of Aberdeen began to act coldly towards him and at one point tried to persuade him to resign superiority of some lands in order that they could be held directly from the Crown.[80] The extent to which Huntly's testimony should be taken as an accurate representation of Haddo's position is hard to say. Huntly clearly retained some bitterness and was writing some ten years after the event. Nevertheless, Haddo's rise, like that of the earl of Aboyne, was indicative of a subtle change in the balance of power in the North-East. The Gordons of Huntly had always had to contend with rival households, but now such households were emerging from within the extended Gordon kin network. The new dynasties of Aboyne and Aberdeen conducted themselves with an independency that

---

75 Fraser, *Sutherland Book*, III, 213–215; WSRO, The Gordon Letters, Goodwood/1166/8 (G. Gordon to [Huntly], 4 December 1682).

76 NLS, Altyne Correspondence, Dep. 175, box 69, letters 1424, 1448, 1487, 1541–1542, 1593 (Huntly to Sir Lewis Gordon, 2 June 1676), (Dunbar to Sir Lewis Gordon, 11 May 1678), (Huntly to Sir Lewis Gordon, 2 April 1678), (Same to same, 25 February 1679), (same to same, 26 May 1679), (same to same, 25 October 1680); NLS, Dep. 175, box 70, letters 1660–1662, 1830–1835 (Huntly to Sir John Gordon, 21 December 1682), (same to same, 12 December 1682 and postscript 14 December 1682), (same to same, 7 December 1682), (Duke of Gordon to same, 3 April 1685), (same to same, 30 April 1685), (same to same, 15 May 1685), (same to same, 21 May 1685), (same to same, 10 September 1685), (same to same, 19 November 1685), (same to same, 12 December 1685).

77 *RPCS, 1678–80*, 311.

78 *CSPD, 1678*, 461; *CSPD, 1680–81*, 537; *CSPD, 1682*, 557; *Letters, illustrative of Public Affairs in Scotland, addressed by Contemporary Statesmen to George, Earl of Aberdeen, Lord High Chancellor of Scotland, 1681–1684*, ed. J. Dunn (Aberdeen, 1851), xxx–xxxiii.

79 See Hopkins, *Glencoe*, 90, 112.

80 WSRO, Goodwood/1428, ff. 6, 12.

had rarely been seen in the Gordon conglomerate prior to the Restoration. Such families could forge their own political destiny and did not have to follow the Huntly line.[81]

To a large extent this was arguably facilitated by the fact that the House of Huntly was no longer the pre-eminent powerhouse of the North that it once had been. Much power remained but the family had less currency than at the time of the Union of the Crowns. Where once the Huntly lords had been leaders of the northern pack, they were now probably merely part of the pack; the fact that families such as the Haddo Gordons had risen to become fellow members of that pack was symptomatic of the change. Another key indicator was the fate of the lost Huntly sheriffships. Where they had once been the sole heredi- tary preserve of that household, they were, by the second half of the seven- teenth century, falling into the hands of other key rival families. In 1661 William Keith, sixth earl Marischal, was granted the sheriffship of Aberdeen during his lifetime.[82] The earl of Aberdeen also became sheriff of Aberdeenshire for a time, as did John Hay, twelfth earl of Errol.[83]

During this period Huntly also struggled to maintain his position in his Highland lordships. The continued holding of courts in Lochaber by successive Mackintosh chiefs (now designated 'of Torcastle') remained a bone of conten- tion. On top of this the Mackintoshes also pursued an ongoing feud with the MacDonalds of Keppoch over disputed rents. Huntly sought to support the cause of the Keppoch men, but his efforts at directly opposing Lachlan Mackin- tosh of Torcastle's expeditions into Lochaber failed. For example, an attempt in 1667 to encourage Lochiel and his Camerons to come out in arms against Torcastle came to nothing. Huntly achieved more success in encouraging dissi- dent Clan Chattan septs such as the Macphersons to remain distanced from Torcastle's chieftainship. He also required that his own Clan Chattan tenants lend Torcastle no support. It is certainly arguable that, when Torcastle received a commission of fire and sword against the Keppoch Macdonalds in 1681, he was unable to fulfil it due to a lack of support on the ground. It can be seen, therefore, that the Highland networking of the Huntly lords retained a degree of potency into the Restoration era. That said, the Mackintosh hold over the stewardship of Lochaber still rankled, particularly given that Huntly failed to buy Torcastle out on at least two occasions.[84]

81 A parallel can be drawn here with the relationship between the House of Argyll and the Campbell earls of Breadalbane.

82 *APS, 1661–69,* 68.

83 *CSPD, 1682,* 479.

84 Mackintosh, *Mackintoshes,* 271–278; Macinnes, *Clanship, Commerce and the House of Stuart,* 42–43; Macfarlane *Genealogical Collections,* I, 383–400; Bulloch, *First Duke of Gordon,* 51–54; *Mackintosh Muniments,* 136. This period also saw what should be regarded as a more minor rift

Also of concern to Huntly was the view the government began to take regarding his role as a Highland power-broker. In 1677 the Privy Council ordered that the castle of Inverlochy be garrisoned with a view to settling disturbances in that part of the world. Despite Huntly being keeper of the castle, the Privy Council did not seek his permission beforehand, the reason being, as John Campbell, earl of Caithness, pointed out, that as it was ultimately a royal possession, it was perfectly in keeping with protocol that a royal force could be stationed there. Huntly saw the matter differently but nevertheless felt obliged to give his blessing to the arrangements, albeit under protest at the manner in which the affair had been conducted.

Perhaps of more immediate concern to Huntly at this time was the Council's decision regarding who should be commissioned for keeping the Highlands and for holding courts in conjunction with this. Huntly and his bailies and followers were passed over in favour of others. Aeneas, Lord MacDonald and James Campbell of Lawers were made joint commissioners for the Highlands, while additional commissions of justiciary went to Archibald, ninth earl of Argyll, Alexander, fifth earl of Moray, Charles, first earl of Aboyne, John, earl of Caithness (later the earl of Breadalbane), and the new governor of Inverlochy – all men with their own Highland agendas.[85]

Huntly's interests in the region were more amply represented in the new set of commissions that were distributed in 1680. Huntly, Argyll, John, first marquess of Atholl, and Kenneth, fourth earl of Seaforth, were each granted an annual sum of £500 sterling (£6,000 Scots) in return for keeping the peace in areas of the Highlands that had been designated for them. However, in Huntly's case there was a catch. His jurisdiction being deemed too large for one man alone, it was decided that it should be split in two, with the earl of Moray being given control of the other half. Huntly's bounds would include the Mearns, Aberdeenshire, Banffshire and the areas of Badenoch and Lochaber lying within the shire of Inverness. Moray was to oversee the shire of Nairn and those parts of the shire of Inverness not granted to Huntly.[86] What this arrangement revealed

---

(at least from Huntly's point of view) between him and Sir Aeneas Macpherson of Invereshie. For a time Macpherson had been Huntly's bailie in Badenoch, but the post had subsequently been granted to William Mackintosh of Borlum, much to the chagrin of the former. From then onwards he regarded Huntly as a mortal enemy and later vented his frustration in a lengthy tract of 1703. See Bulloch, *First Duke of Gordon*, 54–61. For Macpherson's exhaustive diatribe, see A. Macpherson, *The Loyall Dissuasive and other Papers concerning the Affairs of Clan Chattan*, ed. A.D. Murdoch (Edinburgh, 1902).

85 NAS, GD 44/55/1/50–52, 54 (Privy Council to Huntly, 20 September 1677), (Thomas Gordon to Huntly, 21 September 1677), (Mackenzie to Huntly, [24 September 1677]), (Huntly to [Mackenzie], undated).

86 *Historical Notices of Scotish Affairs*, I, 261; *RPCS, 1678–80*, 428–429.

was another aspect of decline. When once the Huntly lords had been granted lieutenancies that encompassed much of the North of Scotland, in 1680 the bounds of the fourth marquess covered considerably less in the way of territory. Moreover, when for many years Huntly and Argyll had been the two main Highland power-brokers, now Seaforth, Atholl and, to a lesser extent, Moray, had succeeded in jostling for position. In terms of the northern Highlands Huntly was now by no means sole 'Cock of the North'.

FALSE DAWN

With the accession of the Catholic monarch, James VII and II, to the thrones of the three kingdoms in 1685 a range of new opportunities did initially open up for the Gordons of Huntly. This change in fortunes had actually been pre-empted the previous year with the elevation of the fourth marquess to the title of duke of Gordon, a promotion masterminded by the new chancellor of Scotland, James Drummond, fourth earl of Perth, who evidently saw Huntly's potential as a useful ally.[87] The new king soon looked to reintroduce discernible facets of Catholicism into public life. He saw to it that the Council Chamber at Holyrood was furnished as a Catholic chapel and even went to the length of allowing a Jesuit printing press to be established there. Moreover, in February 1687 he formally granted a degree of legal toleration for Catholics (as well as for Quakers) in the form of an Indulgence.[88] The actions of his chief ministers also reflected this change. In 1686, the lord chancellor, James Drummond, fourth earl of Perth, and his brother, John, first earl of Melfort, both converted to Catholicism, thus providing an indication of the extent of their loyalty to James as well as of their desire to retain his support.[89] And they continued to favour the duke of Gordon. Indeed in 1686 this alliance between the Drummonds and the Huntly Gordons was sealed with the marriage of Perth to Gordon's second sister, Mary.[90]

One of the first advancements granted to Gordon was a lieutenancy of the northern shires in response to the abortive invasion of the exiled and forfeited Argyll in May 1685.[91] Although Gordon's force never saw action, the idea of a

---

87　R. Hutton, *Charles the Second. King of England, Scotland and Ireland* (Oxford, 1989), 431; *CSPD, 1684–85*, 193; NAS, GD 44/13/3/6; *RPCS, 1684–85*, 54–56.

88　Anson, *Underground Catholicism*, 79–82; T. Harris, *Revolution. The Great Crisis of the British Monarchy, 1685–1720* (London, 2006), 169–171. In June 1687 a revised Indulgence looked to extend toleration to Presbyterians. See T. Harris, *Revolution*, 173.

89　However, they were to have little success in changing the overall negative impression of Catholicism held in Parliament. See R. Hutton, 'The Triple-Crowned Islands', in L.K.J. Glassey (ed.), *The Reigns of Charles II and James VII and II* (Basingstoke and London, 1997), 80.

90　*Chronological Notes of Scottish Affairs, from 1680 till 1701; being chiefly taken from the Diary of Lord Fountainhall*, ed. W. Scott (Edinburgh, 1822), 67.

91　NAS, GD 44/13/3/7; NAS, GD 44/13/4/22.

Catholic being given a military command did generate a degree of criticism.[92] Other favours followed. Over the course of 1685 and 1686 he was made a commissioner of supply for the northern shires, a member of the Privy Council, and a commissioner of the Treasury, all of which were granted without him having to adhere to the Test Oath.[93] During the same period he also received the governorship of Edinburgh Castle and the gift of the lands and barony of Mellerstanes in Berwickshire, the latter being proceeds of the forfeiture of Robert Baillie of Jerviswood for high treason.[94] In addition, in 1687 the king bestowed on Gordon the honour of being made one of the twelve knights of the Order of the Thistle, the ceremony for which featured an oath administered over a Catholic missal.[95]

Although Gordon initially welcomed the moves being made by James towards toleration of Catholics, he soon grew apprehensive as to the speed and manner in which the changes were being introduced.[96] The view of family historian William Gordon that the duke could foresee the coming of the king's own ruin, was probably over-reliant on the benefit of hindsight, nevertheless it was the case that his growing caution did begin to alienate him from James and the Drummond brothers.[97] William Gordon noted that during a visit to the royal court in March 1688, the duke found the king more distanced towards him, something that allegedly stemmed from misrepresentations made by the Drummond brothers.[98] And adding to the tension was the duke of Gordon's attitude towards the bitter dispute that had broken out between Louis XIV of France and Pope Innocent XI. Essentially a split had opened up in Catholic Europe between those who supported the Gallicanism of the French king and those who remained steadfast to the Vatican line. The duke of Gordon backed the latter while James and the Drummond brothers were heavily pro-French in persuasion.[99]

92 *Chronological Notes of Scottish Affairs*, 130. Gordon's was one of three lieutenancies, William, third duke of Hamilton and the marquess of Atholl being granted the other two. See J. [Murray], seventh duke of Atholl, *Chronicles of the Atholl and Tullibardine Families*, 5 vols (Edinburgh, 1908), I, 231–232 (Dumbarton to Atholl, 31 May 1685). For detail on Gordon's uneventful campaign, see *Journal of the Hon. John Erskine of Carnock, 1683–1687*, ed. W. Macleod (Edinburgh, 1893), 130–132.

93 *APS, 1670–86*, 467–469; *Historical Notices of Scotish Affairs*, II, 676, 762; *RPCS, 1686–89*, xxvii.

94 NAS, GD 44/13/3/8; *APS, 1670–86*, 594–595. In a letter to the duke of Queensberry, James revealed that he put the castle into Gordon's hands with a view to encouraging the town to have more regard for royal commands as well as to have a 'civiler' disposition towards Catholics. See W. Fraser, *The Earls of Cromartie, their Kindred, Country and Correspondence*, 2 vols (Edinburgh, 1876), I, cxi (James VII and II to Queensberry, 25 February 1686).

95 NAS, GD 44/13/3/10–12; *Chronological Notes of Scottish Affairs*, 223.

96 For his views on the Test Oath, see Fraser, *Sutherland Book*, I, 309–310.

97 Gordon, *Family of Gordon*, II, 584; Macky, *Memoirs of the Secret Services*, 195.

98 Gordon, *Family of Gordon*, II, 584–585.

99 See S. Pincus, 'The European Catholic Context of the Revolution of 1688–89: Gallicanism, Innocent XI, and Catholic Opposition', in A.I. Macinnes and A.H. Williamson (eds), *Shaping the Stuart World, 1603–1714. The Atlantic Connection* (Leiden, 2006), 79–114.

The tensions were soon reflected by the manner in which James resolved a land dispute that had been ongoing between Gordon and Sir Ewen Cameron of Lochiel. The duke had taken out legal processes against Lochiel over the right of superiority to some of the latter's lands in Lochaber. Following the forfeiture of Argyll, Lochiel had looked to champion his own claims of superiority over land previously held of that noble and, with Gordon also trying to assert his continuing interest in the area, the matter reached an impasse. Eventually, in May 1688 the king decided in Lochiel's favour. Gordon's by then lukewarm attitude towards royal policy on religion and his views on the dispute between the pope and Louis XIV doubtless contributed to the king's decision. Lochiel had now succeeded in obtaining new rights to the disputed lands as well as the right that he and his clan would no longer be accountable to the Gordon's courts – decisions that granted Lochiel a new level of independence.[100] It was another example of the decline of the overall position of the House of Huntly in the Highlands.

Soon overshadowing all of this was the revolutionary process instigated by the landfall in England in November 1688 of Dutch pretender to the Stuart thrones, Prince William of Orange. Discontent had been building in Scotland for some time over the king's policies on religion as well as over the arbitrary manner in which he had tried to push through his agenda. In the Privy Council an anti-Perth faction had finally emerged centring on politicians such as Atholl, Tarbet and Sir John Dalrymple, while on the streets of Glasgow and Edinburgh, popular unrest was much in evidence. By 10 December sufficient pressure had built up for Chancellor Perth to see the need to flee Scotland, a situation mirrored by the final flight of King James to France on the 23rd. It was a situation that those seeking revolutionary change were able to exploit. Following meetings between William and members of the Scots nobility in January 1689 it was agreed that a Scottish Convention of Estates should be called to decide the future of the country. The convention itself, which met in mid-March, soon became Williamite in its agenda, the supporters of King James being too ill-organised to prevent this. By comparison, those in opposition to James were much more driven and focused and soon carried all before them. By the end of March those seeking a change in regime were in control of a newly elected Committee of Estates and on 4 April it was declared that James had forfeited the Crown. William and his wife Mary subsequently accepted the throne as joint sovereigns.[101]

---

100 *Memoirs of Sir Ewen Cameron of Locheil*, ed. J. Macknight (Edinburgh, 1842), 209–210, 220–228; Mackenzie, *History of the Camerons*, 176, 178–179.

101 Young, 'The Scottish Parliament and the Covenanting Heritage of Constitutional Reform', 230–232; D.J. Patrick, 'Unconventional Procedure: Scottish Electoral Politics after the Revolution', in Brown and Mann (eds), *Parliament and Politics in Scotland*, 208–209; Harris,

Throughout this period of uncertainty the duke of Gordon remained governor of Edinburgh Castle. Like many, he seems to have been plagued with indecision over how he should react to events and to what extent he should look out for his own interests. In the initial absence of any instructions from James, Gordon remained willing to countenance rendering up the castle in line with a personal request from William of Orange to do so.[102] Given the assertiveness with which William was beginning to take hold of the reins of government in Scotland, it is evident that Gordon felt suitably justified in complying with this request and terms of surrender were duly drawn up by the newly instituted Convention. It was only at the intervention of the Jacobites John Grahame, Viscount Dundee, and Colin Lindsay, third earl of Balcarres, that Gordon was persuaded to hold out for King James.[103] In a famous meeting at the castle's postern gate high up on the rock, Grahame, then on his way to gather an army for James, reportedly assured the duke that help would soon be on its way.[104] However, following a three-month siege and with no sign of the approach of any Jacobite army, Gordon began to lose his nerve.[105] Finally, with supplies running low and with Williamite siege trenches getting ever closer

---

Revolution, 364–405. The interpretation advocated by scholars such as Young, Patrick and Harris successfully challenges the older accepted version of events in which the Scottish nobles were held to be 'reluctant revolutionaries' who were merely reacting to events in England and who out of self-interest looked to quickly secure a place for themselves within the emerging Williamite polity. See, for example, Donaldson, *Scotland. James V – James VII*, 383; I.B. Cowan, 'The Reluctant Revolutionaries: Scotland in 1688', in E. Cruickshanks (ed.), *By Force or by Default? The Revolution of 1688–1689* (Edinburgh, 1989), 65, 76–77; I.B. Cowan, 'Church and State Reformed? The Revolution of 1688–9 in Scotland', in J.I. Israel (ed.), *The Anglo-Dutch Moment. Essays of the Glorious Revolution and its World Impact* (Cambridge, 1991), 163–166; E. Cruikshanks, *The Glorious Revolution* (Basingstoke, 2000), 48–49; P.W.J. Riley, *King William and the Scottish Politicians* (Edinburgh, 1979), 3, 8.

102 NAS, GD 44/55/1/96 (William of Orange to Gordon, 6 February 1689).

103 *An Account of the Proceedings of the Estates in Scotland, 1689–1690*, ed. E.W.M. Balfour-Melville, 2 vols (Edinburgh, 1954–55), I, 1–2, 7–8, 10–12, 15, 27, 32–33; NLS, Yester Papers, MS 7035, f. 122; *APS, 1689–95*, 14, 17; C. Lindsay, third earl of Balcarres, *Memoirs touching the Revolution in Scotland, 1688–1690 … presented to King James II at St. Germains, 1690* (Edinburgh, 1841), 23–24, 26.

104 C. Lindsay, *Memoirs*, 30. The interview took place on 18 March. See Bulloch, *First Duke of Gordon*, 84–85.

105 Gordon did receive news in late March that James had embarked on an Irish campaign. See *Account of the Proceedings of the Estates*, I, 15; NAS, GD 44/55/1/98 ([L. Luiss?] to Gordon, 3 March 1689). Letters were also sent from James urging him to hold out. See Gordon, *Family of Gordon*, II, 630–632 (James VII and II to Gordon, 29 March 1689), (same to same, 17 May 1689). If Gordon ever received either of them in time, they did not bolster his confidence for long. The contents of the May letter imply that the earlier one may not have been received by Gordon at the intended time.

and the bombardment more damaging, he saw fit to surrender.[106] He delivered up the castle on 13 June.[107]

But Gordon's less than convincing defence of Edinburgh Castle must be judged within the context of the time. In truth, very little in the way of unequivocal, forthright Jacobite support emerged outside of the Highlands in 1689. Dundee did raise some of the clans and achieved a celebrated victory at Killiekrankie on 27 July, but his death in that battle deprived the Jacobite army of a charismatic leader and the campaign soon foundered following defeat at the Battle of Dunkeld on 21 August.[108] Moreover, the efforts of the Jacobite party in the Convention had lacked lustre, and, with the certainty of the Williamites gaining full control, nobles such Charles, sixth earl of Home, and James, fourth earl of Panmure, simply faded into the background and eventually retired to their own houses.[109] Meanwhile, key north-east nobles such as John, twelfth earl of Errol, George, ninth earl Marischal, and George, first earl of Aberdeen, remained quiet, clearly willing at this point to countenance the Williamite takeover.[110] Whatever Jacobite support there was in the northern Lowlands was clearly kept in check by members of the gentry who were enthusiastic for the Revolution. Ludovick Grant of Freuchy, Lord Reay, Lord Strathnaver and

---

106 *Account of the Proceedings of the Estates*, I, 56–57, 105, 110, 125; Gordon, *Family of Gordon*, II, 605. Balcarres made the comment that the duke had failed to make enough provision for an extended siege. See Lindsay, *Memoirs*, 24. The historian C.S. Terry concluded that, in the end, a lack of ammunition was the main problem. See C.S. Terry, 'The Siege of Edinburgh Castle, March–June 1689', *Scottish Historical Review*, vol. 11 (Jan. 1905), 172. Others have concluded that there was little excuse for the capitulation. See, for example, *Original Papers; containing the Secret History of Great Britain, from the Restoration, to the Accession of the House of Hannover. To which are prefixed Extracts from the life of James II as written by himself*, ed. J. Macpherson, 2 vols (London, 1775), I, 211. James Philip, author of the poem *The Grameid*, referred to Gordon being 'inglorious in arms' and 'losing name and fame forever'. See J. Philip, of Almerieclose, *The Grameid. An heroic poem descriptive of the campaign of Viscount Dundee in 1689 and other pieces*, ed. A.D. Murdoch (Edinburgh, 1888), 47. More recently Bruce Lenman has asserted that the Williamite siege of the castle was less than formidable, thus implying a lack of resolution on Gordon's part. See B.P. Lenman, 'The Scottish Nobility and the Revolution of 1688–1690', in R. Beddard (ed.), *The Revolutions of 1688* (Oxford, 1991), 154.

107 *Memoirs of the War carried on in Scotland and Ireland 1689–1691 by Major General Hugh Mackay Commander in Chief of his Majesty's Forces with an Appendix of Original Papers*, eds. J.M. Hog, P.F. Tayler and A. Urquhart (Edinburgh, 1833), 229 (Hamilton to Melville, 14 June 1689). For versions of a contemporary blow-by-blow account of the siege, see Aberdeen University Special Collections, MS 658, 528–671; Gordon, *Family of Gordon*, II, 586–608; *Siege of the Castle of Edinburgh, 1689*, ed. R. Bell (Edinburgh, 1828).

108 Brown, *Kingdom or Province?*, 173–174.

109 Lindsay, *Memoirs*, 35.

110 *Miscellany of the Scottish History Society*, XI, 243 (Claverhouse [Dundee] to Melfort, 27 June 1689).

the master of Forbes could all be counted among this number.[111] A number of those with links to the House of Huntly were also Williamite in sympathy, most notably Sir George Gordon of Edinglassie and Alexander Duff, a bailie to the duke of Gordon.[112] Meanwhile, in the Highlands, the Macphersons would not rise without a specific commission to do so from the duke.[113]

To a certain extent it is arguable that the duke eventually persuaded himself that the threat posed by a Williamite regime remained a lesser evil than the danger of ending up on the losing side in an extended civil war. The House of Huntly had experienced that scenario in the past, much to its cost. During the siege General Mackay wrote a letter to the duke imploring him to prevent his own ruin and reminding him that the Prince of Orange was no man's enemy over matters of religion. Mackay added that Gordon's moderation during the reign of King James would also stand him in good stead.[114] It was thus with hopes of keeping his person and estate intact that he was able to consider his options concerning the idea of surrendering the castle.

Although it stumbled on into 1690, the Jacobite campaign in Scotland was effectively checked following the defeat at Cromdale on 1 May. Two months later James's Irish army was defeated at the Battle of the Boyne. Within a wider European context the Revolution and the Jacobite campaigns had formed part of the bitter war being waged between William and his arch-rival, Louis XIV of France. This carried on for much of the remainder of the decade, but, essentially, with the defeat of the French fleet by the English navy at La Hogue in May 1692, all immediate hopes of rekindling the Scottish and Irish campaigns were dashed.[115] In the Scottish Highlands a handful of clans remained defiant for a time, but by mid-1691 it seemed clear to most that Jacobitism was, for the meantime, a spent force.[116] That summer John Campbell, first earl of Breadalbane, brokered a deal whereby the remaining clan chiefs agreed to submit to

---

111 *Memoirs of the War carried on in Scotland and Ireland*, 8, 13; Lenman, 'Scottish Nobility and the Revolution', 156. Indeed, as Dereck Patrick has noted, there was significant support for the Revolution across the North of Scotland, including in the burgh of Aberdeen. See Patrick, 'Unconventional Procedure', 225, 236–238. For more detail on post-Revolution parliamentary politics across Scotland, see D.J. Patrick, 'People and Parliament in Scotland, 1689–1702' (unpublished PhD thesis, University of St Andrews, 2002).

112 Lenman, 'Scottish Nobility and the Revolution', 155.

113 *Miscellany of the Scottish History Society*, XI, 256 (Claverhouse [Dundee] to Cluny Macpherson, 20 July 1689); Mackintosh, *Mackintoshes*, 284.

114 NAS, GD 44/55/1/99 (Mackay to Gordon, 23 April 1689).

115 Brown, *Kingdom or Province?*, 174. For the importance of the Irish dimension of the conflict, see J.R. Young, 'The Scottish Response to the Siege of Londonderry, 1689–90', in W. Kelly (ed.), *The Sieges of Derry* (Dublin, 2001), 53–74.

116 *Papers illustrative of the Political Condition of the Highlands of Scotland from the Year 1689 to 1696*, ed. J. Gordon (Glasgow, 1845), 9–10 (Hill to Melville, 12 May 1691).

the new regime by the end of the year. A number of clans missed this deadline but only one, the MacIains of Glencoe, was singled out by the government to be made an example of. The infamous Massacre of Glencoe took place on 13 February 1692.[117] The manner in which the Williamite regime could now extend its reach deep into the vastnesses of the West Highlands was perhaps indicative of the overall success of the revolutionary process.

In terms of a religious settlement, William (although himself a Calvinist) had looked to retain the status quo, seeing Episcopalianism as the best means of retaining a degree of control over the Kirk. However, an increasing reliance on the votes of Presbyterians in Parliament resulted in a situation where their demands had to be acknowledged. It also remained the case that the bishops would not give up praying for James VII. In June 1690, therefore, a Presbyterian Church settlement was conceded in return for monetary supply.[118] For Scottish Catholics the year 1689 saw the reassertion of the Penal Laws. However, as with previous years, this meant little in the way of action or reprisals against those of that faith who were prepared to remain at peace with the regime.[119] Nevertheless, Catholics were once again no longer able to hold public office, a marked change in circumstances for the duke of Gordon given the favours showered upon him during the first two years of James's reign. Once again, avenues to power and advancement were being closed off to the Gordon lords.

However, the duke of Gordon's actions (or rather, lack of them) at the Revolution had ensured that, for the most part, what was left of his estates and landed privileges remained intact, as did his titles. One exception to this resulted from the rescinding of the forfeiture of the deceased Robert Baillie of Jerviswood and the return to favour of his son in June 1690. With this action came the restoration of the lands and barony of Mellarstanes, holdings that had so recently been gifted to the duke of Gordon.[120] Essentially, all that had been gained by

---

117 Brown, *Kingdom or Province?*, 175. For an in-depth examination of this event and the build up to it, see Hopkins, *Glencoe*, 308–350.

118 Brown, *Kingdom or Province?*, 176–177. For more background material on religion during the Williamite Revolution, see T. Maxwell, 'Presbyterian and Episcopalian in 1688', *Records of the Scottish Church History Society*, vol. 13 (1959), 25–37; T. Maxwell, 'William III and the Scots Presbyterians', *Records of the Scottish Church History Society*, vol. 15, (1963–65), 117–140, 169–191; L.K.J. Glassey, 'William II and the Settlement of Religion in Scotland, 1688–90', *Records of the Scottish Church History Society*, vol. 23 (1989), 317–329; T. Clarke, 'Williamite Episcopalians and the Glorious Revolution', *Records of the Scottish Church History Society*, vol. 24 (1990), 33–51. For analysis from a three-kingdoms perspective, see T. Harris, 'Incompatible Revolutions?: the Established Church and the Revolutions of 1688–9 in Ireland, England and Scotland', in Macinnes and Ohlmeyer (eds), *The Stuart Kingdoms in the Seventeenth Century*, 204–225.

119 Macinnes, 'Catholic Recusancy', 58.

120 *APS, 1690–95*, 158.

Gordon since 1685 had once again been lost. But the family had not slumped to the depths that it had during the mid-century civil wars. Gordon had chosen not to ruin himself for the Jacobite cause in 1689 and had ensured the survival of his household as a result. In that sense, although the family had declined in relative terms over the course of the century, the situation was not as bad as it had been in 1649 or 1653. A degree of renewal had taken place during the reign of Charles II and James VII and the duke had seen fit to ensure that this was not jeopardised during the Williamite Revolution.

When the duke did come under pressure from the government in the years that followed, it was for his suspected Jacobitism, not for his recusancy. In this he laid himself squarely open to attack, particularly in light of his decision in 1690 to remove himself to the exiled Stuart court at St Germains en Laye. This decision remained a curious one, particularly given the fact that the opportunity had been there to remove himself to his estates and lead as quiet a life as could be managed. But he had been confined to Edinburgh for much of the latter half of 1689 and so, no doubt, had built up a degree of resentment as a result. In February 1690 he had had an audience with William III and II in London, a meeting which, according to John Macky, did not go to the duke's liking, he 'not being received as he thought his family deserved'. On top of this he had also felt compelled to regain James's favour through justifying his surrender of Edinburgh Castle. In this he had little success, and he eventually left St Germains on being told by James that his services were no longer required. He was subsequently arrested in the town of Willingen and by November 1692 was languishing in prison in The Hague.[121] Despite this, his position remained little affected upon his return to Scotland and, although under suspicion from time to time, he remained coolly disposed towards the Jacobite cause for the remainder of his life.[122]

The day to day running of the family went on, but the noble House of Huntly remained a shadow of its former self. The days when the Gordon lords had exercised a commanding power across the North of Scotland and within the corridors of government were long gone. They were no longer the pre-eminent feudal overlords of that part of the world, a fact made apparent by a shrinking support network and the related rise in fortunes of other northern noble

121 Macky, *Memoirs of the Secret Services*, 194; *CSPD, 1689–90*, 442; HMC, Tenth Report, Appendix, part IV, *The Manuscripts of the Earl of Westmorland, Captain Stewart, Lord Strafford, Lord Muncaster and others* (London, 1885), 375; WSRO, Goodwood/1428, f. 17; HMC, *Report on the Manuscripts of the late Allan George Finch esq. of Burley on the Hill, Rutland. Vol. IV 1692 with Addenda 1690 and 1691* (London, 1965), 474–475 (Blathwayt to Nottingham, 27 September 1692), (same to same, 29 September 1692); *Papers illustrative of the Political condition of the Highlands*, 88–89; Bulloch, *First Duke of Gordon*, 91–93.

122 Bulloch, *First Duke of Gordon*, 93–104. He died on 7 December 1716. See *ibid.*, 105.

families. The independence of the earls of Aboyne and the Haddo earls of Aberdeen had become apparent, as had that of the Camerons of Lochiel and the Mackintoshes of Torcastle. Indeed, the Revolution had even revealed how lesser members of the Gordon gentry such as Sir George Gordon of Edinglassie could feel comfortable in adopting a political line that was plainly opposed to that of the House of Huntly. There had been temporary splits in the family in the previous century but by the late seventeenth century they were becoming much more permanent and fundamental in nature. A good example is that of Lord Strathnaver. A staunch Williamite during the Revolution, both he and his father, George, fourteenth earl of Sutherland, had been made commissioners of taxation for putting the kingdom into a state of defence. He also took the opportunity to free himself of his obligations to retain the Gordon surname and remain allied to the House of Huntly.[123] The earls of Sutherland were seeking to distance themselves from the Huntly Gordons once again. The time of the 'Gordon conglomerate' was clearly past and the household was now merely one of a number of families of equivalent power in northern Scotland.

This relatively reduced presence also became evident in the residences maintained by the family. Whereas the first marquess had seen fit to build and keep up a range of palatial homes, by the 1680s Bog of Gight (now becoming known as Gordon Castle) had essentially become the sole pride and joy of the family. In 1641 the mansion at Kandychyle burnt to the ground and was never replaced, while Strathbogie saw no further reconstruction or repair work following the execution of the second marquess in 1649.[124] Buildings were expensive to erect and preserve and remained a massive capital investment.[125] It is perhaps hardly surprising that the duke of Gordon wished to avoid the kind of debt built up by his forebears and so retained a more modest number of holdings.

By the 1690s there had also been a slight change in fortunes in relation to landholding. This becomes apparent when comparing the valuation rolls for 1674 and 1696. Although the figures for the parishes of Gartly and Rhynie/Essie remained the same, and indeed the Dunbennan valuation, somewhat inexplicably, actually rose from £1,610 to £1,800, the Huntly share of the valuations went down in other parishes. In Kinnoir the figure was £830 out of the parish total of £1,260, in Ruthven/Botary it went down to £2,407 out of £3,610 and in Glass it went back down to zero out of a total of £1,800.[126] Evidently, there was

123　Fraser, *Sutherland Book*, I, 319–320.
124　J.G. Michie, *Loch Kinnord* (Aberdeen, 1910), 63; Tabraham, *Huntly Castle*, 11.
125　Brown, *Noble Society in Scotland*, 85–86.
126　Aberdeen City Council Archives, 1/15/1; *List of Pollable Persons within the Shire of Aberdeen, 1696*, ed. J. Stuart, 2 vols (Aberdeen, 1844), 413–463.

a degree of recourse to the practice of either wadsetting or feueing. And there were reverses elsewhere. It has been seen how the duke of Gordon failed to gain superiority over certain lands held by Lochiel in Lochaber; and although he did gain the estate of Mellarstanes in the Borders, he was to hold it only very briefly. Despite repeated attempts, he also failed to buy Mackintosh of Torcastle out of the stewartry of Lochaber. Put simply, whereas the Gordons had gained a good deal of ground during the first twenty years of the reign of Charles II, this proved a peak that they would find hard to maintain following the removal of the Stuarts and the accession of William and Mary to the throne. At any rate, by the late 1680s and 1690s, the family could clearly no longer be described as a great, all-powerful acquisitive dynasty of the first order.

CONCLUSION

The Restoration period provided the House of Huntly with a chance to recover following the tribulations of the Civil Wars. The forfeiture and execution of the marquess of Argyll led to the family regaining the lost estates minus the debts that Argyll had built up on them in the intervening years. The year 1660 also saw the creation of a brand new earldom of Aboyne for Lord Charles Gordon. However, with this elevation, and with the young marquess of Huntly still in his minority, the stage was set for a power struggle between them that would not see a resolution until the early 1670s. For a time the Huntly lands were virtually split in two until a process of revaluation left Aboyne solely with the holdings that appertained directly to his title. Nevertheless, these lands were permanently alienated from the Huntly line and a new independent household had been created in the North-East. During this period a protracted dispute also arose between Huntly and his other surviving uncle, Lord Henry, which eventually saw a settlement that determined monetary portions for the latter and Huntly's three sisters. What remains especially striking was the bitterness with which these two disputes were pursued, which certainly betrayed the fact that the family could hardly be described as being close-knit at the time.

From the 1670s Huntly remained unwilling to put public promotions ahead of his personal adherence to the Catholic faith and so his chances of making an impact on the national stage remained negligible. He thus had little outlet to represent his family's interests within the chambers of power in Edinburgh. This remained in contrast to the opportunities presented to his uncle, Aboyne, who showed himself willing to compromise his beliefs in order to gain advancement. But Huntly was highly active at a regional level, whether using his influence to affect the outcome of local elections or when seeking to maintain his position in the Highlands. He worked hard to maintain links with cadet families like the Gordons of Sutherland. In this he had mixed fortunes; while a closer bond was achieved for a time with this household, other individual lairds and families were drifting a little further from the fold. The key example here was Sir George Gordon of Haddo, who himself was elevated to the peerage as earl of Aberdeen. Huntly also struggled to maintain his position in the Highlands. Relations with the Mackintoshes remained fraught and by 1680 the government was once again looking to reshape traditional Highland power structures. This was made evident with the garrisoning of Inverlochy Castle and the redrawing of Huntly's traditional area of influence so that a new area of responsibility could be created for the earl of Moray. Moreover, whereas for much of the sixteenth century Argyll and Huntly had been the two main standout Highland players, now Seaforth, Atholl and Moray were all vying for contention as well.

Towards the end of the reign of Charles II and during the initial years of the reign of James VII and II, Huntly's political fortunes began to rise, particularly with his elevation to the title of duke of Gordon. However, his questioning of the extent that James should be showing open favour to Catholicism soon left him open to royal displeasure as well as to the machinations of Chancellor Perth and his brother, Melfort. It was noticeable that in the land dispute that developed between Gordon and Lochiel, the king eventually decided matters in favour of the latter. The extent to which Gordon held a grudge about this is uncertain, but with the coming of the Williamite Revolution he was initially torn between remaining loyal to James and pursuing an agenda of self preservation. He eventually decided in favour of the latter option and, although he lost all of the privileges gained during James's reign, he did manage to keep intact what remained of his titles and estates. If nothing else the family had survived, albeit in a reduced state relative to how they had stood in previous centuries. Nevertheless, the era of the 'Cocks o' the North' was clearly well and truly over.

Conclusion

This study has revealed that the seventeenth century was a time of great change for the House of Huntly. The family had survived a very turbulent period in Scotland's history, and from 1690 could look to consolidate what position had been retained in the North of Scotland. And much had been retained; certainly any suggestion that the household had gone into sudden terminal decline or had little power left would be fundamentally wrong. Extensive landholdings were still held across the North-East and in the north-central Highlands, and the Gordon lords, like other Scottish nobles of similar status, maintained their hold over local franchise courts. Some links also remained with a number of the Gordon cadet families and the duke of Gordon yet aspired to the trappings and lifestyle of a top ranking noble.

But evidence of decline was readily apparent, no more so than in the lowland North-East. This was due to the combination of a number of factors. From the early seventeenth century the Crown had attempted to exert more direct influence on the manner in which law and order was enforced in the localities, and although the nobles had remained fully supportive of this move, there had nevertheless been an impact on traditional power structures. Tighter regulations regarding the resolution of feuds had meant that, in certain instances, the nobles were no longer the first recourse when it came to settling matters. In the case of the Gordon lords this inevitably brought about a situation where decisions made by central bodies such as the Privy Council could run counter to their interest. This was highly evident during the Hay feud of 1616–17 and the Frendraught affair of the 1630s. Indeed, with the former, it can be seen how the king's judgement undermined the decisions of Huntly's Sheriff Court of Aberdeenshire. Although there was still a role for the Gordon lords in the resolution of feuds, this steadily became of less importance as the century wore on. Indeed, there seems to be no evidence of their having been involved in such a capacity beyond the 1630s. At any rate, they achieved very little in cases where they were called upon to mediate. This was apparent during the Caithness disputes of the 1610s and 1620s and with regard to the Pitcaple–Frendraught feud of 1630.

Alongside this, the decline in bonding began to undermine traditional alliance networks in the North. Although it is true that many traditional links would have remained intact, others did fall by the wayside. Perhaps most notable for the Gordon lords was the decline from the late 1610s of the long-standing alliance with the Hays of Errol. Certainly by the 1690s this family could no longer be described as the junior partner of the House of Huntly. Much had indeed changed since the two families had stood side by side at the Battle of Glenlivet in 1594. This situation was also reflected within what could once have been termed the 'Gordon conglomerate'. Over the course of the century a number of divisions had become apparent between the Huntly Gordons and some of the cadet families. Among the most notable disputes were those with the Gordons of Park in the 1630s and with the newly formed House of Aboyne from the mid-1660s. From the 1630s relations also became more strained with the Gordons of Sutherland. The Civil Wars of the late 1630s and 1640s certainly brought into sharp relief the fact that this family could no longer automatically be expected to provide political support to the Gordons of Huntly. This was confirmed following the Revolution of 1688–89. The same was true of the Gordon lairds of Haddo, who by the 1680s were beginning to conduct themselves with an independency that had only rarely been glimpsed in the past. Indeed, with their elevation to the peerage as earls of Aberdeen, another rival Gordon household had been created in the North-East.

Also of great import for the Gordons of Huntly was their loss of the sheriff-ships of Aberdeen and Inverness in 1629. Not only had these delivered a guaranteed source of income, they were also a key means by which the Gordons were granted a clear mandate to enforce the law in that part of the world. Moreover, the loss allowed other rival families to move in and gain occupancy of these prestigious and powerful offices. During the reign of Charles II both the Keiths and the Hays of Errol managed at different stages to gain control of the sheriff-ship of Aberdeen. A similar change came with the granting of a lieutenancy of the North to the third earl of Moray in 1625. Although Moray's commission ended up being relatively brief, it did herald a sea change whereby it no longer remained a natural recourse of kings to grant such powers solely to the House of Huntly. The loss of power and prestige implied by all this was only too apparent to the Gordon lords.

This ebbing away of standing was also evident in the Highlands. The lack of constructive Gordon involvement in the royal 'civilising' project of the first decade of the seventeenth century resulted in a decrease in influence in the western Highlands. As a consequence the way was opened up for other families to move in, most notably the Mackenzies of Kintail, who were soon elevated to the peerage as earls of Seaforth. Perhaps most illustrative of the new reality were the Highland commissions granted in 1680. While the Privy Council remained disposed to grant the fourth marquess of Huntly a jurisdiction in the Highlands, this was divided between him and Alexander, fifth earl of Moray. Meanwhile, other jurisdictions were granted to the marquess of Atholl and the earls of Argyll and Seaforth. From around the same time John Campbell of Glenorchy (later first earl of Breadalbane) was also beginning to assert himself as a notable Highland operator. Whereas during the previous century the earls of Huntly and Argyll had reigned supreme as top-ranking power-brokers in the Highlands, by the 1690s others were also jostling for position.

Alongside all this, relations between the House of Huntly and the clans of the lordships of Badenoch and Lochaber remained strained. The great rivalry between the Mackintoshes and the Gordons reignited during the 1610s and the Gordon lords struggled to retain the upper hand in the ensuing confrontations. There were clearly limitations as to what could be achieved either by force or by intrigue and, by the 1690s, little headway had been made against the power of the Mackintosh chiefs. Perhaps most notably, attempts by the Gordon lords to buy the latter out of the stewartry of Lochaber all ended in failure. Relations with Clan Cameron also deteriorated. During the 1610s and 1620s the earl of Enzie conducted expeditions against the Camerons and much bitterness resulted. Moreover, from around the same time Clan Cameron could be found moving much closer to the sphere of influence of the earls of Argyll than had previously been the case. This seems to have had particularly serious repercussions for the second marquess of Huntly during the 1640s. To cap it all was the first duke of Gordon's failure to secure superiority over certain lands pertaining to Ewen Cameron of Lochiel.

All of this reflected a corresponding decline in influence at a national and a trans-national level. The days of the counter-Reformation intriguing of the sixth earl of Huntly certainly remained a thing of the past and, if anything, the continued Catholicism of the first and fourth marquesses of Huntly only compounded a retreat from public affairs. The loss of the sheriffships in 1629 had even been the direct result of the continued recusancy of the first marquess. The Protestant second marquess of Huntly may have had an opportunity to shore up the position of the household, but his adherence to the Royalist cause during the Civil Wars brought defeat, forfeiture and ruin – a situation only reversed with the timely restoration of Charles II in 1660. And despite his staunch Royalism, the second marquess of Huntly was hardly first on the list when Charles I looked to consider who would ultimately lead his forces in Scotland. During the First Bishops' War this honour fell to the marquess of Hamilton, while during the wars of the 1640s it fell to the marquess of Montrose. Nevertheless, the stand taken by the Gordons of Huntly during these conflicts can be seen as their last great hurrah as major political players. By the Williamite Revolution it was clear that neither the means nor the will remained to make any great difference either way to the tide of politics.

Perhaps the biggest failing of the Gordon lords during the seventeenth century was their inability to retain a sustained presence within the power structures of central government, most notably the Scottish Parliament. In large part this was down to the religious and political choices they made, whether the unbending Catholicism of the first marquess and fourth marquess/first duke, or the Royalism of the second maquess. Instead they sought to depend on their regional power alone, something that for the various reasons highlighted was becoming increasingly compromised. Power and influence remained the preserve of the nobility as a whole, but to obtain it individual peers and lairds had to engage themselves at the centres of national power-broking, whether in the Privy Council or the Parliament. Families such as the Hamiltons or the Campbells of Argyll, who were able to do this, remained highly influential at a national level. By contrast, the Gordons became ever more marginalised. The days of the Gordons as the pre-eminent landed magnate family of the North with the ability to retain power through the sword and large retinues were on the wain. They had failed to adapt.

Moreover, while the first duke of Gordon did manage to retain his titles and most of his land following the Revolution of 1688–89, there had been some losses prior to that. The problems brought on by debt and forfeiture in the 1640s had resulted in some lands being permanently alienated from the household. In addition, following the settlement in 1672, Charles, first earl of Aboyne, had secured the part of the Huntly estate that pertained to his title. Although the first duke of Gordon was looking to introduce some improvements on his estates by the 1680s, on the whole the Gordon lords did little to show any real entrepreneurial spirit over the course of the century and did almost nothing to move beyond the boundaries of traditional landowning.

In light of all this, it is clear that the House of Huntly experienced a decline in power during the seventeenth century. Given that the nobility of Scotland retained its position of great power well into the eighteenth century, how, then, should the experience of the House of Huntly be regarded? Should the family merely be looked on as one of a number who had seen better days and whose decline was merely par for the course within a class that, as an overall unit, was prospering? Should the experience of the family be regarded as not special or important in itself? This conclusion would be fine if the House of Huntly *is* to be regarded as a typical Scottish noble family. However, as this book has intended to show, the level of power traditionally enjoyed by the Gordons was atypical, and during the sixteenth century was arguably only comparable to that of the House of Argyll. The House of Huntly was a major player and so any relative reduction in its power should be regarded as important. In essence, this reduction led to a realignment of power in the North whereby the Gordons, although still powerful, became only one of a number of equally influential families. This indicates a key change within the northern nobility that the historiography has hitherto overlooked. Where at one time the Gordons had been the pre-eminent northern magnate household bar none, by the 1690s this position could no longer be maintained. As a unit, the aristocracy did retain its position of pre-eminence in Scottish society but, within its ranks, there had been a noticeable shift in the balance of power.

Through its focus on the Gordons of Huntly this book has also provided a fresh perspective on some of the major themes and events of the seventeenth century. It was a time of much upheaval across Scotland, particularly during the civil wars of the late 1630s, 1640s and early 1650s. Although the Gordons ended up on the losing side in these conflicts, they were nevertheless major players for the king in the North of Scotland. Although this in turn led to a dramatic, if temporary, fall, it also allowed them, for a time, to make the kind of impact at a national level that they so frequently had in past centuries. It was to be their swan song as a major Scottish magnate family.

Bibliography

MANUSCRIPT SOURCES

Aberdeen City Council Archives

1/15/1: Valuation Book of the County of Aberdeen made in the year 1674.
Council Register, LII (1).

Aberdeen University Special Collections

MS 635: A Diary or Spiritwall Exercises Written by Dr John Forbes of Corse and Copied from his Own Manuscript, Anno Dom 1687 and 1690.
MS 658: The Pourtrait of True Loyalty exposed in the Family of Gordon by D. Burnet.
MS 797: Trial of John Meldrum.

Angus Archives, Forfar

Montrose Town Council Minute Book, 1621–1639.

British Library, London

Additional MSS 23114, 23116, 23121–23125, 23128, 23135: The Lauderdale Papers.
Additional MSS 28937, f. 40: Copies of letters to the Earl of Antrim, 1643.
Sloane MSS 650, f. 90: The Marquess Huntlys Oath to the Covenanters.

Drum Castle Archives

Irvine of Drum Papers.

Dundee City Archives

Council Minutes, vol. IV, 1613–1653.

Edinburgh University Special Collections

La.iv.38: Rothes Correspondence.

Inveraray Castle Archives

Miscellaneous bundles, 7, 8, 67, 173.

Lambeth Palace Library, London

MS 3472: Fairhurst Papers.

National Archives of Scotland, Edinburgh

GD 16: Airlie MSS.
GD 44: Gordon MSS.
GD 45: Dalhousie MSS.
GD 84: Reay MSS.
GD 90: Yule Collection.
GD 112: Breadalbane Collection.
GD 220: Montrose MSS.
GD 248: Seafield MSS.
GD 406: Hamilton MSS.
TE 5: Papers relating to Teinds and Teind Administration.

National Library of Scotland, Edinburgh

Adv. MSS 33.1.1: Denmilne Estate Papers.
Dep. 175: Altyne Correspondence.
MS 1672: Campbell of Inverawe Papers.
MS 1915: Antique Papers.
MS 2207: Miscellaneous Papers.
MS 2955: Miscellaneous Manuscripts.
MS 7003–7005, 7035: Yester Papers.
MS 9977: Menzies Papers.
MS 16747: Saltoun Papers.
Wod.Qu.CVI: Wodrow Manuscripts.

Scottish Catholic Archives, Edinburgh

BL1: Blairs Letters.

The National Archives, London

SP78: State Papers Foreign, France.

West Sussex Record Office, Chichester

Goodwood MSS 1166: The Gordon Letters.
Goodwood MS 1428: Incomplete memoir of the first duke of Gordon.
Goodwood MSS 1431: The Montrose Letters.

PAMPHLETS

Anon., *An Act of the Convention of Estates for putting the Kingdome into a posture of defence, for strengthening the Armie and providing of Armes and Ammunition to the Kingdome* (Edinburgh, 1644).

Anon., *A true relation of the happy successe of his maiesties forces in Scotland under the conduct of the Lord James Marquisse of Montrose his excellencie, against the rebels there. Also, causes of a solemne fast and humiliation kept by the rebels in that Kingdom* (1644).

Anon., *Declaration of the Lords of his Majesties Privie Councell and Commissioners for conserving the Articles of the Treatie: for the information of his Majesties Good Subjects of this Kingdome* (Edinburgh, 1643).

Anon., *The copie of a letter showing the true relation of the late and happie victorie received by the marques of Montrose against Generall lieuetenant Baylie, and others of the rebels, at Alfoord, the second of Julie, 1645* (1645).

Anon., *The Declaration and Engagement of the Marquesse of Huntley, the Earle of Atholl, Generall Midletou, and many of the nobility of Scotland that have lately taken up arms for the defence of his Maiesties person and just authority* (1650).

Anon., *The Last Proceedings of the Parliament in Scotland, against the Marquesse of Argyle. Together, with the speech and defence of the said Marquesse, in vindication of himself from the aspersions of his having a hand in the deaths of His late Majesty, James Duke Hamilton, Marquesse Huntley, Marquesse of Montros. And of his dealing with the English after Worcester Fight* (London, 1661).

Anon., *The Order and Solemnitie of the Creation of the High and Mightie Prince Henrie, eldest Sonne to our sacred Soueraigne, Prince of Wales, Duke of Cornewall, Earle of Chester, &c. As it was celebrated in the Parliament House, on Munday the fourth of Iunne last past. Together with the Ceremonies of the Knights of the Bath, and other matters of speciall regard, incident to the same. Whereunto is annexed the Royall Maske, presented by the Queene and her Ladies, on Wednesday at night following* (London, 1610).

Anon., *The true relation of the late and happie victorie obtained by the marques of Montrose his excellencie, his majesties lieuetenant, and Generall Governor of the kingdom of Scotland: against General Lieuetenant Baylie, and others of the rebels, at Kilsyth, 15 August 1645* (1645).

Gordon, G. [second marquess of Huntly], *The Marquesse of Huntley his reply to certaine noblemen, gentlemen, and ministers, Covenanters of Scotland: sent from their associates, to signifie unto him, that it behoved him either to assist their designes, or be carried to prison in the castle of Edinburgh: the 20. of April, 1639. Now published, because of a false copie thereof lately printed without authoritie, or his owne consent* (London, 1640).

Lithgow, W., *Scotland's welcome to her native sonne, and soveraigne lord, King Charles* (Edinburgh, 1633).

PRINTED PRIMARY SOURCES

Aberdeen Council Letters, ed. L.B. Taylor, 4 vols (London, 1942–54).

A Collection of the State Papers of John Thurloe, Esq; Secretary first to the Council of State, and afterwards to the Protectors, Oliver and Richard Cromwell, ed. T. Birch, 7 vols (London, 1742).

A Diary of the Public Correspondence of Sir Thomas Hope of Craighall, 1633–1645, ed. T. Thomson (Edinburgh, 1843).

A Diary of Public Transactions and other Occurrences chiefly in Scotland from January

1650 to June 1667 by John Nicoll, ed. D. Laing (Edinburgh, 1836).

An Account of the Proceedings of the Estates in Scotland, 1689–1690, ed. E.W.M. Balfour-Melville, 2 vols (Edinburgh, 1954–55).

Ancient Criminal Trials in Scotland, ed. R. Pitcairn, 3 vols (Edinburgh, 1833).

Ane Account of the Familie of Innes compiled by Duncan Forbes of Culloden, 1698, ed. C. Innes (Aberdeen, 1864).

A Supplement to Burnet's History of My Own Time derived from his Original Memoirs, his Autobiography, his Letters to Admiral Herbert and his Private Meditations all hitherto unpublished, ed. H.C. Foxcroft (Oxford, 1902).

Baird, W., *Genealogical Collections concerning the Sir-Name of Baird and the Families of Auchmedden, New Byth and Sauchton Hall* (London, 1870).

Balfour, J., *Historical Works*, ed. J. Haig, 4 vols (Edinburgh, 1824–5).

Blakhal, G., *A Brieffe Narration of the Sevices Done to Three Noble Ladyes*, ed. J. Stuart (Aberdeen, 1844).

Burnet, G., *The Memoirs of the Lives and Actions of James and William, Dukes of Hamilton and Castle-Herald* (Oxford, 1852).

Burnet, G., *History of my own Time*, ed. O. Airy, 2 vols (Oxford, 1897).

Calderwood, D., *The History of the Kirk of Scotland*, ed. T. Thomson, 8 vols (Edinburgh, 1842–9).

Calendar of State Papers and Manuscripts, relating to English Affairs, existing in the Archives and Collections of Venice and in other Libraries of Northern Italy, 1202–1675, eds H.F. Brown, R. Brown and A.B. Hinds, 38 vols (London, 1864–1947).

Calendar of State Papers, Domestic Series, of the Reign of Charles I, 1625–49, eds J. Bruce, W.D. Hamilton and S.C. Lomas, 23 vols (London, 1858–97).

Calendar of State Papers, Domestic Series, 1649–60, ed. M.A.E. Green, 13 vols (London, 1875–86).

Calendar of State Papers, Domestic Series, of the Reign of Charles II, 1660–85, eds M.A.E. Green, F.H.B. Daniell and F. Bickley, 28 vols (London, 1860–1939).

Calendar of State Papers, Domestic Series, of the Reign of William and Mary, 1689–95, ed. W.J. Hardy, 5 vols (London, 1895–1906).

Calendar of State Papers, Domestic Series, of the Reign of William III, 1695–1702, eds E. Bateson and W.J. Hardy, 6 vols (London, 1908–37).

Calendar of State Papers relating to Ireland of the Reign of Charles I, 1625–1647, ed. R.P. Mahaffy, 2 vols (London, 1900–1).

Calendar of the Clarendon State Papers preserved in the Bodleian Library, eds O. Ogle, W.H. Bliss, W.D. Macray and F.J. Routledge, 5 vols (Oxford, 1872–1970).

Chronological Notes of Scottish Affairs, from 1680 till 1701; being chiefly taken from the Diary of Lord Fountainhall, ed. W. Scott (Edinburgh, 1822).

Collections for a History of the Shires of Aberdeen and Banff, ed. J. Robertson (Aberdeen, 1843).

Culloden Papers, ed. H.R. Duff (London, 1815).

de Muscry, D.R., *The History of the Troubles of Great Britain*, trans. J. Ogilvie (London, 1735).

Diary of Alexander Jaffray, Provost of Aberdeen, ed. J. Barclay (3rd edn, Aberdeen, 1856).

Diary of Sir Archibald Johnston Lord Wariston, 1639, ed. G.M. Paul (Edinburgh, 1896).

Early Travellers in Scotland, ed. P.H. Brown (Edinburgh, 1891).

Extracts from the Council Register of the Burgh of Aberdeen, 1643–1747, ed. J. Stuart (Edinburgh, 1872).

Extracts from the Presbytery Book of Strathbogie, A.D. 1631–1654, ed. J. Stuart (Aberdeen, 1843).

Extracts from the Records of the Burgh of Edinburgh, 1642-1655, ed. M. Wood (Edinburgh, 1931).

Extracts from the Records of the Synod of Moray, ed. W. Cramond (Elgin, 1906).

Fraser, J., *Chronicles of the Frasers. The Wardlaw Manuscript entitled 'polichronicon seu policratica temporum, or, the True Genealogy of the Frasers', 916–1674*, ed. W. Mackay (Edinburgh, 1905).

Fraser, W., *Memoirs of the Maxwells of Pollock*, 2 vols (Edinburgh, 1863).

Fraser, W., *History of the Carnegies, Earls of Southesk, and of their Kindred*, 2 vols (Edinburgh, 1867).

Fraser, W., *The Book of Carlaverock*, 2 vols (Edinburgh, 1873).

Fraser, W., *The Earls of Cromartie, their Kindred, Country and Correspondence*, 2 vols (Edinburgh, 1876).

Fraser, W., *The Red Book of Menteith*, 2 vols (Edinburgh, 1880).

Fraser, W., *The Chiefs of Grant*, 3 vols (Edinburgh, 1883).

Fraser, W., *Memorials of the Earls of Haddington*, 2 vols (Edinburgh, 1883).

Fraser, W., *Memorials of the Family of Wemyss of Wemyss*, 3 vols (Edinburgh, 1888).

Fraser, W., *The Sutherland Book*, 3 vols (Edinburgh, 1892).

Gordon, J., Parson of Rothiemay, *History of Scots Affairs from 1637 to 1641*, eds J. Robertson and G. Grub, 3 vols (Aberdeen, 1841).

Gordon, R., of Gordonstoun and G. Gordon of Sallach, *A Genealogical History of the Earldom of Sutherland from its Origin to the Year 1630 … with a Continuation to the Year 1651* (Edinburgh, 1813).

Gordon, P., of Ruthven, *A Short Abridgement of Britane's Distemper from 1639 to 1649*, ed. J. Dunn (Aberdeen, 1844).

Gordon, W., *A Concise History of the Ancient and Illustrious Family of Gordon*, 2 vols (Edinburgh, 1726–7).

Guthry, H., *Memoirs … containing an Impartial Relation of the Affairs of Scotland, Civil and Ecclesiastical from the Year 1637 to the Death of King Charles I* (2nd edn, Glasgow, 1747).

Highland Papers, ed. J.R.N. Macphail, 4 vols (Edinburgh, 1914–34).

Historical Manuscripts Commission, Eleventh Report, Appendix, part VI, *The Manuscripts of the Duke of Hamilton* (London, 1887).

Historical Manuscripts Commission, *Report of the Manuscripts of the Earl of Mar and Kellie preserved at Alloa House* (London, 1904).

Historical Manuscripts Commission, *Report on the Manuscripts of the late Allan George Finch esq. of Burley on the Hill, Rutland. Vol. IV 1692 with Addenda 1690 and 1691* (London, 1965).

Historical Manuscripts Commission, *Supplementary Report on the Manuscripts of the Earl of Mar and Kellie preserved at Alloa House, Clackmannanshire* (London, 1930).

Historical Manuscripts Commission, Tenth Report, Appendix, part IV, *The Manuscripts* of the Earl of Westmorland, Captain Stewart, Lord Strafford, Lord Muncaster and others (London, 1885).

Historical Manuscripts Commission, Thirteenth Report, Appendix, part VII, *The Manuscripts of the Earl of Lonsdale* (London, 1893).

Historical Notices of Scotish Affairs selected from the Manuscripts of Sir John Lauder of Fountainhall, Bart., one of the Senators of the College of Justice, 1661–1688, ed. D. Laing, 2 vols (Edinburgh, 1848).

Historical Notices of St Anthony's Monastery, Leith and Rehearsal of Events which occurred in the North of Scotland from 1635 to 1645 in Relation to the National Covenant, ed. C. Rogers (London, 1877).

[Hyde], Edward, earl of Clarendon, *The History of the Rebellion and Civil Wars in England begun in the Year 1641…*, ed. W.D. Macray, 6 vols (Oxford, 1888).

Inquisitiorium ad Capellam domini Regis Retornatarum quae in publicis Archivis Scotiae adhue sevantur, abbreviato, ed. T. Thomson, 3 vols (London, 1811).

Journal of the Hon. John Erskine of Carnock, 1683–1687, ed. W. Macleod (Edinburgh, 1893).

Leith, W.F. (ed.), *Narratives of Scottish Catholics under Mary Stuart and James VI* (Edinburgh, 1885).

Leith, W.F., *Memoirs of Scottish Catholics in the Seventeenth and Eighteenth Centuries*, 2 vols (London, 1909).

Leslie, J., earl of Rothes, *A Relation of Proceedings concerning the Affairs of the Kirk of Scotland from August 1637 to July 1638*, ed. J. Nairne (Edinburgh, 1830).

L'Estrange, H., *The Reign of King Charles: an History Faithfully and Impartially Delivered and Disposed into Annals* (London, 1655).

Letters and Papers of the Verney Family down to the End of the Year 1639, ed. J. Bruce (London, 1880).

Letters and State Papers during the Reign of King James the Sixth, ed. J. Maidment (Edinburgh, 1838).

Letters from Roundhead Officers written from Scotland and chiefly addressed to Captain Adam Baynes, July 1650 – June 1660 ed. J.Y. Akerman (Edinburgh, 1856).

Letters, illustrative of Public Affairs in Scotland, addressed by Contemporary Statesmen to George, Earl of Aberdeen, Lord High Chancellor of Scotland, 1681–1684, ed. J. Dunn (Aberdeen, 1851).

Letters of Sir Robert Moray to the Earl of Kincardine, ed. D. Stevenson (Ashgate, 2007).

Leven and Melville Papers. Letters and State Papers chiefly addressed to George, Earl of Melville, Secretary of State for Scotland, 1689–1691, from the Originals in possession of the Earl of Leven and Melville, ed. W.L. Melville (Edinburgh, 1843).

Lindsay, C., third earl of Balcarres, *Memoirs touching the Revolution in Scotland, 1688–1690 … presented to King James II at St. Germains, 1690* (Edinburgh, 1841).

List of Pollable Persons within the Shire of Aberdeen, 1696, ed. J. Stuart, 2 vols (Aberdeen, 1844).

Macfarlane, W., *Genealogical Collections concerning Families in Scotland*, ed. J.T. Clark, 2 vols (Edinburgh, 1900).

Macky, J., *Memoirs of the Secret Services …during the Reigns of King William, Queen Anne and George I* (London, 1733).

Macpherson, A., *The Loyall Dissuasive and other Papers concerning the Affairs of Clan Chattan*, ed. A.D. Murdoch (Edinburgh, 1902).

Memoirs of Sir Ewen Cameron of Lochiel, ed. J. Macknight (Edinburgh, 1842).

Memoirs of the War carried on in Scotland and Ireland, 1689–1691 by Major General Hugh Mackay, Commander in Chief of his Majesty's Forces with an Appendix of Original Papers, eds J.M. Hog, P.F. Tayler and A. Urquhart (Edinburgh, 1833).

Memorials of Montrose and his Times, ed. M. Napier, 2 vols (Edinburgh, 1848).

Military Memoirs of the Great Civil War, being the Military Memoirs of John Gwynne; and an Account of the Earl of Glencairn's Expedition, as General of his Majesty's Forces, in the Highlands of Scotland, in the Years 1653 and 1654 by a Person who was Eye and Ear Witness to every Transaction, with a Appendix, ed. W. Scott (Edinburgh, 1822).

Miscellany of the Scottish History Society, 11 vols (Edinburgh, 1893–1990).

More Culloden Papers, ed. D. Warrand, 5 vols (Inverness, 1923–30).

[Murray], J., seventh duke of Atholl, *Chronicles of the Atholl and Tullibardine Families*, 5 vols (Edinburgh, 1908).

Orain Iain Luim: Songs of John MacDonald, Bard of Keppoch, ed. A.M. Mackenzie (Edinburgh, 1964).

Original Letters relating to the Ecclesiastical Affairs of Scotland, chiefly written or addressed to his Majesty King James the Sixth after his Accession to the English Throne, ed. B. Botfield, 2 vols (Edinburgh, 1851).

Original Papers; containing the Secret History of Great Britain, from the Restoration, to the Accession of the House of Hannover. To which are prefixed Extracts from the Life of James II as written by himself, ed., J. Macpherson, 2 vols (London, 1775).

Papers illustrative of the Political Condition of the Highlands of Scotland from the Year 1689 to 1696, ed. J. Gordon (Glasgow, 1845).

Philip, J., of Almerieclose, *The Grameid. An heroic Poem descriptive of the Campaign of Viscount Dundee in 1689 and other Pieces*, ed. A.D. Murdoch (Edinburgh, 1888).

Records of Old Aberdeen, 1157–1903, ed. A.M. Munro, 2 vols (Aberdeen, 1899–1909).

Records of the County of Banff, 1660–1770. One Hundred Years of County Government, ed. J. Grant (Aberdeen, 1922).

Records of the Kirk of Scotland containing the Acts and Proceedings of the General Assemblies, from the Year 1638 downwards, as authenticated by the Clerks of Assembly; with Notes and Historical Illustrations, ed. A. Peterkin (Edinburgh, 1843).

Records of the Sheriff Court of Aberdeenshire, ed. D. Littlejohn, 3 vols (Aberdeen, 1904–1907).

Registers of the Great Seal of Scotland, 1306–1668, eds J.H. Stevenson, J.M. Thomson, W.K. Dickson and J.B. Paul, 11 vols (Edinburgh, 1882–1914).

Registers of the Privy Council of Scotland, 1545–1625, ed. D. Masson, 14 vols (Edinburgh, 1877–98).

Registers of the Privy Council of Scotland, 1625–1660, eds D. Masson and P.H. Brown, 8 vols (Edinburgh, 1899–1908).

Registers of the Privy Council of Scotland, 1661–1691, eds E.W.M. Balfour-Melville, M.R. Miller, P.H. Brown and H. Paton, 16 vols (Edinburgh, 1908–70).

Reliquiae Celticae. Texts, Papers and Studies in Gaelic Literature and Philology left by the late Rev. Alexander Cameron, eds A. MacBain and J. Kennedy, 2 vols (Inverness, 1892–94).

Reynolds, J., *Blood for Blood: or Murthers revenged. Briefly, yet lively set forth in thirty tragical histories. To which are added five more, being the sad product of our own times. Viz. K. Charles the Martyr, Montrose and Argyle, Overbury and Turner, Sonds and his two sons, Knight and Butler. With a short appendix to the present age* (Oxford, 1661).

Roll of Alumni in Arts of the University and King's College of Aberdeen, 1596–1860, ed. P.J. Anderson (Aberdeen, 1900).

Row, J. and Row, J., *The History of the Kirk of Scotland from the Year 1558 to August 1637 ... with a Continuation to July 1639*, ed. D. Laing (Edinburgh, 1842).

Scotland and the Commonwealth, 1651–53, ed. C.H. Firth (Edinburgh, 1895).

Scotland and the Protectorate. Letters and Papers relating to the Military Government of Scotland from January 1654 to June 1659, ed. C.H. Firth (Edinburgh, 1899).

Scottish Historical Documents, ed. G. Donaldson (corrected edn, Glasgow, 1974).

Seafield Correspondence from 1685 to 1708, ed. J. Grant (Edinburgh, 1912).

Selected Justiciary Cases, 1624–1650, eds S.A. Gillon and J.I. Irvine, 3 vols (Edinburgh, 1953–74).

Selections from the Records of the Kirk Session, Presbytery and Synod of Aberdeen, ed. J. Stuart (Aberdeen, 1846).

Siege of the Castle of Edinburgh, 1689, ed. R. Bell (Edinburgh, 1828).

Spalding, J., *Memorialls of the Trubles in Scotland and in England, A.D. 1624–A.D. 1645*, ed. J. Stuart, 2 vols (Aberdeen, 1841–2).

Spottiswoode, J., *History of the Church of Scotland*, 3 vols (Edinburgh, 1847–51).

State Papers and Miscellaneous Correspondence of Thomas, Earl of Melros, ed. J. Maidment, 2 vols (Edinburgh, 1837).

'Tables compiled and collected together by the great paines and industrie of Sir Robert Gordon, Knight Baronett of Gordonstoun sone to Alexander, Earl of Southerland, copied out of his papers and continued be Maister Robert Gordon, his son, 1659', ed. J.M. Joass, in J.M. Bulloch (ed.), *The House of Gordon*, 3 vols (Aberdeen, 1903–12), II, 109–52.

The Acts of the Parliament of Scotland, eds T. Thomson and C. Innes, 12 vols (Edinburgh, 1814–72).

The Annals of Banff, ed. W. Cramond, 2 vols (Aberdeen, 1891–93).

The Argyle Papers, ed. J. Maidment (Edinburgh, 1834).

'The Balbithan MS', ed. J.M. Bulloch, in J.M. Bulloch (ed.), *The House of Gordon*, 3 vols (Aberdeen, 1903–12), I, 1–68.

The Blairs Papers (1603–1660), ed. M.V. Hay (London and Edinburgh, 1929).

The Chronicle of Perth; a Register of Remarkable Occurences chiefly connected with that City, from the Year 1210 to 1668, ed. J. Maidment (Edinburgh, 1831).

The Diary of Alexander Brodie of Brodie, 1652–1680 and of his Son, James Brodie of Brodie, 1680–1685 consisting of Extracts from the existing Manuscript, and a Republication of the Volume printed at Edinburgh in the Year 1740, ed. D. Laing (Aberdeen, 1863).

The Diplomatic Correspondence of Jean de Montereul and the Brothers de Bellièvre, French Ambassadors in England and Scotland, 1645–48, ed. J.G. Fotheringham, 2 vols (Edinburgh, 1898–99).

The Earl of Stirling's Register of Royal Letters relative to the Affairs of Scotland and Nova Scotia from 1615 to 1635, ed. C. Rogers, 2 vols (Edinburgh, 1885).

The Greig-Duncan Folk Song Collection, eds P. Shuldham-Shaw, E.B. Lyle, P.A. Hall, E. Petrie, S. Douglas and K. Campbell, 8 vols (Aberdeen and Edinburgh, 1981–2002).

The Hamilton Papers: being Selections from Original Letters in the Possession of his Grace the Duke of Hamilton and Brandon, relating to the Years 1638–1650, ed. S.R. Gardiner (London, 1880).

The Historical Works of Sir James Balfour of Denmylne and Kinnaird, Knight and Baronet; Lord Lyon King at Arms to Charles the First, and Charles the Second, ed. J. Haig, 4 vols (London, 1825).

The Journal of Thomas Cuningham of Campvere, 1640–1654, ed. E.J. Courthope (Edinburgh, 1928).

The Letters and Journals of Robert Baillie, Principal of the University of Glasgow, 1637–1662, ed. D. Laing, 3 vols (Edinburgh, 1841–42).

The Mackintosh Muniments, 1442–1820, preserved in the Charter Room at Moy Hall, Inverness-shire, ed. H. Paton (Edinburgh, 1903).

The Miscellany of the Spalding Club, ed. J. Stuart, 5 vols (Aberdeen, 1841–52).

The Records of Elgin, 1234–1800, eds W. Cramond and S.Ree, 2 vols (Aberdeen, 1903–8).

The Records of the Commissions of the General Assemblies of the Church of Scotland holden in Edinburgh in the Years 1646 and 1647, eds A.F. Mitchell and J. Christie (Edinburgh, 1892).

The Records of the Commissions of the General Assemblies of the Church of Scotland holden in Edinburgh the Years 1648 and 1649, eds. A.F. Mitchell and J. Christie (Edinburgh, 1896).

The Records of the Commissions of the General Assemblies of the Church of Scotland holden in Edinburgh in 1650, in St Andrews and Dundee in 1651 and in Edinburgh in 1652, ed. J. Christie (Edinburgh, 1909).

The Spottiswoode Miscellany: a Collection of Original Papers and Tracts illustrative chiefly of the Civil War and Ecclesiastical History of Scotland, ed. J. Maidment, 2 vols (Edinburgh, 1845).

The Statistical Account of Scotland, 1791–1799, ed. Sir J. Sinclair, 20 vols (Wakefield, 1973–83).

The Thistle of Scotland: A Selection of Ancient Ballads with Notes, ed. A. Laing (Aberdeen, 1823).

The Valuation of the County of Aberdeen for the Year 1667, eds A. and H. Tayler (Aberdeen, 1933).

Wishart, G., *Memoirs of the Most Renowned James Graham, Marquis of Montrose* (Edinburgh, 1819).

REFERENCE WORKS

Matthew, H.C.G. and Harrison, B. (eds), *Oxford Dictionary of National Biography*, 60 vols (Oxford, 2004).

Paul, J.B., *The Scots Peerage*, 9 vols (Edinburgh, 1904–14).

THESES

Adams, S., 'A Regional Road to Revolution: Religion, Politics and Society in South-West Scotland, 1600–1650' (unpublished PhD thesis, University of Edinburgh, 2002).

Hesketh, C., 'The Political Opposition to the Government of Charles I in Scotland' (unpublished PhD thesis, King's College, London, 1999).

Lee, R., 'Government and Politics in Scotland, 1661–1681' (unpublished PhD thesis, University of Glasgow, 1995).

McLennan, B., 'Presbyterianism Challenged: a Study of Catholicism and Episcopacy in the North-East of Scotland, 1560–1650' (unpublished PhD thesis, University of Aberdeen, 1977).

McSeveney, A., 'Non-Conforming Presbyterian Women in Restoration Scotland: 1660–1679' (unpublished PhD thesis, University of Strathclyde, 2005).

Patrick, D.J., 'People and Parliament in Scotland, 1689–1702' (unpublished PhD thesis, University of St Andrews, 2002).

Ross, G., 'The Royal Lieutenancy: Case Studies of the Houses of Argyll and Huntly, 1475–1567' (unpublished MPhil thesis, University of Aberdeen, 2002).

Scally, J., 'The Political Career of James, Third Marquis and First Duke of Hamilton (1606–1649) to 1643' (unpublished PhD thesis, Selwyn College, University of Cambridge, 1992).

BOOKS, ESSAYS AND ARTICLES

Adams, S., 'The Making of the Radical South-West: Charles I and his Scottish Kingdom, 1625–1649', in J.R. Young (ed.), *Celtic Dimensions of the British Civil Wars* (Edinburgh, 1997), 53–74.

Adamson, J., *The Noble Revolt: the Overthrow of Charles I* (London, 2007).

Allardyce, J., *The Family of Burnett of Leys with Collateral Branches* (Aberdeen, 1901).

Anderson, P.D., *Robert Stewart, Earl of Orkney, Lord of Shetland, 1533–1593* (Edinburgh, 1983).

Anderson, P.D., *Black Patie. The Life and Times of Patrick Stewart, Earl of Orkney, Lord of Shetland* (Edinburgh, 1992).

Anson, P.F., *Underground Catholicism in Scotland, 1622–1878* (Montrose, 1970).

Armstrong, R., *Protestant War. The 'British' of Ireland and the Wars of the Three Kingdoms* (Manchester and New York, 2005).

Asch, R.G. (ed.), *Three Nations – a Common History? England, Scotland, Ireland and British History, c.1600–1920* (Bochum, 1993).

Asch, R.G., *Nobilities in Transition, 1550–1700. Courtiers and Rebels in Britain and Europe* (London, 2003).

Aylmer, G.E., 'Collective Mentalities in Mid-Seventeenth-Century England: Royalist Attitudes', *Transactions of the Royal Historical Society*, 5th series, 37 (1987), 1–30.

Barrett, J. and A. Mitchell, *Elgin's Love-Gift: Civil War in Scotland and the Depositions of 1646* (Chichester, 2007).

Bennett, M., *The Civil Wars in Britain and Ireland, 1638–1651* (Oxford, 1997).

Bennett, M., *The Civil Wars Experienced. Britain and Ireland, 1638-1661* (London, 2000).

Boardman, S., 'The Burgh and the Realm: Medieval Politics, c.1100–1500', in E.P.

Dennison, D. Ditchburn and M. Lynch (eds), *Aberdeen before 1800. A New History* (East Linton, 2002), 203–223.

Bogucka, M., 'Scots in Gdansk (Danzig) in the Seventeenth Century', in A.I. Macinnes, T. Riis and F.G. Pedersen (eds), *Ships, Guns and Bibles in the North Sea and the Baltic States, c.1350–c.1700* (East Linton, 2000), 39–46.

Bradshaw, B. and J. Morrill (eds), *The British Problem, c.1534–1707: State Formation in the Atlantic Archipelago* (Basingstoke and London, 1996).

Brown, K.M., *Bloodfeud in Scotland, 1573–1625. Violence, Justice and Politics in an Early Modern Society* (Edinburgh, 1986).

Brown, K.M., 'Burghs, Lords and Feuds in Jacobean Scotland', in M. Lynch (ed.), *The Early Modern Town in Scotland* (London, 1987), 102–124.

Brown, K.M., 'Aristocratic Finances and the Origins of the Scottish Revolution', *English Historical Review*, 104, no. 410 (Jan. 1989), 46–87.

Brown, K.M., 'Noble Indebtedness in Scotland between the Reformation and the Revolution', *Historical Research*, 62, no. 149 (Oct. 1989)), 260–275.

Brown, K.M., 'The Nobility of Jacobean Scotland, 1567–1625', in J. Wormald (ed.), *Scotland Revisited* (London, 1991), 61–72.

Brown, K.M., *Kingdom or Province? Scotland and the Regal Union, 1603–1715* (Basingstoke and London, 1992).

Brown, K.M., 'The Scottish Aristocracy, Anglicization and the Court, 1603–38', *Historical Journal*, 36, no. 3 (1993), 543–576.

Brown, K.M., 'The Origins of a British Aristocracy: Integration and its Limitations before the Treaty of Union', in S.G. Ellis and S. Barber (eds), *Conquest and Union. Fashioning a British State, 1485–1725* (Harlow, 1995), 222–249.

Brown, K.M., *Noble Society in Scotland. Wealth, Family and Culture, from Reformation to Revolution* (Edinburgh, 2000).

Brown, K.M. and A.J. Mann, 'Introduction. Parliament and Politics in Scotland, 1567–1707', in K.M. Brown and A.J. Mann (eds), *Parliament and Politics in Scotland, 1567–1707* (Edinburgh, 2005), 1–56.

Buchan, J., *Montrose* (London, 1928).

Buckroyd, J., *Church and State in Scotland, 1660–1681* (Edinburgh, 1980).

Bulloch, J.M. (ed.), *The House of Gordon*, 3 vols (Aberdeen, 1903–12).

Bulloch, J.M., 'Abergeldie', in J.M. Bulloch (ed.), *The House of Gordon*, 3 vols (Aberdeen, 1903–1912), I, 69–116.

Bulloch, J.M., 'Gight', in J.M. Bulloch (ed.), *The House of Gordon*, 3 vols (Aberdeen, 1903-12), I, 165-310.

Bulloch, J.M., *The Earls of Aboyne* (Huntly, 1908).

Bulloch, J.M., *The First Duke of Gordon* (Huntly, 1908).

Bulloch, J.M., *The Polish 'Marquises of Huntly'* (Peterhead, 1932).

Burgess, G. (ed.), *The New British History. Founding a Modern State, 1603–1715* (London, 1999).

Burgess, G., 'Introduction: The New British History', in G. Burgess (ed.), *The New British History. Founding a Modern State, 1603–1715* (London, 1999), 1–29.

Callander, R., 'The Pattern of Land Ownership in Aberdeenshire in the Seventeenth and Eighteenth Centuries', in D. Stevenson (ed.), *From Lairds to Louns. Country and*

Burgh Life in Aberdeen, 1600–1800 (Aberdeen, 1986), 1–9.

Cameron, J., *James V. The Personal Rule, 1528–1542* (East Linton, 1998).

Cannon, J., 'The British Nobility, 1660–1800', in H.M. Scott (ed.), *The European Nobilities in the Seventeenth and Eighteenth Centuries*, 2 vols (Harlow, 1995), I, 53–81.

Canny, N., 'The Attempted Anglicisation of Ireland in the Seventeenth Century: an Exemplar of "British History"', in R.G. Asch (ed.), *Three Nations – a Common History? England, Scotland, Ireland and British History, c.1600–1920* (Bochum, 1993), 49–82.

Canny, N., *Making Ireland British* (Oxford, 2001).

Carlton, C., 'Civilians', in J. Kenyon and J. Ohlmeyer (eds), *The Civil Wars. A Military History of England, Scotland, and Ireland, 1638–1660* (Oxford, 1998), 272–305.

Cathcart, A., 'Crisis of Identity? Clan Chattan's Response to Government Policy in the Scottish Highlands, c.1580–1609', in S. Murdoch and A. Mackillop (eds), *Fighting for Identity. Scottish Military Experience, c.1550–1900* (Leiden, 2001), 163–184.

Cathcart, A., *Kinship and Clientage. Highland Clanship, 1451–1609* (Leiden, 2006).

Clark, S., *State and Status. The Rise of the State and Aristocratic Power in Western Europe* (Cardiff, 1995).

Clarke, A., 'The Earl of Antrim and the First Bishops' War', *Irish Sword*, vol. 6, no. 23 (1963), 108–115.

Clarke, A., *The Old English in Ireland, 1625–42* (paperback edn, Dublin, 2000).

Clarke, T., 'Williamite Episcopalians and the Glorious Revolution', *Records of the Scottish Church History Society*, vol. 24 (1990), 33–51.

Cowan, E.J., *Montrose. For Covenant and King* (Paperback edn, Edinburgh, 1995).

Cowan, I.B., 'The Five Articles of Perth', in D. Shaw (ed.), *Reformation and Revolution* (Edinburgh, 1967), 160–177.

Cowan, I.B., 'The Reluctant Revolutionaries: Scotland in 1688', in E. Cruikshanks (ed.), *By Force or by Default? The Revolution of 1688–1689* (Edinburgh, 1989), 65–81.

Cowan, I.B., 'Church and State Reformed? The Revolution of 1688–9 in Scotland', in J.I. Israel (ed.), *The Anglo-Dutch Moment. Essays of the Glorious Revolution and its World Impact* (Cambridge, 1991), 163–183.

Croft, P., *King James* (Basingstoke, 2003).

Cruikshanks, E., *The Glorious Revolution* (Basingstoke, 2000).

Cunningham, A., *The Loyal Clans* (Cambridge, 1932).

Curry, P., *Prophecy and Power. Astrology in Early Modern England* (Oxford, 1989).

Cust, R., *Charles I: a Political Life* (Harlow, 2005).

Dawson, J.E.A., *The Politics of Religion in the Age of Mary Queen of Scots. The Earl of Argyll and the Struggle for Britain and Ireland* (Cambridge, 2002).

Desbrisay, G., '"The Civill Warrs did Overrun All": Aberdeen, 1630–1690', in E.P. Dennison, D. Ditchburn and M. Lynch (eds), *Aberdeen before 1800. A New History* (East Linton, 2002), 238–266.

Donald, P., *An Uncounselled King. Charles I and the Scottish Troubles, 1637–1641* (Cambridge, 1990).

Donaldson, G., 'Scotland's Conservative North in the Sixteenth and Seventeenth Centuries', *Transactions of the Royal Historical Society*, 5th series, 16 (1966), 65–79.

Donaldson, G., 'The Scottish Church, 1567–1625', in A.G.R. Smith (ed.), *The Reign of James VI and I* (London and Basingstoke, 1973), 40–56.

Donaldson, G., *Scotland. James V–James VII* (paperback edn, Edinburgh, 1978).

Donaldson, G., *All the Queen's Men. Power and Politics in Mary Stewart's Scotland* (London, 1983).

Dow, F.D., *Cromwellian Scotland, 1651-1660* (Edinburgh, 1979).

Ellis, S.G. 'Introduction. The Concept of British History', in S.G. Ellis and S. Barber (eds), *Conquest and Union. Fashioning a British State, 1485–1725* (Harlow, 1995), 1–7.

Ellis, S.G. and S. Barber (eds), *Conquest and Union. Fashioning a British State, 1485–1725* (Harlow, 1995).

Fissel, M.C., *The Bishops' Wars. Charles I's Campaigns against Scotland, 1638–1640* (Cambridge, 1994).

Ford, J.D., 'Conformity in Conscience: the Structure of the Perth Articles Debate in Scotland, 1618–1638', *Journal of Ecclesiastical History*, 46 (1995), 256–277.

Foster, W.R., *The Church before the Covenants* (Edinburgh and London, 1975).

Franklin, D., *The Scottish Regency of the Earl of Arran. A Study in the Failure of Anglo-Scottish Relations* (Lampeter, 1995).

Furgol, E., 'The Civil Wars in Scotland', in J. Kenyon and J. Ohlmeyer (eds), *The Civil Wars. A Military History of England, Scotland, and Ireland, 1638–1660* (Oxford, 1998), 41-72.

Furgol, E.M., 'The Northern Covenanter Clans, 1639–1651', *Northern Scotland*, vol. 7 (1987), 119–131.

Furgol, E.M., *A Regimental History of the Covenanting Armies, 1639–1651* (Edinburgh, 1990).

Gaffney, V., *The Lordship of Strathavon. Tomintoul under the Gordons* (Aberdeen, 1960).

Gardiner, S.R., *History of the Great Civil War, 1642–1649*, 4 vols (London, 1893).

Geneva, A., *Astrology and the Seventeenth Century Mind. William Lilly and the Language of the Stars* (Manchester, 1995).

Gillespie, R., *Devoted People: Belief and Religion in Early Modern Ireland* (Manchester and New York, 1997).

Glassey, L.K.J., 'William II and the Settlement of Religion in Scotland, 1688–90', *Records of the Scottish Church History Society*, vol. 23 (1989), 317–329.

Glozier, M., 'Scots in the French and Dutch Armies during the Thirty Years' War', in S. Murdoch (ed.), *Scotland and the Thirty Years' War* (Leiden, 2001), 117–141.

Glozier, M., *Scottish Soldiers in France in the Reign of the Sun King. Nursery of Men of Honour* (Leiden, 2004).

Goodare, J., 'The Nobility and the Absolutist State in Scotland, 1584–1638', *History*, 78, no. 253 (June 1993), 161–182.

Goodare, J., 'The Scottish Parliament of 1621', *Historical Journal*, vol. 38, no. 1 (1995), 29–51.

Goodare, J., 'The Statutes of Iona in Context', *Scottish Historical Review*, vol. 77, no. 203 (April 1998), 31–57.

Goodare, J., *State and Society in Early Modern Scotland* (Oxford, 1999).

Goodare, J., 'Scottish Politics in the Reign of James VI', in J. Goodare and M. Lynch (eds), *The Reign of James VI* (East Linton, 2000), 32–54.

Goodare, J., *The Government of Scotland, 1560–1625* (Oxford, 2004).

Goodare, J., 'The Attempted Scottish *Coup* of 1596', in J. Goodare and A.A. MacDonald (eds), *Sixteenth-Century Scotland: Essays in Honour of Michael Lynch* (Leiden, 2008), 311–336.

Goodare, J. and M. Lynch, 'James VI: Universal King?', in J. Goodare and M. Lynch (eds), *The Reign of James VI* (East Linton, 2000), 1–31.

Goodare, J. and M. Lynch, 'The Scottish State and its Borderlands, 1567–1625', in J. Goodare and M. Lynch (eds), *The Reign of James VI* (East Linton, 2000), 186–207.

[Gordon], C., Eleventh Marquis of Huntly, *The Records of Aboyne, 1230–1681* (Aberdeen, 1894).

[Gordon], C., Eleventh Marquis of Huntly, *The Cock o' the North* (London, 1935).

Gordon, C.A., *A Concise History of the Ancient and Illustrious House of Gordon* (Aberdeen, 1890).

Grainger, J.D., *Cromwell against the Scots. The Last Anglo-Scottish War, 1650–1652* (East Linton, 1997).

Grant, R., 'The Brig o' Dee Affair, the Sixth Earl of Huntly and the Politics of the Counter-Reformation', in J. Goodare and M. Lynch (eds), *The Reign of James VI* (East Linton, 2000), 93–109.

Gregory, D., *The History of the Western Highlands and Isles of Scotland from A.D. 80 to A.D. 1493* (2nd edn, London, 1881).

Grosjean, A., 'General Alexander Leslie, the Scottish Covenanters and the Riksråd Debates, 1638–1640', in A.I. Macinnes, T. Riis and F. Pedersen (eds), *Ships, Guns and Bibles in the North Sea and Baltic States, c.1350–c.1700* (East Linton, 2000), 115–138.

Grosjean, A., *An Unofficial Alliance: Scotland and Sweden, 1569–1654* (Leiden, 2003).

Grosjean, A. and S. Murdoch, *Belhelvie: a Millennium of History* (Belhelvie, 2000).

Harris, T., 'Incompatible Revolutions?: the Established Church and the Revolutions of 1688–9 in Ireland, England and Scotland', in A.I. Macinnes and J. Ohlmeyer (eds), *The Stuart Kingdoms in the Seventeenth Century: Awkward Neighbours* (Dublin, 2002), 204–225.

Harris, T., *Restoration. Charles II and his Kingdoms* (London, 2005).

Harris, T., *Revolution. The Great Crisis of the British Monarchy, 1685–1720* (London, 2006).

Hastings, M., *Montrose. The King's Champion* (London, 1977).

Hay, K.M., *The Story of the Hays* (Edinburgh, 1977).

Henderson, G.D., *The Burning Bush. Studies in Scottish Church History* (Edinburgh, 1957).

Hewitt, G.R., *Scotland under Morton, 1572–80* (Edinburgh, 1982).

Hibbard, C.M., *Charles I and the Popish Plot* (Chapel Hill, 1983).

Hill, J.M., *Celtic Warfare, 1595–1763* (Edinburgh, 1986).

Hopkins, P., *Glencoe and the End of the Highland War* (revised reprint, Edinburgh, 1998).

Howard, D., *Scottish Architecture. Reformation to Restoration, 1560–1660* (Edinburgh, 1995).

Hughes, A., *The Causes of the English Civil War* (Basingstoke and London, 1991).

Hutton, R., *Charles the Second. King of England, Scotland and Ireland* (Oxford, 1989).

Hutton, R., 'The Triple-Crowned Islands', in L.K.J. Glassey (ed.), *The Reigns of Charles II and James VII and II* (Basingstoke and London, 1997), 71–89.

Ives, E.D., *The Bonny Earl of Murray. The Man, the Murder, the Ballad* (East Linton, 1997).

Jackson, C., *Restoration Scotland, 1660–1690: Royalist Politics, Religion and Ideas* (Woodbridge, 2003).

James, M., *Society, Politics and Culture: Studies in Early Modern England* (Cambridge, 1986).

Kearney, H., *The British Isles. A History of Four Nations* (Cambridge, 1989).

Kennedy, W., *Annals of Aberdeen, from the Reign of King William the Lion, to the End of the Year 1818*, 2 vols (London, 1818).

King, R., *The Covenanters in the North; or Sketches of the Rise and Progress, North of the Grampians, of the Great Religious and Social Movement of which the Covenant was the Symbol* (Aberdeen, 1846).

Kishlansky, M., *A Monarchy Transformed. Britain, 1603–1714* (London, 1996).

Lee, M., 'James VI and the Aristocracy', *Scotia*, 1, no. 1 (1977), 18–23.

Lee, M., *Government by Pen. Scotland under James VI and I* (London, 1980).

Lee, M., *The Road to Revolution: Scotland under Charles I, 1625–37* (Urbana and Chicago, 1985).

Lee, M., *Great Britain's Solomon: James VI and I in his Three Kingdoms* (Urbana and Chicago, 1990).

Lee, R., 'Retreat from Revolution: the Scottish Parliament and the Restored Monarchy, 1661–1663', in J.R. Young (ed.), *Celtic Dimensions of the British Civil Wars* (Edinburgh, 1997), 185–204.

Lee, S., 'Coclarachie', in J.M. Bulloch (ed.), *The House of Gordon*, 3 vols (Aberdeen, 1903–1912), I, 117–164.

Lenihan, P., '"Celtic" Warfare in the 1640s', in J.R. Young (ed.), *Celtic Dimensions of the Civil Wars* (Edinburgh, 1997), 116–140.

Lenihan, P., 'Confederate Military Strategy, 1643–7', in M. Ó Siochrú (ed.), *Kingdoms in Crisis. Ireland in the late 1640s. Essays in Honour of Dónal Cregan* (Dublin, 2000), 158–175.

Lenihan, P., *Confederate Catholics at War, 1641–49* (Cork, 2001).

Lenman, B.P., 'The Scottish Nobility and the Revolution of 1688–1690', in R. Beddard (ed.), *The Revolutions of 1688* (Oxford, 1991), 137–162.

Leslie, C., *Historical Records of the Family of Leslie from 1067 to 1868–9*, 3 vols (Edinburgh, 1869).

Leslie, J.F., *The Irvines of Drum and Collateral Branches* (Aberdeen, 1909).

Lyall, R.J., 'James VI and the Sixteenth-Century Cultural Crisis', in J. Goodare and M. Lynch (eds), *The Reign of James VI* (East Linton, 2000), 55–70.

Lynch, M., 'The Crown and the Burghs, 1500–1625', in M. Lynch (ed.), *The Early Modern Town in Scotland* (London, 1987), 55–80.

Lynch, M., 'The Early Modern Burgh', in J. Wormald (ed.), *Scotland Revisited* (London, 1991), 73–81.

Lynch, M., *Scotland. A New History* (London, 1992).

Lynch, M., 'James VI and the "Highland Problem"', in J. Goodare and M. Lynch (eds), *The Reign of James VI* (East Linton, 2000), 208–227.

Lynch, M. and H.M. Dingwall, 'Elite Society in Town and Country', in E.P. Dennison, D. Ditchburn and M. Lynch (eds), *Aberdeen before 1800. A New History* (East Linton, 2002), 181–200.

Lynn, J.A., *The French Wars, 1667–1714: the Sun King at War* (Oxford, 2002).

MacCoinnich, A., '"His Spirit was Given only to Warre": Conflict and Identity on the Scottish Gàidhealtachd, c.1580–c.1630', in S. Murdoch and A. Mackillop (eds), *Fighting for Identity. Scottish Military Experience, c.1550–1900* (Leiden, 2002), 133–161.

MacCoinnich, A., 'Native and Stranger: Lewis and the Fishing of the Isles, c.1610–c.1638' (unpublished paper delivered at the Research Institute of Irish and Scottish Studies, Aberdeen, 8 March 2004).

Macdonald, A. and A. Macdonald, *The Clan Donald*, 3 vols (Inverness, 1896–1904).

MacDonald, A.R., *The Jacobean Kirk, 1567–1625. Sovereignty, Polity and Liturgy* (Aldershot, 1998).

MacDonald, A.R., 'James VI and the General Assembly, 1586–1618', in J. Goodare and M. Lynch (eds), *The Reign of James VI* (East Linton, 2000), 170–185.

MacDonald, A.R., 'James VI and I, the Church of Scotland, and British Ecclesiastical Convergence', *Historical Journal*, 48 (2005), 885–903.

MacDonald, F.A., *Missions to the Gaels: Reformation and Counter-Reformation in Ulster and the Highlands and Islands of Scotland, 1560–1760* (Edinburgh, 2006).

Macdougall, N., *James III. A Political Study* (Edinburgh, 1982).

Macdougall, N., *James IV* (East Linton, 1997).

MacGregor, A.G.M., *History of the Clan Gregor*, 2 vols (Edinburgh, 1898–1901).

Macinnes, A.I., 'Scottish Gaeldom, 1638–1651: the Vernacular Response to the Covenanting Dynamic', in J. Dwyer, R.A. Mason and A. Murdoch (eds), *New Perspectives on the Politics and Culture of Early Modern Scotland* (Edinburgh, 1982), 59–94.

Macinnes, A.I., 'Repression and Conciliation: the Highland Dimension, 1660–1688', *Scottish Historical Review*, vol. 65, no. 180 (Oct. 1986), 167–195.

Macinnes, A.I., 'Catholic Recusancy and the Penal Laws, 1603–1707', *Records of the Scottish Church History Society*, 23, part 1 (1987), 27–63.

Macinnes, A.I., *Charles I and the Making of the Covenanting Movement, 1625–1641* (Edinburgh, 1991).

Macinnes, A.I., 'Covenanting, Revolution and Municipal Enterprise', in J. Wormald (ed.), *Scotland Revisited* (London, 1991), 97–106.

Macinnes, A.I., 'Crown, Clans and Fine: the "Civilizing" of Scottish Gaeldom, 1587–1638', *Northern Scotland*, vol. 13 (1993), 31–55.

Macinnes, A.I., 'Gaelic Culture in the Seventeenth Century – Polarization and Assimilation', in S.G. Ellis and S. Barber (eds), *Conquest and Union. Fashioning a British State, 1485–1725* (Harlow, 1995), 162–194.

Macinnes, A.I., *Clanship, Commerce and the House of Stuart, 1603–1788* (East Linton, 1996).

Macinnes, A.I., 'Politically Reactionary Brits?; The Promotion of Anglo-Scottish Union, 1603–1707', in S.J. Connolly (ed.), *Kingdoms United? Great Britain and Ireland since 1500. Integration and Diversity* (Dublin, 1999), 43–55.

Macinnes, A.I., 'Regal Union for Britain, 1603–38', in G. Burgess (ed.), *The New British History. Founding a Modern State, 1603–1715* (London, 1999), 33–64.

Macinnes, A.I., *The British Revolution, 1629–1660* (Basingstoke and New York, 2005).

Macinnes, A.I. and J. Ohlmeyer (eds), *The Stuart Kingdoms in the Seventeeth Century: Awkward Neighbours?* (Dublin, 2001).

MacIntosh, G., 'Arise King John: Commissioner Lauderdale and Parliament in the Restoration Era', in K.M. Brown and A.J. Mann (eds), *Parliament and Politics in Scotland, 1567–1707* (Edinburgh, 2005), 163–183.

MacIntosh, G.H., *The Scottish Parliament under Charles II, 1660–1685* (Edinburgh, 2007).

Mackay, P.H.R., 'The Reception given to the Five Articles of Perth', *Records of the Scottish Church History Society*, 19 (1977), 185–201.

McKean, C., *The Scottish Chateau. The Country House in Renaissance Scotland* (Stroud, 2001).

Mackenzie, A., *History of the Camerons; with Genealogies of the Principal Families of the Name* (Inverness, 1884).

Mackintosh, A.M., *The Mackintoshes and Clan Chattan* (Edinburgh, 1903).

Mackintosh, M., *A History of Inverness* (Inverness, 1939).

McLennan, B., 'The Reformation in the Burgh of Aberdeen', *Northern Scotland*, 2, no. 1 (1974–75), 119–144.

Macmillan, D., *Scottish Art, 1460–2000* (Edinburgh, 1990).

Mann, A.J., '"James VII, King of the Articles": Political Management and Parliamentary Failure', in K.M. Brown and A.J. Mann (eds), *Parliament and Politics in Scotland, 1567–1707* (Edinburgh, 2005), 184–207.

Marren, P., *Grampian Battlefields. The Historic Battles of North-East Scotland from A.D. 84 to 1745* (Aberdeen, 1990).

Marston, J.G., 'Gentry, Honor and Royalism in Early Stuart England', *Journal of British Studies*, 13 (1973), 21–43.

Mathew, D., *Scotland under Charles I* (London, 1955).

Mathew, D., *James I* (London, 1967).

Maxwell, T., 'Presbyterian and Episcopalian in 1688', *Records of the Scottish Church History Society*, vol. 13 (1959), 25–37.

Maxwell, T., 'William III and the Scots Presbyterians', *Records of the Scottish Church History Society*, vol. 15 (1963–65), 117–140, 169–191.

Meikle, M.M., 'The Invisible Divide: the Greater Lairds and the Nobility of Jacobean Scotland', *Scottish Historical Review*, 71, nos. 191/2 (Apr., Oct. 1992), 70–87.

Meikle, M.M., *A British Frontier? Landed Society in the Eastern Anglo-Scottish Borders, 1540–1603* (East Linton, 2004).

Menarry, D.J., 'Debt and the Scottish Landed Elite in the 1650s', in R.J. Morris and L. Kennedy (eds), *Ireland and Scotland: Order and Disorder, 1600–2000* (Edinburgh, 2005), 23–33.

Merriman, M., *The Rough Wooings. Mary Queen of Scots, 1542–1551* (East Linton, 2000).

Michie, J.G., *Loch Kinnord* (Aberdeen, 1910).

Morrill, J., *The Nature of the English Revolution* (Harlow, 1993).

Morrill, J.S. (ed.), *The Scottish National Covenant in its British Context, 1638–51* (Edinburgh, 1990).

Mullen, D.G., *Episcopacy in Scotland: the History of an Idea, 1560–1638* (Edinburgh, 1986).

Murdoch, S., 'Scotland, Scandinavia and the Bishops' Wars, 1638–40', in A.I. Macinnes and J. Ohlmeyer (eds), *The Stuart Kingdoms in the Seventeenth Century: Awkward Neighbours* (Dublin, 2001), 113–134.

Murdoch, S., *Britain, Denmark-Norway and the House of Stuart, 1603–1660* (East Linton, 2003).

Napier, M., *Memoirs of the Marquis of Montrose*, 2 vols (Edinburgh, 1856).

Nenadic, S., *Lairds and Luxury: Highland Gentry in Eighteenth Century Scotland* (Edinburgh, 2007).

Newman, P.R., 'The King's Servants: Conscience, Principle, and Sacrifice in Armed Royalism', in J. Morrill, P. Slack and D. Woolf (eds), *Public Duty and Private Conscience in Seventeenth-Century England* (Oxford, 1993), 225–241.

Newman, P.R., *The Old Service: Royalist Regimental Colonels and the Civil War, 1642–46* (Manchester, 1993).

Ogilvie, J.D., *The Aberdeen Doctors and the National Covenant* (Edinburgh, 1921).

Ohlmeyer, J., 'The Civil Wars in Ireland', in J. Kenyon and J. Ohlmeyer (eds), *The Civil Wars. A Military History of England, Scotland, and Ireland* (Oxford, 1998), 73–102.

Ohlmeyer, J., 'The Wars of the Three Kingdoms', *History Today*, 48, no, 11 (Nov. 1998), 16–22.

Ohlmeyer, J.H., *Civil War and Restoration in the Three Stuart Kingdoms. The Career of Randal MacDonnell, Marquis of Antrim* (Cambridge, 1993).

Ohlmeyer, J.H., '"Civilizinge of those Rude Partes": Colonization within Britain and Ireland, 1580s–1640s', in N. Canny (ed.), *The Origins of Empire. British Overseas Enterprise to the Close of the Seventeenth Century* (Oxford, 1998), 124–147.

Ohlmeyer, J., 'The Baronial Context of the Irish Civil Wars', in J. Adamson (ed.), *The English Civil War: Conflict and Contexts, 1640–49* (Basingstoke, 2009), 106–124.

Ó Siochrú, M., *Confederate Ireland, 1642–1649. A Constitutional and Political Analysis* (Dublin, 1999).

Ó Siochrú, M., *God's Executioner: Oliver Cromwell and the Conquest of Ireland* (London, 2008).

Patrick, D.J., 'Unconventional Procedure: Scottish Electoral Politics after the Revolution', in K.M. Brown and A.J. Mann (eds), *Parliament and Politics in Scotland, 1567–1707* (Edinburgh, 2005), 208–244.

Pincus, S., 'The European Catholic Context of the Revolution of 1688–89: Gallicanism, Innocent XI, and Catholic Opposition', in A.I. Macinnes and A.H. Williamson (eds), *Shaping the Stuart World, 1603–1714. The Atlantic Connection* (Leiden, 2006), 79–114.

Pocock, J.G.A., 'British History: a Plea for a New Subject', *Journal of Modern History*, 47, no. 4 (1975), 601–628.

Potter, H., *Bloodfeud. The Stewarts and Gordons at War in the Age of Mary Queen of Scots* (Stroud, 2002).

Reid, J. *William Davidson of Aberdeen. The First British Professor of Chemistry* (Aberdeen, 1951).

Reid, S., *The Campaigns of Montrose. A Military History of the Civil War in Scotland, 1639–1646* (Edinburgh, 1990).

Reid, S., *Auldearn, 1645. The Marquis of Montrose's Scottish Campaign* (Oxford, 2003).

Riley, P.W.J., *King William and the Scottish Politicians* (Edinburgh, 1979).

Ritchie, P.E., *Mary of Guise in Scotland, 1548–1560* (East Linton, 2002).

Robertson, B., 'The House of Huntly and the First Bishops' War', *Northern Scotland*, 24 (2004), 1–15.

Robertson, B., 'The Gordons of Huntly: a Scottish Noble Household and its European Connections, 1603–1688', in D. Worthington (ed.), *British and Irish Emigrants and Exiles in Europe, 1603–1688* (Leiden, 2010), 181–194.

Royle, T., *Civil War. The Wars of the Three Kingdoms, 1638–1660* (London, 2004).

Rubinstein, H.L., *Captain Luckless: James, First Duke of Hamilton, 1606–1649* (Edinburgh, 1975).

Russell, C., 'The British Problem and the English Civil War', *History*, 72, no. 236 (1987), 395–415.

Russell, C., *The Fall of the British Monarchies, 1637–1642* (Oxford, 1991).

Scally, J., 'Counsel in Crisis: James, Third Marquis of Hamilton and the Bishops' Wars, 1638–1640', in J.R. Young (ed.), *Celtic Dimensions of the British Civil Wars* (Edinburgh, 1997), 18–34.

Scally, J., 'The Rise and Fall of the Covenanter Parliaments, 1639–51', in K.M. Brown and A.J. Mann (eds), *Parliament and Politics in Scotland, 1567–1707* (Edinburgh, 2005), 138–162.

Scott, D., *Politics and War in the Three Stuart Kingdoms, 1637–49* (Basingstoke and New York, 2004).

Scott, H.M., 'Conclusion: the Continuity of Aristocratic Power', in H.M. Scott (ed.), *The European Nobilities in the Seventeenth and Eighteenth Centuries*, 2 vols (Harlow, 1995), II, 274–291.

Scott, H.M. and C. Storrs, 'Introduction: the Consolidation of Noble Power in Europe, c.1600–1800', in H.M. Scott (ed.), *The European Nobilities in the Seventeenth and Eighteenth Centuries*, 2 vols (Harlow, 1995), I, 1–52.

Shaw, L. and J.F.S. Gordon, *The History of the Province of Moray*, 3 vols (Glasgow and London, 1882).

Small, J., 'Notice of William Davidson, M.D.', *Proceedings of the Society of Antiquaries of Scotland*, 10 (1875), 265–280.

Smith, D.L., *A History of the Modern British Isles, 1603–1707. The Double Crown* (Oxford, 1998).

Snow, W.G.S., *The Times, Life and Thought of Patrick Forbes, Bishop of Aberdeen, 1618–1635* (London, 1952).

Sommerville, J.P., 'Absolutism and Royalism', in J.H. Burns and M. Goldie (eds), *The Cambridge History of Political Thought, 1450–1700* (Cambridge, 1991), 347–373.

Spurlock, R.S., *Cromwell and Scotland: Conquest and Religion, 1650–1660* (Edinburgh, 2007).

Stevenson, D., *Scottish Covenanters and Irish Confederates. Scottish-Irish Relations in the Mid-Seventeenth Century* (Belfast, 1981).

Stevenson, D., 'The Century of the Three Kingdoms', *History Today*, 35, no. 3 (March 1985), 28–33.

Stevenson, D., 'Montrose and Dundee', in L. Maclean (ed.), *The Seventeenth Century in the Highlands* (Inverness, 1986), 136–149.

Stevenson, D., 'The Burghs and the Scottish Revolution', in M. Lynch (ed.), *The Early Modern Town in Scotland* (London, 1987), 167–91.

Stevenson, D., *King's College, Aberdeen, 1560–1641: from Protestant Reformation to Covenanting Revolution* (Aberdeen, 1990).

Stevenson, D., 'The English Devil of Keeping State: Elite Manners and the Downfall of Charles I in Scotland', in R. Mason and N. Macdougall (eds), *People and Power in Scotland. Essays in honour of T.C. Smout* (Edinburgh, 1992), 126–144.

Stevenson, D., *Highland Warrior. Alasdair MacColla and the Civil Wars* (Edinburgh, 1994).

Stevenson, D., *King or Covenant? Voices from Civil War* (East Linton, 1996).

Stevenson, D., *Revolution and Counter Revolution in Scotland, 1644–1651* (paperback edn, Edinburgh, 2003).

Stevenson, D., *The Scottish Revolution, 1637–1644. The Triumph of the Covenanters* (paperback edn, Edinburgh, 2003).

Stewart, A., *The Cradle King. A Life of James VI and I* (London, 2003).

Stewart, D., 'The "Aberdeen Doctors" and the Covenanters', *Records of the Scottish Church History Society*, 22 (1986), 35–44.

Stewart, L.A.M., *Urban Politics and the British Civil Wars: Edinburgh, 1617–1653* (Leiden, 2006).

Stewart, L.A.M., 'The Political Repercussions of the Five Articles of Perth: a Reassessment of James VI and I's Religious Policies in Scotland', *Sixteenth Century Journal*, vol. 38, no. 4 (2007), 1013–1036.

Tabraham, C., *Huntly Castle* (rev'd edn, Edinburgh, 1995).

Terry, C.S., 'The Siege of Edinburgh Castle, March–June 1689', *Scottish Historical Review*, vol. 11 (Jan. 1905).

Thomas, K., *Religion and the Decline of Magic. Studies in Popular Beliefs in Sixteenth- and Seventeenth-Century England* (Harmondsworth, 1973).

Wedgwood, C.V., *Montrose* (London, 1952).

Wedgwood, C.V., *The King's War, 1641–1647* (London, 1958).

Wells, V.T., 'Constitutional Conflict after the Union of the Crowns: Contention and Continuity in the Parliaments of 1612 and 1621', in K.M. Brown and A.J. Mann (eds), *Parliament and Politics in Scotland, 1567–1707* (Edinburgh, 2005), 82–100.

Wheeler, J.S., *Cromwell in Ireland* (Dublin, 1999).

Wheeler, J.S., *The Irish and British Wars, 1637–1654: Triumph, Tragedy and Failure* (London, 2002).

White, A., 'The Impact of the Reformation on a Burgh Community: the Case of Aberdeen', in M. Lynch (ed.), *The Early Modern Town in Scotland* (London, 1987), 81–101.

White, A., 'The Menzies Era: Sixteenth-Century Politics', in E.P. Dennison, D. Ditchburn and M. Lynch (eds), *Aberdeen before 1800. A New History* (East Linton, 2002), 224–237.

Whyte, I., *Agriculture and Society in Seventeenth-Century Scotland* (Edinburgh, 1979).

Willcock, J., *The Great Marquess: Life and Times of Archibald, Eighth Earl, and First (and only) Marquess of Argyll (1607–1661)* (Edinburgh and London, 1903).

Williams, R., *Montrose. Cavalier in Mourning* (London, 1975).

Williams, R., *The Heather and the Gale. Clan Donald and Clan Campbell during the Wars of Montrose* (Colonsay, 1997).

Willson, D.H., *King James VI and I* (London, 1959).

Wilson, W., *The House of Airlie*, 2 vols (London, 1924).

Wimberley, D., 'Lesmoir', in J.M. Bulloch (ed.), *The House of Gordon*, 3 vols (Aberdeen, 1903–1912), II, 153–277.

Woolrych, A., *Britain in Revolution, 1625-1660* (Oxford, 2002).

Wormald, J., 'Bloodfeud, Kindred and Government in Early Modern Scotland', *Past and Present*, no. 87 (May 1980), 54–97.

Wormald, J., *Court, Kirk, and Community. Scotland, 1470–1625* (London, 1981).

Wormald, J., *Lords and Men in Scotland: Bonds of Manrent, 1442–1603* (Edinburgh, 1985).

Wormald, J., *Mary Queen of Scots. A Study in Failure* (London, 1988).

Wormald, J., "Tis True I am a Cradle King': the View from the Throne', in J. Goodare and M. Lynch (eds), *The Reign of James VI* (East Linton, 2000), 241–256.

Wormald, J., 'The Headaches of Monarchy: Kingship and the Kirk in the Early Seventeenth Century', in Goodare and MacDonald (eds), *Sixteenth-Century Scotland* (Leiden, 2008), 365–393.

Worthington, D., *Scots in Habsburg Service, 1618–1648* (Leiden, 2004).

Young, J., 'Invasions: Scotland and Ireland, 1641–1691', in P. Lenihan (ed.), *Conquest and Resistance. War in Seventeenth-Century Ireland* (Leiden, 2001), 53–86.

Young, J.R., *The Scottish Parliament, 1639–1661. A Political and Constitutional Analysis* (Edinburgh, 1996).

Young, J.R. (ed.), *Celtic Dimensions of the British Civil Wars* (Edinburgh, 1997).

Young, J.R., 'The Scottish Parliament and the Covenanting Movement: the Emergence of a Scottish Commons', in J.R. Young (ed.), *Celtic Dimensions of the British Civil Wars* (Edinburgh, 1997), 164–184.

Young, J.R., 'The Scottish Parliament in the Seventeenth Century: European Perspectives', in A.I. Macinnes, T. Riis and F.G. Pedersen (eds), *Ships, Guns and Bibles in the North Sea and the Baltic States, c.1350–c.1700* (East Linton, 2000), 139–172.

Young, J.R., 'The Scottish Response to the Siege of Londonderry, 1689–90', in W. Kelly (ed.), *The Sieges of Derry* (Dublin, 2001), 53–74.

Young, J.R., 'The Scottish Parliament and the Covenanting Heritage of Constitutional Reform', in A.I. Macinnes and J. Ohlmeyer (eds), *The Stuart Kingdoms in the Seventeenth Century: Awkward Neighbours* (Dublin, 2002), 226–250.

Young, J.R., 'Charles I and the 1633 Parliament', in K.M. Brown and A.J. Mann (eds), *Parliament and Politics in Scotland, 1567–1707* (Edinburgh, 2005), 101–137.

Index

A Peaceable Warning to the Subjects in Scotland 109

Abbot, George, archbishop of Canterbury 58

Abercromby, Alexander of Birkinbog 127

Aberdeen 12, 15n, 22–3, 27, 30, 32, 35, 55–6, 67, 92, 95, 97, 99–102, 103n, 104–5, 106n, 109–11, 119–20, 123, 126n, 127–30, 137–8, 140–1, 152, 177n

Aberdeen Doctors, the 99, 103, 104n, 109–10, 120

Aberdeenshire 9, 14, 21, 64–5, 69n, 70, 83n, 85, 107, 126, 147, 163, 167–8, 170–1, 183–4

Aboyne 14, 59, 131, 158

Aboyne Castle 59, 148, 151

Achriachan 163

Act Anent Removing and Extinguishing of Deidlie Feuds 51

Act of Classes 145, 147

Act Rescissory 156

Agostini, Gerolamo 127

Airlie Castle 117

Alford 19

Alford, battle of 132, 134

Alsace 82

Alyth 147

Anderson, Walter, minister of Kinellar 104

Angus 106, 108–9, 111, 117, 120

Anna of Denmark 34

Atholl 40, 117

Auchindoun 131

Auchindoun Castle 80, 115, 142n

Auldearn, battle of 132–4

Austria 165

Badenoch 9, 14, 15n, 24–5, 31, 39–40, 42, 47, 59–61, 83, 95, 107, 117–18, 120, 122, 136, 143, 150n, 171, 185

Baillie, Robert 92, 102, 112, 125

Baillie, Robert of Jerviswood 173, 178

Baird, Sir James of Auchmedden 160

Baird, Walter 66

Bairds of Auchmedden 21

Ballantyne, William 152

Banff 111n, 142, 144

Banffshire 9, 107, 126, 147, 167, 171

Barclay, Colonel Harry 140

Barclays 21

Baron, Robert 109

Barra 39n

Belliévre, M. de 142

Belliévre, Pierre de 142

Belormy 116

Benchar 46

Bennachie 19

Benson, Andrew 150

Berwickshire 10, 173

Blackness Castle 28

Blackwater Forest 158, 161

Blair Atholl 129

Blakhal, Gilbert 75, 91–3, 95, 123

Bog of Gight (Gordon Castle) 14, 59, 74, 81, 89, 115, 124n, 127, 138, 142n, 148, 150, 152, 164, 180

Bohemia 165

Botary 163, 180
Bowes, Robert 29
Boyne, battle of the 177
Breadalbane 151
Brechin, battle of 11
Bridge of Dee 27
Bridge of Dee, battle of 101, 103
Brodie, Alexander of Brodie 168
Brodie, Alexander of Lethin 139n
Brodie, James of Brodie 168
Brody, Francis of Ballivat 139
Buchan 18–19, 51, 105, 110
Buchan, Henry 123
Buchanan, Sir John 61n
Burdoune, John 115
Burgie Castle 139
Burgundy 165
Burnet, David 90
Burnet, Gilbert 92
Burnet, James of Craigmyle 106n
Burnet, Thomas of Leys 106n
Butler, James, twelfth earl of Ormond
     142

Cabrach 60, 158, 161
Caerlaverock Castle 114
Cairn o' Mount 15n
Cairngorm Mountains 9, 25
Caithness 15n, 111n, 128
Calderwood, David 34
Cameron, Allan, sixteenth chief of
     Lochiel 28, 44–5, 46n, 47–9
Cameron, Sir Ewen, seventeenth chief of
     Lochiel 149, 170, 174, 181–2, 185
Cameron, John (son of Allan, sixteenth
     chief of Lochiel) 45
Camerons 12, 18, 26, 44–5, 48–9, 61, 76,
     96, 107, 118, 143, 149, 180, 185
Camerons of Erracht 44
Camerons of Glen Nevis 44, 79
Camerons of Kinlochiel 44
Campbell, Anne, second marchioness of
     Huntly 82, 89, 97
Campbell, Archibald, eighth earl and
     Marquess of Argyll 91, 113–18, 120,

123–4, 126, 128, 130–1, 136, 145,
     148–54, 157, 162, 181
Campbell, Archibald, fourth earl of
     Argyll 24n
Campbell, Archibald of Lochnell 18, 24n,
     29–30
Campbell, Archibald, Lord Lorne and
     ninth earl of Argyll 157–8, 159n,
     171–2, 174, 185
Campbell, Archibald, seventh earl of
     Argyll 3, 29–32, 44, 46n, 61, 84, 89
Campbell, Colin, third earl of Argyll 44n
Campbell, Duncan of Glenorchy 18, 24n,
     29–30
Campbell, James of Ardkinglas 29–30
Campbell, James of Lawers 171
Campbell, John of Cawdor 28–9
Campbell, John of Glenorchy, Earl of
     Caithness and first earl of Breadalbane
     170n, 171, 177, 185
Campbell, John of Lundie 29
Campbell, John, second lord Loudoun
     and first earl of Loudoun 114
Campbell, Sir Mungo of Lawers 131
Campbells 29, 127, 131
Campbells of Argyll 8, 24, 27, 32, 39, 43,
     61, 83, 89, 107, 170n, 172, 182, 185–7
Campbeltown 84
Canna 39n
Canongate, Edinburgh 116
Cant, Andrew, minister of Pitsligo 105
Cárdenas, Don Alonso de 91
Carnegie, David, first earl of Southesk
     117
Carnegie, James, Lord Carnegie and
     second earl of Southesk 107
Cassandra 96
Caumont, Jacques-Nompar de, duc de la
     Force 82
Cavendish, William, third earl and first
     duke of Newcastle 124
Charles I 62–5, 67–72, 85, 87–8, 90, 93,
     95–6, 98, 99n, 100–3, 109, 111–15,
     118–22, 125, 127, 135, 137–9, 141–2,
     144–5, 154, 156, 185

Charles II 121, 142, 144–8, 150, 154–5, 157, 159, 161, 166n, 168, 179, 181–2, 184–5
Cheyne, John, provost of Aberdeen 32
Cheynes 21
Clan Chattan 18, 25–6, 28, 32, 49, 71–2, 170
Clan Donald 107
Clan Donald South 38, 40, 43
Clark, William 147n
Coll 15n, 38
Corennie, forest of 20
Corgarff Castle 20
Corrichie, battle of 12, 16–7, 20–2, 24n, 26
Cowper, William, bishop of Galloway 57
Craibstane, battle of 20
Crichton, James, laird of Frendraught 73–8, 80, 85, 105, 130, 183
Crichtons of Frendraught 74–5, 106
Cromar 59
Cromdale, battle of 177
Cromwell, Oliver 121, 145–7, 155
Culloden 46
Culloden House 46–8

Dalrymple, Sir John of Stair 174
Darcy, Captain 140
D'Auvergne, Henri de la Tour, Marshall Turenne 166
David I 10n
Davidson, William 82, 162
Davidsons 25
Declaration of Arbroath 10
Dee, river 84, 120, 162
Deeside 59, 141
Delnabo 79n, 143, 164
Denmark 30
Dick, William of Braid 116, 150
Dickson, David 105n
Donnibristle House 28–9
Douglas family 11
Douglas, George, bishop of Moray 22n
Douglas, James, fourth earl of Morton 12
Douglas, William, eleventh earl of Angus

and Marquess of Douglas 89
Douglas, William, first duke of Queensberry 173n
Douglas, William, tenth earl of Angus 29, 56–7
Drumdelgie 161–3
Druminor Castle 19–20
Drummond, James, fourth earl of Perth 172–4, 182
Drummond, James, Lord Drummond and third earl of Perth 116, 117n
Drummond, John, first earl of Melfort 172–3, 182
Dubh, Donald 24
Duff, Alexander 177
Dugar, John 108
Dumbarton Castle 56
Dumfries 128
Dunbar, battle of 146
Dunbar, Robert of Burgie 139
Dunbars 32
Dunbennan 163, 180
Dundee 20, 82, 104n
Dunkeld, battle of 176
Dunnottar Castle 148n

Edinburgh 50, 54, 63, 78–9, 81, 86, 73n, 88, 104n, 113, 115–16, 146, 167, 173n, 174, 179, 181
Edinburgh Castle 27, 40, 46, 100, 143, 173, 175–7, 179
Eigg 39n
Elgin 23, 42, 59, 69, 82, 106, 123, 139–40, 149, 152
Elgin Cathedral 23
Elizabeth I of England 41
Elphinstone, John, second lord Balmerino 63
Enzie, the 14, 59, 83, 131, 151
Erskine, John, Lord Erskine and fourth earl of Mar 107
Erskine, John, second earl of Mar 13n, 67, 91
Erskine, Sir Robert 19
Erskine, Thomas, first earl of Kellie 60

Essie 83, 163, 180

Farnese, Alexander, Duke of Parma 27
Farquharson, Donald 79
Farquharsons 18
Fife 106
Finlarig Castle 151, 154
First Bishops' War 96, 101, 103, 108, 112, 119, 138, 185
Firth of Forth 28, 111
Five Articles of Perth 54, 58, 99n, 109
Flanders 166
Flodden, battle of 11, 16
Fochabers 83
Forbes, Alexander 19
Forbes, Alexander, Master of Forbes and eleventh lord Forbes 105
Forbes, Alexander of Boyndlie 105
Forbes, Alexander, second lord Pirsligo 105
Forbes, Arthur 20
Forbes, Duncan, provost of Inverness 72
Forbes, John, Master of Forbes and eighth lord Forbes 20, 126, 130
Forbes, John, laird of Pitligo 70
Forbes, John of Corse 109–10
Forbes, John, sixth lord Forbes 19–20
Forbes, Katherine, Lady Rothiemay 74, 77
Forbes, Patrick, bishop of Aberdeen 109
Forbes, William, Master of Forbes and thirteenth lord Forbes 177
Forbes, William, seventh lord Forbes 20
Forbeses 16–18, 20–1, 32, 34, 106, 136
Forbeses of Balfour 21
Forbeses of Brux 21
Forbeses of Corsindawe 21
Forbeses of Monymusk 21
Forbeses of Towie 21
Forres 42, 106
Forther Castle 117
France 70, 80, 82, 93, 114, 124n, 126, 130, 142, 162–3, 165–6, 174
Fraser, Andrew, second lord Fraser 105, 130

Fraser, Hugh, seventh lord Lovat 106
Fraser, James of Wardlaw 132, 143, 167
Fraser, Simon, fifth lord Lovat 28
Fraser, Thomas, laird of Strichen 70, 105
Frasers 106, 136
Frasers of Lovat 18
Frendraught Castle 73, 75, 78, 80–3, 85–6, 89, 183

Gall, Robert (priest) 92
Garioch 105
Gartly 59, 163, 180
Germany 89, 165
Glasgow 56, 88, 99, 104n, 138n, 174
Glass 163, 180
Glen Muick 14, 108, 158, 162
Glen Tanar 14, 108, 158, 162
Glencairn Rising, The 147, 150n, 159
Glencoe, massacre of 178
Glenfiddich 77
Glenlivet 158, 161, 163
Glenlivet, battle of 30–1, 119, 184
Glenluy 45
Gordon 10
Gordon, Sir Adam 10
Gordon, Adam (brother of George, sixth laird of Gight) 49
Gordon, Adam (second son of George, second earl of Huntly) 16
Gordon, Adam (son of George, laird of Auchterless) 79
Gordon, Adam, laird of Park 78, 80
Gordon, Adam of Auchindoun (brother of George, fifth earl of Huntly) 20, 23
Gordon, Adam of Auchindoun (third son of George, first marquess of Huntly) 59, 80
Gordon, Adam, second laird of Ardbroglach 16n
Gordon, Adam, younger of Park 78–9, 81
Gordon, Alexander, eleventh earl of Sutherland 17
Gordon, Alexander, fourth laird of Abergeldie 16n
Gordon, Alexander of Proney 16n

Gordon, Alexander of Tillyminnat 16n
Gordon, Alexander, third earl of Huntly
11, 23n, 25
Gordon, Ann (eldest daughter of George,
second marquess of Huntly) 82, 116
Gordon, Ann (first daughter of George,
first marquess of Huntly) 89
Gordon, Anne (first daughter of Lewis,
third marquess of Huntly) 153, 158–9,
161–2, 181
Gordon Castle *see* Bog of Gight
Gordon, Catherine (fifth daughter of
George, second marquess of Huntly)
82, 158n, 162
Gordon, Charles, first earl of Aboyne 82,
123, 148, 151–2, 157–62, 166–7, 169,
171, 181, 186
Gordon, Duncan of Knowen 16n
Gordon, Elizabeth 10
Gordon, Elizabeth (second daughter of
Alexander, first earl of Huntly) 19n
Gordon, Elizabeth (second daughter of
George, first marquess of Huntly) 89
Gordon, Elizabeth (widow of Alexander
Ogilvy of Findlater) 19n
Gordon, Elizabeth, Lady Frendraught 75
Gordon, Francis (second son of George,
first marquess of Huntly) 89
Gordon, George, Earl of Enzie *see*
Gordon, George, second marquess of
Huntly
Gordon, George, fifth earl of Huntly 12,
23, 26
Gordon, George, first laird of Coclarachie
16n
Gordon, George, fourteenth earl of
Sutherland 180
Gordon, George, fourth earl of Huntly 3,
11–12, 14n, 16–7, 19–23, 24n, 26
Gordon, George, fourth marquess of
Huntly and first duke of Gordon 3, 90,
152, 155, 157–82, 183, 185–6
Gordon, George, laird of Auchterless 79
Gordon, George, laird of Logiealtoun 79
Gordon, George, Lord Gordon, 68n,

82, 100–1, 114–15, 118, 122–3, 126,
129–34, 137, 149, 153–4
Gordon, Sir George of Edinglassie 177,
180
Gordon, George, second earl of Huntly
11, 14n, 19n
Gordon, George, second laird of
Cairnborrow 16n
Gordon, George, second marquess of
Huntly (known as Earl of Enzie prior
to 1636) 37–61, 65, 68–72, 76–7, 80,
82, 84–6, 88–108, 110–19, 122–9, 131,
134, 136–43, 145–6, 149–50, 153–4,
162, 164, 185–6
Gordon, George, seventh laird of Gight
123
Gordon, George, sixth earl and first
marquess of Huntly 3, 9–10, 13,
22–35, 37–45, 48–61, 63–86, 89, 91,
152–3, 163, 185–6
Gordon, George, sixth laird of Gight, 49,
51–2
Gordon, George, third baronet of Haddo
and first earl of Aberdeen 169–70,
176, 182
Gordon, Gilbert of Sallach 78–80, 82, 144
Gordon, Lady Henrietta (daughter of
John, Viscount Melgum and Aboyne)
93
Gordon, Henrietta (second daughter of
George, second marquess of Huntly)
82, 116
Gordon, Lord Henry (fifth son of George,
second marquess of Huntly) 82, 158,
160–2, 181
Gordon, James (eldest son of Adam
Gordon, laird of Park) 79
Gordon, James (Jesuit priest) 33
Gordon, James, first laird of Lesmore 16n
Gordon, Sir James, fifth laird of Lesmore
116, 119
Gordon, James, fourth laird of Haddo
16–7
Gordon, James, laird of Letterfourie
78–80

Gordon, James, Lord Aboyne 68n, 82, 101–3, 108, 111, 114–15, 119, 122, 124–5, 128, 131–2, 134–7, 140, 142–5, 149, 153, 163

Gordon, James of Blelack 16n

Gordon, James of Easter-migvie 16n

Gordon, James, parson of Rothiemay 84, 85n, 89, 97n, 103n, 114, 117n, 118

Gordon, James, third laird of Abergeldie 16n

Gordon, Jane (daughter of George, fourth earl of Huntly) 17

Gordon, Jean (second daughter of John, tenth earl of Sutherland) 17

Gordon, Jean (third daughter of George, second marquess of Huntly) 92, 117

Gordon, Jean (third daughter of Lewis, third marquess of Huntly) 153, 158, 161–2, 164, 181

Gordon, Jean, Lady Strabane 89, 93

Gordon, John (third son of George, fourth earl of Huntly) 12, 19

Gordon, John, fifth laird of Cocklarachy 169

Gordon, John, first baronet of Haddo 103, 127

Gordon, John, laird of Rothiemay 73–4, 79n, 80

Gordon, John, Lord Strathnaver and fifteenth earl of Sutherland 168, 176, 180

Gordon, John of Clubbisgoull 49, 51

Gordon, John, second laird of Pittlurg 16n

Gordon, John, tenth earl of Sutherland 16–17

Gordon, John, thirteenth earl of Sutherland 81, 106, 108, 119, 129

Gordon, John, Viscount Melgum and Aboyne 50, 59, 73–5, 89

Gordon, Laurence (fourth son of George, first marquess of Huntly) 89

Gordon, Lewis, third marquess of Huntly 68n, 82, 118, 130–1, 135, 140, 145–52, 154, 157

Gordon, Margaret (eldest daughter of George, fourth earl of Huntly) 20

Gordon, Mary (fourth daughter of George, second marquess of Huntly) 82

Gordon, Mary (second daughter of Lewis, third marquess of Huntly) 153, 158–9, 161–2, 172, 181

Gordon, Mary (third daughter of George, first marquess of Huntly) 89

Gordon, Colonel Nathaniel 128

Gordon, Patrick, first laird of Craig 16n

Gordon, Patrick of Oxhill 16n

Gordon, Patrick of Ruthven 93–7, 111, 114, 122, 126, 128, 130–2, 134–5, 137–8, 140, 141n

Gordon, Patrick, second laird of Craig 16n

Gordon, Sir Robert of Gordonstoun 32–3, 41n, 45–8, 50–1, 70, 72–5, 108, 116, 119

Gordon, Robert of Straloch 85n, 126, 148, 159

Gordon, Thomas (ninth son of George, fourth earl of Huntly) 17

Gordon, Sir Thomas of Park 151

Gordon, Thomas of Auchiniff 16n

Gordon, William 164–5, 173

Gordon, William, bishop of Aberdeen 22

Gordon, William, first laird of Gight 16n

Gordon, William, first laird of Terpersie 16n

Gordon, William, laird of Rothiemay 73–4

Gordon, Sir William, seventh laird of Lesmore 169

Gordons of Abergeldie 16

Gordons of Aboyne 180, 184

Gordons of Artloch 169

Gordons of Buckie 16, 151

Gordons of Cairnborrow 16

Gordons of Cluny 16

Gordons of Craig 16

Gordons of Gight 16, 107

Gordons of Gordonstoun 169

Gordons of Haddo 16, 107, 169–70, 180, 184
Gordons of Knockespock 169
Gordons of Lesmore 16
Gordons of Letterfourie 16
Gordons of Newton 107
Gordons of Park 79–82, 86, 184
Gordons of Rothiemay 81, 86
Gordons of Sutherland 16–17, 86, 168, 181, 184
Gordonsburgh (at Inverlochy) 84
Gordonstoun 116
Gowrie faction 13
Graham, James, fifth earl and first marquess of Montrose 2n, 5, 95, 100, 102n, 103, 107, 113, 125, 127–41, 144, 149, 153, 185
Graham, William, seventh earl of Menteith 67
Grahame, John, Viscount Dundee 175–6
Grampian Mountains 15n, 25
Grange 161
Grant, James of Carron 73–4, 77n, 79n, 108
Grant, James, seventh laird of Freuchy 106
Grant, John, fifth laird of Freuchy 26, 28, 31, 46–9, 61
Grant, John, laird of Ballindalloch 140, 149
Grant, Sir John, sixth laird of Freuchy 60
Grant, Ludovick, eighth laird of Freuchy 176
Grant, Mary, third marchioness of Huntly 152, 154, 157–60
Grant, Robert 89
Grants of Freuchy 18, 26, 28, 31–2, 141
Guharrig, Donald 143
Guild, William 104, 110
Gunn, Colonel William 103
Guthrie, John, bishop of Moray 108

Hague, The 179
Halidon Hill, battle of 10
Hamilton, Claude, Lord Strabane 89

Hamilton, James, third earl of Arran 22–3
Hamilton, James, third marquess and first duke of Hamilton 91, 100, 102, 103n, 104, 106n, 107n, 108, 110–11, 113, 119–20, 124, 185
Hamilton, Thomas, first earl of Haddington 67
Hamilton, Thomas, second earl of Haddington 114, 117
Hamilton, William, third duke of Hamilton 173n
Hamiltons 17n, 186
Harris 39
Hay, Elizabeth (sister of Nicolas, second earl of Erroll) 19n
Hay, Francis 49
Hay, Francis, ninth earl of Erroll 27, 29–30, 49–51, 56–8, 89
Hay, George, seventh earl of Erroll 19
Hay, Gilbert, eleventh earl of Erroll 105, 119
Hay, John, second earl of Tweedale 157, 160
Hay, John, twelfth earl of Erroll 170, 176
Hay, Margaret (second daughter of George, seventh earl of Erroll) 19
Hay, Nicolas, second earl of Erroll 19n
Hay, Sophia, Lady Melgum and Aboyne 50, 89, 95
Hay, William, Lord Hay 76n
Hay, William of Delgaty 105
Hays of Brunthill 49–50
Hays of Erroll, 18–19, 21, 31, 49–53, 61, 106–7, 119, 183–4
Henderson, Alexander 105n
Henrietta Maria 64, 125, 142, 144
Henry III of France 13
Henry, Prince of Wales 90
Holyrood Palace 172
Home, Charles, sixth earl of Home 176
Home, George, Earl of Dunbar 57
Homildon Hill, battle of 10
Howard, Elizabeth, fourth marchioness of Huntly and first duchess of Gordon 166

Howard, Henry, Duke of Norfolk 166
Howard, Thomas, twentieth earl of
    Arundel 101
Hume, family of 18n
Hungary 165
Huntingtower Castle 13n
Huntly Castle *see* Strathbogie Castle
Hyde, Edward, Earl of Clarendon 90,
    148n
Incident, The 113
Innes, Alexander of Condraught 143
Innes, Robert, younger of that ilk 151
Inneses 32
Innocent XI, pope 173–4
Inverlochy 45, 84, 123
Inverlochy, battle of 131
Inverlochy Castle 171, 182
Inverness 23–4, 72, 106, 111n, 131, 138,
    140–1
Inverness Castle 23n, 24, 59, 100, 106
Inverness-shire 14, 38, 48, 64–5, 69n, 70,
    85, 171, 184
Inverurie 100
Irvine, Alexander, laird of Drum 70, 126
Irvine, Alexander, younger of Drum 128
Irvines 32
Irvines of Drum 107
Irvines of Fedderate 107
Italy 165

Jaffray, Alexander, provost of Aberdeen
    104, 127
James II 11, 14n
James III 11, 12n
James IV 11, 12, 14n, 23n, 36
James V 11, 20, 24n, 44n
James VI and I 4, 9, 12–13, 24, 27–30,
    34–9, 41n, 42–3, 46, 49, 50n, 51–8, 62,
    64, 68–9, 71, 81, 89, 93, 96, 183
James VII and II (Duke of York prior to
    1685) 90, 94, 155, 165, 168n, 172–5,
    177–9, 182
John XXII, pope 10
Johnston, Sir Archibald of Wariston 101n
Johnston, John, sheriff of Aberdeen 70

Johnston, William 104
Johnstone, Robert, provost of Aberdeen
    103
Johnstone, Colonel William 103n
Justice Mills, battle of 129–30, 134

Kandychyle 59, 180
Keith, Elizabeth (daughter of William,
    fourth earl Marischal) 21
Keith, George, ninth earl Marischal 176
Keith, William, fifth earl Marischal 32
Keith, William, fourth earl Marischal 21
Keith, William, sixth earl Marischal 105n,
    106n, 115, 125–6, 149, 170
Keiths 21, 83, 184
Kildrummy 130
Kilkenny 122
Killiecrankie, battle of 176
Kilsyth, battle of 132, 134–5
King's College, Aberdeen 68, 104, 123
King's Covenant 99, 104, 110, 111
Kinnoir 163, 180
Kinrara Manuscript, The 46–7
Kirk Party, The 145–6
Kirkwood, Gilbert of Pilrig 116
Knox, Andrew, bishop of the Isles 40

La Hogue, battle of 177
Lauder, Sir John of Fountainhall 168
Law, James, bishop of Orkney 57
Leinster 122
Leslie, General Alexander 112
Leslie, Lieutenant-General David 135,
    142, 144
Leslie, John (Jesuit priest) 64, 66–7, 69n,
    75, 90
Leslie, John, laird of Pitcaple 74–5, 80
Leslie, John, seventh earl of Rothes 157,
    160
Leslie, John, sixth earl of Rothes 111
Leslie, John, tenth laird of Balquhain 23
Leslie, Patrick, provost of Aberdeen
    103–4, 127
Leslie, William 109
Leslie, William (priest) 64, 69

Leslies 21, 32
Leslies of Balquhain 21n
Leslies of Pitcaple 74, 183
Lesmore Castle 93, 142n
L'Estrange, Hamon 65
Lethin Castle 139-40
Lettoch 164
Lewis 38-40, 43, 106n
Lilburne, Colonel Robert 148
Lindsay, Alexander, first earl of Balcarres 147
Lindsay, Alexander, fourth earl of Crawford 11
Lindsay, Colin, third earl of Balcarres 175, 176n
Lindsay, David, eleventh earl of Crawford 27
Lindsay, David, minister of Belhelvie 104
Lindsay, Thomas 50
Lithgow, William 91
Livingston, Alexander, Lord Livingston and second earl of Linlithgow 68, 89
Loch Kinnord 142n
Lochaber 9, 14, 15n, 24-6, 39-42, 44-5, 47-8, 61, 84, 107, 117-18, 120, 122, 131, 150n, 170-1, 174, 181, 185
Locharkaig 45
Lochawe 131
Lom, Iain 96, 132
London 35, 41n, 113, 115-17, 120, 124
Lords of the Congregation 12
Lordship of the Isles 14, 24-5
Lorraine 82
Louis XIII of France 82, 96
Louis XIV of France 173-4, 177
Lundie, John 104
Lyon, John, second earl of Kinghorn 105n, 107

MacAllan, Donald, Captain of Clanranald 39
Macbeans 25
Macbreck, John (priest) 64
MacColla, Alasdair 127-9, 131, 133-6, 142-4, 153-4

MacDonald, Aeneas, Lord MacDonald 171
MacDonald, Allaster, tenth chief of Keppoch 41-2, 47
MacDonald, Donald, Lord of the Isles 24
MacDonald, Donald Gorm of Sleat 18
MacDonald, Sir James 40-1
MacDonald, Ranald, eleventh chief of Keppoch 41-2, 79, 117
MacDonalds 39
MacDonalds of Clanranald 24
MacDonalds of Islay and Kintyre *see* Clan Donald South
MacDonalds of Keppoch 26, 31, 42, 107, 170
MacDonnell, Randal, second earl and first marquess of Antrim 5n, 100, 107, 124-5, 127, 129, 135, 144, 153
Macgillvrays 25
MacGregor, Patrick Roy 167
MacGregors 38, 73, 77, 79, 108, 123
MacIains of Ardnamurchan 38
MacIains of Glencoe 78, 178
Macinneses 84
Mackay, Donald, first lord Reay 108, 128, 139, 141n
Mackay, Sir Donald of Farr 60
Mackay, George, third lord Reay 176
Mackay, Major-General Hugh 177
Mackay, John, Master of Reay and second lord Reay 129n
Mackenzie, Colin, second lord Kintail and first earl of Seaforth 43, 47, 49, 60-1
Mackenzie, George, second earl of Seaforth 106, 139-40
Mackenzie, Sir George, Viscount Tarbet 167, 174
Mackenzie, Kenneth, first lord Kintail 40, 43
Mackenzie, Kenneth, fourth earl of Seaforth 171-2, 182, 185
Mackenzies of Kintail 18, 32, 43, 61, 83-4, 184

Mackintosh, Duncan (uncle of Lachlan, seventeenth chief of Mackintosh) 46

Mackintosh, Lachlan of Dunnachton, sixteenth chief of Mackintosh 25, 31–2

Mackintosh, Lachlan of Dunnachton, seventeenth chief of Mackintosh 41n, 42, 45–9, 52

Mackintosh, Lachlan of Dunnachton and Torcastle, nineteenth chief of Mackintosh 170, 181

Mackintosh, William of Borlum 171n

Mackintosh, William of Dunnachton, fifteenth chief of Mackintosh 25n, 26

Mackintosh, William of Dunnachton and Torcastle, eighteenth chief of Mackintosh 83, 107

Mackintoshes 18, 25–6, 28, 31–2, 34, 45–9, 60–1, 71, 73n, 83, 96, 107, 170, 180, 182, 185

Macleod, Torquil 24

Macleod, Torquil of Lewis 18

Macleods of Lewis 24, 38, 40

MacMhiurich, Niall 132

MacNeill, Rory of Barra 39

Macphails 25

Macpherson, Sir Aeneas of Invereshie 171n

Macphersons 25, 28, 32, 107, 170, 177

MacQueens 25

Maastricht 165

Macky, John 166, 179

Maitland, Sir John of Thirlstane 28

Maitland, John, second earl and Duke of Lauderdale 8, 156, 159–60, 166

Malcolm III 10n

Mamore 45

Mar 105, 117

Marian Civil War 20, 21n, 23

Marischal College, Aberdeen 32

Mary of Guise 12, 25n

Mary, Queen of Scots 12

Mary II 174, 181

Maule, Henry of Dunbar 83

Maule, James, fourth earl of Panmure 176

Maurice, Prince 128

Maxwell, Robert, first earl of Nithsdale 114, 124–5

Maxwells of Nithsdale 58

Mazarin, Cardinal Jules 143n

Mearns, The 32, 105–6, 111, 120, 126, 171

Megray Hill, battle of 101

Meldrum, John of Reidhill 74–6, 77n

Melgund 83

Melgund Castle 83

Mellerstanes 173, 178, 181

Melvill, Thomas, minister of Dyce 104

Melvin, Andrew, minister of Bacnchory-Devenick 104

Menzies family of Pitfoddels 22, 32

Menzies, Gilbert of Pitfoddels 23

Menzies, Lieutenant-Colonel James 143

Middleton, John, first earl of Middleton 137, 140–1, 143, 146, 148n, 149, 156, 159–60

Moidart, John, chief of Clanranald 12, 26

Monro, Colonel Robert 113–15, 120, 123

Monroes 32

Montereul, Jean de 92, 143n

Montrose 104, 128

Monymusk 19

Moray 57, 59, 67, 108, 111n, 116, 129, 138–40, 149n

Moray Firth 83, 140

Morayshire 25, 28

Morinsh 149

Mounth, The 14, 15n, 128

Murray, John, first marquess of Atholl 171–2, 173n, 174, 182, 185

Murray, Patrick, first earl of Tullibardine 40, 48, 108

Nairnshire 171

National Covenant, the 63, 87–8, 99n, 103–7, 110–14, 117–9, 126n

Negative Confession, the 99n, 109–10

Netherlands 119, 145

Nevie 164

New Aberdeen 105, 147n

New Model Army 145
Newark 141
Newbury, first battle of 130
Newcastle 101n, 142
Nicoll, John 147n
North Esk, river 15n
Northern Band, the 146

Ogilvie, Alexander of Findlater 19n
Ogilvie, Sir George of Banff 103n
Ogilvies of Banff 106
Ogilvies of Findlater 106
Ogilvy, James, eighth lord Ogilvy and second earl of Airlie 108, 109n, 125, 135–6
Ogilvy, James, first earl of Airlie 109n, 124
Ogilvys of Airlie 117
Ogston 116
Old Aberdeen 59, 105, 122, 126
O'Neill, Sir Phelim 89
Orkney 60, 61n
Otterburn, battle of 10
Overton, Colonel Robert 147
Oxford 126, 160

Pacification of Berwick 101, 112
Paris 20, 95n, 144
Paris, university of 13
Perth 13n, 56, 104n
Perthshire 18, 106, 108
Peterhead 149
Philiphaugh, battle of 135, 137, 144, 153
Pinkie, battle of 11, 16
Plewlands 59, 116
Pluscardine Rising, The 146
Poland 158, 162

Raasay 39n
Rannoch 117
Ravenscraig 149
Reformation of 1560 12
Reid, Robert, minister of Banchory-Trinity 104
Reynolds, John 137n

Rhind, David 115
Rhind, John 115
Rhynie 83, 163, 180
Ridge, Avary 124
Robert the Bruce 10
Robertson, Isobel 123
Robertson, William, minister of Footdee 104
Robertsons of Struan 18
Ross 111n
Ross, Alexander 109
Rothes 140
Rum 39n
Ruthven 161, 163, 180
Ruthven Castle 14, 31, 59, 95, 143
Ruthven in Badenoch 83
Ruthven, William, first earl of Gowrie 13n

Sauchieburn, battle of 12n
Scroggie, Alexander 109
Second Bishops' War 112
Sempil, Hugh (priest) 91
Seton, Alexander 11
Seton, Alexander, first earl of Dunfermline 43, 58
Seton [later Gordon], Alexander, first earl of Huntly 11, 14n, 19, 23n
Seton, George, Lord Seton 116
Seton, George, third earl of Winton 116
Seton, James, fourth earl of Dunfermline 164
Shetland 60, 61n
Sibbald, James 109
Sinclair, George, fifth earl of Caithness 50–1, 106, 108, 183
Sinclair, John, Master of Berriedale 108
Sinclair, William, Lord Berriedale 50, 108
Sinclairs of Caithness 50–1
Skye 39
Slains Castle 18, 30
Society and Company of Boyes 52
Solemn League and Covenant 125–7, 131, 137, 146, 153

Spain 29, 30n, 32, 58, 114, 152
Spalding, John 74, 78, 79n, 97, 105, 113, 117n, 119, 122, 126–7, 141n
Spanish Armada 27
Spey, river 22, 27, 84, 106, 120, 140–1
Speyside 25
Spire 82
Spottiswoode, John, archbishop of Glasgow (archbishop of St Andrews from 1615) 57, 67
Spynie Palace 22n, 27, 108, 140
St Andrews, University of 165
St Germains en Laye 179
St Kilda 39n
St Machar Church, Old Aberdeen 97
Start, the 146
Statutes of Iona 40
Stewart, Alexander, fifth earl of Moray 171–2, 182, 185
Stewart, Andrew, Lord Ochiltree 40
Stewart, Elizabeth (daughter of James, first earl of Moray) 21–2
Stewart, Esmé, first duke of Lennox 13
Stewart, Francis, fifth earl of Bothwell 27–8, 30
Stewart, Henrietta, first marchioness of Huntly 13, 67, 115, 124
Stewart, James, first earl of Moray 12, 21, 22n, 26
Stewart, James, first lord Doune 21
Stewart, James, fourth duke of Lennox and first duke of Richmond 124
Stewart, James, second earl of Moray 21–2, 27–31, 75
Stewart, James, third earl of Moray 46, 71–3, 75, 85, 89, 95, 106, 184
Stewart, John, fifth earl of Atholl 28
Stewart, John, first earl of Traquair 112, 150
Stewart, Ludovick, second duke of Lennox 28, 30, 38
Stewarts of Moray 21, 34
Stirling Castle 56
Stonehaven 101
Stornaway 83–4

Strathavon 79n, 108, 131, 143, 158, 161, 163
Strathbogie 10, 14, 20, 60, 131, 151, 152n, 163
Strathbogie Castle (Huntly Castle) 14, 30, 33, 59, 65, 79, 82, 97, 113, 115, 122–3, 141, 142n, 150, 153, 164, 180
Strathdee 108
Strathdon 19, 59
Strathnaver 128, 129n, 137, 146
Strathspey 138
Sutherland 30, 111
Sutherland, Elizabeth, Countess of Sutherland 16
Sweden 100

Tay, river 104
Taylor, John 59, 95
Test Oath 173
Thirty Years' War 66, 89
Tibbermore, battle of 129, 134n
Tillyangus, battle of 20
Tongue 128
Torrisoule 79
Torterston 149
Toschach, John 75–6, 77n
Tower of London 115
Tudor, Margaret 11, 36
Turriff 100–2, 119

Uist 39
Ulster 37–8, 122, 124

Verney, Sir Edmund 102

Wakefield, Mary 150
Wallace, Captain James 115
Wardhouse Castle 142n
Warsaw 162
Wars of Independence 10
Wemyss, David, Lord Elcho 107
Wester Campdal 163
Western Isles 15n, 38–40, 56, 127
Westminster 90
Whitehall 62, 145

William III and II (Prince of Orange) 3,
  156, 166, 174–5, 177–9, 181
William the Conqueror 10
Williamite Revolution 8, 178n, 179, 182,
  184, 186
Willingen 179

Wishart, George 95n, 132–3, 134n, 135,
  137–8, 139n
Worcester, battle of 147

Yarmouth 101
York 102, 124